PUBLICATIONS

OF THE

NAVY RECORDS SOCIETY

VOL. 164

THE NAVAL MISCELLANY
VOLUME VIII

The NAVY RECORDS SOCIETY was established in 1893 for the purpose of printing unpublished manuscripts and rare works of naval interest. The Society is open to all who are interested in naval history, and any person wishing to become a member should either complete the online application form on the Society's website, www. navyrecords.org.uk, or apply to the Hon. Secretary, The Mill, Stanford Dingley, Reading, RG7 6LS, United Kingdom, email address robinbrodhurst@ gmail.com. The annual subscription is £40, which entitles the member to receive one free copy of each work issued by the Society in that year, and to buy earlier issues at much reduced prices.

SUBSCRIPTIONS should be sent to the Membership Secretary, 19 Montrose Close, Whitehill, Bordon, Hants, GU35 9RG.

THE COUNCIL OF THE NAVY RECORDS SOCIETY wish it to be clearly understood that they are not answerable for any opinions and observations which may appear in the Society's publications. For these the editors of the several works are entirely responsible.

THE NAVAL MISCELLANY
VOLUME VIII

Edited by

BRIAN VALE, C.B.E., B.A., M.Phil.

PUBLISHED BY ROUTLEDGE
FOR THE NAVY RECORDS SOCIETY
2017

Routledge
Taylor & Francis Group

LONDON AND NEW YORK

First published 2017
by Routledge
2 Park Square, Milton Park, Abingdon, Oxon OX14 4RN

and by Routledge
711 Third Avenue, New York, NY 10017

Routledge is an imprint of the Taylor & Francis Group, an informa business

British Library Cataloguing-in-Publication Data
A catalogue record for this book is available from the British Library

Library of Congress Cataloging-in-Publication Data
A catalog record for this book has been requested

ISBN: 978-1-138-21979-3 (hbk)
ISBN: 978-1-315-18433-3 (ebk)

Typeset in Times New Roman
by Apex CoVantage, LLC

Printed in the United Kingdom
by Henry Ling Limited

This volume is dedicated to John Hussey,
a distinguished historian and long-time member
and generous supporter of the Society.

CONTENTS

PREFACE

The contents of this, the eighth of the Navy Records Society's *Naval Miscellany* series, chronicles the activities and adventures of the Royal Navy, its officials, its officers and its men – both in British employment and out of it – over a period of some six hundred years. Ranging from the reign of Edward III to that of Edward VIII, its contents shine a spotlight into hitherto partially understood corners of naval history, from the maintenance and victualling of the Royal fleet of the fourteenth century to the diplomatic and personal minefields encountered by officers when escorting the Emperor Haile Selassie into exile following the Italian invasion of Abyssinia.

Thomas de Snetesham was one of the first to hold the title of Clerk of the King's Ships. His duties covered the building and repair of royal ships, their care and maintenance when in harbour or laid up, and the supply of victuals and naval stores. The documents printed here give extensive details and enable the reader to form an impression of how mariners, dockyard artisans and royal officials kept Edwards III's fleet seaworthy. Snetesham's papers provide insights into the operation of shipyards, the nature of the work force, the design of the ships themselves, the nature of their equipment and the source of naval supplies. Of particular interest is the earliest documented mention of a timing device and a form of magnetic compass to be used on an English ship.

Much has been written about *Mary Rose* following the raising of Henry VIII's favourite flagship from the mud of the Solent in 1982. The material found and the supporting documentation have enabled a picture to be formed of the structure of the vessel, her armament, the life of her crew and how she worked as a functioning warship. But not all the detail has been settled, and the documents which form the second contribution to this volume fill some of these gaps. The victualling account, for example, shows exactly the official scale of rations in terms of such things as bread, meat, fish and beer. Likewise, the shipwrights' report not only confirms the form of *Mary Rose*'s missing stem, but shows that alterations were being considered to the bow section of conventional English sailing ships at the time to give them the notoriously effective forward-firing capability of the galley. Other documents illustrate the command structures in place; and give lists of captains without ships; ships without captains; and appointments already made. They also provide confirmation that the captain of *Mary Rose* was undoubtedly Sir George Carew. Finally, Sir John Oglander's narrative of the Battle of the Solent is included – a document which, although it must be treated with caution, gives much local detail.

Three hundred years later, Captain Archibald Kennedy must have thought himself lucky in 1763 to have been posted as senior naval officer to New York, an area with which he had strong personal connections. He owned estates there; he had an American wife; and his father had earlier served as Collector of Customs. However, it was a far from happy time. His arrival coincided with the determination of the British Government to enforce the Navigation Laws, particularly in relation to the importation of sugar from the French and Spanish West Indies, and to raise money locally to defray the costs of the colony's protection by imposing the notorious Stamp Act. In the middle of competing forces in the eye of a storm which, ten years later, was to trigger the American War of Independence, Kennedy was dismissed from his post for non-cooperation with the local authorities by refusing to take the stamped papers which were the target of mob protest onto his ship. Returning to London with copies of every document relating to these events – most of which are reproduced here – he was able to clear his name and was reinstated in his post.

At about the same period, there emerged a desire among thinking professionals to improve the Royal Navy's fighting effectiveness not only through technical advances but by supplementing – or indeed replacing – the old haphazard system of officer training with a more systematic method based on an assessment of the skills and qualities they needed. The 1780 *Essay* printed here, written by naval chaplain, and erstwhile naval surgeon, the Reverend James Ramsay, was an important manifestation of this strategy. Backed by senior officers like Sir Charles Middleton and Admiral Richard Kempenfelt – both members of the growing 'evangelical' movement within the service – it was inevitable that piety and religious observance were seen as important elements in the qualities needed for leadership. But Ramsay's book was not a religious tract. In part it was a thoughtful and practical analysis of how the navy could be improved by changes in management, tactics, recruitment and signalling; but in the main its principal thrust lay in the idea that the 'complete' sea officer was a man who was not only competent in ship-handling, cool under fire and brave, but was also solicitous of the welfare of his men, able to gain their willing obedience and the possessor of a host of gentlemanly social, conversational and linguistic skills. The modern value of Ramsay's book lies not only in its influence, but in the light it shines on the style and attitudes of the Georgian navy as viewed by an informed and professional observer.

For the general reader, the traditional story of the Anglo-American War of 1812–14 has reflected myth rather than reality. It is only in recent years that interest has been moved from strategically unimportant victories by American warships against smaller British opponents to the defeat of the invasion of Canada – a major America war aim – and the application of a remorseless British blockade which destroyed American maritime trade and government revenue. Credit for bringing the Americans to the conference table by turning the final screw of blockade and making coastal raids almost at will, has tended to be given to two active and aggressive admirals, Alexander Cochrane and George Cockburn. The performance of Sir John Borlase Warren, who commanded in the difficult first two years of the war, has been portrayed as more disappointing. Our fifth contribution shows this view to be mistaken. Warren was specifically selected following the American declaration of war because he had both the diplomatic and service experience that was judged to be needed in a political and military situation that was confused. Unfortunately, Warren's orders to both negotiate and blockade were contradictory; he was responsible for an unrealistically huge area of command stretching from Halifax to the West Indies; he lacked local repair facilities; was short of manpower; and had too few ships to seal the huge coastline of the USA and guarantee the protection of British trade against swarms of privateers. With Britain's attention focused on the major conflict with Napoleon, Warren made the most of the resources that could be spared, imposed as tight a blockade as was possible, and took hundreds of privateers. Unfortunately, the powers that be in London failed to fully appreciate either the severe practical and operational problems facing Warren or the extent of his achievement, and his recall on an operational technically had all the appearance of a reproof.

For the country at large, the end of the Napoleonic War may have been a cause for satisfaction, but for most officers and men of the navy it meant half-pay or unemployment. By 1822 the number of men in service had fallen by four-fifths to 23,000 and there was employment for less than 15 per cent of serving officers. Many found alternative careers in Britain; but a number took their skills overseas, most notably to the fashionable wars of liberation then taking place throughout South America. Our sixth contribution gives a glimpse of the professional life of one such man, John Pascoe Grenfell of the Brazilian Navy. Brazil, like Chile, Peru and the United Provinces (later Argentina), was essentially a continental country with no maritime tradition. To man the new navy needed to defeat the Portuguese at sea, the Brazilian authorities turned to foreign, largely British, recruitment to fill the gap. It was a wise choice. Not only did the new Brazilian Navy secure a staggering victory under Lord Cochrane in the War of Independence, but scores of British officers and men stayed on to serve for the next forty years. As the Grenfell contribution shows, they not only filled vacancies; but brought with them professional skill, experience in ship management, confidence in victory and an aggressive style which, in Grenfell's case, led to the loss of an arm.

Criticisms of public policy by political opponents and those with different administrative priorities are to be expected in the British Parliamentary system. What gave the 'usual' complaints against Lord Northbrook – that he was more interested in colonial than naval affairs and that his Liberal zeal for reducing public expenditure had sacrificed the navy's global position – was that it was taken up and amplified by the 'muck-raking' journalist W.T. Stead in the *Pall Mall Gazette* in 1884. Backed by information provided by those with political or personal axes to grind, it provoked a major 'naval scare' that the navy was falling badly behind other powers. In a political atmosphere where it was ungentlemanly to stoop to defend oneself in the public prints, these criticisms went largely unanswered with the result that the reputations of Northbrook and his talented subordinates have suffered ever since. Our seventh contribution is focused on the 'handover' Memorandum prepared by Northbrook in 1885. This document was not written as a public defence of his policies. It was – typically – an internal and entirely factual paper designed to inform the incoming Conservative administration in detail of the actions of its predecessor. Its value to historians is that it demonstrates that Northbrook and his colleagues were innocent of Stead's misleading strictures and that, far from allowing Britain's naval supremacy to dwindle, their programmes had had the opposite effect.

The impotence of the League of Nations and the appeasing instincts of Britain and France in the face of the invasion of Ethiopia by Fascist Italy reflect little credit on anyone. However, a sense of fair play, plus an Imperial instinct triggered by the fact that the defeated Head of State was an Emperor, caused the British to agree to convey the refugee Haile Selassie to a place of safety, first to Palestine, then to Gibraltar from whence he was to proceed privately to England. Caution as well as humanity dictated that until the Imperial party was clear of the Mediterranean it should be transported discreetly by warship. Our final contribution describes the voyage and the politics which surrounded it and features the witty and humane report of the captain of HMS *Enterprise* who was responsible for the first part of the trip and who, on arrival at Djibuti expecting to embark a party of 12 persons, found himself confronted with 150 plus two lion cubs and a dog. Of interest is the contrast between the cool and legalistic reactions of Foreign Office diplomats who, with one apprehensive eye on Italy, wanted total discretion and anonymity; the actions of local colonial officials whose automatic instinct to the arrival of a crowned head was to lay on guards of honour and national anthems; and the attitude of officers of the Royal Navy who were largely sympathetic to the pathos of the event, amazed by the exotic manifestation of the Ethiopian court in exile and struck by both the personal charm of Haile Selassie and the good looks of some of the princesses.

I would like to thank at a personal level all the contributors to this volume who dedicated themselves not only to producing expert and important material, but did so in a way that required minimal editorial intervention. In particular, I would like to acknowledge the contribution of Professor David Loades who sadly passed away before this volume could be published. The piece on the *Mary Rose*, in which he collaborated, is an excellent example of the scholarship and erudition with which he has illuminated the publications of the Society over many years.

On behalf of the Navy Records Society, I would also like to thank the many public archives, libraries and the private collections which were generous enough as to provide access to the material. These comprised in Britain, The National Archives Kew, the British Library, the Libraries of the Universities of Cambridge and Liverpool, the Isle of Wight Record Office, the Cecil Papers at Hatfield House, and the South American Papers in possession of the Grenfell family; in the USA, the Watkinson Library at Trinity College, Hartford, Connecticut and the Providence Public Library, Rhode Island; and in Brazil, the Arquivo Nacional, Rio de Janerio. Full details can be found in each contribution.

Brian Vale

GLOSSARY OF ABBREVIATIONS

AC	Annals of Congress
Adm	Admiral
AN	Arquivo Nacional, Rio de Janeiro
AMR	*The Archaeology of the Mary Rose*
AoF	Admiral of the Fleet
BCS	Battle Cruiser Squadron
BL	British Library
BTM	*Before the Mast*
Capt	Captain
Cdr	Commander
Cdre	Commodore
C-in-C	Commander-in-Chief
CCR	Calendar of Close Rolls
CFR	Calendar of Fine Rolls
CO	Commanding Officer
Col	Colonel
CPR	Calendar of Patent Rolls
(D)	Destroyers
DF	Destroyer Flotilla
Dir	Director
E	Exchequer, Pipe Office, Declared Accounts (in Rolls)
ECCO	Eighteenth Century Collections Online
FAA	Fleet Air Arm
Gen	General
HCA	High Court of Admiralty, Deposition Books
HM	His Majesty's
LMR	*Letters from the Mary Rose*
LP	*Letters and Papers, Henry VIII*
Lt	Lieutenant
Lt Cdr	Lieutenant Commander
MTB	Motor Torpedo Boat
NEM	*The Navy of Edward VI and Mary I*
NLS	National Library of Scotland
NMBS	Naval and Military Bible Society

NMM	National Maritime Museum
NRS	Navy Records Society
PPL	Providence Public Library
RA	Rear Admiral
RAC	Rear Admiral Commanding
RAF	Royal Air Force
RN	Royal Navy
SBNO	Senior British Naval Officer
Sec	Secretary
SNO	Senior Naval Officer
SP	State Papers, Henry VIII
Sub-Lt	Sub-Lieutenant
TNA	The National Archives
VA	Vice Admiral
ULLSCA	University of Liverpool Library Special Collections and Archives

I

ACCOUNTS FROM THE EARLY YEARS OF THE OFFICE OF THE CLERK OF THE KING'S SHIPS; THOMAS DE SNETESHAM'S ACCOUNTS FOR 1344–45 AND 1350–54

Edited by Susan Rose

Two separate accounts have been transcribed and translated here. Both are preserved in The National Archives at Kew and come from the records of the Exchequer. Both date from the reign of Edward III and relate to the affairs of Thomas de Snetesham who was Clerk of the King's Ships in the early years of this office. He was first appointed in 1336 but at times shared the title and the duties of the office with William de Clewere and Matthew de Torksey whose accounts at times cover periods overlapping with those of Snetesham. Similarly towards the end of the reign of Edward III the office seems to have been shared to some extent between Robert Crull and John de Haytfield.

The duties of the office seem not to have been clearly defined until the end of the century with each clerk having a slightly different set of responsibilities. Generally, the duties of the Clerk of the King's Ships extended to the repair of royal ships, sometimes to the building of a new one, the provision of supplies like cordage and caulking materials and occasionally victuals, and the organisation of ship keepers to care for the vessels when they were in harbour or laid up in an anchorage. The Clerks were not concerned with operational matters although some mention is often made of the voyages for which a vessel was being prepared. A particular value of these accounts is to allow some conclusions to be drawn about the ships themselves, their design and their equipment. They also allow us to understand how a medieval monarchy approached the expensive and onerous task of keeping a royal fleet in a seaworthy condition and the way in which this had become of much greater concern than previously in the reign of Edward III.

The first account edited comes from the Accounts Various class of the Exchequer (TNA E101) and consists of the particulars of account kept by Snetesham for the year 18 Edward III, that is 25 January

1344–25 January 1345. He is described as Clerk of the ship *George*, not as Clerk of the King's Ships in this particular instance. From the account it is not clear whether this refers to the ship called *George*, formerly in French ownership, which was captured at the battle of Sluys by the English and which sank in Winchelsea harbour in 1346. It could equally be another vessel, the *George Beauchamp*, which was in the service of the Crown at around the same date. Although ships' clerks are often described as the predecessors of pursers it is not clear if Snetesham went to sea in this ship. He was also described in 1338 as Clerk of the King's Ship *Christopher,* but again there is no evidence that this necessarily implied that he went to sea in this vessel.[1]

This is not the only surviving particulars of account relating to Snetesham's period of office as Clerk of the King's Ships. There are others for the years 1336–47, 1338, 1340–43, and 1345–46. All contain much the same information about money spent on ship repairs and mariners' wages. Extracts from that for 1345–46, were published in an appendix to Volume II of Sir Nicholas Harris Nicolas's *History of the Royal Navy* as long ago as 1847. Much of the account is very similar to that printed here but there is a paragraph of greater interest. This records the purchase of various items at Sluys in Flanders. Included are a number of hour glasses and also an item which Harris translated as 'the amending of divers instruments belonging to the ship [the *George*]' at a cost of 7d and finally 'twelve stones called adamants called sailstones bought there 6s'. David Waters mentioned this document in a footnote in *The Art of Navigation in England in Elizabethan and Early Stuart Times*[2] but stated that the date was wrong and should be amended to 1410–12. This has probably prevented the recognition that this is the earliest mention of both a timing device and some form of magnetic compass on an English ship. The date of 1410–12 related to the mention of a compass in an inventory of a royal ship for these years. Because of the importance of this confirmation that navigation including the use of a compass was undertaken in England in as early as the first half of the fourteenth century, the whole of this paragraph has also been retranscribed and retranslated here as a separate short item.

The particulars of account were the papers, kept by the accountant either in his own hand or by a junior clerk, which would later be presented at the Exchequer for audit and payment. Only when the barons

---

[1]The National Archives (hereafter TNA): E101/21/80.
[2]David W. Waters, *The Art of Navigation in England in Elizabethan and Early Stuart Times* (London, 1958).

of the Exchequer were satisfied that all was in order and it was clear whether the accountant had a claim against the Crown or was in arrears himself, would the accounts be written up in a somewhat abbreviated format on the relevant roll. The second account included is that on the Pipe Roll for 1357–58.[1] It consists of Snetesham's finalised accounts for 1350–54. The delay between the end of the accounting period and the enrolment of the agreed accounts was not unusual. There would in all probability have been a further delay before Snetesham received the £42 15s 1¼d which, in this instance, was due to him from the Crown. The second section of the Pipe Roll account is made up of an exhaustive and repetitive inventory of all the stores in the hands of the office of the King's Ships during this accounting period, the use made of them, and finally what remained to be handed over to Matthew de Torksey who took over responsibility from Snetesham with regard to the items listed as remaining. This inventory section provides further information regarding the equipment to be found on ships at this date and also allows us to appreciate in a small way how ships were maintained. It includes many technical terms not all of which are as yet fully understood. These are listed in the Glossary with an explanation where this is possible. The last part of this inventory, however, the items handed over to Torksey, has not been transcribed as it repeats the material in the first two parts.

Very little is known about Snetesham himself. He was certainly in holy orders, a clerk in both medieval senses of the term. He may well have come from the Norfolk village now known as Snettisham, not far from Hunstanton. He certainly had connections with this part of the country since he was presented to the living of Rushton in Lincolnshire in 1336.[2] In the following year he was also presented to the living of Freshwater in the Isle of Wight, a parish which had been part of the temporalities of

---

[1] The Pipe Rolls, TNA class E372 (so-called because they resembled a pipe when rolled up), are the original class of documents kept by the Exchequer. They exist in a continuous series from the reign of Henry II to that of William IV. There is also a single roll from the reign of Henry I. The rolls record county by county the income of the Crown and authorised expenditure set against this income, in accounts submitted by the sheriff. Separate from this section were the foreign accounts which dealt with matters such as the army and navy, royal works and the like. The Snetesham accounts are found in this section which came after all the various county accounts. This section became so bulky by the fourteenth century, making the rolls very unwieldy, that in 1368 a separate set of rolls, the Rolls of Foreign Accounts (TNA class E364) was started. The final accounts of Clerks of the King's Ships can be found in this class from 1372 to 1452.

[2] Calendar of Patent Rolls (hereafter CPR), 1334–38, p. 4.

Carisbroke Priory.[1] This might have fitted in rather more easily with his work for the king's ships, which were mostly based on the south coast. We have no evidence, however, that he was active in either living.

His other appearances in royal records are more clearly related to his work as an active member of the general machinery of government. He was, for example, involved in the royal use of Italian merchant houses to finance the wars with France. The Bardi provided £50 to Snetesham to pay men at arms at Hull in 1338; these men were guarding wool for export with the proceeds of its sale also intended to provide war finance.[2] In 1339 the collector of customs at Lincoln was ordered to allow Snetesham and others to send wool to Antwerp for the same purpose.[3] In the same year he was helping to get one Robert Deth from Maidstone released from prison in the town. Deth had refused to go to sea on the *Cog Thomas*. Snetesham and the ship's master Richard Fille undertook to ensure that Deth obeyed orders and purged his contempt. This man must have been more than a common seaman for the matter to reach Chancery and to be enrolled in the Close Rolls, perhaps a navigator or pilot.[4] Snetesham's commission in 1338 to investigate a possible case of piracy by royal mariners against ships of the Count of Guelders and to ascertain the whereabouts of the missing cargoes was the kind of duty which fell to the lot of most clerks of the King's ships.[5]

The final settlement of his accounts was perhaps made more difficult by an incident which apparently took place some time after 1338 and which came to royal attention in August 1357. Snetesham was granted a pardon because he was unable to provide any details of the income and expenditure of his office when he was Clerk of the King's Ships between 1336 and 1338. The pardon states that all his rolls and memoranda were lost when the ship carrying them was taken by enemy vessels off Zealand. He, therefore, had no receipts for any of the money received from the Exchequer, the King's Chamber or the Keeper of the Wardrobe in this period and thus could not finalise his accounts. It is not clear why these documents were on board a ship or ships but it is certainly the case that accounts for the years in question do not exist.[6] There are no notices of

[1]CPR, 1334–38, p. 507.
[2]Calendar of Chancery Rolls (hereafter CCR), 1337–39, p. 589.
[3]Calendar of Fine Rolls (hereafter CFR), 1337–47, p. 153.
[4]CCR, 1339–41, p. 159.
[5]CPR, 1338–40, p. 143.
[6]CPR, 1354–58, p. 608. This pardon explains the apparent disappearance of the records for this year noted in a set of accounts for 1363–67 relating to Robert Crull's tenure of the post of Clerk of the King's Ships, TNA: E101/29/4.

Snetesham's death or his reasons for relinquishing the clerkship but it seems likely that he may have left royal service for whatever reason in the late 1350s.

It should be noted that, while both accounts translated here relate to periods when Edward III was actively exploring the best use to make of royal ships, these accounts have very little to say on this topic. A full and soundly researched account of the naval exploits of this period can be found in Graham Cushway's *Edward III and the War at Sea: the English Navy, 1327–77*.[1] As far as maritime activities are concerned, 1344–45, the year to which the particular account relates, was a relatively quiet one. Although efforts were made to put together a fleet of requisitioned vessels they seem to have come to nothing, largely because of the reluctance of ship owners to support yet another campaign. In this year Snetesham's main concern was to oversee the building of a vessel described as a flune at Vauxhall on the Thames above London. This ship type is not common and mentions are confined to the mid-fourteenth century. There is little information about the design; it was clearly not very big (the costs incurred in this instance were round about a hundred pounds) but was not intended only for inland waters since two vessels of this type are recorded as preparing to sail to Brittany in the same account. There is no mention of any masts, spars or sails or rigging or of any oars for the flune in this account but this may reflect the stage which building had reached rather than any lack of these essential features of medieval ships. The hull was clinker-built in the usual fashion for this period.

Other expenditure relates to a group of ships setting forth for Gascony and also the provision of victuals for two others (both called flunes) by the Abbey at Beaulieu. The assumption is that these ships were setting forth from the Beaulieu River. The victuals included flour, beer, cider, beef, mutton, fish and onions as well as firewood for the galley. The Abbot of Beaulieu also provided Thomas with cash for sailors' wages by means of indentures between Thomas and himself.

The final section of these particulars relates to the refurbishment of personal armour intended for ships' crews. Considerable effort was devoted to the basinets or light steel helmets provided which were burnished and also decorated with white and red leather. Some sort of plate armour was also renovated for the crews of royal ships.

---

[1]Graham Cushway, *Edward III and the War at Sea: the English Navy, 1327–77* (Woodbridge, 2011).

The second account translated here is Snetesham's final accounts from the Pipe Roll for the period from 26 February 24 Edward III (1350) till 24 June 27 Edward III (1353), a period of 3 years, 16 weeks and 4 days; the office was then handed over to Matthew de Torksey.[1] This was a period which included the engagement of *Les Espagnols sur Mer*, also known as the Battle of Winchelsea. This was a major encounter which ended with the English taking twenty-four large Spanish ships during a running boarding action on the high seas, probably the first time something like this was attempted. Froissart provided a dramatic and colourful account of the battle in his Chronicle which included the *Cog Thomas* under the command of the King himself deliberately ramming an enemy vessel and causing a considerable amount of damage to both ships.[2] This battle leaves no trace in Snetesham's accounts; there is no sudden increase in money for the office after August (the battle took place on 29 August); receipts continue at much the same rate as before. No ships apparently needed sudden urgent repairs. One explanation for this is that William Clewer also accounted as Clerk of the King's Ships in these years and his accounts contain rather more information about vessels damaged in the fight against the *Espagnols* (in fact Castilians allied to France).[3] There is also the possibility that Froissart's account is somewhat overblown. The later years covered by this Pipe Roll account, 1351–53, were years of truce or of a lower level of conflict. What look like routine repairs were undertaken, with the provision of ovens in the *Cog Thomas* in 1350 and in the *George* in 1351 as special projects. We may speculate that the need for these is perhaps an indication that elite passengers were expected on board who required a higher standard of living than that usually provided for mariners.

The accounts, however, despite this lack of material about the operation of royal ships allow the reader to build up a picture of the operation of ship yards at this period. There is information about the sources of naval supplies and about the equipment to be found on these vessels and about the work force. Some of the technical language is still obscure but even so much can be learnt from this material.

---

[1] Some selectioms from Torksey's accounts are transcribed in B. Sandahl, *Middle English Sea Terms, III Standing and Running Rigging* (Uppsala, 1982), Appendices 6.1, 2.3, on pp. 150–52.

[2] Geoffrey Brereton (ed.), *Froissart Chronicles* (London, 1968), pp. 113–19.

[3] TNA: E101/24/14.

The Editing of the Accounts

Both documents are originally in Latin, but technical terms for which the clerk could find no Latin equivalent are usually in English. If the meaning of a term is unknown or uncertain it is printed in italics. These terms can be found in the Glossary below with a suggested meaning where this is available. Also in the Glossary are technical terms which are now archaic but whose meaning is clear. Place names are modernised as are the first names of individuals named. Surnames are as written in the MS. The names of ships are in italics with modernised spelling.

Glossary

Armid	Connected with building; meaning unknown
Babeyne/beneyne	Brushwood tied up with only one withy
Bacinett/basinet	A small light steel helmet, usually with a visor in front
Bast	A bolt rope of soft-laid rot-proofed hemp
Bemes	Beams; strong thick pieces of timber stretched across the hull from side to side to support the deck
Berders	Ship's carpenters working on the hull planking
Berling	A pole or spar; may have been used for bearing off a vessel from a wharf
Bever	Material used for awnings
Boiropes	A rope attaching a buoy to an anchor
Bolstres	Small pieces of soft wood used to prevent cables or other things chafing against structural timbers
Caggyngcable	Probably a cable used with the anchor
Cavil	A wooden peg or wedge
Cortic	Tree bark
Dedmennesheyne	A flattened block of wood with holes, usually three in number, to receive the lanyards but without sheaves
Elbowlynes	A kind of measuring line or sounding line
Endelangtrowes	A fore and aft strengthening timber
Endlof	Possibly a variant of the above
Estrichbord	Board imported from the Baltic
Filace	Rope yarn
Firnaculis	Unknown
Forchekes	Unknown
Gemae	Rosin
Gliphes	Unknown; connected with building
Glot	A term for the size of nails

Haires/ hayres	Hurdles; support for an awning
Halfes	Possibly the same as 'halse' the final planks of a strake abutting on the stem and stern posts
Hankes	Possibly reef points or cringles
Hurdis	Palisade or bulwarks fitted to the waist of a ship
Jonkes	Junk; old cordage
Knows	Knees; angled timbers to support the deck beams
Koke/Kokks	Possibly cock boat
Legg	A prop
Lollers	Tacks
Luch	Anchor
Lynes	Small ropes
Midglot	Middle sized nails
Nailtols	Nail tools? A device for masking nails
Planchbord	Thick cut board
Plator	Plate armour
Ran	Rouen; used for cordage etc. imported from Normandy
Rastres	Unknown
Righoltbord	Softwood boards from Riga
Rivesinges	Modern risings; a strake supporting the thwarts
Salecos beres	Wicker baskets
Salo	Salt
Scaltrowe	Shaltree; a pole used for moving a vessel
Seyfflnes	Rope; use unknown
Shaffhokes	A sickle shaped hook attached to the yards for cutting the rigging of an opponent when running up to board her
Sherwynd	Part of a mechanism for raising the mast or other heavy gear
Skegge	The after keg or after-part of the keel
Sketfattes	Vats for necessary purposes
Stempne locks	Connected with the stem piece which unites the bows of a ship
Straie	Unknown
Stup	Tow
Susternes	Connected with the parrel; perhaps a special kind of double block or a pair of thimbles lashed together
Swyvels	Swivel
Tabula	Usual meaning table; here a stand
Talchid	Firewood
Talwode	Firewood

Tieldes	Awnings
Trac	Perhaps a sledge; something drawn or pulled along
Trief	A square sail without bonnets
Trisrop	Rope for hoisting a boat on board
Tynclenail	A nail used in connection with the tingle, the board which covered the space formed by the stem and the continuation of the gunwales
Uptighes	Upties; ropes that tie up the yards
Utmell head	Unknown
Virons	Avirons, that is oars
Washours	Washers
Wegges	Wedges
Welsdysshbord	Board from the forests of the Weald in Kent and Sussex
Woles	Rope wound tightly around a mast or yard for support or as a repair
Wrong hokes	Connected with wrongs or floor timbers
Wynches	Winches
Wyveling	Caulking material

1. *Particulars of the receipts of Thomas de Snetesham lately Clerk of the Royal Ship called the* George *from 25th January in the 18th year of Edward III after the Conquest, King of England finishing on 24th day of the same month of the same year*[1]

[TNA: E 101/24/7]

Receipts of Money

The same Thomas de Snetesham accounts that he has received from Nicolas Pyk on 9th June at Westminster from moneys received by him from Thomas de Hatfelde at the receipt of money of the King's Chamber for the making of a certain *flune* for the King. £6.

The same from the same on the same day of the same month at London for the making of the same *flune*. £4.

The same from the same on the 5th of the same month at Westminster for the same works. £10.

The same from the same 27th of the same month for the said works. £10.

(The money was received from Thomas de Hatfeld via the same Nicholas).[2]

The same from Nicholas Pyk of London on 9th September in victuals and money for the wages of various sailors setting forth with certain royal ships to Gascony by order under the privy seal among the writs for that term. £113.

The same from the Abbot of Beaulieu and the Convent in the same place on 18th June for the wages of sailors on board the royal ships the *George*, the *Marie* and the *Laurence* for the time they were anchored at Burselden in Hampshire and off the Isle of Wight as stated in letters under the great seal remaining in the Hanaper among the orders of this term. £20 12s 8d.

And from the same Abbot and Convent of the same place for the wages of the said sailors on the said ships as appears in two indentures drawn up between the masters of the same ships and one between the said Thomas and the Abbot, remaining in the Hanaper of this term with letters under the privy seal among the orders for this term. £21 0s 2d.

Total of receipts.

Total £126 12s 10d.[3]

---

[1]The regnal year of Edward III began on 25 January so this account covers one complete year.
[2]Note in the right-hand margin.
[3]Note in the left-hand margin.

Particulars of the account of Thomas de Snetesham
Clerk of the George from 25 January in the year of the King
as above and beginning on the said 18 and finishing 24 of
the same month in the same year

Wages of royal sailors[1]

The same Thomas de Snetesham accounts that he expended on the wages of Robert Saloman master of the royal ship *George,* 2 constables and 2 carpenters each taking 6d per day and 80 sailors each taking 3d per day and 2 boys each at 1½d per day while on board the said ship on a certain voyage to be made to Gascony lasting from 16th September in the above year to 20th October next following (both days included) for 35 days. £39 16s 3d.

The same Thomas de Snetesham accounts that he expended on the wages of Adam Cogge master of the royal ship called *Denys* and Wilfred de Swerdeston clerk of the same 2 constables 1 carpenter 80 sailors, 2 boys, all receiving per day as above, while on board the said ship going as above in the said period. £39 16s 3d.

The same Thomas accounts that he expended to Robert Wygeyn master of a royal ship called the *Passenger* and Reginald of Ferrara clerk of the same for their wages and 30 sailors 1 boy each receiving per day as above while on board the same ship as above at the same period. £15 – 22½d.

The same Thomas accounts that he has expended to William Piers master of a royal ship called the *Robinet* for his wages receiving 6d per day and 17 sailors each receiving 3d per day while on board the said ship as above for the said period. £8 6s 3d.

The same Thomas accounts that he has expended to John William, master of a royal ship called the *Messager* for his wages receiving 6d per day 20 sailors each receiving 3d per day as above while on board the said ship as above for the said period. £9 12s 6d.[2]

Total £ 112 13s 1½d.[3]

Victuals received by Adam Cogge from the Abbot of Beaulieu.[4]
7 quarters of flour price 32s 6d.

---

[1]Note in the left-hand margin.
[2]£10 15d has been crossed out and £9 12s 6d substituted.
[3]£113 19½d has been crossed out and £112 13s 1½d substituted.
[4]This heading and the details of victuals supplied are in a note in the left-hand margin.

9 barrels beer price 33s.
1 pipe cider price 9s.
9 beef carcasses price 33s.
18 carcasses mutton price 9s.
And ½ quarter fish price 2s.
500 *talwode* price 3s.

The same Thomas de Snetesham accounts that he paid to the foresaid Adam Cogge master of a certain royal *flune* called the *Laurence* for his sustenance and that of 40 sailors while on board the ship for a voyage to Brittany by order of the said Lord King that the said Adam should obtain victuals form the Abbot of Beaulieu given on 14th November in the said year as appears in 2 indentures that were made between the said Abbot and the said master remaining in the hanaper of Easter term dated 18th June in the said year as required by letter of privy seal; and the total cost of the said victuals was accounted for by the said Thomas de Snetesham in the rolls of the Exchequer noted above among the Receipts. £6 6d.

Victuals delivered to John Salman[1]
4 quarters flour 20s.
2 barrels beer price 140s.
Salt fish price 13s 4d.
500 Onions price 5s.
500 billet price 6s 8d.
In money 6s 8d.

The same Thomas accounts that he expended to John Salman master of a certain royal *flune* called the *Marie* for the sustenance if himself and 30 sailors while on board the same ship for the voyage aforesaid by order of the King in victuals and money received by the said Thomas from the Abbot of Beaulieu as above and also noted at the Exchequer 18th June by writ under the great seal. £4 11s 7d.

Wages[2]
The same Thomas de Snetesham accounts that he paid to Robert Saloman master of the royal ship called the *George* Thomas Monete constable and 14 sailors, ordered by the King to remain on the same ship for her safe-keeping at Burselden in Hampshire from 21st October to 13th

---

[1]This and the preceding heading is a note in the left-hand margin.
[2]Marginal note.

January[1] then next following each receiving per day as above for 96 days inclusive. £19 4d.

Wages[2]

The same Thomas accounts for his own wages receiving 6d per day from 25th January in the said year to 24th of the same month in the same year for 364 days inclusive. £9 2s 7d.

Purchases[3]

The same Thomas accounts that he has spent on 2 pieces of timber bought and used on 7th June for 1 beam for a certain *flune* being newly built at Vauxhall[4] by order of the King 10s.

Also for the carriage of the same from Southwark to Vauxhall 4d.

Also for 2 *skegges* bought and used 6s 8d.

Also for the carriage of the same from London to Vauxhall 3d.

Also for 2 pieces called *susternes* and 1 post bought and used 4s 3d.

Also for 153 pieces of timber called *wrong hokes knows forchekes halfes stampne loks* each at 6d bought and used for the said *flune* at Newhithe[5] 76s 6d.

Also for the carriage of the same from Newhithe to Vauxhall 8s.

Also in moving the same from the place where they were bought at Newhithe to the boats 10d.

Also in 4 pieces bought at Southwark for *rivesing* then sawn for the said *flune* 13s. 4d

Also for the carriage of the same to the said place 6d.

Also for the purchase of 12 pieces of timber called *bemes* and *endelangtrowes* for the said *flune* 12s.

Also for 100 pieces made in *rastres* for shores and *legges* bought there 22s 10d

Also for the carriage of the same out from Southwark to the said place 6d.

Also for 1 piece of timber for 1 rack then to be made 3s.

Also for 4 pieces of timber bought in Southwark for *hurdis* of the same 4s 10d

Also for the carriage of the same 2d.

[1]This has been corrected from 23.

[2]Marginal note.

[3]Marginal note.

[4]The MS reads Fakenshall, an archaic spelling of Vauxhall.

[5]Newhithe (New Hythe) in Kent, near Maidstone on the Medway.

Also for 200 boards called *Weldisshbord* bought from various men in London and in various places 32s.

Also for 100 boards called *righoltbord* 50s.

Also for 50 *estrich bords* for *hurdis* of the said *flune* bought and used 6s 8d.

Also for the carriage of the same boards from London to Vauxhall with 4 carts 16d.

Also 1 last of pitch containing 12 barrels with carriage 24s 6d.

Also for 2 barrels of tar bought for 5s.

Also for 2000 *wyveling* bought at 2s 9d a thousand 5s 6d.

And for 6 jars of oil price per jar 10d 5s.

Also for 100 lbs rosin bought and used 3s 4d.

Also for 200 spikes bought and used 20d.

Also for 1300 nails bought at the price per 100 5d 5s 5d.

And for 2000 bought at 16d per thousand 2s 8d.

And for 1500 nails bought for 17½d.

And for 4303 quarters of clench and *anned* bought in the Weald price per thousand 10s 44s 10½d.

Also for empty coffers bought for *saleco beres* 4s 6d.

And for making them 14d.

Also for 74 *planchbord*s bought and used for *berdyng* and *endlof* for the said *flune* price each 5d 33s 10d.

Also for the carriage of the same from London to Vauxhall in 3 carts 12d.

And for 100lbs of iron bought and used for various works then undertaken to wit bolts and ironwork for the rudder with the making 6s 11d.

Carpenters' wages[1]

The same Thomas de Snetesham accounts that he paid to John Miche Peter Talborch Richard Ballard William de Stone William de Bedeford Nicholas Dyleswych Willian Farman and Solomon Brennyng shipwrights and *berders* working on said *flune* at Vauxhall at a rate of 6d per day for 24 working days between 22nd June and 4th August in the said year £4 16s.

And the same Thomas accounts for the wages of John Godland John Stokflet Thomas Hugo Michael Salaman of Sarre John Colyn William Morice Arnold Pacce carpenters and clenchers working there for the said period each receiving 5d per day £4.

Also the same Thomas accounts for the wages of Wilfred Palmer John Geffrey Roger Palmer Thomas Morice Franceys Carpenter John Pesak

---

[1]Note in the left-hand margin.

Henry Sivert Hugo Edmund carpenters and holders working there on the said *flune* for the said period each receiving 4d per day 64s.

Also for the wages of Thomas Gaiwood remaining there looking after the purchases and assisting the carpenters for the said period in the same place receiving 3d per day. 6s.

And the same Thomas accounts for the wages of 2 men sawing revesyng and weyres for the said *flune* 6 days within the said period receiving 10d per day 5s.

Total £12 11s.

Various necessaries bought for various armaments belonging to royal ships.[1]

The same Thomas accounts for 100 ells of canvas bought from Alan Gille and used in the repairs and improvements of various *plator* and *bacinett* on board various ships of the Lord King between 29th February in the said year and 24 March next following 32s.

And for 6000 nails for the said *plat* bought and used at a price per 100 10d 5d.

And for white and red leather bought and used for decorating *basinet* 2s.

And for white thread bought and used 11d.

And in 3lb white leather bought and used for the *plat* and *bas* aforesaid 8d.

And for 2 pots of oil bought for the same and used 2s.

And for 4 lb varnish bought and used for the same 12d.

And for 150 staples bought for the same and used 12d.

And for 100 *firnaculi*s 16d.

And in a russet coffer bought and used for the same 12d.

And for 1 quarter of coal bought for the same and used 8d.

Total 39s 2d.

Wages of various workers working on these armaments belonging to the ships of the Lord King at the Tower of London.[2]

And the same Thomas accounts that he has paid to Peter Lenglys while at the Tower of London to supervise and work on the said *plat* and *basinet* for 12 days receiving 6d per day 6s.

And for the wages of Henry Roye John of Totenhal Jacob Springet Roger de Donne each receiving 4d per day working there on the work as above for the same period 16s.

---

[1]Note in the left-hand margin.
[2]Note in the left-hand margin.

And for the wages of 4 men remaining there to finish and burnish the said *bascinett* each receiving 3d per day for 10 working days 10s.

And for the wages of 2 tailors working on the covering of the said *plat* and the decorating of the *bascinetts* each receiving 3d per day for 12 days 6s.

Total 38s.

Overall total of expenses £187 17s 10½d And he should have more 165s ½d.[1]

2.   *The enrolled accounts of Thomas de Snetesham*
clerk of the king's ships in the reign of Edward III
for the years 1350–53

[TNA: E372/203].

The account of Thomas de Snetesham, clerk of the king's ships and barges concerning various purchases provisions and equipment bought and provided for the royal ships pinnaces and barges by the terms of a writ under the great seal dated 9 July 31 Edward III (1357) which is enrolled among the King's Remembrancer's Memoranda for Trinity Term in the same year among the fees. In this writ is stated that the King on 1st March in the 24th year of his reign verbally ordered the afore-said Thomas to provide the equipment and other things necessary for the operation of the royal ships and barges, and carpenters and other work-men needed for the required work to be employed and paid at the King's wages. Later by another royal writ open under the great seal given 8th February 26 Edward III, enrolled among the writs of the same year, the King assigned the said Thomas to make provisions in the aforesaid mat-ter and the King ordered the Treasurer and barons of the Exchequer that the said Thomas's account for the period, in which he was required to make provision either on his own initiative permitted to him orally by the King or made by virtue of the grant made to him at a later date, should be audited under oath and due and reasonable allowances made to him.

Concerning these purchases provisions, gear, equipment and other necessities for the royal ships pinnaces and barges he accounts from the said 1st March in the said year on which day he received the said office by oral order of the King from Nicholas Pike, the clerk before him in

---

[1]Note in the left-hand margin.

the said office to 24 June in the year 27 Edward III, that is for 3 years, 16 weeks and 4 days. He then handed over the said office to Matthew de Torkeseye the clerk after him by royal writ in an order and indenture then made between the said Matthew and Thomas. From which day the said Matthew makes account elsewhere in this roll.[1]

Receipts[2] in year 24
The same accounts for the receipt of £6 from Robert of Mildenhale, receiver of moneys in the King's Chamber on 26th February 24 Edward III for the repair of various ships as contained in the roll of particulars delivered to the Treasury

And for £10 received from the same Robert on the same day for the same ship repairs as noted therein.

And for £10 received from the same Robert on 13th March for the repair of ships as noted therein.

And for £20 received from the same Robert on 21st March for the aforesaid purpose as noted therein.

And for £6 13s 4d received from the same Robert on 3rd April 24 Edward III for the same purpose as noted therein.

And for £10 received from the same of the same[3] for ship repairs as noted therein.

And For £30 received from the same Robert on 17th of the same month for the repair of various royal ships as noted therein.

And for £40 received 26th of the same month for the repair of royal ships as noted therein.

And for 60s received from the same Robert 8th May of the same year by the hands of William Rider for the wages of sailors taking a certain ship, the *Mariole*, from Sandwich to London as noted therein.

And for £55 received from the same Robert 15th May of the same year by the hands of Pelegerin of St Luke for the purchase of a certain ship called the *St Jake* and for various other provisions to be made as[4] noted therein.

And for 55s received from the same Robert on the same day for the wages of the said Thomas as noted therein.

---

[1]The accounts of Matthew de Torksey for 1358–59 are on TNA Pipe Roll E372/203 on membranes 33 and 34; for 1361–62 on E372/206 and for 1362–63 on E372/207.
[2]Marginal note.
[3]That is on the same day from the same person.
[4]The next word has been scratched out in the MS.

And for £30 received from the same Robert on 28th May for the purchase of a certain ship of Bayonne as noted therein.

And for £14 received from the same Robert on 5th June in the same year for taking various ships from Sandwich to London as noted therein.

And for £10 received from the same Robert on the 22nd of the same month for repairs to various royal ships as noted therein.

And for £16 15s 6d received from the same Robert on 11th July in the same year for the same purpose as noted therein.

And for 44s received from the same Robert on 13th of the same month for the wages of the said Thomas as noted therein.

And for £20 received from the same Robert on the same day for the repair of the royal ships as noted therein.

And for £40 received from the same Robert on 14th August in the same year for the aforesaid purpose as noted therein.

And for 21s received from the same Robert on the same day by the hands of Thomas Saltfletby for his wages and those of 4 colleagues going from London to Sandwich in a certain ship called the *Porteyoie* as noted therein.

And for 21s received from the same Robert on 3rd September in the same year by the hands of the same Thomas for the wages of the same Thomas and his said colleagues going to Wynchelsee in the same ship as noted therein.

And for £40 received from the same Robert for the repair of royal ships as noted therein.

And for £20 received from the same Robert on 16th October in the same year for the abovesaid purpose as noted therein.

And for £66 13s 4d received from the same Robert on 10th November in the same year for the purpose as above as noted therein.

And for £20 received from the same Robert on 13th of the same month for the above purpose as noted therein.

And for £33 6s 8d received from the same Robert on 11th January for the same purpose as noted therein,

And for £40 from the same Robert on 12th February in the 25th Year for the purpose above as noted therein.

And for £30 received from the same Robert on 26th February for the same purpose as noted therein.

And for £25 received from Richard of Norwich on the 21st August in the 24th year abovesaid by the hands of Thomas Brembre as noted therein.

And for £4 received from the same Richard 7th September in the same year by the hands of William Bassyngden master of a ship called *Goldberete* for the wages of William himself and his colleagues as noted therein.

And for 60s received from ?the same Richard on the same day by the hands of the said William Basshyngden for making various purchases as noted therein.

Total Receipts   £610 9s 10d   Concerning which

Expenses[1]

The same Thomas accounts for 260 pieces of timber 30 cartloads of timber bought by the cartload 250 pieces of timber called *legg* 1301 *shipboards* 207 *righolt boards* 1400 *estricboard* 92 *planchboards* 18 empty tuns 7200 biletts for *cavil* then to be made 108 *talchid* bought and provided between the said 1st March 24 Edward II and the last day of February next following for the repair and improvement for the ships called *Cog Thomas*, *Edward*, and *Michel* and various other royal ships flunes barges and boats built and repaired within the period aforesaid £113 9s as contained in the roll of particulars delivered to the Treasury.

The same Thomas must answer for this timber boards *legg* barrels billets and *talschid* and he does so below.

And for 396 pieces of elm timber bought and provided for the construction of various buildings at Ratcliff for the expediting of the work on the said royal ships £7 9s 8d in the same period as noted therein. He certifies that this timber has been used for the construction of the same building by order of the king in the said period as noted therein.

And for 92,850 various nails, 24 locks, 12 haspes, 29 iron staples 5 pairs of hinges bought and provided for the repair and improvement of the said royal ships in the aforesaid period £ 21 10s 9¼d.

The same Thomas must answer concerning these nails locks and other things and he does so below.

And for 12877 lb of iron bought and provided for the repair of the said royal ships in the same period £50 6s 11¼d. as noted therein

The same Thomas must answer for this iron and he does so below.

And for 2 masts 1 spar called a sailyard 378 *virons* bought and provided for the said royal ships in the said period £27 16s 3d as noted therein.

And for 70 *tieldes* half a roll of *bever* bought and provided for *tieldes* and sails to be made for the said royal ships and boats £7 6s 6d.

The same Thomas must answer for these *tieldes* and *bever* and he does so below.

And also for 46 barrels of pitch 2 lasts 3 barrels of tar, each last holding 12 barrels, 9 weys 5½ stones of lubrication 950 lb of rosin And in

---

[1]Marginal note; the letter R (for *reddit* he answers) also appears in the margin for every item purchased for which Thomas is held liable.

wadding for oil grease and glue and [*blank*] bought and provided for caulking the royal ships barges and boats £33 10s 9¼d in the same period as noted therein.

The same Thomas must answer for this pitch tar lubrication and rosin and he does so below.

And for 20lb white lead 87lb vermilion 20lb plaster and 3lb varnish bought and provided for painting the royal ships 111s 1d in the same period as noted therein.

The same Thomas must answer for this white lead vermilion plaster and varnish and he does so below.

And for English and Flemish tiles plaster and saltpetre bought and provided for making a certain oven in the ship called *Cog Thomas* with the carriage of the tiles and stone from the place where they were bought and provided to Ratcliff, 12s 8½d in the said period as noted therein.

And for 3 anchors with 3 pieces of wood for the same bought and provided in the said period 58s 4d as noted therein.

The said Thomas must answer for these anchors and he does so below.

And for 85 scoops 15 shovels and 9 *trac* bought and provided for the said ships in the said period 19s 9d as noted therein.

The same Thomas must answer for these scoops and shovels and he does so below.

And for 2260 ells of canvas 20 ells of thread called *fillace* bought for the sails made for the said ships 4915 4 clewes and 40 skeins of white yarn bought and provided for cables and ropes then made for the said ships together with the transport and carriage of the canvas and yarn form where it was bought to Ratcliff £44 18s 7½d in the said period as noted therein.

The same Thomas must answer and he does so below.

And for 7 great cables 16 small cables 885 lb ropes 4 *lynes* and ropes of bast bought and provided for the said ships with the transport and carriage of the same from the place where they were bought to Ratcliff within the said period £22 19d as noted therein.

The same Thomas must answer for these cables and ropes and he does so below.

And if 1 anvil and 1 pair of bellows with 2 *tabula* for bellows bought and provided for the royal works at Ratcliff with the transport of the same to Ratcliff from the place where they were bought 60s 10d as noted therein.

The same Thomas must answer for this anvil and bellows and he does so below.

And for lathes, *armid* poles nails *utmell* and *gliphs* and *straie* bought and provided for the repair of the buildings at Ratcliff £15 2s 11d in the said period as noted therein.

All these things are accounted for in the expenses for the repair of royal buildings in the same place at the said time as noted above.

And for 2 ships from Bayonne with all their equipment except for 1 boat bought by oral order of the King £55 as noted therein.

The same Thomas must answer for these ships and he does so below.

And for 1 small boat bought for the ship called *Gabriel* 16s 8d as noted therein.

And for the transport and boat dues for certain sails various *scaltrowes berling* and other things from the places where they were bought to Ratcliff 8s 9½d in the same period as noted therein.

And for the making of a certain oven for the ship called the *Cog Thomas* together with the making of 700 wooden *cavil* out of royal timber 6s 8d as noted therein.

And for the wages of various carpenters sawyers and others working there on the repair of royal ships and the royal buildings at Ratcliff together with the wages of sailors living on board the ships between 1st March 24 Edward III and the said last day of February next following £215 4s 9¾d as noted therein.

And William de Bassyngden master of the ship called the *Goldberete* in money paid to him on the said 7th September by the hands of Richard of Norwich for his wages in 2 instalments (concerning which money the same Thomas is held liable above in the Receipts of money) because the said William has not yet settled with the said Thomas £7 as noted above.

The same William must answer and he does so below.

Total Expenses £ 635 12s 8d.   He is still due £25 2s 10d as allocated to the same Thomas below after the expenses of year 27.

Receipts year 25[1]

The same received £50 from Robert of Mildenhale receiver of money in the King's Chamber for the repair of various royal ships on 19th March in year 25 as contained in the roll of particulars which has been delivered to the Treasury.

And £63 13s 4d received from the same Robert 12 April for the said purpose as noted therein.

And for £60 received from the same Robert 1st May for the repair of royal ships as noted therein.

And for £91 15s received form the same Robert 18th May for the same purpose as noted therein.

And for £60 received from the same Robert 9th June for the same purpose as noted therein.

And for £16 10s 10d received from the same Robert 20th of the same month for the same purpose as noted therein.

---

[1]Marginal note.

And for £20 received from the same Robert 9th July in the same year 25 for the same purpose as noted therein.

And for £40 received from the same Robert 23rd of the same month for the above purpose as noted therein.

And for £20 received from the same Robert 10th August in the same year 25 for the purpose explained above as noted therein.

And for £20 received from the same Robert 23rd of the same month for the said purpose as noted therein.

And for £38 13s 4d received from the same Robert 2nd October in the same year for the said purpose as noted therein.

And for £33 10s received from the same Robert 8th of the same month for the said purpose as noted therein.

And for £20 received from the same Robert 21st of the same month for the said purpose as noted therein.

And for £22 received from the said Robert 18th January year [*blank*] for the said purpose as noted therein

And for £40 received from the same Robert 13th February in year 26 for the repair of royal ships as noted therein.

And for £40 received from the same Robert 26th of the same February in the same year for the same purpose as noted therein.

Total Receipts £637 2s 6d.

Foreign Receipts[1]

The same accounts for £4 received from Simon de Reyngham in October of the said year 25 for a certain old mast sold to him as noted therein.

And for £4 13s 4d received from the royal fine for a certain transgression committed by Thomas Saltfletby and his companions on board a certain royal ship called *Porteioye* coming in the said ship from Calais to London as noted therein.

And for 9s received from Bartholomew Stigeyn for the freight charges of the passager called *Le Berthen* seeking billets in Essex as noted therein.

And for 3s 4d received from a certain Greenwich man for a certain old boat sold to him as noted therein.

And for 70s received for 1000 *talwod* and 5 *baneyne* coming from the loppings of oaks sold as noted therein.

Total foreign receipts £12 15s 8d.

Overall total of receipts £649 18s 2d.   Concerning which

[1]Marginal note.

Expenses year 25[1]

The same accounts for 586 pieces of timber 100 poles for *birlings* 700 *righolt boards* 150 *shipboards* 5777 *estrichboards* 140 *plaunchboards* 150 *talwod* bought and provided between 1st March year 25 and the last day of February for the making repair and improvement of various royal ships, to wit the *Edward, Jerusalem, Welifare, Philip,* and the *Cog John* and various other royal flunes barges and boats with the carriage of the said timber board and *talwod* from various places where it was bought in the same period to Ratcliff, £130 10s 6d as noted therein.

And the same Thomas must answer for this timber board and *talwod* and does so below.

And for 96725 nails, 4800 tree nails, 4 dozen and 7 pairs of hinges 16 haspes 36 stapuls 6 locks and 2 iron plates bought and provided for the repair of the said royal ships in the same period. £18 6s 3½d with the carriage of the same nails from the places where they were bought and provided to Ratcliff as noted therein.

And the same Thomas must answer for these nails hinges and other things and does so below.

And for 2000lb of iron bought and provided for making various necessities for the repair of the said ships with the carriage of this iron from London to Ratcliff 100s 4d in the same period as noted therein.

And the same Thomas must answer for this iron and does so below.

And for 1 mast 4 anchors 4 cables 559 *virons* bought and provided for the royal ships in the same period £38 19s 9d. as noted therein.

The same Thomas must answer for this mast, anchors, cables and *virons* and does so below.

And for 217 *tieldes* and *hayres* 3 rolls of *bever* 1167 ells of canvas 48 skeins of half pound yarn and 26 cloves of *fillace* bought and provided for the repair of the said royal ships £60 6s 11d in the said period with the carriage of the same things from the various places where they were bought and provided to Ratcliff as noted therein.

The same Thomas must answer for this awning haircloth and other things and he does so below.

And for 5 lasts 1 barrel of pitch, 15 barrels, 4½ gallons of tar, 18 wedges, 8½ hundreds of wax, 1300lb rosin, 76 gallons of oil, towe, *bremyng* and *streia* bought and provided for the repair and improvement of the said royal ships flunes and boats £ 36 2s 10d together with the carriage of the same things from the places where they were bought and provided to Ratcliff in the same period as noted therein.

---

[1]Marginal note. The letter R (*reddit*) is placed in the margin against every item for which Thomas had to answer.

The same Thomas must answer for these barrels of pitch tar wax rosin and oil and he does so below.

And for 30lb vermilion, ½lb of orpiment, 114lb of plaster 3 dozen and 10 metal foils in various colours bought and provided for painting the said royal ships £4 3s 1½d with the painting of 8 shields of the royal arms on the ship called *Edward* in the period as noted therein.

The same Thomas must answer for this vermilion orpiment plaster and metal foil and he does so below.

And for 2 anchors with 1 stock for the anchor bought and provided in the same period 16s 6d as noted therein.

The same Thomas must answer for the anchors and he does so below.

And for 28 wooden vessels called bails bought and provided for the same ships together with the repair of various wooden vessels in the same period 19s 2d as noted therein.

The same Thomas must answer for the bails and he does so below.

And for 6 cables 15 ropes called hausers 33 other ropes 14 *lynes* 843lb of cordage 1103 quarters of ½ yarn for cordage various other cordage and ropes of *bast* bought and provided for the said ships together with the carriage of the same from the places where it was bought to Ratcliff £33 10s 8¾d in the same period as noted therein.

And the same Thomas must answer for these cables and ropes and does so below.

And for 30 qua. of sea coal bought and provided for the King's forge at Ratcliff in the same period £4 10s 11d together with the weighing and carriage of the said coal from the said places where it was bought to Ratcliff as noted therein.

The said Thomas must answer for this coal and he does so below.

And for tiles stone lime *straie* and iron bought to make an oven on the *George* 34s 8d as noted therein.

And for the ballast of the said ship with the carriage of a certain windlass from Lesnes to Ratcliff 16s 2d as noted therein.

And for 6 ox skins 24 calfskins bought and provided in the same period 37s as noted therein. This same leather was bought and used in the making of *kokeror* for the said ships within the said period as he declared on oath as noted therein.

And for 15 cauldrons 7 kettles 2 lead cisterns 17 dozen lanterns and 36 hammers 25 small hatchets and 8 shafhokes bought and provided for the fitting out of the said royal ships £16 13s 10d as noted therein.

The same Thomas must answer for these cauldrons kettles and other things and does so below.

And for 4 pairs of cart wheels bought and provided for the transport of large timber 22s 10d as noted therein.

The same Thomas must answer for these wheels and does so below.

And for 1 boat bought for a ship called the *Cog Thomas* in the same period 20s as noted therein. This was delivered to the master of the said ship called the *Cog Thomas* as he declared on oath as noted therein.

And also for the wages of various carpenters smiths painters and other workmen working on the repair and maintenance of the said royal ships flunes barges and boats between the said 1st March in the said 25th year and the said last day of February in the following 26th year on various operations accounted for in the said ships and boats in the said period £351 14s.

Total Expenses £ 707 11s 11¾d And he should have more £57 13s 9¾d; this is allocated to the said Thomas below.

Receipts year 26[1]

The same accounts for £13 6s 8d received from Robert de Mildenhalle receiver of money in the King's Chamber 6th August year 26 for the repair of various royal ships and boats as contained in the roll of particulars delivered to the Treasury.

And for £8 3s 8d received from the same Robert 15th September in the same year for the repair of the said ships as noted therein.

And for £10 9d received from the same Robert 25th of the same month for the above purposes as noted therein.

And for £16 6s 8d received from the same Robert 16th October in the same year for the said purposes as noted therein.

And for £12 received from the same Robert 31st of the same month for the said purposes as noted therein.

And for £40 received from the same Robert for the said purpose as noted therein.

And 106s 8d received from the same Robert by the hands of John Stodeye on the same day to buy cordage for the royal ships as noted therein.

And for £44 received from the same Robert 28th November in the same year 26 as noted therein.

And for £25 6s 8d received for the same Robert 4th December in the same year by the hands of Adam de Bury for the purchase of timber as noted therein.

And for £24 received from the same Robert 13th December by the hands of Thomas Blod for the purchase of timber bought from the same at Lesnes as noted therein.

---

[1]Marginal note.

And for £80 received from the same Robert 22nd of the same month by the hands of Bartholomew Streyn for the purchase of cordage to be made at Bordeaux as noted therein.

And for £40 received from the same Robert 21st January in year 26 by his own hands as noted therein.

And for £50 received from the same Robert 10th February in year 27 for the repair of the said royal ships as noted therein.

And for £6 13s 4d received from Richard of Norwich 1st May for the provision of cables other necessaries.

And for £159 12s 8d received from John Malewayn being the price of various necessaries bought by the said John for the repair of royal ships as noted therein.

And for £53 6s 8d received from John de Wesenham in May in the year 26 abovesaid as noted therein.

And for 112s received from Richard de Norwich for the purchase of boards and [*illegible word*] as noted therein.

And for £13 6s 8d received from John de Wesenham 1st August in the said year as noted therein.

And for £10 received from the same John 26th August in the same year as noted therein.

And for £6 16s received from the same John the price of 234 boards bought from the same in the same year as noted therein.

And for £17 16s received from the same John the price of various necessaries bought in Flanders by the hands of Hamo Lovetot in the same year as noted therein.

Total Receipts   £641 14s 5d.

Foreign Receipts[1]

And the same accounts for 100s received in settlement of the sale proceeds of 110 oaks felled in the park of Lesnes for the works of the royal ships as noted therein.

And for 16s received from the sale of *cortic* coming from the issues of the same wood as noted therein.

And for £4 5s received for 1700 *talwod* made of the loppings coming from the said 110 oaks as noted therein.

And for £7 received from the sale of 3500 *talwod* coming from the issues of the said 110 oaks as noted therein.

And for 52s received for 301 quarters of *babeyne* made from the loppings of the said oaks as noted therein.

---

[1]Marginal note.

And for 8s 6d received from Bartholomew Stigeyn for the freight of the *Hakebot* of Poole to the *cravens* in the Vintry of London as noted therein.

And 20s received from Bartholomew Vanhale for damage to 1 cable delivered to him by Bartholomew Stigeyn to be taken from Bordeaux to London as noted therein.

Total Receipts £21 2s 6d.

Overall total receipts £6452 16s 11d   Concerning which

Expenses for year 26[1]

The same accounts for 109 oaks bought and provided for the repair of the royal ships to wit *la Jonette*, which was made out of the *Cog darundell*, the *Cog Thomas Beauchamp*, the *Gladwyre*, the *Isabel*, the *Cog John*, the *Jerusalem* and making and repairing various other royal ships and boats, £52 8s 4d between 1st March in the said year 26 and the last day of February in the following year, as noted therein.

The said Thomas must answer and he answers below.

And for 207 pieces of timber 32 cartloads of timber bought by the cartload 1923 shipboards 900 *estrchboards* 400 *righolt* board 100 planchboards 12 empty tuns 10800 billet for making wedges bought and provided for the repair of the said royal ships together with the carriage of the same from various places where they were bought and provided to Ratcliff £116 3s 4d in the same period as noted therein.

The same Thomas must answer for this timber, board and billets and he does so below.

And in 2 pairs of hinges 12 staples and hasps 57,575 nails bought and provided for the works of the said royal ships together with the carriage of the nails from various places where they were bought to Ratcliff. £8 19s 3d in the said period as noted therein.

The same Thomas must answer for these hinges staples haps and nails and he does so below.

And for 24000 and 233 lbs of iron bought and provided for making various ironwork for the said royal ships £67 11s 9¼d together with the carriage and transport of the same iron from various places where it was bought to Ratcliff in the same period as noted therein.

The same Thomas must answer for this iron and he does so below.

And for 1 mast with 1 rother 200 pieces of wood for oars[2] and 7 oars bought for the *Philip* within the same period £7 4s 5d as noted therein.

---

[1]Marginal note; as before the letter R in the margin denotes an item for which Thomas must answer.

[2]The term used in the MS is *viron* from the French *aviron*.

The same Thomas must answer for this mast and oars and he does so below.

And for 5 anchors 9 anchor stocks bought and provided for the said royal ships in the same period 69s 6d as noted therein.

The same Thomas must answer for the anchors and he does so below.

And for 68 *tieldes* 16 dozen and 6 *haeres* 40 rolls of *bever* 2119 ells of canvas 4450lbs 7 clews of yarn 3 quarters 9 cloves of *filace* bought and provided for the repair of the said royal ships in the said period £131 8s 9d with the carriage of the same *tieldes*, *bever*, canvas and thread from the various places where they were bought to Ratcliff as noted therein.

The same Thomas must answer for these *tieldes*, *bever*, canvas and thread and does so below.

And for 3 lasts of pitch 2 lasts of tar, the last containing 12 barrels, 13 weyes of wax 528 lbs of rosin 3 barrels and 14 pitchers of oil bought and provided for the repair of the said royal ships together with the carriage of the said things from the places where they were bought and provided to Ratcliff in the said period £35 5s 5d as noted therein.

The same Thomas must answer for this tar pitch wax rosin and oil and does so below.

And for 6 lb of vermilion bought for painting the said royal ships in the same period 8s as noted therein.

The same Thomas must answer for this vermilion and does so below.

And for 2 cables 4 hausers 12 lines 4 ropes 96 lb of cordage bought and provided in the same period for repairing the said ships together with carriage of the same from the places where it was bought to Ratcliff £6 14s 3d as noted therein.

The same Thomas must answer for these cables ropes and lines and does so below.

And for 2 cauldrons 2 kettles 26 lanterns 2 lead cisterns 5 small hatchets 1 large hammer 1 small hammer bought and provided for the fitting out of the said royal ships within the said period £4 5s 11d as noted therein.

The same Thomas must answer for these cauldrons kettles lanterns hatchets and hammers and does so below.

And for 1 iron saw 14 scoops 12 shovels bought in the same period 8s 9d as noted therein.

The same Thomas must answer for the saw and does so below.

And for 2 cart bodies, 2 carts bought without wheels, for the transport of large timber 16s 8d in the same period as noted therein.

The same Thomas must answer for the carts and does so below.

And for tiles and *salo* bought for the repair of the hearth in the ship called *La Jonette* in the said period 9s as noted therein.

And for the wages of various carpenters smiths painters and other workmen working on the repair and refurbishment of the said royal ships from the said 1st March in year 26 and the said last day of February next following in year 27 together with various works for the said ships done as required in the said period £310   12¼d as noted therein.

Total Expenses £745 8s 3½d; and he should have more £82 11s 4½d which is allocated to the same Thomas below.

Receipts year 27[1]
The same accounts for £37 13s 11½d received from Robert of Mildenhale, receiver of money in the King's Chamber 22nd March in year 27 for the repair of various royal ships barges and boats as noted therein.

And for £30 received from the same Robert 10th March in the same year for the repair of the said royal ships as noted therein.

And for £30 received from the said Robert 21 March for the above purpose as noted therein.

And for £100 received from the said Robert 25th of the same month by the hands of Robetr of Hull for various necessities for the repair of the said ships as noted therein.

And for £45 received from the same Robert 19th April by his own hands for the repair of various royal ships as noted therein.

And for £38 10s 4d received from William of Rothewell 4th May by the hands of John of Ellerton a royal man of arms as noted therein.

And for £30 received from the same William 11th May as noted therein.

And for £6 10s received from the same William 3rd June by the hands of John Clark of Hampton for the carriage of a certain mast from Hampton to London as noted therein.

And for £40 received from the same William 9th June as noted therein.

And for £20 received from the same William 26th of the same month as noted therein.

And for £9 10s 3d received from the same William 27th June as noted therein

Total Receipts £387 4s 6½d.

Foreign Receipts[2]
And the same accounts for 10s received from the interest on 60 *floren de scuto*[3] received from Robert of Hull as noted therein.

And for 35s 6d received for 150 lbs of lime coming from 403 quarters of *grossi lim inferi* bought as noted therein.

---

[1]Marginal note.
[2]Marginal note.
[3]Ecus; the French currency.

And for 40s received from the sale of old cordage called *jonkes* almost rotten as noted therein.

And for £4 received from the sale of timber coming from old royal ships as noted therein.

And for 13s 4d received from the sale of a certain old sail of the ship called *La Welifare* as noted therein.

Total receipts £8 18s 10d.

Overall total receipts £396 3s 4½d.   Concerning which

Expenses for year 27[1]

The same accounts for 22 oaks bought and provided for the repair of various royal ships to wit the ship called the *Nawe Saint Marie,* and the *Redcog* and various other ships flunes barges and boats between the said 1st March in year 27 to 24th June next following, 33s as noted therein.

The same Thomas must answer for these oaks and he does so below.

And for 696 pieces of timber with 2 cartloads of timber bought by the cartload 100 ship boards 603 quarters of *righolt board* 1023 e*stric board* and *wainscot* 4300 billet 125 *talwod* bought and provided for the repair of the said royal ships together with the carriage of the same timber boards and billets for the places where they were bought to Ratcliff £71 9s 1½d in the same period as noted therein.

The same Thomas must answer for this timber boards billets and *talwod* and does so below.

And in 104000 nails bought and provided for the repair of the aforesaid ships flunes and boats within the said period £14 8s 2d as noted therein.

The same Thomas must answer for these nails and does so below.

And in 18 stones of iron bought and provided for the making of 3 *swyvels* for towing 2 masts from Hartlepool and 1 mast from Scarborough in the same period 24s as noted therein.

The same Thomas must answer for these *swyvels* and does so below.

And for 3 masts with 2 spars called sailyards bought in Hartlepool and Scarborough together with the cost of towing the same from the aforesaid places where they were bought and first made to Ratcliff £28 as noted therein.

The same Thomas must answer for and he answers below.

And for 600 oars bought and provided for the said royal flunes barges and boats in the said period £35 16s 4d as noted therein.

He answers below for these.

[1]Marginal note; the letter R is written alongside items for which Thomas must answer.

And for 8 cables 2 hausers 4 ropes 12 *elbowlynes* bought and provided for the said royal ships together with the carriage of the same cables and cordage from the said places where they were bought and first made to Ratcliff in the same period £52 16s 11d as noted therein.

The same Thomas must answer for these cables ropes and lines and he answers below.

And for 10 quarters of seacoal bought for the royal forge at Ratcliff with the weighing and transport of the same by boat from London to Ratcliff in the same period 19s 5d as noted therein.

The same Thomas must answer for this coal and he answers below.

And for 1 chisel bought for a certain lathe at Ratcliff for working on boards 6d as noted therein.

The same Thomas must answer for this chisel and does so below.

And in 1000 [*word illegible*] for covering walls within the same period 10s as noted therein.

And in 28 pots of oil 3 lasts of tar containing 36 barrels 3 lasts of pitch each last containing 12 barrels 403 quarters of lime called *stup* bought and provided for the repair and improvement of the said royal ships within the same period £14 17s as noted therein.

The same Thomas must answer for this oil tar and pitch and does so below.

And in the wages of various carpenters smiths painters and other workmen working on the improvement and repair of the royal ships between the last day of February in the year 27 aforesaid and the 24th June next following together with various works for the same royal ships undertaken by assessed payments within the same period £179 9s 11½d as noted therein.

And to John of Elerton, royal sergeant at arms, for all the money lacking in the particular accounts of the said John amounting to the sum of £38 10s 4d received by the same from William de Rothwell receiver of money in the King's Chamber for doing various things and placed to the debit of the said Thomas of Snetesham as an advance and for which he was debited at the Receipt of the Chamber 40s.

The said John should answer and he does so on the dorse of this roll.

And to Robert of Hull sailor for all the money lacking in the particular accounts of Robert himself which total of £100 received from Robert of Mildenhall receiver of the King's Chamber in year 27 for various items provided in Flanders, made for the royal ships and debited to the said Thomas of Snetesham as an advance and for which he is debited at the Receipt of Money £7 16s 7d.

The said Robert of Hull must answer and he does so on the dorse of the roll.

Total expenses £411 12s and he should have more £14 17s 7½d.
And £25 2s 10d the balance due on his account for year 24.
And £57 13s 9¾d the balance due on his account for year 25.
And £82 11s 4½d the balance due on his account for year 26.

Joint total of the balances due including £18 5s 7¾d which are owing to various creditors whose names are noted on the dorse of the roll of this account called le *parcos*

£137 10s 6d.

And so the balance due to him is £42 15s 1¼d.

Old memoranda; timber boards and billets[1]

The same accounts for old timber coming from old royal ships to wit the *Cog Darundell*, the *Nawe Saint Marie*, the *Belebaw*, the *Edward*, and various other royal ships flunes barges and boats broken up within the said period. He accounts for this timber which was wholly used on the repair and improvement of various royal ships flunes barges and boats rebuilt and repaired between the first day of March in year 24 and 24th June in year 27 according to the old memoranda because it was sold within the said period for £4.[2]

He was debited concerning this sum above in money received in year 27 as noted therein.

The same accounts for 260 pieces of timber, 30 cartloads of timber bought by the cartload 250 *legg* 1031 ship boards 207 *righolt boards* 1460 *estrichboards* 92 *plaunchboards* 18 empty barrels 7200 billets 108 *talschid* received from the purchases of year 24 as noted above.

And 586 pieces of timber 100 poles for *birling* 700 *righolt boards* 150 ship boards 5777 *estrcichboards* 140 *plaunchboards* 150 *talwod* received from the purchases as noted above in year 25.

And for 55 pieces of timber given to the King by the Archbishop of Canterbury.

And for 6 pieces of timber given to the King by the Bishop of Rochester.

And for 21 pieces of timber given to the King by the Earl of Pembroke as noted therein.

And for 207 pieces of timber 32 cartloads of timber bought by the cartload 1923 shipboards 900 *estrich boards* 400 *righolt boards*

---

[1] Marginal note.
[2] Right-hand marginal note; this balances (Et eqz).

100 *plaunchboards* 12 empty barrels 10800 billets received from the purchases in year 26 as noted above.

And for 696 pieces of timber [*fold in MS*][1] 2 cartloads of timber bought by the cartload 100 shipboards 603 quarters of *righolt board* 1023 *estrichboard* 4300 billets 125 *talschid* received from the purchases in year 27 as noted above.

And for 1144 *plaunchboard* of timber [*fold*] within the period of the account as noted therein.

And for 45 pieces of timber coming from 21 oaks given to the King by Isabella Queen of England, 12 oaks given to the King by the Earl of Stafford and 12 oaks given to the King by the Abbot of Waltham as noted therein.

And for old timber coming from various broken up royal ships.

Totals Pieces of timber 1876

Cartloads of timber 64

Legg 350

Shipboards 3000 [*fold*]

Righoltboards 1903 quarters and 7

Estrichboard 9140

Plaunchboard 1476

Barrels [*fold*] 30

Talwod ? [*fold*]

Billets 22,300

Concerning these materials:

The same renders account for the repair and building of various ships flunes craiers barges and boats which were to be built and repaired between the said 26th February in year 24 abovesaid and 24th June in year 27; 1923 pieces of timber 64 cartloads of timber 154 poles and *legg* 2216 shipboards 1620 boards of *righolt boards* 8007 *estrichboards* 1054 *plaunchboards* 30 empty barrels 383 *talwod* [*fold*] billets as noted therein.

And the same delivered to the same Matthew of Torkeseye 453 pieces of timber which included 272 spars 196 *legg* 988 shipboard 373 boards of *righolt board* 1133 *estrichboard* 422 *plaunchboard* [*fold*] 2400 billets of which 248 were worked as per the aforesaid indenture.

The same Matthew must answer for these pieces *legg* boards billets and does so on the dorse of the roll.

---

[1]Here and in several instances below a fold in the parchment obscures a word.

Nails and various other ironwork[1]

The same renders account for 92,950 various nails 24 locks 12 haspes 29 staples and 5 pairs of hinges received from the purchases in year 24 as noted above.

And for 96725 nails 4800 trenails 4 dozen and 7 pairs of garnets 16 haspes 36 staples 6 locks and 2 iron lanterns received from the purchases in year 26 as noted above.

And for 2 pairs of hinges 12 staples and hasps 57575 nails received from the purchase in year 26 as noted above.

And for 104,050 nails received from the purchase in year 27 as noted above.

And for nails with rivets called *cleynch* and *anned* made of iron bought earlier for the King weighing 1400lbs in the accounting period.

And for 11500lbs of old nails called *cleynch* and *anned* coming from the old royal ship broken up within the same period.

And for 106lbs of large *spikyng* coming from a certain ship called *Cog Darundell*.

And for 2610lbs of various bolts and ironwork coming from old ships broken up within the said period as noted therein.

Totals

Nails 351250

Clench and *anned* 25606 lbs

Locks 30

Old ironwork 2610 lbs

Trenails 4800

Staples and haspes 105

Hinges and garnets 62

Concerning these materials:

The same accounts that he used for the repair and refurbishment of various ships flunes barges and boats built and repaired between the said 26th February in the said 24th Year and the said 24th June in year 27 abovesaid, 291,378 nails 769 lbs of nails called *cleynch* and *anned* a hundred for 125lb, 105 staples and hasps 62 pairs of hinges and garnets as noted therein.

And he accounts for the delivery to the said Matthew of 59972 various nails to wit clench for *kokkes* 220 nails 47 *anned* 15325 nails of large *glot* 23924 nails called *middglot* 20413 nails of *tynalenaill*.

[1]Marginal note.

Also 453 lbs of clench and *anned* coming from iron bought earlier 503 quarters 14lbs of old *cleynch* and *anned* newly worked and 7110 lbs coming from old clench and *anned* and other ironwork coming from old broken up royal ships by the said indenture as noted therein.

The said Matthew must answer for these said nails and he does so, on the dorse of this roll.[1]

[2]The same render account for 12877lbs of iron received from purchases in year 24 as noted in another part of this roll.

And for 2000 lbs of iron received from purchases in year 25 as noted therein.

And for 24233 lbs of iron received from purchases in year 26 as noted therein.

Total receipts 39110 lbs of iron.

The same accounts for the making of large nails, *ryvets* called *cleynch* and *anned* bolts and various other ironwork for the royal ships barges and boats to be built and repaired in the said period using 34629 lbs of iron as noted therein.

And he accounts that he has delivered to the said Matthew de Torkeseye 4401lbs of iron in 65 bars by the abovesaid indenture.

The said Matthew must account for this iron and he does so below.

[3]The same accounts for 2 masts 1 spar called sail yard 378 oars received from purchases in year 24 as noted in another part of the roll.

And for 1 mast 559 oars received from purchases in year 25 as noted therein.

And for 1 mast 1 rudder 206 pieces of timber for oars and 7 oars bought in year

26 as noted therein.

And for 9 spars called sail yards coming from various royal ships.

And for 3 masts 2 spars and 600 oar blanks received by purchase in year 27 as noted therein

And for 15 masts coming from various old ships broken up in various places as noted therein.

Totals masts 22

Spars called sail yards 13

---

[1]Account continues on the dorse of the roll.

[2]Marginal note; iron. The letter R is also placed in the margin against every item for which the accountant must answer and the note 'this balances' in the left-hand margin when the quantities of material used or delivered to Torksey correspond to those purchased or received.

[3]Marginal note; masts.

Oars 1744
Rudder 1

Concerning these materials:

The same accounts that he had placed 6 masts in 6 royal ships in the said period.

And he accounts that he had used and delivered to various mariners for the said royal flunes barges and boats 954 oars.

And he accounts that he had placed the said rudder in a certain ships called the *Jonett* as mentioned in the said roll of particulars.

And 1 mast which was rotten was sawn up for boards for the said ships then being built as noted therein.

And he accounts that he delivered to the said Matthew 15 masts 12 spars called sail yards 910 oars and oar blanks and 6 trestle tables boards made out of the said mast by the said indenture as noted therein.

The same Matthew must answer for these masts sailyards oars and boards and he does so below.

[1]And the same renders account for 70 *tieldes* half a roll of *bever* 1260 ells of canvas of filace received from the purchases of year 24 as noted in another part of the roll.

And for 217 *tieldes* and *haires* 3 rolls of *bever* 1167 ells of canvas 26 cloves of filace received in the purchases of year 25 as noted therein.

And for 68 *tieldes* 16 dozen and 6 *haires* rolls of *bever* 21219 ells of canvas 203 quarters and 10 cloves of filace received in the purchases of year 26 as noted therein.

Totals *haires* and *tieldes* 553

Rolls of *bever* 43½

Ells of canvas 4536

Filace 203 quarters 56 cloves

Concerning these materials

The same accounts that these have been used as awnings for various royal ships and in making and repairing sails for the same royal ships within the same period; awnings 514 *tieldes* 16 rolls 43 ells of *bever* 3511 ells of canvas 56 cloves and 50 lbs of filace. And he accounts that he delivered to Matthew of Torkeseye 39 *tieldes* 27 rolls and 27 ells of *bever* 1025 ells of canvas 228lbs of filace.

The same Matthew must answer for the *tieldes bever* canvas and filace and he does so below.

---

[1]Marginal note; tieldes.

[1]The same accounts for one old sail of the ship called *La Welifare* as contained in the said roll of particulars. He accounts for the sale of this sail; the same Thomas accounted for the money among[2] the Money Received in year 27 as noted in another part of this roll.

And the same accounts for 494 lbs of yarn 4 cloves and 40 skeynes of yarn received by purchase in year 24 as noted in another part of the roll.

And for 10466 lbs received from Thomas Cary sheriff of Somerset and Dorset by 3 indentures in 22 sarplers freighted with cordage (concerning which there are 2 indentures for 7920 lbs of yarn).[3]

And for 1103 quarters and a half of 1½ lb thread 48 skeynes of half pound thread received by purchase in year 25 as noted therein.

And for 4450 lbs 1 8 cloves of thread received from the purchases of year 26 as noted therein.

Yarn total: 21018 of 'half' thread 12 cloves 88 skeynes of yarn

Concerning these materials

The same accounts for the making of various cables hausers *uptighes boiropes* and various other cordage made for the said royal ships in the said period 17018 lbs of 'half' and 12 cloves of thread.

He accounts for these cables hausers and ropes being placed and used in the various said royal ships in the said period as he declared under oath.

And in the making and repair of various sails for the said royal ships ordered to be made and repaired and improved within the said period 88 skeynes of sail thread as mentioned in the said roll of particulars.

And he accounts that he delivered to the same Matthes of Torkeseye 40010 lbs of yarn in 10 sarplers made up of 90 ells of canvas by the said indenture as noted therein.

The same Matthew must answer for this thread and the sarplers and he does so below.

[4]The same accounts for 3 anchors received by purchase in year 24 as noted in another part of the roll.

And for 6 anchors received by purchase in year 25 as noted therein.

And for 5 anchors 9 anchor stocks received by purchase in year 26 as noted therein.

And for 37 anchors received for various royal ships.

---

[1]Marginal note; sail.
[2]Marginal note; yarn.
[3]Matter in brackets added over an omission mark to the MS.
[4]Marginal note; anchors.

And for 1 iron anchor broken in 2 pieces.

And for 1 piece of 1 anchor 8½ feet long.

And for 2 pieces of 2 anchors 1 was 13 feet long and the other 12 feet long.

And for 2 anchors broken in 4 pieces 1 *luch* and 1 iron ring for the head.

And 1 anchor with 1 *suavel* without a ring at the head.

Total 51 whole anchors, 1 broken anchor and 7 pieces of various anchors.

Concerning this material

The same accounts that he delivered 12 anchors for the fitting out of various royal ships in the said period as noted in the said roll of particulars.

And he accounts that he delivered to the said Matthew de Torkeseye 42 whole anchors of which 3 were small, 1 iron anchor broken in 2 pieces 1 piece of an anchor 8½ feet long 2 pieces of 2 anchors of which 1 was 13 feet long and 1 12 feet long and 2 anchors broken in 4 pieces which were lacking 1 stock and 1 ring at the head and 1 anchor with 1 *suawel.*

The same Matthew must answer for these anchors and pieces of iron and he does so below.

Pitch and tar[1]

The same accounts for 46 barrels of pitch 2 lasts and 3 barrels of tar, the last containing 12 barrels, 9 weys 6 stone 7lbs of grease 950 lbs of rosin *stup* oil varnish *gemae* and cole received by purchase in year 24 and noted in another part of the roll.

And for 5 lasts 1 barrel of pitch 15 barrels 5 pots of tar 18 weys ½ clove of wax 1300 lbs of rosin 76 pots of oil received by purchase in year 25 as noted therein.

And for 3 lasts of pitch 2 lasts of tar 13 weys of wax 528 lbs of rosin 3 barrels and 14 pots of oil received by purchase in year 26 as noted therein.

And for 3 lasts of pitch 3 lasts of tar 28 pots of oil 403 quarters of *stup* received by purchase in year 27 as noted therein.

Totals

Pitch 14 lasts 11 barrels

[1]Marginal note.

Tar 8½ lasts 4½ pots
Wax 40 weys 9 stone 10½ lbs
Rosin 2778 lbs
Oil 3 barrels 118 pots
Stup 403 quarters.

Concerning these materials

The same accounts that he used for the repair of the said ships flunes craiers barges and boats of the said King in the said period 8 lasts 2 barrels of pitch 6 lasts 7 barrels 4 gallons of tar 26 weys 4 stones wax 2784 lbs of rosin 3 barrels 118 gallons of oil 303 quarters of *stup* in repairs and improvements ordered in the said period as noted in the said roll of particulars.

And he accounts that he delivered to the said Matthew 14 barrels of pitch of middle size 5 lasts 7 barrels of small size 1 last 3 barrels of tar of middle size 8 barrels of tar of large size 106 lbs of rosin by the said indenture as noted therein.

The said Matthew must answer for these barrels of pitch lasts of tar pounds of rosin and he does so below.

Painting[1]

The same accounts for 20 lbs of white lead 87 lbs of vermilion 20 lbs of plaster 3 lbs of varnish received by purchase in year 24 as noted in another part of the roll.

And in 30 lbs of vermilion ½lb of orpiment 114 lbs of plaster and 3 dozen and 10 leaves of tin of various colours received by purchase in year 25 as noted therein.

And for 140lbs of vermilion received from John of Cologne in the same year 25And for 7lbs of vermilion by purchase in year 26 as noted therein.

Totals
White lead 20 lbs
Vermilion 263 lbs
Orpiment ½lb
Plaster 134 lbs
Varnish 3 lbs
Tin 46 sheets

[1]Marginal note.

All of this material was completely used up in the painting of the said royal ships within the said period as described by him on oath in the said roll of particulars.

Cables[1]

The same accounts for 8 great cables 16 small cables 885 lbs of rope and 80 *lynes* and ropes of bast received by purchase in year 24 as noted in another part of the roll.

And for 6 cables 15 ropes called hausers 33 other ropes 14 lines 843 lbs of cordage received by purchase in year 25 as noted therein.

And for 2 cables 4 hausers 12 lines 4 ropes 91 lbs of cordage received by purchase in year 26 as noted therein.

And for 8 cables 2 hausers 4 ropes 12 elbowlines received by purchase in year 27 as noted therein.

And for 6 cables 2 upties 2 hausers received from John Charnele by the hands of Bartholomew Stigeyn.

Totals
Great cables 29
Small cables 16
Hausers 23
Upties 2
Ropes 56
Lines 44
Cordage by weight 1827 lbs

Concerning this material

The same accounts that he has used in the repair of various royal ships *flunes* and cogs in the aforesaid period 20 great cables 13 small cables 21 hausers 56 ropes 44 lines and 1809 lbs of cordage.

And he delivered to the said Matthew 9 large white cables 5 small cables of which 2 called upties were of white yarn and 2 great hausers by the same indenture.

The said Matthew must answer for these cables upties and hausers and he does so below.

Tools for the smithy[2]

The same accounts for 1 anvil and 1 pair of bellows and 2 parts of boards for bellows received by purchase in year 24 as noted in another part of the roll.

---

[1]Marginal note.
[2]Marginal note.

And for 8 tools called *slegg* 4 large tongs 5 small tongs 4 hand hammers 4 *nailtols* 1 bighorn 1 bellows 2 tools for beating hot iron 2 punches for making holes in iron 2 *washours* 2 hearth stones 2 *bolstres* 1 *petra vertibilis* with 2 *wynches* and iron axes 2 iron *wegges* made out of the King's iron bought as above.

All these tools the accountant delivered to the said Matthew by the above indenture as noted in the said roll of particulars.

The same Matthew must answer for these tools and he does so below.

Ships[1]

The same accounts for 2 ships received as purchases in year 24 as noted in another part of the roll.

Total 2 ships.

Concerning these

The same accounts that he delivered to Thomas Clerk of Greenwich and John Sprignan 1 ship by personal order of the King as he declared on oath as noted in the said roll of particulars by the testimony of Regina de Ferrers.

And he accounts that he delivered to John Mareys keeper of the royal manor of Rotherhithe and Richard Albon carpenter the hulk of 1 ship for the repair of the wharf at Rotherhithe by personal order of the King as he declared on oath as noted therein.

As regards the cables ropes anchors and other equipment of the ship the same Thomas has been debited above among ropes and anchors. As regards the hulk of the same ship the same John and Richard must answer and they do so below.

Cauldrons[2]

The same accounts for 15 pots 7 kettles 2 lead cisterns 17 dozen lanterns 36 hammers 25 small hatchets and 8 shaffhokes received by purchase in year 25 as noted in another part of the roll.

And for 2 pots 2 kettles 2 lead cisterns 26 lanterns 5 hatchets and 2 hammers received by purchase in year 26 as noted therein.

TotalsPots 17

Kettles 9

Cisterns 4

Lanterns 230

Hammers 38

[1]Marginal note.
[2]Marginal note.

Hatchets 30
Shaffhokes 8

Concerning these items

The same accounts that he has delivered to various masters of various ships for the equipping of the same 26 pots 9 kettles 4 lead cisterns 230 lanterns 36 hammers 27 hatchets and 8 shaffhokes as noted in the said roll of particulars.

And he accounts that he delivered to the said Matthew 1 big pot for pitch 2 hammers 3 hatchets by the said indenture as noted therein.

The said Matthew must answer for this pot hammers and hatchets and he does so below.

Coal[1]

The same accounts for 80 quarters of sea coal found in a certain ship called the *Falcon* forfeited to the King in year 25 as noted in the said roll of particulars.

And for 30 quarters of sea coal received by purchase in year 25 as noted.

And for 10 quarters of sea coal received by purchase in year 27 as noted in the same place.

Total 120 quarters of sea coal.

Concerning this sea coal

The same accounts that 80 quarters of coal was used by 3 royal smiths at Ratcliff in the making of various iron bolts nails with rivets called clench and anned and various other pieces of ironwork for the said royal ships being built or repaired in the same period as noted in the said roll of particulars.

And he delivered 40 quarters of sea coal to the same Matthew by the said indenture as noted therein.

The same Matthew must answer and he does so below.

Carts with wheels[2]

The same accounts for 2 carts and 3 pairs of wheels bought for the same carts for 1 wagon to transport large timber as noted in the same roll of particular.

And for 1 cart made for the royal timber in the same period as noted therein.

---

[1]Marginal note.
[2]Marginal note.

Total carts 3
Whccls 4 pairs

Concerning this

The same accounts that he wore out in the carriage of timber in the accounting period 3 pairs of wheels as noted in the said roll of particulars.

And he accounts that he delivered to the said Matthew 3 carts and 1 pair of wheels by the said indcnturc.

The said Matthew must answer and he does so below.

Scoops[1]

The same accounts for 85 scoops and *sketfattes* and 15 shovels bought in year 24 as noted in another part of the roll.

And for 14 scoops 12 shovels and 1 saw received by purchase in year 26 (therein).[2]

And for 1 iron chisel bought for working a certain lathe for working on boards in year 27 as noted therein.

Totals
Scoops 99
Shovels 27
Saw 1
Chisel 1

Concerning these tools

The same accounts that he wore out 75 scoops 3 shovels in the said period as noted in the said roll of particulars.

And he accounts that he delivered to the said Matthew 12 shovels and 10 *sketfattes* 1 saw and 1 chisel by the said indenture as noted therein.

The said Matthew must answer for these shovels and *sketfattes* saw and chisel and does so below.

Bails[3]

The same accounts for 28 bails received by purchase in the year 25 as noted in another part of the roll. They were used in equipping various royal ships in the accounting period as he declared on oath.

---

[1]Marginal note.
[2]Added over an omission mark to the MS.
[3]Marginal note.

Swivels[1]

The same accounts for 5 iron swivels weighing 134 lbs made of the King's iron for towing masts in year 27 as noted in another part of the roll. These were delivered to the same Matthew de Torkseye by the said indenture as noted in the said roll of particulars.

Oaks[2]

The same accounts for 109 oaks received by purchase in year 26 as noted in another part of the roll.

And for 32 oaks received by purchase in year 27 as noted therein. All these oaks with their trimmings were wholly used in the repair and improvement of the said various royal ships in the accounting period as noted in the said roll of particulars.

The same accounts for the work on the trimming and shaping of the said oaks; and for 6200 *talwod* 1801 quarters of *baveyn* coming from the said the loppings of the said 9 oaks.

He accounts for the sale of all of this with the price debited in another part of the roll in the section money received in year 26.

He does not answer for the profit coming from the oaks given to the King by Isabella Queen of England Ralph Earl of Stafford or the Abbot of Waltham because this was all accounted for among their fees as he declared on oath.

The same accounts for 2 iron chains weighing 100lbs 1 crow weighing 28 lbs 1 tripod weighing 39 lbs 7 shaffhokes made of the King's iron.

And for 1 lath with 1 *stipit* for working boards made from the King's timber.

And 2 couples of Handropes 1 pair of backstays 1 pulley for the wind-lass with 1 hinge 1 rack with fixings 3 *seyffnes* 1 strikrope 3 ropes for *steys* 1 boyrope 2 white cables 2 sheets 3 handropes found in a certain ship called the *Bilebaw*.

And for 1 pair of backsteyes 5 handropes 1 uptie of *Ran* 1 rack with its fittings 2 pulleys with 2 brass wheels 1 old hammer on a certain ship called the *Cog darundell*.

And for 11 couples of handropes 1 handrops single 1 couple backsteys 1 couple steyes with 1 *sherwynd* 2 polancres 2 sheets of *Ran* 1 rack with fittings 1 hinge for 1 *tristrope* for a certain boat with 1 pulley 3 old painters for the head of an anchor 1 old bowrope 3 stetyng with 4 pulleys

---

[1]Marginal note.
[2]Marginal note.

1 trusserope girding[1] 1 botrope 1 handrope 1 uptie 1 wyndyng rope 3 cables 1 pot 16 spoke 3 boyes 2 streamers 2 standards on board a certain ship called *la Cog Thomas Beauchamp*.

And for 3 white cables 2 upties 2 bolynes 2 yardropes 2 polancreropes 3 steyes 12 couple handropes 2 couple of backsteyes 1 *trief* with the bonnet in bad condition 1 rack with fittings 4 white hausers 2 pairs of *dedmennesheye* of which 1 with an iron chain on board a certain ship called the *Naw Seint Marie*.

And 1 uptie with 1 pulley 4 couple handropes 1 couple backsteys 1 trief for a certain boat.

And 2 couple handropes 1 couple backsteys 1 stertrope 1 rack with fittings.

And 1 rack with fittings 2 upties 4 steys 11 couple handropes 1 polancrerope 1 henge with the pulleys for 1 polancre 1 couple backsteys 1 piece of an uptie of 5 fathoms 1 new white uptie 4 pulleys for stetyngs 2 strigrope 2 lollers 1 wyndyng rope 1 yerdrope 2 crosspulleys 4 peyntours 2 stetyngs 1 topline 1 piece of rope of 3 fathoms 1 trusserope 1 slyngrope 1 start rope 1 boyrope 1 wyndyngpulley 4 cables 1 *caggyngcable* 2 *woles* for the topcastle 2 shetes 1 streamer 2 standards 9 lanterns in bad condition 1 fane without cloth on board a ship called *Cog John*.

And 2 couple handropes 1 steye with 1 pulley 1 uptie with 2 pulleys on board a certain boat of the same ship.

And 8 couple handropes 3 steyes 1 couple backsteyes 2 upties 2 sheets 2 *lollers* 2 trussropes with 4 pulleys for the polancrerope with the stropp 2 stetes 2 bonelines 2 boyropes 1 stropp for the polancre without the rope 1 girtdyng 1 yerdrope 1 henge of a piece of cable 1 handrope 1 rack with fittings for a mast 1 cranelyne 3 white cables 1 *tref* with 1 bonnet 1 kettle in bad repair 1 *hanegor* 1 hammer 1 gauge 1 hatchet 1 wyndyng pulley 16 oars 10 cast of *tields* 6 new *tieldes* 1 old tankard 1 bail on board a certain ship called *Redcog*.

And for 4 couple of handropes 1 steigh 1 upteigh 1 rack for the mast on board the boat of the same ship 1 capstan 19 haukes.

And for old timber which was on board the ships called *Redcog Isabel Naw Seint Marie* and *Bilebawe* of which was delivered to the said Matthew Torkeseye clerk by the said indenture.

The same Matthew must answer and he does so below.

---

[1]No quantity given in the MS.

[*Note*. Torksey's answer for all the goods handed over to
him repeats the above and is therefore not transcribed as it does
not add any new information.]

William Bassyngden master of a royal ship called the *Goldbirete* owes
£7 as money advanced to him on the said 7th September year 24 by
Richard of Norwich on account of the said William's wages in 2 particulars for which money the same Thomas was debited in another part of
the roll among money received in the same year 24.

And he must answer in the following roll in the section for London.

John Ellerton a royal man at arms owes 40s in money given to him as
an advance for all the money owing in the particulars of the said John
part of a certain sum of £38 10s 4d by the same received from William
de Rothwell at the Receipt of money of the King's Chamber to provide various things for the King's ships. In respect of this money the
same Thomas was held liable on another part of the roll among moneys
received in year 27.

And he will answer in the following roll in the section for London.

Robert of Hull royal mariner owes £7 16s 7d in money given to him as
an advance on all the money owing in the particulars of the said Robert
part of a certain sum of £100 received by the same Robert of Hull from
Robert of Mildenhall at the receipt of money of the King's Chamber
for providing various things in Flanders for the royal ships. The same
Thomas was held liable in another part of the roll for this money in
money received in year 27.

And he will answer on the next roll in the section for London.

3.   *Extract from Snetesham's particulars, 1345–46*

[TNA: E101/25/7]

[This short extract from Snetesham's particulars for the years 19 and
20 Edward III (1345 and 1346) is included because of the importance
of the reference to lodestones at this comparatively early date. The
remainder of the account is very similar to that included here as the
first document. It records payment for a voyage of the George from
Burseldon to Sandwich where the King boarded the ship and then on
to Sluys in Flanders. This took eight days. The return journey was to
London after the vessel had been at Sluys for some months. Payments
are included for the pilots who took the ship out of Burseldon into
the Solent and from the Downs into Sandwich. Snetesham may have
been on board himself and may have been personally responsible for

the purchases listed below. The 'timers' were sand glasses probably used for timing the length of each tack in conjunction with a traverse board. The word used in the MS is orlog. The word adamant which can mean diamond was also used for lodestone at this period. A godet was a drinking vessel.]

Necessaries bought for the royal ships
The same Thomas accounts that he spent at Sluys in Flanders on 12 glass timers bought by order of the King, each costing 4½ *groots*[1] which makes a total in sterling of 9s.

And for 4 timers of the same sort bought at 5 *groots* each which makes a total in sterling of 3s 4d.

And for 9 godets called *ffleyghes* bought by royal order at 7d each total 5s. 3d.

And for 7 godets bought at 5d. each 2s 11d.

And for 1 large godet bought for the King 12d.

And for the repair of various instrumnets belonging to the ship 7d.

And for 12 stones called adamant called sailstones bought for 6s.

And for 4 lanterns bought in the same place for the said ship 3s. 4d.

And for 2 large lanterns bought in the same place for the said ship 4s. Total 35s 5d.

---

[1]The usual unit of the currency widely used in the Low Countries.

II

MORE DOCUMENTS FOR THE LAST CAMPAIGN OF THE *MARY ROSE*

Edited by C.S. Knighton and Dominic Fontana,
with the assistance of David Loades

These papers are supplementary to those published in association with the Mary Rose Trust a decade ago.[1] They are not strictly new discoveries, having come from catalogued collections. It was rather that the cataloguing was inadequate or positively misleading, so that the relevance of the materials to *Mary Rose* had not been recognised.[2]

Sinking [by Professor Loades]

Mary Rose sank in the context of the so-called 'Battle of the Solent' between 18 and 21 July 1545. Claude d'Annebault, the Admiral of France, had assembled a great fleet of over 150 ships and 25 galleys with the objective of taking Portsmouth and immobilising the English fleet. The purpose of this exercise was not so much to take an English port as to secure a bargaining counter for the return of Boulogne, which had been in English hands since the previous year.[3] Taking out the English fleet was likewise designed to cut the lines of supply by which the garrison of Boulogne had been maintained, and thus facilitate its recapture. Having failed to check d'Annebault's preparations by a raid on the Seine a few

---

[1] C.S. Knighton and D. Loades, *Letters from the Mary Rose* (Stroud, 2002) [hereafter *LMR*]. For the present purpose names of ships and captains are rendered in modern forms, though verbal alternatives (as *'Great'/'Grand Mistress'*) are kept as they occur; variant spellings of the MS sources are given in the index.

[2] The fundamental source for the study of *Mary Rose* is the five-volume report of the Mary Rose Trust, *The Archaeology of the Mary Rose* (Portsmouth, 2003–11) [hereafter *AMR*]. The principal monographs are A. McKee, *How We Found the Mary Rose* (London, 1982), M. Rule, *The* Mary Rose: *The Excavation and Raising of Henry VIII's Flagship* (London, 1982), E. Bradford, *The Story of the* Mary Rose (London, 1982) and D. Childs, *The Warship Mary Rose: The Life and Times of King Henry VIII's Flagship* (Barnsley, 2007); most of the documentary evidence was printed in *LMR*.

[3] J.S. Brewer, J. Gairdner and R.H. Brodie (eds), *Letters and Papers, Foreign and Domestic, of the Reign of Henry VIII* (1862–1932) [hereafter *LP*], xix, I, no. 932; II, nos 35, 164, 424. R.J. Knecht, *Francis I* (1982), p. 368.

days earlier, Lord Admiral Lisle with the English fleet was at Spithead or within the harbour of Portsmouth, prepared to withstand the French assault.[1] Meanwhile King Henry with a large army was encamped beside the town, with the same object in view. On 18 July the King dined on the flagship *Henry Grace à Dieu* (*Great Harry*) as the guest of the Lord Admiral. However he did not remain on board overnight, so his departure cannot have precipitated the dramatic events the following day.

On Sunday 19 July, the wind then being light and fitful, d'Annebault began the assault by sending in his galleys, with their formidable forward-firing guns, to attack the becalmed English warships. Lisle had only a few galleasses and rowbarges to withstand this attack, and would probably have been overwhelmed if the wind had not freshened sufficiently to enable the full English fleet to move out against the galleys, which thereupon retreated. But it was in the course of this action that *Mary Rose* was lost. Having discharged a broadside, an attempted manoeuvre resulted in the open gunports being forced below the waterline on the lee side and the sea rapidly entered. The ship was unable to regain an even keel, and sank in a few minutes, taking most of her crew of 500 with her, including the captain Sir George Carew.[2] The wind then dropped again, and further action became impossible, so on 20 August d'Annebault concentrated his energies on landings on the Isle of Wight, as Sir John Oglander's account makes clear [7]. These landing parties met with mixed fortunes, and on the 21st, the weather still being unhelpful and the plague beginning to stir among his crews, the French Admiral retreated, recovering his landing parties (or what was left of them) on the way.

Because *Mary Rose* had sunk in comparatively shallow water, it was at first hoped that she could be raised; and the Duke of Suffolk, who had overall responsibility for the defence of Portsmouth, set salvage in motion. The King has been an aghast spectator of the accident, and he may well have insisted that this be done. Two Venetian salvors were engaged and provided with three hulks, and great cables to pass under the wreck. The idea was to fasten these cables to two of the hulks at low tide, and then to rely upon the incoming tide to raise all three. However they started by trying to drag her upright, and in the process broke off the foremast. On 9 August they reported their failure and asked for the use of the hulks for another six days. It was now apparently intended to drag *Mary Rose*

---

[1]Lisle's fleet has been estimated as high as 200; but the core of fighting ships was at most 68, and that included very few oared warships; hence Oglander's comment about his relative weakness (Doc. No. 7).

[2]In contemporary reports the number of survivors ranges between 25 and 40: *LMR*, pp. 118, 120.

into shallower water, and to recover her from there. The extra days were granted, partly because of the value of the ship, and partly because of the 'goodly ordnance that is in her'. As late as 25 August hopes were still high, and a letter from the King of that date refers to a new mast for the ship, presumably to repair the broken foremast. However, after that there is silence. Some of the guns were apparently recovered, but the Venetians were paid off during December, having confessed their failure. How close they had come to success was revealed in 1982, when the wreck was lifted, because the great cables with which it had been intended to lift here were then found in place. P. Marsden, *Sealed by Time: The Loss and Recovery of the* Mary Rose (AMR, vol. 1: Portsmouth, 2003), fig. 13.2 on p. 131. Quite why their plan failed is not known, but it may have been some problem with connecting the cables to the hulks.

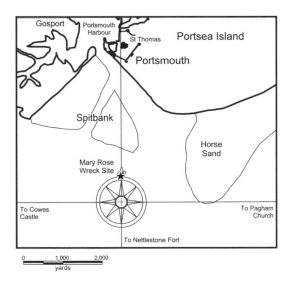

The relationship of the compass rose on D623 and the wreck site of the *Mary Rose.*

(Map and note by Dr Fontana)

Chart D623 (the earliest in the United Kingdom Hydrographic Office collection, *c.* 1586 × 1620) shows Portsmouth Harbour and its entrance, and may indicate that late Tudor seafarers were able to locate the *Mary Rose* wreck site. A compass rose is placed in a very specific geographical position. From its centre, pencil lines extend east and west, north and south. The line running north is aligned to the tower of St Thomas's church in Old Portsmouth, a prominent feature in the landscape. Clearly, this is not a navigation mark, for following this route would cause a vessel to run aground on the shallow water of Spitbank. Intriguingly, the fleur-de-lis of the compass rose, which functions as the north arrow, is placed along this line and marks precisely the *Mary Rose* wreck site point. The scale distance from the centre of the compass rose to the fleur-de-lis measures exactly 750 yards or ⅜ of one nautical mile.

The location of the central point of the compass rose can be located out at sea by taking direct sightlines to the west to Cowes Castle and to the east to the tower of Pagham church on the Selsey peninsula. The line which extends directly south from the centre of the compass rose aligns with the site of Nettlestone Fort on the north coast of the Isle of Wight. Therefore, a mariner could easily find the centre of the compass rose by using line of sight to place himself where these four shore-based features intersect. Using this position as his starting point, a mariner could then head directly northwards towards the church tower of St Thomas for 750 yards, which would lead his vessel directly across the wreck site of *Mary Rose*.

Whether this was the intended purpose of the compass rose and its markings or is merely a coincidence is uncertain but nonetheless, it is a practical means of locating the wreck site.

The government did not altogether give up on *Mary Rose*, and in July 1546 engaged the services of another Italian, Piero Paolo Corsi, to try again. Corsi brought in his team of divers, but his brief seems to have been limited.[1] In May 1547 and August 1549 he was paid £20 and £50 respectively for recovering ordnance, but nothing was said of any attempts to raise the ship herself.[2] Thereafter the wreck seems to have been abandoned, although the memory of her presence and the cause of her loss were not forgotten. Rather surprisingly, Sir William Monson, writing in the early seventeenth century, said that he had seen 'parts of the ribs of this ship' with his own eyes,[3] although how that could have come about is not recorded. In 1836 some fishermen's nets were snagged on the remains, and the Deane brothers succeeded in recovering a few more guns, but nothing was done to disturb the time capsule until serious archaeological investigation began with Alexander McKee's rediscovery of the wreck in 1971. Since then countless artefacts and organic remains have been brought to the surface, and reconstructions of the men, their lifestyles and their diet have become possible.

---

[1] G. Ungerer, 'Recovering a black African's voice in an English lawsuit: Jacques Francis and the salvage operations of the *Mary Rose*, and the *Sancta Maria and Sanctus Edwardus*, 1545–ca.1550', *Medieval and Renaissance Drama in England*, 17, ed. J. Pitcher and S.P. Cerasano (Madison/Teaneck, NJ, 2005), pp. 255–71, printing as appendix (pp. 265–6) HCA 13/93, ff. 202v–203, a deposition of 8 Feb. 1548 referring to Corsi's salvage activities off the Isle of Wight in the previous summer. Although the deposition does not refer specifically to *Mary Rose*, Ungerer's article (appearing after the publication of *LMR*) adds greatly to our understanding of the Tudor salvage operation.

[2] *LMR*, pp. 131–2.

[3] M. Oppenheim (ed), *The Naval Tracts of Sir William Monson*, vol. 2 (NRS, vol. 23, 1902), p. 265.

Victualling

The great quantity of animal and fish bones recovered from *Mary Rose* has been examined in painstaking detail, along with traces of an astonishing variety of vegetable matter.[1] This information is not only of huge importance in itself; but because we are what we eat, it combines with the skeleton evidence to tell us what the men of *Mary Rose* ate and how that affected what they were. Yet this detailed examination of *Mary Rose*'s larders has not been matched by a thorough search of the archives. There is not as much there as would have been the case had the ship survived a little longer, because in the aftermath of the 1545 campaign the naval administration was put on a more business-like footing, with the setting up of the body which came to be known as the Navy Board. Fuller records were duly kept, and from 1547 those in charge of naval victualling accounted regularly to the Exchequer. Save for a small gap in Mary's reign these accounts are complete for the rest of the century, so that we can say with some precision how the Elizabethan navy was fed.[2]

There are some earlier papers relating to victualling, indeed to the victualling of *Mary Rose* herself. Otherwise *Mary Rose* historians have had to make assumptions based on much later material, such as a memorandum drawn up by Lord Burghley just before the Armada, and descriptions of naval rations from Pepys's era and beyond.[3] The gap is usefully filled by [1] below, which has long been accessible in Cambridge University Library, but which had failed to attract attention to itself. The fulsome title was printed in the great calendar of Henrician documents, but nothing more.[4]

The MS is handsomely written by a professional scribe of the mid-sixteenth century; the first part details the victualling of the fleet during the 1545–46 campaign; the latter part concerns provisioning an army intended for Berwick in 1557. The purpose for which these two elements were combined is unknown, as is the manuscript's route to Cambridge. The 1545–46 material is in five ostensibly interlocking sections: a list of the fleet; the range of prices paid for each commodity and the wages of those who prepared them ashore at Portsmouth; the quantities

---

[1] J. Gardiner with M.J. Allen, *Before the Mast: Life and Death aboard the* Mary Rose (*AMR*, vol. 4: Portsmouth, 2005) [hereafter *BTM*]; with references to the research of the many contributors.

[2] The first five victuallers' accounts have now been printed: C.S. Knighton and D. Loades (eds), *The Navy of Edward VI and Mary I* (NRS, vol. 157, 2011) [hereafter *NEM*], pp. 171–268, 435–52.

[3] For example *BTM*, pp. 603–5; Childs, *Mary Rose*, pp. 90–91.

[4] *LP*, xxi, I, no. 1256.

of each commodity; and finally the total sums paid for the various food-stuffs and their containers.

The fleet comprised 156 ships carrying 17,800 men. Only just over a third of the vessels were owned by the King; the rest were merchant-men on long-term loan, ships owned by senior commanders, and a much larger group of little craft from the West Country, requisitioned at the height of the emergency. This fleet was never together at any one time: the West Country ships did not arrive until after the Battle of the Solent, and some of the King's rowbarges had not then been built. None of the ships listed would have served for the whole 515 days covered by the account, and we cannot say for how long any particular ship was at sea: such data only becomes available in the Navy Treasurer's accounts of the 1560s.[1] So it is not possible to use this account to calculate how much food was supplied to any one ship.

There are other limitations and cautions. For some items we have quantities but no prices; for others prices but no quantities. Even where we have all the elements for a calculation, they may not reconcile. One needs to be alert to the intermittent use of the 'great hundred' for certain commodities. This normally means 120, but in computations of pounds weight c represents neither 100 lb nor 120 but the cwt of 112 lb.[2] Hops were bought at 18s the '$ma. c.$'. So the total quantity of hops bought, expressed as 62,410 pounds is probably 69,898 lb [computed as (624 × 112) + 10]. However, the total price for hops is £221 9s 8d, though the weight stated at 18s makes just over £561 by any calculation.

The explanation is that the Cambridge MS is compiled from several separate elements while omitting others. Much of the data comes from an Exchequer account – submitted by George Paulet, Navy Victualler at Portsmouth, and covering almost exactly the same period as the Cambridge document, 1 January 1545 to 11 July 1546.[3] This is the only one of its kind, and has also been overlooked in all previous studies of *Mary Rose*. Paulet's account gives much fuller details about the sources and distribution of supplies. It reveals there was often a considerable difference between the quantities the Navy bought and the quantities actually sent to the ships.

For example the Cambridge MS says that 125,912 stockfish were bought, 75 per cent of the individually counted fish. Paulet's account gives the same figure, but also says how they were sourced (14,229 from John Myll and Thomas Welles of Southampton, 75,000 from John

---

[1] C.S. Knighton and D. Loades (eds), *Elizabethan Naval Administration* (NRS, vol. 160, 2013), pp. 538–41.
[2] See the examples in *NEM,* pp. xxxv–xxxviii.
[3] E 351/2477.

Hopkins of London, and so forth). It also shows that less than half these fish reached the fleet; 1,029 were lost before they reached Portsmouth, 20,000 were sent to London, 10,000 to Dover, 30,000 to Berwick; 1,855 were sold off as surplus, and the accountant still had 7,009 in stock. Only 56,019 went towards naval rations, and – at one fish to four men per meal, and five fish meals a week – that would have served 17,800 men for a fortnight.[1] The serving of these provisions cannot be more precisely determined. It is nevertheless possible to attempt some correlation between the quantities in these accounts and the fragments which have survived in *Mary Rose*. This is best illustrated by staying with fish.

The gadoids – the cod in its various forms – dominated the market. They account for 93.62 per cent of identifiable fish remains from *Mary Rose*.[2] Hake and pollack each formed just under 2 per cent of the purchases, and are each just under 1 per cent of the *Mary Rose* fish remains.[3] Conger is the largest of the minor league, with 4.24 per cent of the surviving bones, representing 3.4 per cent of the purchases. It should not be surprising to find history and archaeology in agreement; but it is reassuring when they are so.

Hitherto the daily ration of food aboard *Mary Rose* has been a matter of conjecture.[4] The Cambridge MS provides the reality, under the heading 'Quantities and rates of meat and drink that was allowed to every man in the said ships'. The main ration is one piece of powdered beef per man a day; the carcase, with the bones and neck removed, is said to make 122 pieces. A pound of pork (called bacon) might be substituted for the beef, and this alternative was demonstrably available aboard *Mary Rose*. But there is nothing to support speculation, based on much later practice, that pork was served on specific days, one of them being Monday; and that therefore the pork bones found in cask 81A3346 were from meat being soaked for Monday 20 July 1545.[5] The only stipulation is that fish was served on Wednesday, Friday and Saturday. So we may be sure that for their last supper the men of *Mary Rose* ate fish. On Sunday night the tables were turned.

Adapting

It has long been known that the forward-firing capability of the galley was such a menace that much effort and ingenuity was employed

---

[1] *BTM*, p. 604.

[2] Ibid., table 14.7 on p. 578; combining total percentages for bones certainly identifiable as cod (89.51) and gadidae (4.11).

[3] Hake 0.8 per cent and pollack 0.9 per cent by the same reckoning from the same source.

[4] Ibid., p. 604, table 14.13, 'Probable rations per man for the *Mary Rose*'.

[5] Ibid., p. 574.

to match it from conventional ships.[1] However the evidence for this was largely theoretical. It was therefore of considerable interest to find specific proposals for adapting three ships to achieve forward fire [2].[2] This paper in the Library at Hatfield House had been catalogued by the Historical Manuscripts Commission under the year 1557 (with a query) as 'View of repairs of certain ships, by James Baker, Benjamin Gonson, &c. – *Undated*.'[3] This was seen while looking for items to include in *The Navy of Edward VI and Mary I* but it was immediately evident that it belongs to the 1540s, and demonstrates drastic attempts to alter the structure of three ships to achieve forward fire. James Baker was Henry VIII's master shipwright, and disappears from view after 1546; Gonson, was to be Treasurer of the Navy from 1548 to 1567, but it was as Surveyor that he was first formally appointed in 1546, and it is likely that this confirmed a function he was already performing in 1545.[4] The HMC editors presumably thought that the *Mary Rose* mentioned in the report was the second of the name, launched in 1557. Yet this is manifestly a report on adapting ships not newly building them, and there can be no doubt that it refers to the original *Mary Rose* of 1511, along with *New Bark* of *c.* 1523 and *Jennet* of 1538–39.[5] Furthermore it seems almost certain that this drastic surgery was being considered not long before the Battle of the Solent. Just a few weeks later, when there was still some prospect of salvaging *Mary Rose*, James Baker was ordered to continue with work on *New Bark* and *Jennet* [3].

The larger significance of the shipwrights' report is it that, alongside the recovery of the stem, it has prompted a re-evaluation of the (missing) bow section of *Mary Rose*, the deployment of her ordnance, and therefore her fighting capability. The interpretation confirms the image familiar from the Anthony Roll (though there shown in reverse) of two tiers of guns firing forward from the sterncastle past a slender forecastle.[6]

---

[1]N.A.M. Rodger, 'The development of naval gunnery, 1450–1650', *The Mariner's Mirror*, 82 (1996), pp. 301–24.

[2]This document is printed in original spelling and more fully discussed in C. S. Knighton and A. Hildred, 'Overgunning the *Mary Rose*: the King was warned', *Journal of the Ordnance Society*, 24 (2017 for 2012), pp. 5–17.

[3]*Catalogue of the Manuscripts of the Most Hon. the Marquess of Salisbury, K.G., etc., preserved at Hatfield House, Hertfordshire* (Historical Manuscripts Commission, 1883–1976), i, p. 146.

[4]Full details of Gonson's appointments and general career are given in *NEM*, pp. 545–6.

[5]Specifications and service careers of these ships are given in *NEM*, pp. 488–9, 494, 499–500.

[6]A. Hildred (ed), *Weapons of Warre: The Armaments of the Mary Rose* (*AMR*, vol. 3, Portsmouth, 2011), pp. 942–4; G. Hunt, *The Sea Painter's World: The New Maritime Art of Geoff Hunt 2003–2010* (Greenwich, 2011), pp. 49–53.

Commanding

Also found misplaced in the Hatfield calendar was a command list [4]. With *Mary Rose* in second position this cannot belong to 1547 as the calendar suggests. In fact it must date immediately before the Battle of the Solent: it slots into place in a sequence of other lists in the public records, the first group of which are printed here for comparison [5]. These comprise a list of ships with captains already appointed; a list of ships awaiting captains (among them *Mary Rose*), and a list of captains awaiting ships (among them Sir George Carew). The Hatfield list has the command structure in place, with Carew in the vice-flagship. It must therefore date from immediately before the battle. In conjunction with details from a list after the battle, dated 10 August, some significant changes of command can be plotted [6]. The letter referring to the repair of *Jennet* and *New Bark* [3] adds some detail to this process.

The Hatfield list should also serve to eliminate the baseless but pervasive claim that *Mary Rose*'s last captain was not Carew but Roger Grenville, father of Sir Richard of *Revenge*.[1] There is actually no archival evidence to connect Grenville with the ship, let alone its command. He is, however, known to have gone down with her – and is indeed the only individual, apart from the captain, who can be certainly named among the casualties. This is known from Richard Carew's *Survey of Cornwall*, first published in 1602, where the dutiful example of Grenville's father is said to have:

> encouraged his sonne Roger the more hardily to hazard, & the more willingly to resign his life in the vnfortunate Mary Rose.[2]

The first printed accounts of the sinking all follow the same form, of which two versions will suffice. First Cooper:

> At which time of the Kynges abode there [Portsmouth], a goodlye shippe of Englande called the Mary Rose, with Sir George Karew the captain, and many other gentlemen, was drowned in the middes of the haven by great foly and negligence.[3]

Then Stow:

> The 20. of July the King being at Portsmouth, a goodly shippe of England called the Mary Rose, with Sir George Carrow the captain

[1]Rule, *Mary Rose*, pp. 59, 60, 61; Bradford, *Mary Rose*, pp. 40, 56; Childs, *Mary Rose*, p. 65.
[2]R. Carew, *The Survey of Cornwall* (edn 1769), p. 81.
[3]T. Cooper, *Chronicle* (1560), f. 325v.

and manie Other gentleman, were drowned in the midst of the haven, by great negligence.[1]

The first work to connect this passage with Richard Carew's reference to the death of Roger Grenville is a biographical dictionary of 1757, in its article on Sir Richard Grenville:

> On the twentieth of July . . . Sir George Carew, who commanded her, Sir Roger Grenville, with many other persons of distinction, in all to the number of four hundred, were miserably drowned in the port.[2]

Apart from the doubtful knighthood,[3] this is a good and proper weaving of the two elements of evidence (as cited) – Cooper/Stow and Carew's.

But in 1871 Edward Arber, reprinting the account of the last fight of *Revenge*, refers to the captain's father as 'himself a captain, in the navy, and lost his life, as Carew tells us, in the unfortunate Mary Rose'.[4] Then in 1890, Sir John Laughton, writing Sir Richard Grenville's life for the *Dictionary of National Biography*, finally connected up the wrong dots by stating unequivocally that his subject:

> was the son of Roger Greynvile, who commanded and was lost in the Mary Rose in 1545.

For this Laughton cites the *Biographia Britannica* of 1757, and one can only suppose that his eye had been misled by the juxtaposition of 'commanded' and 'Grenville'. Whatever its prompting, Laughton's statement has passed into general currency, and into the particular literature of *Mary Rose*. In consequence one of the early Mary Rose Trust vessels was named *Roger Grenville*.

Since Grenville has nevertheless wandered into the picture, attempts have been made find him a place in it. Some have supposed that Carew as Vice-Admiral would have had a subordinate captain in command of his ship. However, at this time only the Lord Admiral ever had such an officer.[5] Another suggestion is that Carew was captain and Grenville was

---

[1] J. Stow, *Annals* (1605), p. 992.

[2] *Biographia Britannica* (1757), iv, p. 2282 note [*B*].

[3] R. Granville, *The History of the Granville Family* (Exeter, 1895), p. 82, asserts that Roger Grenville, an Esquire of the Body to Henry VIII, was indeed knighted, but there is no support for this elsewhere.

[4] E. Arber, *English Reprints* no. 29 (1871), p. 10.

[5] Not until 1596–99 can instances be found of other Admirals having what would now be termed flag captains below them: M. Oppenheim (ed.), *The Naval Tracts of Sir William Monson* (NRS, vols 22–3, 43, 45, 47, 1902–14), i, pp. 344, 358; ii, pp. 21, 38.

master.[1] Quite apart from the fact that there is no documentary support for this, Grenville was not a professional seaman but a gentleman and a courtier. For that very reason he was almost certainly aboard as a military commander, and as such a 'captain'. This point has been noted,[2] but it is irrelevant to the misunderstanding which has made him out to be captain of the ship.

Fighting

This group of texts is completed by Sir John Ogander's narrative of the Battle of the Solent [7]. The writer was born in 1585, son of Sir William Oglander of Nunwell in the parish of Brading, and Anne Dillington of Knighton. He was educated at Winchester, Balliol and the Middle Temple, and knighted in 1605. From 1620 to 1623 he was deputy Governor of Portsmouth, selling the office which was too expensive to maintain. In 1624 he became Deputy Governor of the Isle of Wight, and sat for Yarmouth in Charles I's early Parliaments. As a staunch royalist he was relieved of his command during the Civil War and was three times arrested; while at liberty he paid several visits to the imprisoned King at Carisbrooke.[3] Oglander was a prodigious collector of historical information about the island, and filled several volumes with his notes. The narrative of the 1545 attack is important as the only source for much local detail; but it must be treated with caution. The Victorian editor who printed other selections from the Oglander MSS warned that much of Sir John's writing consisted of 'conjectures . . . often erroneous, and disproved by modern research'.[4] His explanation of the *Mary Rose* disaster has found no supporters.

Acknowledgements

We acknowledge with thanks permission of the Comptroller of Her Majesty's Stationery Office to publish material from the public records; we are likewise grateful to the Most Honourable the Marquess of Salisbury, and to His Lordship's former Librarian and Archivist Mr R. Harcourt Williams; to Mrs F. Oglander, and the Isle

---

[1]McKee, *How We Found the* Mary Rose, p. 25; Marsden, *Sealed by Time*, p. 18.

[2]D. R. Banting, *An Introduction to the Life and Times of George Carew, Vice Admiral of the* Mary Rose (2007), p. 38.

[3]*Oxford Dictionary of National Biography* (Oxford, 2004).

[4]W. H. Long (ed.), *The Oglander Memoirs: Extracts from the MSS. of Sir J. Oglander, Kt.* (London, Portsmouth and Newport, 1888), pp. i–ii.

of Wight County Record Office; and to the Syndics of Cambridge University Library.

Documents printed in this article or cited in the footnotes are, except where otherwise stated below, in The National Archives (formerly and now incorporating the Public Record Office); with the Departmental Abbreviations below:

E 351   Exchequer, Pipe Office, Declared Accounts (in Rolls)
HCA 13   High Court of Admiralty, Deposition Books
SP 1   State Papers, Henry VIII

1. *Victualler's Account*

[Cambridge University Library, MS Dd.13.25   12 February 1545–11
(*LP*, xxi, I, no. 1256)][1]   July 1546

[f. 3] Portsmouth   *anno* 36.37.38

The declaration of names of such ships as did serve in the wars against France from the 12th of February in the 36th year of the reign of our late sovereign lord of famous memory King Henry the eight [*1545*] until the 11th day of July in the 38th year of his said Highness's reign [*1546*], being one whole year and 21ty weeks, with such number of men as every of them had in them the same time of service, together with the rate and proportions allowed for everyone, one man by the day, and also the prices of wheat, malt, peasen, fitches [*vetch*], hay, straw, empty butts, pipes, hogsheads, barrels new and old, land carriages and water carriages, with the wages of clerks, bakers, brewers, coopers and others belonging to the same, with other sundry notes as shall appear [distinctly *altered to*] distinct particularly hereafter following.

---

[1]Formally written throughout in the same mid-sixteenth-century hand, generously spaced with ornate initials and braces. On the verso of the first original leaf in a then contemporary hand: 'On Tuesday the 23 of Nov. 1658 was the funerall of Oliver Ld Protector of England'. On the second verso, in (? another) seventeenth-century hand: 'A declaration of the ships against France from Feb. xijth 36th of Hen. 8th to the xjth of July 38th of the said K'. Formerly bound with Dd.13.214. Calendared under date 11 July 1546, merely transcribing the full title of the first section, but adding '*Written about 1550*', doubtless prompted by reference to Winchester as Lord Treasurer (1550–72), though his marquessate was not conferred until October 1551. This transcription omits sub-totals for each page of the MS.

The *Henry Grace à Dieu* – 700 men. The *Mary Rose* – 500 men. The *Christopher of Danzig* – 500 men. The *Venetian Great* – 500 men. [f. 3v] The *Sampson* – 500 men. The *Argosy* from Hampton – 450 men. The *Peter Pomegranate* – 300 men. The *Swallow* – 310 men. The *Great Galley* – 350 men. The Galleon of Hamburg – 306 men. The *Jesus of Lübeck* – 300 men. The *Matthew Henry* – 300 men. The *Pauncy* – 300 men. The *Morion of Danzig* – 300 men. The *Matthew Gonson* – 300 men. The *Argosy* from London – 300 men. The *Mary of Hamburg* – 350 men. [f. 4] The *Struse of Danzig* – 250 men. The *Pelican of Danzig* – 250 men. The *Salamander* – 250 men. The *Galley Subtle* – 250 men. The *Grand Mistress* – 250 men. The *Sweepstake* – 240 men. The *Saviour of Bristol* – 240 men. The *Less Galley* – 240 men. The *Thomas Tipkins* – 240 men. The *Greyhound* – 240 men. The *Anne Lisle* – 236 men. The *George Bonaventure* – 220 men. The *Minion* – 220 men. The *Evangelist Judde* – 220 men. [f. 4v] The *Mary George of Rye* – 215 men. The *Anne Gallant* – 200 men. The *Tricell of Danzig* – 180 men. The *Spaniard of Deva* – 250 men. The *George Brigges* – 144 men. The *Falcon Lisle* – 160 men. The *Trinity of Totnes* – 146 men. The *Henry of Bristol* – 140 men. The *Margaret of Bristol* – 140 men. The *Trinity Caerleon* – 140 men. The *Unicorn* – 140 men. The *Trinity Reneger* – 140 men. The *Pilgrim of Dartmouth* – 140 men. The *New Bark* – 140 men. [f. 5] The *Mary Fortune of Lowestoft* – 140 men. The *Trinity Henry* – 120 men. The *Trinity Smythe* – 120 men. The *Rose Lion* – 120 men. The *James of Rosendaal* – 120 men. The *James of Arnemuiden* – 120 men. The *Jennet* – 120 men. The *Evangelist Norton* – 120 men. The *Magdalene Dryver* – 120 men. The *Mary Fortune Vaughan* – 120 men. The *Christopher Bennet* – 120 men. The *James Sowthwell* – 118 men. The *Michael of Newcastle* – 116 men. The *Dragon* – 110 men. [f. 5v] The *Mary James of Bristol* – 110 men. The *James of Bristol* – 110 men. The *Mary Conception of Bristol* – 110 men. The *Mary Bulloyn of Barnstaple* – 100 men. The *Christopher Constable* – 100 men. The *Thomas Magdalene* – 100 men. The *Row Galley* – 94 men. The *Peter of Lowestoft* – 95 men. The *Mary Martin of London* – 90 men. The *Primrose* – 80 men. The *Mary George of Bristol* – 80 men. The *Martyn Bulley* – 80 men. The *Sampson of Tergoes* – 80 men. The *Anne of Arnemuiden* – 80 men. The *Mary James* – 80 men. [f. 6] The *Phoenix* – 80 men. The *Mary and John of London* – 80 men. The *Lartique* – 80 men. The *Jesus Bonaventure of Hampton* – 80 men. The *Galley Reneger* – 80 men. The *Falcon* – 80 men. The *Mary of Greenwich* – 70 men. The *Roo* – 70 men. The *Julian of Dartmouth* – 70 men. The *Marlion* – 70 men. The *Michael of Dartmouth* – 70 men. The *Saker* – 60 men. The *Primrose* – 60 men. The *Trinity of Fowey* – 60 men. [f. 6v] The *George of Falmouth* – 56 men. The *George of Dittisham* – 56 men. The *George of Totnes* – 56 men. The *Clement of Mount's Bay* – 56 men. The *Mary Waller of Hastings* – 52 men. The *Hind* – 50 men. The *Brigantine* – 50 men. The *Matthew Winter* – 51 men. The Spanish pinnace – 45 men. The *Mary* of London – 40 men. The *Erasmus of Hampton* – 40 men. The *Hooper of Looe* – 39 men. The *Trinity of Rye* – 38 men. [f. 7] The *George of Rye* – 37 men. The *Magdalene of Rye* – 37 men. The Lord Admiral's prize – 37 men. The *Eagle* of Sir Thomas Clere – 35 men. The *Unicorn of Poole* – 32 men. The *James of Rye* – 30 men. The *James Fletcher of Rye* – 30 men. The *Jesus of Rye* – 30 men. The *Hare of London* – 30 men. The Renegers' foist – 26 men. The *Hoy Bark* – 25 men. The *Katherine of* [*Le*] *Croisic* – 25 men. The King's shallop – 24 men. The *Pinnace Reneger* – 24 men. [f. 7] The *Lawrence of Looe* – 24 men. The *Falcon of Plymouth* – 24 men. The *Pickpurse of Plymouth* – 21 men. The *Pinnace of Rye* – 20 men. The *Mary Grace of Aldeburgh* – 20 men. The *Richard Fortune of Calais* – 20 men. The *Great Pinnace of Lowestoft* – 20 men. The *John of Rye* – 18 men. The *Michael Hyckes of Looe* – 18 men. The *Mary Germyne of Calais* – 18 men. The *Clement of London* – 18 men. The *James of Hull* – 17 men. The *Mary Martyne of Calais* – 16 men. The *Mary Thomas of Leigh* – 16 men. [f. 8] The *Redbreast* – 16 men. The *Mary Pity of London* – 16 men. The *Shoulder of Mutton* – 15 men. The *Trinity of Barking* – 14 men. The *Bonaventure Maynerd* – 14 men. The *Jesus of Calais* – 14 men. The *Mary of Looe* – 14 men. The *Mary Grace of Lowestoft* – 12 men. The *Thomas of Newcastle* – 12 men. The *Elizabeth of Manningtree* – 12 men. The *Edward of Southwold* – 11 men. The *Bosse Sampson* – 11 men. The *Mary Katherine of Leigh* – 11 men. [f. 8v] The *Jesus of Leigh* – 10 men. The *Anthony of Leigh* – 10 men. The *Mary Fortune of Newcastle* – 10 men. The *Edward of Hull* – 10 men. The *Mary Figge of Plymouth* – 10 men. The *Christopher of Ipswich* – 10 men. The *John of Harwich* – 10 men. The *Michael of Yarmouth* – 9 men. The *John of Maldon* – 9 men. The *Mary Katherine of Dunwich* – 9 men. The *Mary Gryffen of London* – 8 men. The *James of London* – 8 men. [f. 9] The *James of Dover* – 7 men. The *Margaret of Ipswich* – 7 men.

Summa totalis of the men and ships that served in the King's Majesty's army royal at the seas and victualled in Portsmouth in the 36th,[1] 37th and 38 years of His Majesty's reign, *viz.*: Ships – 156. Men – 17,800.

---

[1]MS. *xxxjth* for *xxxvjth*.

[f. 9v] Quantities and rates of meat and drink that was allowed to every man in the said ships at the sea for one day, and the sorts thereof, as hereafter followeth, *viz*.:

Biscuit. Bread allowed for a man one day is one pound, which should be in biscuit well baken [*sic*] and dried in the number of eight cakes: *one pound in eight cakes.*

Fresh bread. Fresh bread instead thereof if any captain would have fresh bread, for whose use it was ordained, then was delivered instead of one pound of biscuit one loaf of bread, which should weigh two pounds: *this loaf of 2 pound must serve for 2 pound of biscuit.*

Beer. Beer is allowed for a man one day one gallon, which allowances was thought necessary in consideration of the leakage upon the beer: *one gallon for a man.*

[f. 10] *The contents of the pipe, barrel and hogshead.* The content of the pipe was rated at: *120 gallons.*

The hogshead was rated for the contents: *60 gallons.*

The Humber barrel was rated at: *36 gallons.*

Powdered beef. Powdered beef is allowed for a man the day one piece, which did weigh being fresh two pounds.

The carcase of an ox is cut into 122 pieces, the chines, marrow bones ('maryebones') and 'flaile' [? *flayed*] bones taken away, and also the neck: *one piece for a man the day.*

The pipe wherein powdered beef is packed did use to contain 422 pieces. And the hogshead 200 pieces: *pipes wherein the beef was packed.*

Fresh beef. Fresh is allowed one pound instead of a piece of powdered beef, and so it was rated: *one pound instead of one piece of powdered beef.*

[f. 10v] *Bacon.* Bacon is allowed instead of a piece of powdered beef and a pound of fresh beef one pound of bacon: *one pound of bacon for a man one day.*

White herring. White herrings be allowed ten to serve for a mess in the time of Lent: *ten herrings for a mess.*

Fish, butter and cheese. Saltfish was appointed three days in the week, that is to say Wednesdays two meals, Friday one meal, and Saturday two meals. The Wednesday dinner and supper is allowed for four men one mess of fish and one pound of cheese, and so likewise the Saturday. The Friday is but one meal, and for four men is allowed one mess of fish and one pound of butter, and no cheese. The stockfish is but a small fish, and therefore often times he is served one fish for a mess. The saltfish is considered by the purser when he cometh to the storehouse for it, what messes the fish will make: *the rate of three fish days in the week and the allowance for it.*

[f. 11] *What weight of biscuit the quarter of meal maketh.* Every quarter of meal made in the King's Majesty's bakehouse at Portsmouth: *255 weight of biscuit.*[1]

The quarter of meal made in biscuit and baked in the country to the King's Majesty's use: *200 weight of biscuit.*

Malt. Every quarter of malt did make in the King's Majesty's brewhouse at Portsmouth: *4 Humber barrels of beer.*

Hops. Hops to every quarter of malt brewed in the King's brewhouse at Portsmouth: *7 pounds.*

Grain used for beer-corn. Wheat. Oats. Beans. Maslin.

Every brewing was delivered 20 quarters of malt, and in beer-corn for the same 5 quarters of wheat and oats together, or: beans and maslin together, which is to every quarter of malt 2 bushels of beer-corn: *2 bushels of beer-corn to every quarter of malt.*

[f. 11v] Prices of wheat, rye, oats, beans, peasen, hops, fitches, straw, hay, faggots, billets, tallwood, and other necessaries for the furnishing of the said ships and army.

Wheat. Was bought in several shires at sundry prices: *at 16s the quarter, at 12s the quarter.*

Rye. Was bought in divers places at sundry prices, that is to say: *for 13½d the bushel.*

Malt. Was bought also at several prices, that is to say: *at 12s the quarter, at 8s the quarter.*

Beans and pease. Pease and beans in the straw were bought at several prices: *at 7s the load, at 6s 8d the load.*

Fitches. Fitches was bought at several prices: *at 7s the load, at 6s 8d the load.*

Hops. Was bought: *at 18s the 'ma. c.'* [great hundred]

[f. 12] *Tallwood.* Was bought at several prices: *at 7s the load, at 5s the load.*

Billets. Was bought: *at 3s 4d the 1,000.*

Faggots. Was bought: *at 20d the 100.*

Hay. Hay for carthorses was bought at several prices, *viz.*: *at 10s the load, at 8s the load.*

Straw. Straw for the stable and other necessaries: *at 2s the load.*

Barrels. The new Humber barrel was bought: *at 12d the barrel, at 10d the barrel, at 9d the barrel.*

---

[1]Usually meaning 2 hundredweight (of 112 lb) plus 55 lb, so by our reckoning 279 lb.

Hogsheads. The hogsheads, being old, at: *at 10d the hogshead.*
[f. 12v] *Butts and barrel boards.* The old pipe or butt: *at 20d the piece.* The new barrel boards: *at 20s the 1,000, and 12s the 1,000.*

Hoops. The dozen of trussing hoops for pipe and hogshead, at: *at 18d.* The hundred pipe hoops: *at 18s the 100.*

Drawing of beer. Every ship steward hath for drawing of every one tun of beer spent in the ship – *4d.*

Necessaries for the ships. Every ship had money allowed him for necessaries of the same, that is for a man one penny in the week to provide wood, lights and bowls of wood to drink in, with other things, which portion was allowed every ship according to the number of their men: *1d a man the week.*

[f. 13] *The bakehouse.* The master baker had: *10d the day.* And the rest: *8d the day.* The furners had: *9d the day. And find themselves.*

The brewhouse. The master brewer had: *12d the day.* The underbrewer: *10d the day.* All their men: *8d the day.* The coopers: *7d the day.* The mill horse-keeper: *6d the day.* The miller: *8d the day.* Labourers: *5d the day.* The overseers of the brewhouse: *2s the day.* Keepers and measurers of grain: *5d the day.* Horse hired to grind malt: *2d the quarter. And find themselves.*

[f. 13v] *Clerks' wages.* The clerks making provision and proportions for the ships and keeping the accounts of all other provisions: *20d the day.*

Packers of beef. The packers of beef in butts, pipes and hogsheads had: *4d for the pipe making.*

Slaughtermen. Slaughtermen had: *6d the day.*

Clerk of the bakehouse. The clerks of the bakehouse had: *8d the day. And find themselves.*

Brewing in the country. If any brewing were made in the country for these wares, then was there allowed them for every quarter brewing: *12d the quarter.*

Storehouses. The hire of storehouses and barns to put in provision were allowed 5s the month: *5s the month.*

[f. 14] *Land carriages.* Carriages of provision from London to Portsmouth: *4d the mile.*

Carriages. And from sundry places nigh about Portsmouth: *2d the mile.*

Lighters. Carriages or lighters hired to carry provisions from place to place were at 12d for the tonnage of his such boat or crayer for a month, and 5s for a man's wages, and 6s 8d for a man's meat and drink one month: *12d his tonnage, 5s his wages, 6s 8d his board: for a month.*

Hoys. The hire of Flanders hoys for storehouses, whereof were a number hired by the month, and according to his burthen he was allowed as if he were of 60 tuns, then hath he for the tun wages and meat for himself and his men one month – *£4.*

[f. 14v] What sorts of grain and the number of the quarters, as also what oxen, bacon, butter, cheese, and fish of divers sorts, with other necessaries that were provided at Portsmouth for the victualling of the said ships and army.

   Wheat: 2,519 quarters 2 bushels 2 pecks.
   Malt: 6,900 quarters 7 bushels half a peck.
   Barley: 518 quarters 2 bushels.
   Oats: 918 quarters 2 bushels 2 pecks.
   Beans: 88 quarters 2 bushels.
[f. 15] Maslin: 886 quarters 3 bushels 2 pecks.
   Pease: 919 quarters 3 bushels 2 pecks
   Bran: 285 quarters.
   Horse-bread: 965 dozen [*fodder of compacted beans, bran &c.*].
   Biscuit: 1,517,961 pounds [*perhaps 15,179 cwt 61 lbs*]
   Beer: 3,980 tuns 2 hogsheads 1 barrel.
   Hops: 62,410 pounds [*perhaps 624 cwt 10 lbs*].
   Oxen: 583.
[f. 15v] Salt beef: 1,695 pieces.
   Fresh beef: 39,490 pounds [*perhaps 394 cwt, 90 lbs*].
   Butter: 291 barrels, 31 pounds in every barrel.
   Bacon: 16,215 pounds [*perhaps 162 cwt 15 lbs*].
   Stockfish: 125,912 fishes.
   Mud-fish: 3,000 fishes [*fish dwelling in mud*].
   Martinmas ('Martlemas') beef: 55 pieces [*beef salted around St Martin's day, 11 November*].
   Pollacks: 4,002 fishes.
[f. 16] Haberdine: 1,240 fishes [*large cod*].
   Congers: 6,480 fishes.
   Dry hakes: 2,614 fishes.
   Newlands: 1,299 fishes [*Newfoundland fish*].
   Cods: 6,984 fishes.
   Wet newland: 7,082 fishes [*MS here and next 'Bett~' in error; wet fish being those preserved in salt or brine*].
   Wet hakes: 1,444 fishes.
   Sprats: 37 cades.
[f. 16v] Lings: 30,054 fishes.
   Bay-salt: 2,134 quarters [*salt extracted from sea water*].
   Billets: 254,200 billets [*chopped wood*].
   Faggots: 6,050.

Pipes, hogsheads and pipestaves: 33,614 'pa.'
Twigs for ho[*ops*]: 465,200 twigs.
Casks – 1,531 tuns, 2 barrels.
Carthorses – 26 horses.

[f. 17] Money disbursed for the said provision of corn, oxen, butter, beef, bacon, cheese, with divers and sundry kinds of fishes, clerks' bakers', brewers' and other labourers' wages at Portsmouth for the victualling of the said ships.

In primis wheat: £314 11s 11½d. Item malt: £462 5s 10d. Item wheat flour: £4 17s 6d. Item barley: £109 15s. Item oats: £52 8s 2d. [f. 17v] Item rye and maslin: £412 8s 10½d. Item bran: £18 14s 6d. Item horse-bread: £29 18s 10d. Item biscuit: £86 10s. Item beer: £690 10s 11d. Item oxen: £680 12s 4d. Item salt beef: £289 9s 5½d. Item butter: £360 10s 8d. [f. 18] Item cheese: £259 15s 4d. Item bacon: £354 8s 6d. Item hops: £221 9s 8d. Item stockfish: £4 10s 4d. Item mud-fish: £3 4s 4d. Item dry hakes: £80 11s. Item wet hakes: £4 6s 9d. Item haberdine: £421 4s 2d. [f. 18v] Item lings: £580: 7s 9d. Item white herrings: £64 4s. Item cods: £105 13s 4d. Item bay salt: £216. Item tallwood: £34 11s 2d. Item faggots: £60 19s 4d. Item billets: £60 10s. Item carthorses: 42s 10d.

[f. 19] *Summa totalis* of the money disbursed for the aforesaid provision of grain and victuals for the same ships amounteth to: £7,823 9s 9d.

Necessaries belonging to the bakehouse and brewhouse. Item for hoops, hedging timber, canvas for biscuit bags, coopers' twigs, ashen staves, empty casks, shovels, pick-axes, leather and buskins, locks, bins ('bynges') for bread and other necessary,[1] as appeareth by the book of particulars: £995 1s 9d.

Grain. Item for grinding of grain, *viz.* wheat, barley, malt &c.: £84 18s 1d.

[f. 19v] *Carriages.* Item to divers persons for the freights and land carriages of all sorts of grain, victuals, hoops, casks and other necessaries from sundry places unto the said town of Portsmouth, as also to sundry others for attending the victualling of the said navy at the sea: £1,404 18s 4d.

Storehouses. Item paid for rent of divers houses to keep the foresaid provision in during the abiding at Portsmouth – £34 18s.

Purveyors. Item paid for the charges of divers purveyors of oxen and steers, powderers and packers of beef, coopers, carriers of bay

---

[1]*Sic*, but probably copyist's error for 'necessaries'.

salt, labourers, and other necessaries belonging to that service at Portsmouth: £212 4s 10d.

[f. 20] *Wages.* Item the wages of clerks, bakers, brewers, millers, and other workmen during the time of this provision making at Portsmouth, and until such time as it was shipped: £1,910 14s 0½d.

Conduct money. Item for the conducting of the said provision into the ships: £18 14s.

Diet. Item the accountants' diet: £288 0s 10d.

Riding charges. Item paid for riding charges: £84 19s 6d.

Prest money. Item prest money – £310 3s 3d.

[f. 20v] The whole sum of money disbursed for the provision of oxen, corn, butter, beef, cheese, divers sorts of fish, with other necessaries for the bakehouse and brewhouse at Portsmouth, grinding of grain, carriages, hire of storehouses, purveyors' wages, conduct money, diet of the accountants, riding charges, prest money, with divers other provisions for the said navy in the 36th, 37th and 38th years of His Majesty's reign: £13,200 11s 4d.

[*The remainder of the MS concerns provisioning for 12,000 men to defend Berwick against an anticipated siege when Queen Mary's war with France began in summer 1557.*[1]]

[f. 21] A rate and proportion of victualling of 12,000 men for 4 months, declaring the provisions of the week and month particularly, and appointed for the said men to defend Berwick, unto which the Scots determined to lay siege, which came not to pass, and yet the victuals provided; which proportion was made by the Right Honourable Lord Marquess of Winchester and High Treasurer of England, *viz.*:

This number of 6,000 quarters of wheat for 12,000 men 4 months is full furnished at Berwick and Newcastle.

For 4,000 men, after one peck a man for the week: 125 quarters.

For 8,000 men by the week: 250 quarters.

For 12,000 men by the week: 375 quarters.

For 12,000 men by the month: 1,500 quarters.

For 12,000 men for 2 months: 3,000 quarters.

For 12,000 men 4 months: 6,000 quarters.

[f. 21v] This number of 7,000 quarters of [*malt*] for 12,000 men 4 months is full furnished at Berwick and Newcastle.

[1]*NEM*, p. 342 and n. 3.

Malt for the said 12,000 men for 4 months: 7,000 quarters.

Hops. Hops after 6 pounds to the quarter of malt for the 4 months: 8,300 pounds.

Oxen. This 9,600 oxen will be borne with the market and the forays [*MS*. 'forrles' *but cf. below*] out of Scotland, with the provision of the 2,400 oxen for 4 months. For 12,000 men one week, accounting 300 pounds to every ox: 600 oxen.

For 12,000 men one month, after the rate of 600 for a week: 2,400 oxen.

For 12,000 men 4 months, after the rate of 2,400 for a month: 9,600 oxen.

[f. 22] *Sheep*. These 12,000 sheep, with the markets and forays ('forreis') will serve the 4 months, except there be a siege.

For one week of sheep: 3,000.

For 12,000 men one month: 12,000.

Saltfish. Haberdine. Consider the store and plenty of the country, and then this will serve, except there be a siege.

For 2 days in the weeks, after half a saltfish a mess: 6,000 fishes.

And for the said men one month: 24,000 fishes.

And for the said men 4 months: 96,000 fishes.

For 2 days in the week, cutting 3 mess of a fish: 2,880 fishes.

And for the said men 2 months: 11,580 fishes.

And for the said men 4 months: 46,080 fishes.

[f. 22v] *Butter*. Butter for 12,000 men 2 days in the week, after half a pound for a man, is: 6,000 pounds.

And for the said 12,000 men for one month: 24,000 pounds.

And for the said 12,000 men for 4 months: 96[,000] pounds.

Summa: 96[,000] pounds, which be barrels after 240 pounds in a barrel: 400 barrels.

Cheese. Cheese for 12,000 men for 2 days in the week, after one pound for a man: 12,000 pounds.

And for the said 12,000 men for one month: 48,000 pounds.

And for the said 12,000 men for 4 months: 192[,000] pounds.

[f. 23] *Summa* of 192,000 pounds of cheese, after the rate of 210 pounds to the wey: 800 wey.

These 2,000 quarters of oats and 600 quarters of beans, with new corn and grass, will serve:

Oats. For 4,000 [men *deleted*] horses by the week, after one bushel for a horse: 500 quarters.

And for the said 4,000 horses one month: 2,000 quarters.

Beans for 4,000 horses one month, after the rate before written, is: 600 quarters.

[ff. 23v–41 *blank*]

2. *Shipwrights' Report*

[Hatfield House, Cecil Papers 201/127   ? June 1545
(HMC *Salisbury*, i, p.146)][1]

King's]s Majesty of ships following by John
. .]es, James Baker, Benjamin Gonson and
. . . *that i*]s to say:

The Mary Rose   First the[*re can be*] no more [*or*]dnance laid at the luff without
the taking away of 2 kn[*ees*] and the spoiling of the clamps
that [*c*]o[*v*]ereth the bits, which will be a great weakening
to the same part of the ship.

Item, she hath right over the luff two whole slings lying
forwards over quarter-wise, and at the barbican head
likewise forward over 2 culverins, and the decks over
the same shooting likewise forward over 2 sakers.

The Jennet   Item, her foremast cannot well be otherwise translated
for lack of breadth on the bow, and now shooteth forward
over of either side the foremast one saker.

The New Bark   Item, she hath forwards over of one side the foremast a demi
culverin and over the other side a saker lying, as we suppose,
. . . er to pass than to translate the said foremast where is
[*room*] for 2 demi culverins, if it may please Your Grace.

3. *Lord Admiral Lisle to Secretary Paget*

[SP 1/205, ff. 118–119v (new foliation) (LP, xx, II, no. 62)]   7 August 1545

Master Secretary, after my very hearty commendations, having seen
your letters of the 6th of this present, whereby amongst other things it
appeareth that the King's Majesty's pleasure is I should put the book
of the names of ships and captains in other form, and to place every
captain according as they were appointed at such time as His Majesty did place Peter Carew to the *Mistress*, and also to set upon every

---

[1]MS dated in modern pencil '?1557' (supplied by previous Hatfield Librarian, following
the position in the nineteenth-century Calendar).

ship the captain's name that is or then was, although they be dead or gone, with also a titling upon the same ships of such men's names as I think meet to serve.[1] As touching the alteration of the captains, I require you to signify unto His Highness that there is no alterations since His Majesty's last appointment of them, saving that Peter Carew, when he perceived that we were like to fight with the French army at their being here, and remembering that he was in a ship able to board one of the greatest of the enemy's [*or* enemies] and what might be thought in him to forsake such a ship (of himself, whereas before he did desire the other), which petitions now besought me that he might not be shifted out of his ship, for that he trusted to do His Majesty good service in her.[2] So that (perceiving him so loath to depart from the said ship and the time then being very short to make any alteration) I thought it best to let every captain remain in their former places (whereof then I did send His Majesty word by Sir Thomas Clere). And so doth the whole number of ships remain at this present without changing of any captain except only such as be gone sick, and one that is dead.

And where His Majesty's pleasure is that I should make a titling of other captains' names which I think meet to serve in those ships that want their captains, I assure you (Mr Secretary) I cannot call to remembrance out of this army of two that is meet for that purpose, albeit there is no doubt but there be divers that could and would be glad to serve, but I cannot call them to memory; yet have I studied with myself as much as I can possibly for it. As touching the *Argosy* that Sir Robert Stafford was in,[3] I intend to place one Thomas Apowen, a servant of His Majesty [in her *inserted*], which is an expert gentleman in this feat and a hardy man, being before but in one of the mean ships of Bristol, which ship a meaner man may serve in.[4] And as touching the *Matthew Gonson* I am minded that John Winter (if he amend, who is now in an ague) shall be placed in her if His Majesty's pleasure

---

[1] On 3 Aug Lisle had responded to the King's request for a list of ships; but this did not name the captains: *LP*, xx, II, no. 27. Two days later he explained the omission; having spied the approaching reinforcements from the West Country, he had hastened to inspect them, in the process 'forgetting to finish the book': ibid., no. 39. The full list was completed on 10 Aug: ibid., no. 88 (printed in full in *State Papers during the Reign of Henry VIII* (Record Commission, 1830–52), i, pp. 810–13; incorporated into Doc. No. 6 below.

[2] Carew remains in place in the *Great Venetian* in the list of 10 Aug (Doc. No. 6)[6].

[3] The London *Argosy* of 300 men as listed in Doc. No. 1.

[4] Stafford featured in the July list (Doc. No. 5). Thomas Apowen (here 'Abowyn') duly appears as captain of the *Argosy* (of London) in the list of 10 Aug [6].

so be.[1] And the gentleman which was one of the Rhodes who hath made means to serve the King's Majesty (as in my former letters I did advertise you) shall be in the *Small Galley*. He is called a very hardy man and one that hath been brought up in the feat of the sea. His name is Anthony Hussye.[2] I require you that I may have a letter under the Stamp[3] to deliver him at his coming, if it be the King's Majesty's pleasure that he shall serve.

And as concerning all the new ships, I know none other way (I mean those that come out of the West parts and such of London as were victuallers that want captains) but to place them [as *deleted*] with mean men to be their captains, as serving men and yeomen that be most meet for the purpose. And if it shall stand with His Majesty's pleasure that one man shall have the charge of all the rowing pieces, and to be as it were a wing to the army (seeing that Mr Carew is [to *deleted*] so loath to depart out of the great ship that he is in, which proceedeth of a good heart) I think William Tirrell the most fittest gentleman in all the army for that purpose, if it may so like His Highness, for he is a man that hath seen the feat of the galleys, and is a sure man and a diligent in any thing that he is committed unto.

And whereas I do perceive His Majesty's pleasure is [that *deleted*] to have James Baker and the other shipwrights here to go [about *deleted*] in hand with the trimming of the *Jennet*, the *New Bark* and the bark with salt, since His Majesty's removing from hence I have sundry times communed with the said Baker and declared His Highness's pleasure unto him in that behalf, and he saith that for his life he shall not be able to being them to His Majesty's purpose in one month; for the upper overlop of the *New Bark* must be clean taken down and the prize in like manner, their overlops be so near togethers that men cannot else row in them. And if he should begin to alter them and could not make them ready to depart with the army, the want of such two ships would be a great weakening to the same, the which I require you to signify unto His Majesty, and also

---

[1] In the 10 Aug list the *Matthew* is commanded by Gawain Carew; Winter was still in the grip of a 'fervent burning ague' on 12 Aug, though three days later he reported himself 'whole' though 'somewhat weak': *LP*, xx, II, nos. 108 (Lisle to King, 12 Aug), 135 (Winter to St John, 15 Aug).

[2] On 5 Aug, Lisle reported that Hussye, 'that was one of the Rodes' (i.e. a former Knight of St John), had been sent for from Poole to take over this command: *LP*, xx, II, no. 39. This man is distinguished from an Admiralty official of the same name: cf. index to *LP*, xx (pt II, p. 740).

[3] In Henry VIII's later years certain documents were authenticated by stamping an impression of the King's signature, inked over by one of the Principal Secretaries (an act of treason for which they were regularly pardoned).

that His Highness's army shall, God willing, be ready to depart hence by Wednesday next, and sooner if it may be possible. The *Argosy*'s mast is not yet up, but this day it will be set up at the furthest, and there is as much done by my Lord Great Master[1] and my Lord Chamberlain[2] for the advancement of our setting forth as may be.

Further these may be to desire you to signify unto the King's Majesty that yesterday (being a very calm) three of the French galleys appeared at St Helens Point, and one of the boats of Rye being abroad came in a pace and had much ado to escape; the said galleys followed her almost against St Helens haven. But the *Mistress*, the *Anne Gallant*, the *Greyhound* and the *Falcon* canvassed them away again, whose coming I suppose was but to escry what we did here and what order we kept. But I think they liked not the sight that they saw, for they might see a greater number of sails than at their last being here. We fear nothing but when their Admiral [*four words repeated then deleted*] shall hear the news, he will not long after tarry in the Narrow Seas. If he do (God willing) there may be a better attempt made unto the King's Majesty of him than he hath yet made to his master. As knoweth the living God, who send you as well to fare as I would myself.

Scribbled[3] at Portsmouth, the 7th of August.

> Your loving friend,
> John Lisle.

4. *Command Lists*

[SP 1/245, ff. 23–25 (new foliation)   June–July 1545
(*LP Addenda*, no. 1697)]

[*List 1 (f. 23) with the King's ships to which captains had been appointed*]

Captains	Ships	Tuns	Men
The Lord Admiral	The *Peter*	600	400
The Lord Clinton	The *Great Galley*	500	300
The Lord William [Howard]	The *Pauncy*	400	300
Sir John Berkeley	The *Salamander*	300	220
Sir John Luttrell	The *Mary Hambrough*	400	246

[1]Charles Brandon, Duke of Suffolk.
[2]William Paulet, Lord St John, later first Marquess of Winchester.
[3]Meaning only that it was a draft; repetition of a few words shows that it was a fair copy before signature.

Sir George Cornwall	The *Sweepstake*	300	230
Andrew Dudley	The *Swallow*	240	154
Anselm Guise	The *Dragon*	140	110
William Tirrell	The *New Bark*	160	120
Baldwin Willoughby	The *Jennet*	160	120
Dunstan Newdigate	The *Lion*	120	100
Richard Grey	The *Falcon Lisle*	200	160
Gilbert Grice	The *Anne Lisle*	200	160
John Winter	The *Less Galley*	300	250

The 6 ships of Bristol, every of
them having 120 men,
summa   720

The 5 boats of Rye, every of them
having 40 men, one with another
summa   200

Summa of sails – 25.   *Summa totalis* of men   3,788

[List 2 (f. 24) of *King's ships to which captains had not yet been assigned*][1]

Ships	Tuns	Men
The *Henry Grace à Dieu*	1000	700
The *Mary Rose*	700	500
The *Jesus of Lübeck*	600	300
The *Matthew Gonson*	500	300
The *Great Venetian*	700	400
The *Argosy*	500	300
[The *Struse of Danzig*	400	250][2]
The great galleon made at Smallhythe	300	250
The less galleon made there	200	160
The new galleon made at Deptford	120	100
The King's galliot	80	60
The shallop made at Deptford	60	50
The great pinnace	60	50

[1]There is also a fragment of a related list in Hatfield, Cecil Papers, 201/50, detailing ordnance remaining or taken from the King's galliot, the Great pinnace, the Shallop at Deptford, *Marlion* and the *Shallop Hutton*.
[2]Inserted without adjustment of the totals below.

| The *Marlion* | 50 | 50 |
| The *Shallop Hutton* | 30 | 30 |

Summa of ships – 14.   *Summa* of men –   3,250

[*List 3 (f. 25) with captains to be appointed to commands*]

Captains for ships	Captains for galliots and shallops

Sir George Carew   Richard Broke   } Rhodians[1]
Sir Charles Howard   Ambrose Cave   }
Sir William Woodhouse   Robert Reneger of Hampton
Sir Edmund Wyndham   Richard Williams, one of the Grooms
                                         of the Chamber

Sir John Clere
Peter Carew   Thomas Roodes   } of the Guard
Gawain Carew   William Hall   }
William Pickering,   Richard Fletcher of Rye
   Sir William
Pickering's son   Thomas Harding
Cuthbert Paston, one of   Thomas Hutton
   the Pensioners
William Broke, Surveyor of the Ships
John Chichester of the West Country
Thomas Sherbourne of Norfolk
Thomas Beeston, one of the
   Queen's Ushers
Thomas Cotton

[*A fourth list in this group (f. 26) lists ships marked 'b' for battle and
'w' for wing; the substance is printed in LP*]

5. Command lists

[Hatfield House, Cecil Papers, *201/51–3*   July 1545
(HMC Salisbury, I, p. 52)][2]

Captains	Ships	Tuns	Men

---

[1]Knights of St John, who were generally put in command of oared vessels.
[2]MS dated 1547 in modern pencil, to follow Calendar.

Lord Admiral[1]	The *Henry Grace à Dieu*	1,000	730
Sir George Carew	The *Mary Rose*	700	500
Peter Carew	The *Great Venetian*	700	450
Sir John Clere	The *Peter Pomegranate*	600	400
Sir W. Woodhouse	The *Matthew*	600	300
Gawain Carew	The *Great Galley*	500	300
Mr St Clere	The *Jesus of Lübeck*	700	300
Robert Stafford	The *Argosy*	500	300
Francis English	The *Sampson of 'Ynquys'*[2]	700	300
[Henr]y Fraunces[3]	The *Morion of Danzig*	500	250
John Chichester	The *Struse of Danzig*	450	250
Lord Clinton	The *Pauncy*	450	300
Roger Basing	The *Great Mistress*	450	250
Sir John Luttrell[4]	The *Mary Hambrough*	400	246
Robert Legg	The *Anne Gallant*	400	200
Clement Paston	The *Pelican of Danzig*	400	210
John Winter	The *Less Galley*	400	240
Arthur Winter	The *Saviour of Bristol*	340	200
Sir George Cornwall	The *Sweepstake*	300	240
Morgan Mathew	The *Salamander*	300	220
Thomas Cotton	The *Minion*	300	220
Edward Jones	The *Galley Subtle*	300	250
Thomas Heneage	The *Tricell of Danzig*	300	180
Thomas Beeston	The *Spaniard of Deva*	260	120
Andrew Dudley	The *Swallow*	240	160
Richard Broke	The *Unicorn*	240	160
Richard Grey	The *Falcon Lisle*	200	160
Gilbert Grice	The *Anne Lisle*	200	160
William Tirrell	The *New Bark*	200	120
William Broke	The *Greyhound*	200	120
William Harvest	The *Henry of Bristol*	180	120
Thomas Apowell	The *Trinity Caerleon*	180	120
Edward Butler	The *Margaret*	180	120
Baldwin Willoughby	The *Jennet*	180	120
Robert Reneger	The *Trinity [Reneger]*[5]	180	120

[1]John Dudley, Viscount Lisle (later Duke of Northumberland), executed 1553.
[2]Otherwise 'of Lübeck'.
[3]Originally written 'William Candish' [Cavendish], the surname deleted and '-y Fraunces' added above.
[4]MS. 'Batrell'.
[5]MS. 'bovag'.

Thomas Robertes	The *Mary George of Rye*	180	116
Thomas Gye	The *Thomas Tipkins*	180	120
John Norton	The *Evangelist Norton*	160	120
William Cavendish[1]	The *Christopher Bennet*	180	120
William Grainger	The *George Brigges*	140	100
[blank] Boyce	The *Evangelist Judde*	160	110
James Spencer	The *Thomas Magdalene*	130	100
John Roodes	The *Mary Fortune*	120	90
Thomas Lokyer	The *Trinity Smythe*	140	100
William Courtenay	The *Mary James*	140	100
Thomas Dale	The *Mary Conception*	140	100
Anselm Guise	The *Dragon*	140	110
John Cutt	The *Pilgrim of Dartmouth*	140	100
Dunstan Newdigate	The *Lion*	140	100
Thomas Harding	The *Falcon*	100	60
John Apmerik	The *Lartique*	100	80
John Crocher	The *Mary Martin*	100	90
William Hatcher	The *Jesus Reneger*	140	80
Thomas Sherbourne	The *Thomas of Greenwich*	80	70
Walter Soly	The *Roo*	90	80
John Burley	The *Saker*	60	60
William Haw	The *Hind*	80	50
Richard Fletcher	The *Marlion*	60	50
John Basing	The *Brigantine*	40	50
John Cowper	The last pinnace[2]	60	45
Thomas Hutton	The *Hare*	30	30

Boats of Rye

Andrew Church	The *George*	–	37
[blank] Blakey	The *Magdalene*	–	37
Blake Jonson	The *Jesus*	–	30
John Bredes	The *James*	–	30
James Jonson	The *Mary George*	–	30
David Worth	The *Trinity of Rye*		30
[blank]	The *Mary James Fletcher*	–	30

[1]Written over 'Henry Frauncis' deleted.
[2]Assumed to be *Less Pinnace*, which is listed with the same complement on 3 Aug: SP 1/205, ff. 48–49: *LP*, xx, II, no. 27(2); in Anthony Roll (no. 42), the ship of this name is 40 tons/44 men.

Ships and boats of war – 68
Men – 10,811

Victuallers to follow the fleet

William Driver	The *Magdalene Driver*	100	30
[*blank*] Cheyny	The *Peter of Lowestoft*	120	35
William Baker	The *Mary and John*	100	30
[*blank*] Hutson	The *Mary Fortune of Lowestoft*	100	30
William Lee	The *Martyn Bulley*	130	35
[*blank*]	The *Galley Reneger*	120	35

6. *Summary of Command lists*

June–August 1545

[The swung dash (~) indicates the name as in the preceding column.]

June/July [Doc. No. 4 *above*]	July [Doc. No. 5 *above*]	10 August[1]	
Henry Grace à Dieu[2]	[*vacant*]	Lord Admiral	~
Mary Rose	[*vacant*]	Sir George Carew[3]	
Peter Pomegranate	Lord Admiral	Sir John Clere	~
Matthew	[*vacant*]	Sir W. Woodhouse[4]	Gawain Carew
Great Galley/Bark	Lord Clinton	Gawain Carew	Thos Wyndham
Jesus of Lübeck	[*vacant*]	John St Clere	~
Pauncy	Lord William Howard	Lord Clinton	~
Morion	Henry Francis	Thomas Francis	
Struse of Danzig	[*vacant*]	John Chichester	~
Mary Hambrough	Sir John Luttrell	~	~
Less Galley/Bark	John Winter	Winter	Roger Basing
Sweepstake	Sir George Cornwall	~	~
Minion		Thomas Cotton	~
Lartique		John Apmerik	~

[1]SP 1/205, ff. 171–173v, 168 (misbound) [*LP*, xx, II, no. 88]

[2]First group here printed (King's great ships and pinnaces) in the order of the Anthony Roll: see C.S. Knighton and D. Loades (eds), *The Anthony Roll of Henry VIII's Navy* (NRS, Occasional Publication no. 2, 2000); fuller details of most ships in *NEM*, Appendix 1.

[3]Lost with his ship 19 July.

[4]Reported as being very sick, 1 Aug; on the following day the Lord Admiral recommended his replacement by Mr Constable or 'yong Mr Carye' (i.e. Gawain Carew): *LP*: xx, II, nos 3, 16.

Mary James		William Courtenay	~
Grand Mistress		Roger Basing	William Tirrell
Anne Gallant		Robert Legge	~
Salamander	Sir John Berkeley	Morgan Matthew	~
Unicorn		Richard Broke	~
Swallow	Andrew Dudley	~	~
Galley Subtle		Edward Jones	~
New Bark	William Tirrell	~	Edmund Hussye
Greyhound		William Broke	~
Jennet	Baldwin Willoughby	~	~
Lion	Dunstan Newdigate	~	~
Dragon	Anselm Guise	~	~
Falcon		Thomas Harding	~
Saker		John Burley	~
Hind		William Haw	~ (Haull)
Roo		Walter Soly	~
Phoenix Hertford			Edward Woulf
Marlion	[*vacant*]	Richard Fletcher	~
Less Pinnace		John Cowper	William Bell
Brigantine		John Basing	~
Hare		Thomas Hutton	~
Falcon Lisle	Richard Grey	~	~
Anne Lisle	Gilbert Grice	~	~
Great Venetian[1]	[*vacant*]	Peter Carew	~
Argosy	[*vacant*]	Robert Stafford	Thomas Apowen
Great Galleon of Smallhythe	[*vacant*]		
Less	[*vacant*]		
New galleon Deptford	[*vacant*]		
King's galliot	[*vacant*]		
Shallop Deptford	[*vacant*]		
Saviour of Bristol		Arthur Winter	~
Painted hulk	[*vacant*]		
Spaniard of Deva[2]	[*vacant*]	Thomas Beeston	~
Ship of Montrego	[*vacant*]		
New galleon of Kent	[*vacant*]		
Less new galley	[*vacant*]		
Ships of Bristol	[*vacant*]		

---

[1]Identified as *Maryen de Pawlo* [*Marian de Paulo*], 700 tons, in list of 19 April: *LP*, xx, I, no. 543.

[2]Given as *Ship of Dover* in *LP*.

Sampson of Lübeck	F. English[1]	Thomas Bell *vice* Apowen
Pelican of Danzig	Clement Paston	~
Tricell of Danzig	Thomas Heneage	~
Henry of Bristol	William Harvest	John Elyott
Trinity Caerleon	Thomas Apowell	Anthony Carvanian
Margaret of Bristol	Edward Butler	William Butler
Trinity Reneger	Robert Reneger	~
Mary George of Rye	Thomas Robertes	~
Thomas Tipkins	Thomas Gye	~
Evangelist Norton	John Norton	Edward Treford
Christopher Bennett	William Cavendish	Geoffrey Vaughan
George Brigges	William Grainger	~ ('Raunger')
Evangelist Judde	[*blank*] Boyce	~ (Thomas Boyce)
Thomas Magdalene	James Spencer	~
Mary Fortune	John Roodes	Thomas Roodes
Trinity Smythe	Thomas Lokyer[2]	James Parker
Mary Conception	Thomas Dale	
Pilgrim of Dartmiuth	John Cutt	~
Mary Martin	John Crocher	~
Jesus Reneger	William Hatcher	
Thomas of Greenwich	Thomas Sherbourne	
boats of Rye		
George	Andrew Church	~
Magdalene	[*blank*] Blakey	~ (William Blakye)
Jesus	Blake Jonson	~
James	John Bredes	
Mary George (II)	James Jonson	~
Trinity	David Worth	(David North)
Mary James Fletcher	[*blank*]	John Emerye
victuallers		
Magdalene Driver	William Driver	~
Mary and John	[*blank*] Cheyny	~ (Thomas Cheyny)
Mary Fortune of Lowestoft	[*blank*] Hutson	~ ('Hudson')
Martyn Bulley	William Lee	~
Galley Reneger	[*blank*]	John Reneger
Mary of Greenwich		William Cavendish
Renegers' Pinnace		Christopher Stoughton
Argosy of Hampton		Sir Thomas Clere
Galleon of Hambrough		Thomas Sherbourne
Mary Bulloyn		Francis Barney
Unicorn of Poole		Luke Lambarde

[1]Reported as departed sick on 1 Aug: *LP*, xx, II, no. 3.
[2]Lockyer of Bristol, one of the guard and 'a very good captain', reported dead 1 Aug: *LP*, xx, II, no. 3.

James of London	Henry Goldyng
Michael of Newcastle	William Harman
Trinity of Fowey	Anthony Dogate
Galleon of Lyme	Richard Myller
Falcon of Plymouth	Thomas Nycoll
Pickpurse	John Peers
Grey of Lowestoft	William Graye
Shoulder of Mutton	David Lloyd
Redbreast	John Austyn
Trinity of Totnes	John Wallwyn
Julian of Dartmouth	Thos Fletcher
Nicholas of Dartmouth	Matthew Hull
Mary Katherine of London	John Toppe
Marlion Russell	James Spicer
George of Falmouth	John Calerde
George of Totnes	George Stuckley
George of Dittisham	Giles Calawey
Hackney of Plymouth	Walter Hollyes
Figge of Plymouth	Leonard Willes
Mary Winter of Plymouth	William Stephen
George of Dartmouth	Thomas Gooddale
Mary of Fowey	Thomas Hollyes
James of Fowey	Thomas Cock
George of Truro	Richard Whyte
Katherine Whyte of Looe	Thomas Even
Mary of Hastings	Oliver Burton
Cakaphogo	Thomas Norres

7. *Sir John Oglander's narrative of the invasion of the Isle of Wight*

[Isle of Wight Record Office, OG/AA/28, ff. 21–22][1]   July 1545

[f. 21] In Henry the 8th reign the French King provided a great fleet to invade England, which came unto the Isle of Wight in [strength into

---

[1]First printed by P.G. Stone in 'Two accounts of the French descent on the Isle of Wight under Claude d'Annebault, July, 1545. Extracted from the Memoirs of Martin Du Bellay, 1513–46, and from the MSS. of Sir John Oglander, Kt., 1585–1655, with a digest of the two accounts', *Isle of Wight County Press* (Nov 1907); subsequently reissued as a separate pamphlet. The MS, though undoubtedly contemporary with its compiler, has been carelessly copied from an earlier version, with numerous mistakes and *lacunae*, here corrected or supplied in italic within square brackets. Dr Fontana brought Stone's transcript to the attention of the Mary Rose Trust, and subsequently located the original MS on which the present version is based.

corrected to] July. You shall [*see by*] the French their own relation which is most commonly with advantage *le nombre des navires ordonnez pour l'armée montoit à cent cinquante gros vaisseaux ronds, sans compter soixante flouins, et vingt cinq galleres*.[1] All this great fleet weighed anchor at Havre de Grace on the 16th day of July 1545 and came all to an anchor before St Helens on the 18th of the said July 1545; the commander was the Admiral of Annebault.[2] There was a little skirmish between our ships which then lay at Portsmouth, being in number 60; but it is true that we were too weak and withdrew within the Horse,[3] but it is to be observed that both we and the Frenchmen lost each one the best ship in their fleet without shooting one shot. The French ship being called *La Maistresse*, wherein all the treasure was for payment of the Navy, sunk down into the sea near St Helens; the reason was that going out of the harbour at Honfleur she touched against the ground, which so opened her joints, and the water getting in, became so leaky that there she sunk down; the men were most saved and all the money. We lost the *Mary Rose*, one of our own best ships, in this manner (although the French vainly write that they sunk her). The one day before he determined to fight with the French, [*the King*] dined aboard the said *Mary Rose*, there giving order for the better ordering of the said battle. All things despatched and the King returning, the many people that was then aboard all flocked to that side to see the King go [off *corrected to*] out, whereon the weight of them brought the ship to one side, and the ordnance being unbreeched rolled to that side also; the ports being open, the sea came in and presently sunk her. Although infinite numbers were in the sea, [*yet*][4] not many drowned by reason of the multitude of small boats. It was remarkable that the two best ships of both fleets, the Mistress of France and the Queen of England,[5] should both so accidentally miscarry. Out of doubt it [*was*] a warning given by God to the Princes that they should be less prodigal of Christian blood. We will leave critics to make comments upon it and return to [f. 21v] our discourse. It is true there were many skirmishes, but the weather was so calm that

---

[1]M. Du Bellay, *Les Memoires de Mess. Martin Du Bellay Seigneur de Langey* (Paris, 1569) [hereafter Du Bellay], p. 339 ('The number of ships designated for the armada amounted to 150 great round ships, not counting sixty pinnaces, and 25 galleys').

[2]Claude d'Annebault, Admiral of France from 1543 until his death in 1552; at the conclusion of hostilities one of the peace negotiators, and sent to England in Aug 1546 as special ambassador to celebrate the treaty of Ardres: cf. *NEM*, p. 142 & n. 1.

[3]Horse Sand in the Solent, east of the channel into Portsmouth Harbour.

[4]MS. 'it'.

[5]Clearly understanding the ship to have been named after the King's sister Mary, Queen of France.

we durst not come forth but on advantages in the calms, their galleys being too hard for us. The chief commanders of the French under the Admiral were the Seigneur de Boutières,[1] the Baron of Curton,[2] the Prior of Capua, brother of Seigneur Piero Strozzi;[3] all which gave their advice, that they should land in the Isle of Wight, hoping that when the King saw his country afire he would draw out his ships to relieve them, for his Majesty then lay at Portsmouth. They landed in three several places all at one time, purposely to divide our forces. Pierre Strozzi landed at [Bembridge *corrected to*] St Helens, where [*there*][4] was a little fort and beat our men, being divided from the fort, into the woods. The Seigneur de Tais, General of the Foot, landed at Bonchurch, where there was a hot skirmish between them and us, and on either party many was slain of both sides. We had there most of the companies of Hampshire, where Captain Fischer,[5] being a fat gentleman and not able to make his retreat up the hill (for they put our men to rout) cried out 'A 100[li] for a horse' but in that confusion no horse could be gotten for a kingdom. Whether he was taken prisoner (which is the most likeliest, and that he died at sea) or what became of him we could never hear, although search was made here and inquiry in France. Of the French not many of quality were slain nor many hurt. The Seigneur de Moneins[6] was shot through the right hand. The third landing was made near Sandham by Captain[s] Marsay and Pierebon, who were both wounded and beaten back, with slaughter of many, to their ships. They all did little; they returned to their fleet. Afterwards they landed again in Bembridge, where Seigneur de Tais commanded in chief. They marched up as high as [the top of *inserted*] Bembridge Down before they were by us set on. We, lying in ambush on the other side, fell upon them both with foot and some horse (that we had mustered up amongst the carts), killed many, took prisoners, and drove the rest down as far as their ships, killing them all the ways. But then

---

[1]Guigues de Guiffrey, Baron de Boutières, commanding the right wing; a veteran of Pavia (1525), who had won repute for leading cavalry at Cérisoles (1544): C. de La Roncière, *Histoire de la Marine Française* (Paris, 1899–1932), iii, p. 421.

[2]Joachim de Chabannes, Baron de Curton, commanding the left wing; another veteran military commander: *ibid.*

[3]Leone Strozzi (d. 1554), Italian mercenary commander in French service, and brother of Piero *alias* Pietro (d. 1558); the MS uses French taken from Du Bellay (p. 340) '*le prieur de Capouë frere du Seigneur Pierre Strosse*', but this became a little muddled in Stone's transcription.

[4]MS 'then'.

[5]Robert Fyssher, who commanded the Island militia: J. Goodwin, *Bonchurch from A–Z* (Bonchurch, 1992), p. 7.

[6]Probably Jean de Royère.

[f. 22] the Admiral, having notice of it, commanded all ashore to their succour, and our King also sent word to us that we should retreat in order, seeking to draw all their strength ashore far from their ships, hoping for a favourable [*wind*] to bring his fleet in the interim to surprise theirs. Whereupon we retreated and skirmished with them as far as Yarbridge [*and*] gave them leave to burn all Bembridge and Yaverland. But the wind being still calm and not serving for our fleet, we [in *deleted*] beat them back again to their ships. Afterwards, seeing they durst not assail our ships lying within the Spit, the French entered into council what course they should take. Many were of opinion that they should fortify St Helens and Bembridge, and to that purpose to leave behind them of soldiers and pioneers 6000; but the Seigneur de Tais and Seigneur Remy were of another opinion and dissuaded them from it: first, that they could hardly spare so many men without hazard of their ships; secondly, they could not leave victuals sufficient; next they [*would*] leave them to great and eminent danger after the remove of their fleet. These and many more reasons, as the winter coming on and their having no good places of shelter, dissuaded [*them*] from that foolish opinion. So they set sail, and coasting the Island the Knight de Aux[1] landed somewhere in the south part of the Island (it is not certainly known, but most likely near Bonchurch). Going ashore to take in fresh water [*he*] was assailed by us; his company all fled, and he being shot in the knee with an arrow could not fly, whereupon some countryfellow (I can imagine him no better), he calling for ransom, clove his head with his brown bill. He was as brave a man as any amongst the French and Captain of the galleys, for whom there was much lamentation. He was buried, as I take it, in Bonchurch. And this was the last assault our island hath it had.[2]

---

[1]Pierre de Blacas d'Aulps, Knight of St John, appointed Captain-General of the Galleys of the Ponant (i.e. west, as opposed to Levant), 10 Dec 1544: La Roncière, p. 414 and n. 5.

[2]There is a summary account in another of Oglander's MSS (Isle of Wight Record Office, OG/AA/1, p. 3): 'In Hen. the 8th reign *anno Dom.* [*blank*] the French invaded the Island, landed at St Helens and came through Bembridge to Yaverland, and burned all as they went, but at Yarbridge we resisted them, beat them back to their ships and slew Monsieuir de Alxe [*dAulps*].'

III

THE ROYAL NAVY AND THE ENFORCEMENT OF THE STAMP ACT, 1764–65: THE ACCOUNT OF CAPTAIN ARCHIBALD KENNEDY RN

Edited by Byrne McLeod

While investigating a tranche of captains in the mid-eighteenth century in The National Archives, a unique cache of documents was found in the letters to the Admiralty in Captain Archibald Kennedy's file.[1] The importance of these documents is that they reveal the events in New York and the eastern seaboard of North America during the Stamp Act crisis which occupied the last three months of 1765, as they impinged on a naval captain – not a politician, colonial official or merchant. This perspective is different from that usually described in histories and is worthy of a wider audience.

Captain Kennedy was senior naval officer at New York from 1763, and most of his correspondence with the Admiralty had to do with the difficulties of impressing men from the merchant vessels trading in and out of New York. Trade was booming in the years after what was known in America as the French and Indian War and in Britain as the Seven Years' War. Merchant vessel owners could afford to pay their crews more than the navy offered, which made manning his vessels difficult. Kennedy reported to his Commander-in-Chief Lord Colvill, stationed in Halifax, and copied his letters to the Admiralty when it seemed likely that ships would reach England more quickly than ice-bound Halifax. He deployed the three sloops he had at his disposal as best he could to meet the many conflicting demands of the local colonial officials.

In 1764 everything changed. The Grenville administration had long planned to recoup from the colonists themselves some of the costs of protecting the American colonies from the French. Leading lawyers from the colonies, such as John Tabor Kempe, the young Attorney General in New York, had discussed this in London. Politicians in Britain anticipated no difficulty in levying taxes in America. If they had realised

---

[1] The National Archives Series 1/2012 Captains' Letters K 1763–70.

that the cost of collecting customs dues charged on American trade was three times the amount that officials raised in money they might have thought again. It is easy with hindsight to see that politicians in London should have paid more attention to the warnings of colonial administrators in America who were unable to persuade the colonial assemblies to vote them any income. Trading with the enemy was not confined to the American colonies: the Irish supplied beef to the French army despite being much more closely governed than the colonies were.[1] The strong Irish element in New York society was powerful amongst the trading community, and displayed vigorous contempt for British navigation laws. Evading the navigation acts prepared the colonies for rebellion.

The original Dutch community in New York was still strongly represented amongst the leading merchants, and saw no reason to stop trading with Holland or with Dutch interests in the West Indies. The collector of customs in New York was a royal appointment. Holder of this office for two decades was an earlier generation of Archibald Kennedy, father of the naval captain. Collector Kennedy (hereafter referred to as Kennedy Snr) reported:

> We have reason to believe that there has been for some time lately carried on, a clandestine illegal trade, by some of the traders of this place, to Holland and other parts.[2]

The merchants of New York did not consider themselves to be traitors, despite the fact that their trade with the French West Indian islands had continued throughout the war. They were not conspiring with enemies to betray England: trading with the neutral Danish, Dutch or Spanish did not constitute 'adhering to the king's enemies', and they also outfitted colonial and British troops as well as victualling British warships. The profit on trade was even higher during war than in peacetime, as prices could be inflated. General Loudoun denounced the 'lawless set of smugglers, who continually supply the enemy with what provisions they want, and bring back their goods in barter for them'.[3] The merchants were daring and resourceful, and their commercial impulse was irresistible. Trading through the Spanish port of Monte Christi made it the busiest sea port in the North Atlantic, with merchant vessels unloading into local coasting

[1]Neil R. Stout, *The Royal Navy in America, 1760–1775* (Annapolis, 1973), p. 18.

[2]Thomas M. Truxes, *Defying Empire: Trading with the Enemy in Colonial New York* (Yale, 2008), p. 44.

[3]Theodore Draper, *A Struggle for Power: The American Revolution* (Preston, 1997), p. 176.

vessels goods destined for both French and British purchasers. Against his better judgement, the collector of customs appealed for co-operation:

> to prevent, as far as it in our power, that flagitious practice of carrying provisions to the enemy; which, besides the iniquity of supplying our enemies, our own navy and troops may in all probability want.[1]

Kennedy Snr knew that the city's trading patterns were deeply embedded and that to succeed he would have to combat not only the economic foundations of the city, but the intertwined political and social hierarchies. Kennedy Snr wrote and published in New York a series of papers on the problems of controlling trade from a distance, typical of which was the 1750 pamphlet *Observations on the Importance of the Northern Colonies under Proper Regulations*. He believed that restrictions on trade would only frustrate the commercial development of the intertwined economies, and would be of limited value in England. Despite his misgivings, shortly before he died in 1763 Kennedy Snr published an appeal in the *New York Gazette* for informants:

> some of our traders have for some time carried on . . . a correspondence with enemy . . . and supplied them with provisions . . . whoever will assist in detecting such scandalous and infamous practices, they need not doubt of the protection of the government or of being thankfully rewarded

Kennedy Snr was not supported by his lieutenant governor, Cadwallader Colden. Asked by the Board of Trade for a report on the situation in New York, Colden disingenuously claimed that he was 'entirely a stranger' to the city's trade, despite his son Alexander's being a high-ranking customs official. Colden also claimed that the trade with the French islands had effectually stopped as a result of the many seizures by the navy, by which 'some of the merchants have been entirely ruined and all of them have suffered greatly'.[2]

The customs house at Perth Amboy, New Jersey, was visited regularly by vessels bound for quite different destinations. Corrupt customs officials provided clearances from Perth Amboy so that a vessel which arrived with a legitimate declaration for a local destination would leave with the same cargo now cleared for the onward voyage to a forbidden port. This was evidence of collusion with the officials of the customs

[1] Truxes, *Defying Empire*, p. 12.
[2] Truxes, *Defying Empire*, p. 112.

house. However, customs officials did not all collude with smugglers. Kennedy Snr advised Admiral Colvill of possible ways in which loopholes in the current laws could be closed, and suggested features which became law in the 1764 Sugar Act. One of these was that bonds be given for non-enumerated cargoes, a second was that ships clearing from England for the colonies should load their whole cargoes in England. Persuaded by General Amherst, Kennedy Snr also appealed to the public for information:

> Whoever will discover to me, or any other of the officers of his Majesty's customs, the landing of any foreign rum, sugar or molasses within this district, before entry made and the duties paid, shall upon condemnation and charges deducted, receive one third part of the whole, with the thanks, doubtless, of his country.[1]

Once the new legislation was in place, Admiral Holmes, Commander-in-Chief in Jamaica, ordered all vessels leaving the Spanish ports of Monte Christi and Hispaniola to be seized. This halted the trade temporarily, but without ratification from the government the action was of limited significance. When taken to the Court of Prize Appeals in London the seizures were reversed: the customs house in London had granted clearances and the trade was insured by English underwriters. During the whole of the war period British courts upheld French property rights and London merchant bankers provided financial services for French correspondents.[2] The only seizures which were condemned were those taken to courts in Jamaica where the local merchants made sure that the illicit trade was punished.

Progress was made, in that the bogus trade by which merchant ships were protected by flags of truce was brought to an end. Until the navy took over returning prisoners of war, if merchant ships carried as few as one or two prisoners of war, they could sail under a flag of truce and trade with impunity. The fact that they had been preyed on by local English privateers as well, rendered this trade less profitable.

The new provisions started with the customs officials themselves. Accustomed as these men had been to drawing salaries without physically being in the colonies at all, they were now required to be in place or have their employment terminated. In return, they were protected under new court rulings whereby the violator of the law had to put up £60 security for court expenses even if he was found innocent. Rewards

---

[1]Truxes, *Defying Empire*, p. 10.
[2]Truxes, *Defying Empire*, p. 5.

were given for information on 'compounding'. This was an old device by which customs officials and smugglers settled out of court if the value of the goods was low. It was accepted that the official charged a figure less than prohibitory.

The new Customs Act extended the 'hovering' provision to small vessels which were taken while 'loitering' within two leagues of the coast. Ships loading sugar, rum or molasses had to have a certificate signed by a justice of the peace showing the origin, quality and quantity of their cargo 'in words at length and not in figures' – to make altering the manifest impossible. Ships could not unload until this certificate had been produced to the customs collector. Ships carrying enumerated commodities had to post bonds that the goods would be landed only in British territory. Any goods not covered by the 'cockets' could be seized. Small vessels, of less than 100 tons, were forbidden from importing the easily smuggled goods of brandy, rum, spirits, tea and tobacco. The most important provision of the new act was that proceeds from the seizures at sea were to be shared equally between the naval officers involved and the King, each getting a 'moiety'. Once the customs officers lost their one-third share therefore, there was competition between the land- and sea-based officials and not co-operation. Colonial governors were not happy at having lost their income: the London Customs Board reminded governors that their oaths required them to enforce the trade laws whether or not they profited from them.

The final loophole was closed when a Vice Admiralty Court for All America was established at Halifax to replace the compromised colonial courts. In the Vice Admiralty Court the seizures were examined and released or condemned. There was considerable resistance against this: Halifax was far to the north and the delay in taking seized vessels there was considerable. Once one merchant vessel had been taken the rest knew that the coast was again clear of snooping naval vessels.

The Sugar Act of 1764 was only the beginning. A further tax, with much wider implications, was to follow in a year's time. It did not occur to the British Government that the Stamp Act would arouse such resentment.[1] Embossed Revenue-stamped paper for legal documents had been in daily use in England since 1694, raising money which went straight to the Government. The colony of Massachusetts issued stamped paper from 1757 and so did the colony of New York. The British Government's new Stamp Act covered every occasion on which paper was used in the

---

[1]E.S. Morgan, *Prologue to Revolution Sources and Documents on the Stamp Act Crisis, 1764–1766* (New York, 1959), p. 24.

commercial or legal world, and included newspapers, playing cards and dice: this was not a tax which an individual could avoid by changing patterns of consumption. The Stamp Act was to come into force on 1 November 1765, which gave time for supplies of the stamped paper to cross the Atlantic, for the distributors of the paper to organise their stocks, and for the assemblies to find alternative ways of raising the necessary funds to support the expenses of a defensive military force. This delay also gave time for comment from the American colonies: the colonies were not, however, expressly asked for a response.[1]

Resistance to the Stamp Act was loudest in the ports where there was a concentration of lawyers, merchants, newspapers and agents of all kinds, all of whom depended for their livelihood on trade. The delay had given time for the Stamp Act Congress to be organised in New York. The delegates elected by nine colonial assemblies met in secret from 7 to 24 October, and resolved on fourteen points of protest.[2] The date on which the legislation was due to come into force was unfortunate. It was customary to celebrate the anniversary of Guy Fawkes publicly with huge bonfires, for which material was gathered some time in advance.

It was at this point that Captain Archibald Kennedy, son of the late customs collector, became involved. Captain Kennedy had served with brilliance throughout the Seven Years' War, stationed mainly off the Portuguese coast, cruising against French privateers and demonstrating courage, independence and outstanding professional ability. As senior officer on the New York station Kennedy had at his disposal only three sloops [A]. One of these, the *Hawke* under Captain Brown, captured the merchant vessel *New York* as she headed for Perth Amboy loaded with rum, molasses, Bordeaux wine and French soap. John Tabor Kempe, the Attorney General, advised Brown to prosecute, but he was sued by the Franklin brothers, the owners of the *New York*.

In an extraordinary judgement, New York's Judge Morris attested that the vessel had been bound for the Isle of Man and acquitted the Franklins, leaving Brown arrested on a damages suit of £10,500. Cadwallader Colden got in on the act by complaining that the *Hawke* was not at sea. When Captain Kennedy ordered Brown to put to sea the merchants filed a new suit against Brown and had him thrown into gaol. Kennedy ordered his own first lieutenant to take the *Hawke* to sea instead, so the merchants had Brown released. The owners of the molasses and rum sued Brown for £4,046 in damages. John Tabor Kempe refused to

---

[1]Morgan, *Sources and Documents*, p. 26.
[2]Morgan, *Sources and Documents*, p. 62.

advance Brown money for an appeal, so that eventually when he was ordered back to England he had to sell his share of the cargo to help cover his losses. As Captain Kennedy explained to the Admiralty, if he had not personally put up the bail for Brown, he would never have been freed.

The hostility towards the navy's actions was exemplified by the hapless Brown's experiences. The merchants were powerful members of local society and were prepared to go to any lengths to maintain their extremely profitable trade with the French sugar islands. Moreover, the merchants used the courts as their most effective weapon against the navy. The courts were no protection for the naval officers engaged in stopping illegal trading. There was the hostility of Judge Morris, who threatened to take out an injunction to stop the navy moving *Hawke* out of his jurisdiction and then took evidence from himself in his own court before finding in favour of the merchants. On a second occasion Captain Hawker of the sloop *Sardoine* (pronounced 'sardine') was left to pay the difference between the costs of the court and the fine imposed, after Judge Morris had taken two months to enumerate more fees than had ever previously been charged.

A further factor militating against the navy was the lack of support from New York's Attorney General, who at first advised Brown to prosecute and then decided that he was at fault for having left New York, before finally refusing to advance him money for an appeal. Not even the lieutenant governor, Cadwallader Colden, supported the navy. Governors had expected to get rich from seizures, but their share was now taken by the navy. Colden accused Lord Colvill, Commander-in-Chief in Halifax, of intimidating Judge Morris out of his rightful 'reward'. There was some justification for this as Colvill had made it clear to the Admiralty that he took the job as Commander-in-Chief North America in order to get the 'advantage' such a commission promised him. In 1755 he asked for the King's share to be given to him instead of to the province, governor, customs collector or squadron commander, and urged that the new Vice Admiralty Court for All America be set up in Halifax, where he was based.

Finally, the collusion of some customs officials with the merchants was exemplified by the deviations via Perth Amboy of merchant vessels whose cargoes were of mixed derivation. Brown's experiences, which would have been widely discussed, might have reduced the determination of other captains to enforce the regulations.

The long eastern seaboard provided some excellent harbours, but also thousands of creeks, inlets and bays in which small vessels could be loaded or unloaded or simply hidden from sight until the coast was clear.

Once there was a distinction as far as seizures were concerned between those on land and those on the sea, Colvill recognised that:

> American Lawyers, Judges and Governors will not allow us any benefit from the last new act, as they may say that nothing is the sea but that part of the ocean which is without the coast.

So in 1765 a further Act defined seizure at sea as:

> all seizures made by the commanders, or officers of his Majesty's ships or vessels of war, duly authorized for the purpose, anywhere at sea in or upon any river and which shall not actually be made on shore, within any British colony or plantation in America.[1]

Captain Kennedy paid from his own funds for small vessels which could pursue the smugglers in close inshore work. Other captains billed the Navy Board for similar expenses.[2]

Captain Kennedy does not mention the New York Stamp Act Congress. It was outside his remit. What did matter to him were the concerns of the venerable Cadwallader Colden, again reinstated as the lieutenant governor of New York until the arrival from London of Sir Henry Moore, the governor designate of New York. Colden told Kennedy about the resignation of Mr McEver, the stamp distributor for the province on New York [2]. The position of Stamp Distributor was central to Britain's planning. The intention was that each local incumbent would have power, prestige and income derived from levying a locally raised tax which would provide about a third of the cost of supporting the colonial army.[3]

Kennedy's documents are evidence of the value of the navy to the colonial authorities – for as long as the ships were not immobilised by ice in the Hudson River. The appeals [30] made by the various authorities along the eastern seaboard show that they were accustomed to asking for and receiving help from the navy, and New York was not the only province anticipating problems when the stamped paper arrived. A letter [31] dated 2 September, and written by Zacharia Hood, the Distributor in Maryland, was concerned that there was no place of safety for the

---

[1]Stout, *Royal Navy*, p. 53.

[2]Julian Gwyn, 'The Royal Navy in North America 1712–1776' in Jeremy Black and Philip Woodfine (eds), *The British Navy and the Use of Naval Power in the Eighteenth Century* (New York, 1988), p. 143.

[3]Peter D.G. Thomas, 'The Grenville Program, 1763–1765' in Jack P. Greene and J.R. Pole (eds), *The Blackwell Encyclopaedia of the American Revolution* (Cambridge, MA, 1991), pp. 110–11.

stamped paper when it arrived. Hood had been advised by General Gage to ask Kennedy for the protection of a naval vessel.

On 5 September, Kennedy ordered *Hawke* to the Hook, and *Guarland* to the Narrows, to identify and escort the vessel carrying the stamped paper into safety [3, 4]. When the *Edward* arrived Kennedy had the cargo unloaded so that the bales of paper could be taken off, despite the owners threatening to sue him for ordering their vessel to be delayed and her cargo handled in this way. When she left again for England she carried with her the fourteen-point Declaration of Rights and Grievances, the work of the Stamp Act Congress. Kennedy's letter to the Admiralty detailing the problems he faced was sent to Secretary Conway for the information of the King.

Kennedy's preparations had been made only just in time. On Thursday 31 October a crowd of about four or five hundred men flexed their muscles by behaving 'riotously'. They threatened Colden, his son Alexander and Major James of the Fort, but dispersed without doing any mischief except breaking a few windows and pulling down a little bawdyhouse. Major James had once boasted that he could subdue the city with two dozen troops, but feared that he would not be able to stave off an attack on the Fort.[1]

Colden asked for marines [5] and assistance in securing the Fort [6, 7, 8], which Kennedy agreed to supply. However, the next request was for Kennedy to take the stamped papers on board *Coventry* [9], and this was denied [10]. The Mayor and Commonalty of the city then wrote to ask for Kennedy's co-operation [11]. Kennedy was only authorised to take orders from the Governor, and explained this, together with the fact that taking the stamped paper on board would not keep it safe at all [16]. His decision was approved of by Lord Colvill [17]. His refusal, however, caused Colden to write to the Admiralty saying that Kennedy had refused to assist him. They responded by sending out a replacement for Kennedy as he had shown 'a want of zeal for his Majesty's service'.

Kennedy set to work immediately and in four days, before he left for England in the packet, he gathered together copies of all the letters which had been written before and during the critical days at the end of October, including a letter [E] from Colden correcting the impression he had given of Kennedy's behaviour. Kennedy paid his own fare in the packet as well as that of his servant and clerk, and had time during the

---

[1] Fred Anderson, *Crucible of War: The Seven Years' War and the Fate of the Empire in British North America 1754–1766* (London, 2000), pp. 643–4.

crossing to write a lengthy letter [F] in which the tumultuous events are catalogued dispassionately and the thirty-five documents he enclosed are itemised. Documents which would have appeared as numbers 33 and 34 were not included, perhaps because he no longer thought them relevant. Other minor mistakes in numbering by the normally careful Kennedy have been adjusted.

The Admiralty, for once, admitted that an error of judgement had been made and reinstated Kennedy, not just to full pay but, as he insisted, back to his ship and to his station in New York.

The cumulative effect of the resistance to the Stamp Act had caused it to be repealed by the time Kennedy left New York. It was not until ten years later that the feelings so vividly described in Kennedy's documents began the war which finally separated the colonies from British rule. The significance of this cache of documents is that the role of the navy in these events has not been properly appreciated.

It was ironic in Kennedy's case that he was so closely caught up in the events of 1765 from the perspective of a naval officer and those of 1776 from the perspective of a landed gentleman. When he retired from the navy in 1768 it was to spend more time on his private affairs in New York, where he owned substantial properties. When the war broke out in the next decade he attempted to remain neutral, with allegiance on both sides. However, he was captured by the rebels and held for three years, being moved constantly to prevent his being released. Kennedy's new house in New York, No. 1 Broadway, was occupied during the war. His houses at Second River were plundered, and property to a value of £25,000 taken away or destroyed. Eventually Kennedy was permitted to go back to England on condition that he took no part in the war. Archibald Kennedy eventually succeeded in 1794 to the ancient Scottish titles of 11th Earl of Cassillis and 13th Lord Kennedy and died two years later.

PART 1

The sequence of letters A–C were written by Kennedy to the Admiralty between 20 November 1764 and 10 February 1765, in the normal course of his duty, giving his reasons for his actions and providing the background to the events which provoked the later behaviour of 'the mob'. The letter D was written by Kennedy to the Admiralty on his return to London, explaining why he had been determined to refute the accusation that he had failed in his duty. Letter E is Cadwallader Colden's denial that Kennedy had not done his duty. Document F is the summary of events written by Kennedy with his numbered list of supporting documents numbered 1–37.

A. *Captain Kennedy to Admiralty*

New York
20 November 1764
[received 15 February 1765]

I beg you will be pleased to inform their Lordships that on the 15th instant I ordered the sloop *Hawke* Capt. Brown to cruise between Sandy Hook and Great Egg harbour for the most effectual prevention of smuggling which is still much practised here and the parts adjacent, notwithstanding the utmost care and precaution is used by both by his Majesty's ships and the Customhouse to prevent it.

On his being ordered to sea he was re-arrested and carried to jail, for ten thousand and odd pounds at the suit of Messrs Franklin and White to answer the damages that may be given, on account of the seizure he some time ago made of the ship *New York* and cargo the merit of which cause he has already laid before their Lordships and the Commissioners of the Customs. Their reason for re-arresting him at that time appeared plainly to me to be that they might prevent his Majesty's service from being executed, or as they are some of those people that have been principally concerned in carrying on the illicit trade from this place, to give them in his absence an opportunity of running the cargoes of some vessels said to be expected, I beg their Lordships will be pleased to direct some more effectual measures for protecting the sea officers in case of seizure, otherwise it will be impossible for any officer to execute his duty in this place where the minds of the people are so much inflamed against them that I believe on the most trivial motion they would give most unreasonable damage against the Crown and officers of the Crown. I hope their Lordships will consider the present circumstances of Captain Brown's case as it is entirely owing to his strictly performing his duty and in my opinion has done no more than any good officer would. I have ordered Lt John James of the *Coventry* to command the *Hawk* during her cruise and on her return shall send her to Amboy if possible to lay there during the winter, the Collector of that port having wrote me for assistance to enable him to perform his duty.

I constantly acquaint Lord Colvill with the transactions that happen at this port. I should not on this occasion have troubled the Lordships, as it is only a copy of what I have wrote to his Lordship were it not the immediate opportunity I have of sending it, which Lord Colvill may not have for some time and his having entrusted me with the command of the ships on the New York station.

B.   *Captain Kennedy to Admiralty*

New York
15 January 1765
[received 14 March 1765]

I have to inform their Lordships that I have received their order of 26 October enclosing an order of the King in Council, likewise that as the Customs House had granted clearances to many vessels after the first of November on unstamped paper the stamped paper had been received for the use of this province is lodged in the City hall under the care of the Corporation. I wrote to Governor Moore on this head and finding it his opinion as well as my own that such Clearances were illegal, I ordered that all vessels attempting to sail with those clearances should be detained. On the 2 inst. the river being full of ice I was by the severity of the weather obliged to order the *Coventry* and *Guarland* alongside the wharfs, since which many vessels have escaped, as they will not allow our boats to stop them. It will not be in the power of the Kings ships to be of any great service during the winter, but shall as early as the weather will permit haul into the stream again when every assistance the ships can possibly give shall be given the Governor for enforcing the laws or preserving the peace. The mob a few days ago burnt ten boxes of stamped paper that came in the last vessel from England, Haviland master, and from them I have received some letters, threats and menacing advertisements have been put up. Flatter myself their Lordships will approve of my conduct would not now have troubled them as I constantly correspond with my Lord Colvill and whom I have informed of all the above transactions at this port to the 24th of December, only the uncertainty of his having an early opportunity of laying before their Lordships the present state of matters here . . .

PS enclosed an extract from an advertisement put up this morning at the coffee house.

Sir Henry Moore having offered a reward of £100 and his Majestys pardon to any one that should discover any of those that were concerned in burning the stamped papers that came over in *Haviland*.

The following is an extract from an advertisement that was put up at the coffee house in consequence of the above reward being offered in the public papers:

That they will consider any one who is aiding or assisting to promote the Stamp Act, in whatever Clothes he may appear, as an enemy to his Country and devote him to destruction.

That they applaud and approve of the conduct of those patriotic heroes who burnt the stamps in Havilands ship, that they will defend them with their lives and fortunes, notwithstanding Sir Henry Moores proclamation.

That the sons of liberty in Albany and Connecticut have offered their assistance, and will be ready at a call from those of New York.

That the friends of the Stamp Act being desirous to deprive the Americans of *Tryals* by Jurys are themselves unworthy of such a privilege and ought therefore to suffer without jurys.

[The turn-back on this letter directed the clerks to send copies of the letter and its enclosure to Secretary of State Conway for the information of the King.]

C.   *Captain Kennedy to Admiralty*

New York
10 February 1765
[received 4 April 1765]

In answer to yours of the 15 November I beg you will be pleased to acquaint their Lordships that I impressed eleven men from the ship *America*, but so far in my opinion was the master of her from thinking it a hardship that he declared he intended to have put several of them on board the King's ships, and only requested one of them to be returned him which was immediately complied with. The inclemency of the weather during a great part of the winter on this station renders it impossible for any ships during that season to remain in the stream. They are obliged to haul alongside of wharfs for security, so it is not in the power of man in that case to prevent seamen from running away, especially considering the high wages and other inducements the merchants give them, in reality upon the whole the merchants are no loosers by it for if the ships of war impress from them, they inveigle the seamen from the men of war when they are in want. Not one of his Majestys ships who are stationed at any of the trading ports in North America would ever be able to proceed on service after laying up one winter if they did not impress. Last spring I was obliged to hire a vessel to raise men for manning the ships that were here, of which I formerly acquainted their Lordships. As I am now under orders from Lord Colvill to join him early in the spring or as soon as the weather will permit I will be under the necessity of doing the same before I can possibly proceed to sea with his Majestys ship.

D.   *Captain Kennedy to Admiralty*

London
7 May 1766

I have received your letter of 14 December last informing me that their Lordships had thought proper to supercede me from the command of the *Coventry* on account of authentick advices having been received that the Lieutenant Governor of New York having requested me to take on board the ship I commanded the stamps which had been sent thither for the use of that Province, in order to secure them from the violence of the people, I absolutely refused to receive them and that they were of opinion that by such refusal I did not show that zeal for his Majestys service which, as Captain of the Kings ship I should have shown at such a conjunction.

As I should be very sorry to think that any part of my conduct had given just cause for my falling under their Lordships censure, I by the first packet returned to England in order to have an opportunity of clearing myself to their Lordships of a charge so injurious to the honor and character as want of zeal for His Majestys service, from the enclosed copy of a letter from Governor Colden to the Hon. Henry Seymour Conway Esq., it will appear that I never absolutely refused to receive them, and from the other original letters and papers which you will find enclosed, it will plainly appear that I did take every possible and some very effectual measures for enforcing that Act, nor do I know of single step that I did take that I have not my Lord Colvill's approbation of, I beg you will be pleased to communicate this to their Lordships, who I flatter myself on a thorough examination of the enclosed papers will be convinced that the censure I have fallen under has arose from a misrepresentation of my conduct to them.

[The turn-back on this letter reads: '3 Jan. Let him know their Lordships are satisfied with his conduct for the reasons contained in his letter and the enclosed papers and they will take an early opportunity of employing him.']

E.   *Cadwallader Colden to the Rt. Hon. Henry Seymour Conway*

New York
28 March 1766

I was extremely surprised when Captain Kennedy informed me that he was superceded in command of his Majesty's ship *Coventry*, on a complaint of his having refused to take the stamped paper on my request. I did not mention Captain Kennedy's name nor anything of the officers of the navy in my letters of 5th and 9th of November which it is supposed have occasioned his Majesty's displeasure, and in my letter immediately preceding of the 26th October you will find sir that my sentiments were very different by the following paragraph of it viz: <u>I am the more particular in this account that you may have some conception of the difficulties I labour under from the want of assistance where I had the best reason to expect it. At the same time I have the pleasure to assure you that the officers of the navy and army with great alacrity give me every assistance I require</u>. This letter went by Captain Dover of the Royal Artillery in an Artillery transport which I am informed did not arrive till some time after you had received my despatches of the 9th November in which the minutes of the Council were enclosed and which I suspect to have given rise to some mistake.

In those minutes a Minute of the common council of the city is recited, in which it is said I was willing to deliver up the stamps to Mr Kennedy and that he had refused their earnest request to receive them, it is true I should have yielded to the proposal of delivering them to Captain Kennedy had he consented to receive them, but as I did not think it necessary for his Majesty's service or prudent for Captain Kennedy to receive them, I did not at any time join in desiring him to take them. They in desperation sent some of their members to desire him to receive the stamps, but I suppose he thought he had no connection with them. I have been obliged sir to give you the trouble of reading so much words but I was unwilling to enter into a minute detail of circumstances where I did not apprehend it to be necessary, and I did not then imagine the circumstances of Captain Kennedy's declining to take the stamped paper to be such, but now justice to him makes it necessary to trouble you with a minute detail of this matter.

The next day after the mob insulted their Governor on the 1st November in the manner set out in my letters of the 5th and 9th of that month they were the whole day collected in bodies throughout the town which appeared to be in the greatest confusion and tumult. I called together his Majesty's Council and laid before them the situation I was in, and desired their advice as appears by the minutes of that day. They unanimously agreed and proposed to me as an expedient which in their opinion would entirely quiet the mob, that I should declare that I would not distribute the stamps or act further till Sir Henry Moore arrived, who was then expected every hour, they insisted that I could in no manner be blamed for declaring I would not act in an a matter in which every man knew it was not in my power to act, as no one would or durst receive a stamped paper, it was now near night and the mob becoming very numerous and riotous, I was pressed to pacify the people, and the strong desire I had to deliver up the Administration in quietness to my successor, with other reasons which I have mentioned to you Sir in my letter of 21 February induced me hastily to comply with the unanimous advice of the Council, who went out instantly to the mob, and declared to them what I had agreed to, on which a general Huzza was given they dispersed in all appearance well satisfied, I am confident the peace of the city would have been restored by this concession, had peace and quietness been consistent with the purposes of the directors of the mob, which by the sequel plainly appeared was not.

The city remained quiet and easy one day during which the Directors had found another expedient to excite tumults, by making a demand that the stamped papers should be sent on board the *Coventry* I then plainly saw their intentions and that no yielding would satisfy them and that it only served to increase their demands and insults however I was desirous that the whole load should not be taken upon my shoulders and I called the Council in hopes they would assist me in taking some share of it, but when I told them plainly what I thought were the intentions of these riotous proceedings but I was disappointed, they advised me to write to Captain Kennedy to receive the stamps. In my letter to Captain Kennedy I mentioned the request of the Gentlemen of the Council that he would receive the stamps on board in order to quiet the minds of the people, I did not join myself in the request for the following reasons

1st   I thought the stamps at least as safe in the fort as on board his ship and their demand to have them sent on board *Coventry* was for no other purpose than to insult the Government.

2nd   I suspected that one view in desiring the stamps to be sent on board the *Coventry* was with hopes of having them delivered up by Captain Kennedy to preserve his private property in the city which is considerable and which otherwise the mob would destroy. I was confirmed in this suspicion when a gentleman came into the fort with others that came to me to persuade me to send the stamps on board the *Coventry* openly said he would sooner loose his right hand than advise Captain Kennedy to take them. I knew he was Captain Kennedy's friend and I believed he was in the secret of the directors of the mob. I would not therefore desire Captain Kennedy to do a thing which he believed would bring ruinous distress upon him, when the public service and his duty did not require it.

3rd   Lastly the stamps could not be so safely on board the *Coventry* as in the fort as winter approached, when the ship must be brought to one of the wharfs in the town, the guns must be put on shore, and the officers could not prevent the men from leaving the ship or from being seduced by the people of the town, it is well known sailors easily may be seduced.

Captain Kennedy in his answer did not absolutely refuse to take stamps on board, but gave reasons why he thought it unnecessary and the Gentlemen of the Council did not advise any reply, or further requisition from him, they even desired no minutes might be made of their request which as the motion had come from them I consented to.

The opinion I had conceived of the purposes pursued by the Directors of the mob is strongly confirmed by what has happened since the arrival of Sir Henry Moore. He has yielded everything in order to quiet the minds of the people, and notwithstanding of this, riots and mobs have continued as frequent and as much insulting on Government as ever, the only difference is, they have not been directed personally against them, as they ever did against me.

I flatter myself you will sir excuse the trouble which I think in justice to Captain Kennedy an honest man cannot avoid, but it is done with humble submission . . .

[*Clerk's writing on cover page*: 'Papers received in 1766 from Capt Kennedy in justification of his conduct in New York touching his refusal to take Stamps on board the *Coventry*.']

F.   *Summary of events written by Captain Kennedy with his numbered list of supporting documents*

As the reason assigned in Mr Stephens letter (1) dated 14 December 1765 for superceding Captain Kennedy from the command of his Majestys ship the *Coventry* is that an application made to him by Lieutenant Governor Colden to take on board his Majesty's ships the stamped paper he absolutely refused complying with his request and thereby discovered a want of zeal for his Majesty's service.

It becomes necessary for him in order to acquit himself of so groundless and injurious charges set forth in the fullest and clearest manner, the whole tenor of his conduct relative to the said stamp papers.

The following state thereof will fully elucidate the part he acted respecting those belonging to the Province of New York.

On the 3rd September Governor Colden informed him by letter (2) of the resignation of Mr McEver the stamp distributor for this Province, of his apprehensions that a design was formed to destroy the stamps on their arrival, proposing some measures in order to prevent any such design being put in execution and desiring a consultation with him on

what might be proper for his Majesty's service, on receipt of Governor
Colden's letter he immediately waited on him, and having concerted
and determined on such means as would most effectually preserve the
stamped papers from the intended destruction. On the 5th he ordered
his Majesty's sloop *Hawke* to the Hook, giving Captain Brown instructions (3) to examine with the utmost strictness all vessels coming into
the Hook from the sea and on finding the vessel in which the stamped
papers were, immediately to weigh and conduct her through the narrows to the *Guarland*. Same day ordered the Hon. Captain St John of his
Majesty's ship the *Guarland* who then lay off the watering place Staten
Island near the narrows (4) to examine all vessels coming from sea and
acquainting him that I had ordered Captain Brown on his finding the
vessel importing the stamps to conduct her to him when they both were
to proceed with her into the North River and bring her to an anchor off
and as nigh to Fort George as possible in order under the cover of their
guns to send an officer to acquaint the Governor with their proceedings and to use every means for preserving the papers for his Majesty's
service.

By desire of General Gage and Governor Colden, that one ship should
cover the Kings wharf where a great part of the military stores are lodged,
to defend them from the mob, or be ready to receive them on board the
Coventry dropt abreast of and as nigh to as possible the Kings Wharf.

In this situation the Kings ships lay examining all the vessels that
came into the Port until the 23rd of October when the ship *Edward* Captain Davis she having seven packages of stamped paper on board, was
conducted by the *Guarland* and *Hawke* into the North River brought to
an anchor nigh the fort and under cover of their guns one package that
could be got at immediately sent into the fort, as the others were under a
great part of her cargo all the necessary assistance was given him by the
ships in unstowing his hold to get at them and the sloop *Gaspée* Lieutenant Allen ordered alongside the ship *Edward* to take into him part of
the cargo if they would not be got at without, notwithstanding the owners
threatened to prosecute him for detaining the vessel by unstowing her
hold, when the packages were found they were by the ships boats sent
on board the *Guarland* from whence they at the request of the Governor
were next day about twelve landed and lodged in the fort, at which landing he was present.

On 1st November he received a letter from the Governor (5) acquainting him the magistrates had informed him that they were very apprehensive of a mob that night and desiring him to send the marines from on
board the ships to reinforce the regular troops, in consequence of which
he ordered Lt Owin (6, 7) and twenty four marines to be landed from the

ship and to follow the Governors orders acquainting the Governor that by so doing he should leave the ships without marine sentries (8).

On 2nd November he received another letter from Governor Colden (9) informing him that the Gentlemen of the Council were desirous that the stamped paper in the fort should be put on board one of the men of war, and desiring to know whether he would order them to be received or not. To which he answered (10) that as they were already lodged in Fort George a place of security sufficient to protect them from any attempt the mob could possibly make to destroy them he could not see any plausible reason for moving them, that the very attempting to move them must be attended with greater risque than they would possibly be exposed to while in the fort, that whenever necessity required he should be ready to give all the assistance in his power.

On 4th November he received a letter from John Cruger Esq Mayor of the City of New York (11) in behalf of the Corporation, repeating the Governor's proposal and desiring him to take the stamped paper on board his ship, but as by his instructions (12) he is only authorised to consult with the Governor or the Kings Council he acquainted the gentlemen therewith (13) and declined treating with them on the subject, especially as the Governor and his Majesty's Council were on the spot and no reasons were by the City Council assigned for their request besides the objections made the preceding day to Governor Colden's application were by them tacitly assented to.

As these last transactions are supposed to have given rise to the censure that has fallen on Captain Kennedys conduct, and for which he has been superceded in his command, it is necessary to be more particular in animadverting on them and to observe that the letter (5) from Governor Colden appears only to contain a desire of the Council in which he did not join, and the following affidavit plainly shows the Governor himself in every way averse to such a step.

Be it remembered that on the 29th March 1766 (14) personally came and appeared before me Francis Filkins Aldrman of the City of New York and one of his Majesty's Justices of the Peace for said City and County Mr George Stoney Lieutenant of his Majesty's ship the *Coventry* and made oath on the Holy Evangelist of Almighty God that he the said George Stoney being charged by Captain Archibald Kennedy with the delivering of a letter to the Honourable Cadwallader Colden Esq his Majesty's Governor and Commander in Chief of the Province of New York did on the 2nd November deliver said letter to the said Governor accordingly and that he understood the said letter to be an answer to a letter received by the said Captain Kennedy in which he had been desired by his Majesty's Council to receive on board his Majesty's ships the stamped papers and that the said answer so by him delivered contained reasons from the said Kennedy against the propriety of moving said stamped papers out of his Majesty's fort, that the said Governor after receiving and perusing the said answer did declare to and assure the said Stoney that the request of the Council signified by him to Captain Kennedy was contrary to his opinion, that he conceived no place could be more safe and secure for lodging the stamped papers than the fort where they then were deposited or words to that purpose.

[*Signed*] Francis Filkins   George Stoney

Nay further the Governor had mentioned his objections to the Council and now by them was desired to make no minute of the transaction, which desire he complied with as the whole was a motion of theirs and no suggestion of his to them as he ever judged those papers more secure in the fort than they would be in any ship at a wharf, which he observed must soon be the case.

It is necessary to observe that Captain Kennedy's answer (10) does not contain a refusal to take them on board the King's ship but only his reasons with regard to the inexpediency of that measure as they were lodged in a place of security and the great risque that would attend their removal for the mob at that time were all round the fort, and positively declared their intention to destroy them.

The minute on the minutes of the Kings Council where Captain Kennedy is said absolutely to have refused to receive that stamped papers is only a minute of the City Chamber used as a preamble to the security given by the Governor for the said papers and as such entered on the minutes of his Majestys Council as appears from (13) extracted and delivered to me by Governor Colden from the Council minutes and how ill founded is very plain for what goes before and (11) to which is subjoined the Mayors Certificate that it was the only correspondence or transaction that passed between the Mayor, Aldermen and Commonalty of the City of New York relative to the stamped papers.

Captain Kennedy also considered that from the severity of the climate the ships before the end of December would be absolutely obliged to come to the wharf, and would then in that defenceless state be inevitably exposed to the fury of the Mob, who he had occasion to doubt would take every measure in their power to have the stamps delivered up to them or aim at destroying the ship as having the stamps on board, that most of his men were impressed consequently could not have that confidence in them that so critical a situation would require, these considerations having great weight with him he judged it his duty to urge the inexpediency of receiving them and on his Majesty's Council considering the danger they must, on removing them from the fort be exposed to, would if they differed in opinion give some reasons for their desire but as they were so far from further urging their removal that they desired the minute might be made of their application he never supposed they acquiesced to his objections.

In my letter to Lord Colvill of November the 4th (15) I informed him of my having objected to the receiving of the stamped papers on board with my reasons for so doing, but I had more fully laid them before him in a former letter (No 16) in regard of the New Jersey stamps in case they might be sent with those for the city of New York in his answer (17) he refers to his letter in relation to Kings ships taking on board those belonging to New Jersey where he is pleased to observe that the reasons given for declining to receive the New Jersey stamped papers are very plain, that he thought he should take no charge of them, unless the Governor of New York should absolutely refuse to receive them into the fort, that the Governors house in the fort was a much properer place for depositing the stamps than any ship and the more so as the fort was full of men and military stores to give the greater security to the important trusts.

Which appreciation of his conduct by my Lord Colvill's knowing the removal of them was contrary to this opinion or that of Governor Colden the great risque that must have attended their removal and the small space of time he with certainty could have defended them appear to Captain Kennedy sufficient grounds for having pointed out to the Council the inexpediency of the measure they proposed, instead of inconsiderately receiving them.

That his apprehension of the most outrageous attacks of the mob upon his Majesty's ships was well founded will fully appear from their conduct since respecting the stamped papers for notwithstanding the Mayor and Aldermen of the City at the request of the principal leaders of the mob apply for and obtain from the Governor the stamps, after giving security for payment of the amount of the same in case of their being destroyed or sent out of the province as appears from their letter to the Governor and his answer and their receipt and security for the papers (10) (Extracted by Mr G Cartland clerk of the City from the minutes of the Council) they deposited them in the City Hall, nevertheless in violation of the engagement a firm design was formed to break open the Hall doors but were prevented from executing that design by some of the most resolute of the inhabitants who were possessed of considerable property the Corporation found it absolutely necessary next day to apply to ask these citizens who had property and whose estates would have been liable by a taxation to pay for the value of those papers to know whether they approved of their being given up, it being voted in the negative, they were moved into a more secure place and a guard from the militia besides a considerable number of the Gentlemen of the city found absolutely necessary for their safety neither of which measures is there the least occasion to suppose would have been taken had the city not been liable to make good their value or had they been on board any of his Majesty's ships.

It is further to be observed that during the commotion when the fort was invested by the mob, and an assault expected that Captain Kennedy stationed the ships in such a manner (19) as was judged the most effectual for assisting the Garrison.

Likewise that as he judged the ships at any rate unsafe in the wharf in the winter may lay in safety and out of danger from the mob he applied to have his Majesty's ships there but could not obtain it as appears from (20) and there is nigh town a place called Turtle Bay where two ships in the winter season may be in safety out of the ice, he applied to have his Majestys ships there, but could not obtain it as appears from No 20.

From this period to the 10 December nothing further was transacted by Captain Kennedy in relation to the stamped papers of this Colony, but at that time having found that several vessels then in the harbour had been cleared at the Customs House on unstamped paper which clearances being in his opinion illegal, he judged it necessary to consult the Collector of the Customs respecting them (21) as an officer of the Revenue and as his Majesty's representative (22) but from their behaviour (23, 24) and finding himself left to the exercise of his own judgement he resolved to do his duty without being influenced either by the threat of the populace or the example of others immovably fixed that he had no right to dispense with any Act of the British legislature and though the utmost effort were used to provoke him to the contrary and notwithstanding the advanced season of the year the excess of the weather and the ice making in the river in the night which severity at any other time would have induced him to bring the ships to the wharf, he ordered his Majesty's ship the *Guarland* (25) to anchor in the mouth of the harbour, and the *Coventry* to the eastward of the wharf with orders to stop all vessels going out of the port with clearances on unstamped paper, this measure occasioned the most violent commotions amongst the citizens of all rank, but unmoved at their threats both against person and property, he continued the ships at their stations, effectively preventing all merchant vessels from sailing. On 23rd he received a letter (26) signed by many of the merchants complaining of his conduct and requiring an explanation in answer to which (27) he observed his stopping the vessels not having legal clearances was a point of duty which he could not think they would wish him to violate. He continued the ships in the stream till the 2nd January when the weather made it absolutely necessary for their safety to come to the wharfs, and the *Guarland* had nigh been lost before she could haul in.

He wrote my Lord Colvill of these transactions (28) and received his answer (No 29) in which his Lordship, after approving his conduct as a sea officer, observed that he has no orders in regard to this Act, as likewise that the Distributor of stamps at Halifax had orders to prosecute no vessel on account of the want of or not using stamps.

State of Captain Kennedy's conduct
Respecting the New Jersey stamped papers

His Excellency William Franklin Esquire Governor of the Province of New Jersey by letter (30) dated Burlington October the 1st 1765, acquaints Captain Kennedy that he had wrote to Governor Colden requesting that if the stamped papers for New Jersey should arrive at New York that he would order them to be taken care of and lodged in Fort George till proper measures could be taken to bring them with safety into that Province that Governor Colden assured him he would do all in his power to preserve them in case of their coming into that place, but as the fort was full of men and military stores he had no place to lodge the stamps in but the Governor's house which might be very inconvenient to Sir Henry Moore who would probably come in the same ship with the stamped paper that he therefore submitted it to Governor Franklins consideration whether it would not be as safe and more convenient to have the New Jersey stamps put on board one of his Majesty's frigates at New York who might land them at any time and place that might be proper and therefore requested to Captain Kennedy that he would give the necessary orders for having the stamped papers for Jersey in case of their arrival in New York (and that they could not conveniently be lodged in the Fort) put on board one of the Kings frigates till other measures could be taken for their security.

In answer to which Captain Kennedy replied on the 4th October (16) that he had waited on Governor Colden and represented to him the many inconveniences that would attend taking the stamped papers on board any of his Majesty's ships, there being no place on board where any quantity could be put where it would not run the risque of being damped or otherwise so damaged as might render it useless, that all the ships were on immediate service and on orders received from my Lord Colvill obliged without delay to proceed to sea that in winter they lay at the wharf and could then afford no protection for as most of the men were impressed in the spring, many at the first opportunity would desert and while it was impossible at a wharf to prevent, however in case Mr Colden should still refuse receiving them into the Fort he might depend on all the assistance in his power for protecting them and the ship that imported them that he would thoroughly consider of the methods he would take as also of the propriety of receiving them on board of the Kings ships on which head he should write my Lord Colvill but that he could and would protect the ship importing them as long as the weather would admit of his laying in the stream.

On the 13th October he wrote to Lord Colvill (16a) and transmitted copies of Governor Franklins letter and his answer and desiring his lordship's directions as to what he judged proper to be done in regard of the New Jersey stamps.

To which his Lordship by letter dated November 5th (17) answered that the reasons he had given for declining to receive the New Jersey stamps were very plain and that he should take no charge of them unless the Governor should absolutely refuse to receive them into the Fort or give other reasons for declining than are set forth in Governor Franklins letter, that surely the Governors house in the Fort was a much more proper place for depositing the stamps than any ship, and the more so as they were full of men and military stores to give the greatest security to the important trust that Mr Colden had assured Mr Franklin that he would do all in his power to have the New Jersey stamps preserved if they came to New York and that there was no doubt of his having that power whilst he commanded the Fort that he would therefore make use of his own prudence and give all necessary assistance in preserving the stamps or conveying them to the place of their destination provided such preservation or conveyance cannot be obtained from any other quarter.

From the preceding narrative it fully appears that Captain Kennedy was ready and disposed to give all the assistance in his power for protecting and securing the stamp papers belonging to the Province of New Jersey.

That the reason urged by Mr Colden was only a supposition that they would be inconvenient to Sir Henry Moore on his arrival and not from any danger he conceived they would be in whilst in the fort.

That Mr Franklin's request to have them taken on board the Kings ships was with a proviso, that they could not be lodged conveniently in the Fort, and therefore reasonable to think he would have given a preference to their being put there even before he had heard Captain Kennedy's reasoning on the risque and impropriety of their being taken on board the ships.

That Captain Kennedy was resolved to protect both the stamps and vessel that brought them as long as he could lay in the stream, in the meanwhile would consider of the propriety of taking them on board the

Kings ships, on which he would and immediately did write to my Lord Colvill who it appears approved of his conduct.

State of Captain Kennedy's conduct
Respecting the Maryland stamped papers

On 2nd September Mr Zacharia Hood, Distributor of Stamps for the province of Maryland, who had fled from that country and was just arrived at York, by letter from Fort George (31) acquainted Captain Kennedy of his having made application to General Gage for a ship of war to protect the stamps expected from England for Maryland but that General Gage had returned for answer that he had no command over the ships of war and therefore Mr Hood proposed to Captain Kennedy that he would order a sloop of war to lay off Annapolis and have them lodged on board her when they arrived and from whence he proposed to distribute them agreeable to the nature of his office.

In answer to which he informed him (32) that the ships stationed at this fort, the *Sardoine* at Philadelphia were intended for the protection of the trade and the security of the Province of New York, New Jersey and Delaware River, that from Delaware to the Capes of Virginia was immediately under Captain Stirling in the *Rainbow*, that application having been made to him by the Governor of this Province for the aid of his Majesty's ships here, and they stationed accordingly, that therefore it was not in his power to grant him the assistance he required.

On 13th October Captain Kennedy transmitted copies of the preceding letters to my Lord Colvill (16a) the receipt of which his Lordship acknowledged in his letter (17) referring him to what he had already wrote on that subject, which it contained in a letter (35) dated Halifax October 13th 1765 in which his Lordship after remarking on the situation of the ships on the Virginia station observes I would have you send the *Guarland* or *Hawke* to Annapolis and continue there whilst it may be necessary provided either of them can be of more essential service in that Province than in the neighbourhood of New York. I do not mean that a Kings ship should be turned into an office for the distribution of stamps but that the Captain should give all assistance to Governor Sharp at a time when the executive power is found too weak to enforce a due obedience to the Law.

After receipt of this Captain Kennedy received another from Mr Hood (36) informing him he likewise had had a letter from Lord Colvill in relation to what he had wrote to Captain Kennedy but as the stamps for Maryland were on board the *Sardoine* Captain Hawker and in safety he believed it would be for the good of his Majestys service and the peace

of his country, that nothing now was done till the law was generally com-
plyed with all over the rest of the Colonies.

Notwithstanding which application as he was studious to avoid giving
any plea to the people of Maryland for doing business as usual, under
pretence of having no stamp. He immediately ordered the *Hawke* sloop
to Newcastle on the Delaware (37) to take on board her the papers for
Maryland and to proceed with it to Annapolis which was accordingly
done, and is an evident proof he was not wanting in the zealous exertion
of the powers he was vested with, to remove any pretence which might
be made to evade a compliance with sanctity of the British Legislature.

PART 2

Documents 1–37 were collected by Kennedy before he left New York,
and represent his evidence that his actions had been misrepresented.

1. *Philip Stephens, Secretary to the Admiralty
to Captain Kennedy,* Coventry, *New York*

14 December 1765

Authentick advices having been received that the Lieutenant Governor
of New York having requested you to take onboard the ship you command the stamps which had been sent thither for the use of that Province
in order to secure them from the violences of the People, you absolutely
refused to receive the same on board; I am commanded by my Lords
Commissioners of the Admiralty to acquaint you that they are of opinion
that by such refusal you did not show that zeal for his Majesty's service
which, as captain of the King's ship, you should have shown at such a
conjuncture, and that they have therefore thought fit to appoint Captain
Corner (by whom you will receive this) to supercede you in the command of the *Coventry*.

2. *Cadwallader Colden to Captain Kennedy*

Fort George, New York
3 September 1765

Mr McEvers having resigned his office of Distributor of Stamps ordered
me to take care of the stamps when they arrive, I am very desirous to
advise with you for this purpose for I know not how I can do it without
your assistance. Mr McEvers, in his letter to me tells me that his friends
assure him that there is a design to destroy the stamps at their arrival,

and he is confirmed on the truth of this by the many inflammatory papers published in this place, tending to excite sedition. As I know not in what vessel the stamps may come, I think it may be of use to prevent any wicked design of destroying the stamps to give orders to the officers under your command to speak with every vessel on board of which the stamps may be, as soon as possible after the vessels arrive within the Hook, and to inform the master of the vessel on board of which the stamps are, of his danger, and that the vessel be brought to an anchor under your protection, till such time as proper methods can be taken for securing the stamps from any violences. I shall stay in town until Saturday morning and shall be very glad of consulting with you on what may be proper for his Majesty's service on his occasion.

3, 4. *Captain Kennedy to Captain St John,* Guarland
and Captain Brown, Hawke

5 September 1765

Whereas I have received information from undoubted authority that there is a design formed for destroying the stamps that are soon expected for this place immediately on their arrival.

You are hereby required and directed to use the utmost of your endeavours to speak with everything coming through the narrows from the sea, and as soon as possible to get on board such ship or vessel in which the said stamps may be shipped in case she may have escaped his Majestys sloop *Hawke* at Sandy Hook, whose Commander I have given orders to for this purpose, and to conduct her to you above the narrows and there to deliver her into your charge when you will immediately proceed with her into the North River and bring her to an anchor off the Fort, as near as possible you can with safety, and to be under the cover of your guns. Then you will send an officer to acquaint the Governor of your proceedings and use every means in your power for securing the said stamps from any violence until they may be properly secured for his Majesty's service for which this shall be your order.

5. *Cadwallader Colden to Captain Kennedy*

Fort George
1 November 1765

The magistrates of the City have informed me that they are apprehensive of a mob this night. As we have not a sufficient number of the regular troops to secure the Fort and at the same time to suppress any sedition I must beg the favour of your sending the marines on board his Majesty's ships to reinforce the troops in the Fort.

6. *Captain Kennedy to Capt St John,* Guarland

1 November 1765

Governor Colden having by letter of this date requested the assistance of the marines from his Majesty's ships to aid the regular troops in securing the Fort and suppressing any Mob that may happen, the Magistrates of the City having informed him they are apprehensive such a thing will this night.

You are hereby required and directed to send a Sergeant and twelve marines from his Majesty's ship *Guarland* under your command to Fort George where they are to put themselves under the command of Lt Owin of the marines and follow his orders.

7. *Captain Kennedy to Capt St John,* Guarland

4 November 1765

The following is the Lieutenant Governor's request which you are hereby required and directed to comply with. A white flagg hoisted on the flag staff in the Fort, in the day time shall be a signal that a boat is wanted at the flatt rock near the SW bastion of the Fort. Two lanthorns hoisted one above another shall be a signal for the same in the night.

8. *Captain Kennedy to Governor Colden*

1 November 1765

I have yours of this date informing me there is some reason to be apprehensive of a mob this night and desiring you may have the marines to reinforce the Fort.

In consequence of which I have ordered Lt Owin and twenty four marines to be land [*sic*] from his Majesty's ships and to follow your orders, you may at all times depend on every assistance in my power for the good of his Majesty's service but must beg you will consider that by doing this I leave the ships without marine sentrys and as most of our men are imprest there is danger of their deserting.

9.   *Cadwallader Colden to Captain Kennedy*

2 November 1765

The Gentlemen of the Council are desirous that the stamped papers now in the Fort, should be put on board one of the men of war, and I desire to know as soon as possible from you whether or not you will order them to be received on board.

10.   *Captain Kennedy to Governor Colden*

2 November 1765

I have this instant received yours of this date informing me it is the desire of the Council that the stamp papers should be sent on board one of the Kings ships.

As they are already lodged in Fort George a place of sufficient security to protect them from any attack the mob can make to destroy them I cannot see any plausible reason for moving them, and indeed the very attempting to move them must be attended with much greater risque than they can possibly be exposed to while there. I shall ever be ready when necessity requires to give you all the assistance in my power.

11.   *Copy of a letter written by Mayor John Cruger on behalf of the Commonalty of City of New York to Captain Kennedy Monday evening Council Chamber*

4 November 1765

Sir, such is a the calamitous situation of this city that we find ourselves obliged by a deputation from our Board, to entreat you to consent to the Lieutenant Governor's proposal of placing the stamps in one of the ships under your command. This Board will be extremely glad to meet you in their chamber in the morning at nine o'clock to receive your determination on this subject and we hope in tenderness to the safety of the inhabitants and the public repose you'll favour us with your presence and assistance.

12.   *Captain Kennedy's answer to the above letter*

28 March 1766

As I am only authorised by my instructions to consult with the Governor and Council I cannot receive any proposals of this nature from your chamber, or give any answer to the letter I have the honour of receiving from you, dated Monday evening. I have the honour to be, gentlemen.

This is to certify that the above letters are true copies of those passed between Captain Kennedy of his Majesty's ship *Coventry* and the Mayor Aldermen and Commonality of the City of New York and that they are the only correspondence that passed between them on the subject of the stamped paper.

13.   *At a Council held at Fort George in the*
City of New York 5th November 1765
Present: The Hon. Cadwallader Colden Esq Lieutenant
Governor etc., Messrs Horsmanden, Smith, Watts, Walton,
Delancey, Anthirp, Reades, and Morris

His Honour the Governor General laid before the Board the Minutes of this day of the Common Council of this City, to the purport and effect following, which he said he had acquainted the gentlemen who attended him, that he would lay before the Council, that is to say: 'This board taking into serious consideration the intimation that his Honour the Lieutenant Governor was willing to deliver the stamped paper now in Fort George to Capt Kennedy or any other of the Commanders of the Kings Ships now in the harbour, and that Capt Kennedy in answer to their earnest request signified to him last night that he cannot and will not receive the stamped paper. It is therefore resolved that that it appears to this Board absolutely necessary to remove the present dissatisfaction and save the city from the most distressing confusion, that a Committee immediately wait upon his Honour and in the most respectful manner acquaint him of the present dangerous state of things and request that for the peace of the city and the preventing any effusion of blood he would be pleased to direct that the stamped paper be delivered into the care of the Corporation to be deposited in the City hall and guarded by the City Watch and the Board do further resolve and engage to make good all such sums of money as might be raised by the distribution of the said stamps as shall be destroyed or carried out of the Province.'

And thereupon his Honour was pleased to observe to the council that he had taken an oath to do his utmost that all and every the clauses in the Act of Parliament be punctually and bona fide observed as far as appertained to him, that it appeared to him that the power of the Corporation alone would be sufficient to preserve the stamps from being destroyed, it was nighest the same power added to the strength of the garrison must be sufficient to protect them against any forces. That the demands of the populace would end here, and that the measures proposed if yielded to by him might draw the government into still greater contempt and his compliance be construed as a breach of his oath, and then his Honour was pleased to refer the matter to the consideration of the Council.

The Council on due deliberation declared they were thoroughly sensible of the weight of his Honours reasons, but that the city appeared to them to be in perfect anarchy and the power of government either military or civil unequal to the protection of the inhabitants from the ravages and violence of the populace. That the evil, if not speedily removed would soon be greatly increased by vagabonds who would flock hither from all parts of the Province. That the Commander in Chief of his majesty's forces had given his opinion that the stamps should be removed on board one of the Kings ships, although Captain Kennedy had thought proper to refuse to take charge of them. That the destruction of the great part of the city would be involved in the necessary defence of the Fort, and that they conceive it more advisable to yield to the necessity of the times, than by a contrary resolution abandon the inhabitants to the consequence of an attack upon the Fort, which his Honour himself apprehended, and the Council feared would actually be attempted. That the Council are sensible his Honour hath taken every method consistent with his duty prudence and humanity to carry the law into execution. That more is not in his power, and therefore that they do unanimously advise his Honour upon the assurance given by the corporation who are willing to receive and defend the stamps, and in case of loss to be answerable for all damages, to deliver the stamped paper and parchment into their care and custody.

14.   *Affidavit of Lieutenant George Stoney*
dated 29 March 1766 sworn before Mr Francis
Filkins Esq, Alderman of the City of New York

[Not reproduced as printed in full in Captain Kennedy's narrative.]

15.   *Captain Kennedy to Lord Colvill*

4 November 1765

My Lord, I have received your letters of 11th and 13th October, have ordered the *Hawke* sloop to Newcastle on Delaware to take on board her the stamp paper intended for Maryland and to proceed with it to Annapolis, as the Act took place on the 1st I have paid no regard to Zacharia Hood second letter to me as I judged it necessary the paper be sent to the

Province that they might not have reason to plead the want of stamps as the cause of their evading or opposing that Law.

With regard to Captain Wallace of the *Tryal* stopping at Boston in consequence of a request by letter from General Gage, though the *Coventry* and *Guarland* were both present when he received it and the said letter communicated to me, I desire to inform you that the letter I did not see. General Gage made an apology to me for having applied to him, the reason he gave for having applied to him was my not being in town the day the *Tryal* arrived and he informed she was to stop at Boston and Halifax.

I in compliance with Governor Colden's first letter ordered a party of marines but as he afterwards judged it not to be necessary they were not sent, as to his second letter I excused myself from taking the stamps as they were lodged in a place of security and if taken was uncertain when they might judge proper to have them landed again and there is no such thing as securing them aboard of ship when alongside a wharf, which must now soon be the case, besides by his directions they had been landed from the ships, after they had been taken on board them from the merchant vessel that imported them.

On 31st Oct. a mob of about four or five hundred got together behaved riotously, threat [*sic*] the Lieutenant Governor his son and Major James, but dispersed without doing any mischief except breaking few windows and pulling a little bawdyhouse down. Next day they assembled to the number of five or six thousand and pulled down part of the fencing that is round the garrison, abused the Lieutenant Governor most grossly, broke into his stables and from thence carried away his chariot two sleighs and another gentlemans chair merely because it was his stables, all which they burnt almost under the very walls of the garrison, and hanged and burnt in effigy the Governor, Lord Bute and the devil, the Governor distributing the stamps, afterwards went to Major James house and entirely burnt and destroyed his furniture, drank his wine etc to the amount of £1,500 sterling then returned to the house of the Governors son, Mr Alexander Colden which they with great difficulty were prevented from destroying by some of the merchants in town, next day sent a most threatening letter to the Governor, informing him if he did not solemnly swear that he would neither distribute the stamps himself nor appoint anyone to distribute the stamps, they would burn him in reality and destroy the houses of everyone connected with him and publick advertisements were pasted up in different parts of the town to much the same purport. After the Council had the next day sat a considerable number of hours, the expedient they fell upon as the only means of quieting the populace was that the Lieutenant Governor should declare that he would give no orders for nor in any measure intermeddle with the distribution of the stamps but that business should go on in the usual and accustomed manner till the arrival of Sir Henry Moore who was daily expected which declaration was publickly read and by that means a much more numerous mob than that of the day before and from their threats much more mischievously inclined dispersed. I from their threats ran a very great risque of having my new house in town burnt with everything in it, which would have hurt me to a very considerable amount. Enclosed is the state and condition of his Majestys ships and copies of sundry letters from Governor Colden, Captain Hawker and Mr Hood, as likewise a copy of my letter to the Governor on his applying to have the stamp papers sent on board one of the ships.

16.   *Captain Kennedy to Governor Franklin*

4 October 1765

On my receiving yours of 1st instant [No 30] I waited on Governor Colden and expressed to him the necessity of lodging the stamp paper intended for New Jersey in case of its arrival here in Fort George as there is no place of defence in the Province of the Jerseys where it can with safety, at same time acquainted him with the many inconveniences that would attend taking them on board any of his Majestys ships of war there being no place on board where any quantity of paper could be put where it would not run the risque of being damped and otherwise so damaged as might render it useless. You are likewise to consider that all the ships are on immediate service, and on any orders received from my Lord Colvill obliged to proceed to sea without delay, in the winter lay at the wharf where they could afford no protection for as most of the men are impressed in the spring many at the first opportunity desert and there is no preventing them when at a wharf, however in case Mr Colden should still refuse receiving them into the Fort, you may depend on all the assistance in my power for protecting the stamped paper and ship that brings them, but must more thoroughly consider of the methods which I can take, as likewise of the propriety of taking them on board any of the Kings ships, on which head I shall write my Lord Colvill. The ship bringing them I can and will protect as long as the weather will admit of my laying in the stream.

16a.   *Captain Kennedy to Lord Colvill*

13 October 1765

Enclosed you have a copy of a letter from Governor Franklin of New Jersey and likewise the copy of one from the stamp collector of Maryland and my answer to each, should be glad if your Lordship would direct what you judge will be proper to be done in regard of the stamp paper for New Jersey. By the same opportunity you have the state and condition of his Majesty's ships here.

17.   *Lord Colvill to Captain Kennedy*

Romney, Halifax
5 November 1765

Yesterday I received your letter and the copies of the letters therein contained and an abstract of weekly accounts. The reasons are very plain which you gave for declining to receive the New Jersey Stamps, and I think you should take no charge of them unless the Governor absolutely refuses to receive them into the Fort, or gives other reasons for his declining it than are set forth in Governor Franklins letter: surely the Governor's house in one of his Majesty's Forts is a much properer place for depositing the stamps than in any ship, and the more so as the Fort is full of men and military stores, to give the greater security to the important trust: besides there is no part of Sir Henry Moore's Character which should make it apprehended that he would be displeased with such a measure, or that he would think it anyways inconvenient to him. Mr Colden has assured Mr Franklin that he will do all in his power to have the New Jersey stamps preserved if they come to New York and there can be no doubt of his having this power whilst he commands the Fort. You will therefore please to make use of your own prudence in this affair and give all necessary assistance in preserving the stamps, or conveying them to the places of their destination in your neighbourhood, provided such preservation or conveyance cannot be obtained with more propriety from any other quarter. It is unnecessary for me to say anything on the subject of the letter you received from Mr Zacharia Hood Distributor of Stamps for Maryland, as I have already written to you on that head.

17a.   *Lord Colvill to Captain Kennedy*

Romney, Halifax
25 November 1765

I have read your letter of 4th instant giving me an account of the riotous proceedings of the mob at New York and other matters relating to the stamped paper but as I have already communicated my thoughts to you on this subject in my letter of the 5th instant I have nothing more to add now, but to inform you that I have transmitted a concise account of these transactions to the Secretary of the Admiralty.

18. *Council meeting with John Cruger Mayor,*
all the Aldermen and assistants

5 November 1765

This Board taking into serious consideration the intimation that his Honour the Lieutenant Governor was willing to deliver the stamped paper now in Fort George to Captain Kennedy, or any other of the commanders of the Kings ships in the harbour and that Captain Kennedy in answer to their earnest request signified to him last night informs that he cannot and will not receive the stamped paper. It is therefore resolved that it appears that this Board absolutely requisite to remove the present dissatisfaction and save the city from the most distressing confusion that a Committee immediately wait upon his Honour and in the most respectful manner acquaint him of the present dangerous state of things and request that for the peace of the city and the preventing an effusion of blood, he would be pleased to direct that the stamped paper be delivered into the care of the Corporation to be deposited in the City Hall and guarded by the City Watch. And this board do further resolve and engage to make good all such sums of money as might be raised by the distribution of such of the said stamps as shall be lost, destroyed or carried out of the province; and the said Committee having waited on his said Honour with the above resolve, reported to this Board that his Honour accepted of the same, and returned for answer, in the words following: Fort George Nov 5th Mr Mayor and gentlemen of the Corporation, In consequence of your earnest request and engagement to make good all such sums of money as might be raised by the distribution of such of the stamps sent over for the use of the province as shall be lost destroyed or carried out of the Province, and in consequence of the unanimous advice of his Majestys council and the concurrence of the Commander in Chief of the strong laws, and to prevent the effusion of blood and the calamities of civil war which might ensue by my withholding them from you, I now deliver to you the packages of stamped paper and parchment that were deposited in my hands, in this his Majesty's fort, and I doubt not you will take that charge and care of them conformable to your engagement to me. I am with great regard gentlemen your most obedient humble servant, Cadwallader Colden

At which time his honour requested that the mayor would give him a receipt in the words following which the mayor executed accordingly on behalf of the corporation: viz: Received of the Hon. Cadwallader Colden Esq his Majestys Lieutenant Governor and Commander in Chief of the Province of New York, seven packages containing stamped paper and parchment, all marked No 1 IME New York, which I promise in behalf of the Corporation of the city of New York, to take charge and care of, and to be accountable in case they shall be destroyed or carried out of the province as particularly set forth and declared in the minutes of the common court of the said corporation of this day, witness my hand in the City of New York this first day of November 1765.

19.   *Map attached showing disposition of ships on night of 1 November 1765*[1]

20.   *James Furnis, Office of Ordnance, to Captain Kennedy*

26 November 1765

On the 16th instant Captain St John applied to me in your name requesting his Majesty's ships might be laid up at the ordnance wharf at Turtle Bay, as it was your opinion the said ships would not be safe at the usual wharfs at the city, should any tumult arise and at the same time mentioned the protection we might have from your marines in case his Majestys ordnance stores, at that place, should be attempted to be plundered or destroyed, to which application for the preservation of his Majestys ships and protection of his Majestys ordnance stores, I then consented.

As since that time all the artillery ammunition and ordnance stores lately sent into Fort George for the defence thereof which gave so much disgust to the people have by the Commander in Chief's orders been taken from thence and deposited in the places from whence they were taken, it is not now thought his Majestys ordnance stores, either at this place or at Turtle Bay, are in danger from the people of this place, and having considered the fatal consequences which might arise by the explosion of fourteen hundred barrels of gunpowder deposited in a slight magazine contiguous to the wharfs by the forces on board the ships and irregularity of the seamen when on shore.

As it is my duty to take every method for the preservation of his Majesty's ordnance stores, I have therefore communicated the same to the Commander in Chief, and have his approbation to acquaint you the

[1]TNA: MPI 1/168.

consequence of his Majesty's ships wintering at Turtle Bay might be so fatal to both departments of his Majestys service that it would be highly improper the said ships should be laid up at that place during the winter.

21. *Captain Kennedy to Andrew Elliot Esq*

New York
10 December 1765

As there is at present several vessels in the Port which have been cleared at the Customs House on unstamped paper since that act ought to have taken place I desire to know in what light I am to hold these Clearances and whither I as Commanding officer by sea at this Port will in your opinion be excusable to the Commissioners of the Customs in allowing them to proceed to sea. I have wrote Governor Moore on the same head.

22. *Captain Kennedy to Sir Henry Moore*

New York
10 December 1765

As there is at present several vessels ready to proceed to sea, which vessels have loaded and been cleared at the Customs House of this port on unstamped paper since that act ought to have taken place.

I desire to know whether with your approbation I am to deem these clearances sufficiently legal for me as the Commanding Officer by sea at this port to permit these vessels to proceed to sea on their intended voyages.

23. *Andrew Elliot and Samuel Moore, Collectors of Customs, to Captain Kennedy*

Custom House
10 December 1765

Your letter of this date to the Collector is now before us, in answer to which we beg leave to observe that by a late Act of Parliament all cocketts and clearances granted in America after the 1st day of November last ought to be upon stampt paper, but the present situation of affairs in this Province (to which you can be no stranger) has obliged us since the 5th instant to grant cocketts and clearance upon unstampt paper when demanded neither was this step taken by us without the approbation of the Surveyor General of this District, therefore in what light you are to hold these clearances so granted by us must leave you to determine.

24.   Governor Moore's answer to Captain Kennedy's letter of 10 December 1765

That he has consulted him upon a point in law which he would not take upon himself to judge of, that therefore an answer in writing was unnecessary.

That Clearances without stamps were illegal.

That he did no business relative to his department nor would he do anything without stamps that required them.

That even the Courts of Prerogative and Chancery were shut up and on application in regard to a suit in Chancery, of some of the witnesses being old, infirm and uncertain of life desiring some authority to take their depositions he had refused without stamps.

That if a merchant he would not venture any of his vessels to sea.

Begged Captain Kennedy would excuse his not having answered his letter.

The above is a true copy of his answer as delivered to me by Lt George Stoney and since granted by the Governor to contain the purport of what he said.

25.   Captain Kennedy to Captain St John, Guarland

11 December 1765

Whereas the Governor of this province deems all clearances granted by the Customs House here as illegal which are given on unstamped paper since 1st November

You are hereby required and directed diligently to examine all vessels coming to or going from this port, and detain all such as you shall judge illegally cleared, for which this shall be your order.

26.   Thirty-four merchants of New York to Captain Kennedy

28 December 1765

Sir, the customs house of this port is now shut in consequence of the conduct observed by the officers of his Majestys ships stationed here. It seems strange that this port is not open to outward bound vessels at the same time that vessels cleared at different ports for this place without stampt papers arrive daily.

The inconvenience arising to the trading interest of this place from this restraint is very considerable, therefore the merchants in general here would take kind from you an explanation of this matter there being at present near forty sail of vessels loaded and loading some of which have perishable cargoes on board.

Our collector has received a letter from Philadelphia acquainting him that that port was open on the 23 instant.

You'll oblige us in furnishing us with a satisfactory answer on this subject by the return of the bearer. We hope you will do everything in your power consistent with your duty in favour of the trade of this place. P.S. In consequence of your order to Capt St John the Collector has this day refused giving any more clearances.

27.   *Captain Kennedy to merchants*

24 December 1765

Your letter of yesterday's date desiring an explanation of my conduct as Commander of his Majestys ships here in preventing vessels not having legal clearances from going to sea, I have just received.

In answer to which give me leave to observe that I am greatly surprised the merchants of New York could imagine I would act officiously in laying restraints upon the trade of this place, having as I think never given the least reason for such a suggestion to the contrary I have ever been ready to the utmost of my power to give the trade of this city all due protection. And as to the part I have acted in stopping vessels not having legal clearances I persuade myself you will be fully satisfied with the propriety of it, when I assure you that if I was to act otherwise it would be highly inconsistent with my duty, which I cannot conceive the merchants of New York would ever wish me to violate.

I beg leave to assure you that I shall always cheerfully do everything in my power consistent with my duty to favour the trades of this place, to which I sincerely wish the greatest prosperity.

28.   *Captain Kennedy to Lord Colvill*

10 December 1765

My Lord, I am honoured with yours of the 5th ultimo after the delivery of the stamped paper to the Corporation of the City. On the city's security everything remained quiet here till the 4th instant that the Custom house cleared and entered vessels on unstamped paper contrary to the late Act, on which occasion I wrote Sir Henry Moore and the Collector of Customs. Enclosed you have my letters to them and their answers to me. I likewise consulted with the Attorney General and on the whole judged it necessary to acquaint the masters of merchant vessels that if any of them attempted going to sea with illegal or unstamped papers I should be obliged to seize them, more particularly as the Governor refused giving them a *transire* or let pass without stamps. Capt Hawker has written to me in regard to the detaining of vessels and I have referred him to the opinion of the Attorney General, and his own judgement. I flatter myself what I have done will meet with your approbation, in which case I must beg you will send me an order for detaining the shipping for if known that I acted without your orders the mob will be so enraged I know not what they may attempt. I have already received some threats and a letter or two on the subject, yet it is the only way I see for enforcing the Act, till his Majesty and Council give some more effectual orders for doing it, but it will not be long in my power to detain for after I go alongside the wharfs they will not permit my boats to board them.

29. *Lord Colvill to Captain Kennedy*

8 February 1766

On the 5th instant I received your letter of 10th December enclosing copies of letters between you the officers of the Customs and Sir Henry Moore and acquainting me that after advising with the Attorney General you had judged it necessary to inform the masters of vessels that if any of them attempted going to sea with unstamped papers, you should be obliged to seize them and desiring an order from me for that purpose.

In answer to your letter I am to observe that I have no instructions relative to the stamp act. The Governor of New York looked upon it as an improper subject for him to write to you about, therefore made an apology for not answering your letter, thinking it was on a point of law wherein he did not chuse to give his opinion. Had you sent me the opinion of the Attorney General it would have had great weight with me. The Officers of the Customs in their answer to your letter confess that with the approbation of the Surveyor General, they have submitted to the necessity of the times and granted Cockets and Clearances on paper without stamps; but I observe they will not give you the opinion you desire with regard to your being answerable to the

Commissioners of the Customs in allowing vessels with such clearances to proceed to sea.

Tis probable that Sir Henry Moore considering the present state of affairs in his government though he owns the illegality of such clearances, has prudential or political reasons for not giving his opinion, or approbation, in the case you proposed to him, and it could scarcely be expected that the officers of the Customs at New York should say in what light their commissioners would look upon the conduct of a commanding sea officer in so nice a point. But I will readily give you my opinion.

The clearances in question cannot on any account whatsoever be deemed legal; and a sea officer must be justifiable in endeavouring to defeat the purpose of all who break the law on the element he occupies. All the business of entrances, clearances cockets and such like belongs to the Custom house department on shore, and a sea officers deputation from the commissioners does not require him to interfere in these matters or in any shape to control the land officers he must be sufficiently excusable to them for letting the collector, controller etc go on in their own way with the approbation of their surveyor general and I am confirmed in this opinion by the third article of the instructions which were delivered to the sea officers with their deputations.

The Distributor of Stamps for the province of Nova Scotia has received orders from his board not to prosecute any one for carrying on business with common paper which by the late act ought to be on stamped paper.

30. *William Franklin, Governor of New Jersey,*
to Captain Kennedy

Burlington
1 October 1765

By the advice of his Majesty's council of this Colony I wrote to Governor Colden, requesting that if the stamp papers for New Jersey should arrive at New York, that he would be pleased to order them to be taken care of and lodged in the Fort until proper measures could be taken to bring them with safety into this Province. In answer to which the governor has assured me that 'He will do all in his power to have them preserved in case they come to that place. But as the fort is now full of men and military stores so that he has no place to lodge the stamps but in the Governors house which may be very inconvenient to Sir Henry Moore who will probably come in the same ship with the stamps he submits it to my consideration whether it would not be as safe and more convenient to have the New Jersey stamps sent on board one of the Kings frigates now at New York who may land them at any time and place which may be proper.'

I must therefore request of you, sir, that you would give the necessary orders for having the stamped paper for New Jersey in case of their arrival in New York, and that they cannot be lodged conveniently in the Fort, put on board one of the Kings frigate until other measures can be taken for their security.

I should not propose to give you this trouble, but that the preservation of the stamps is a matter of importance to his Majesty's Revenue and that we have no fort or place of defence within the province.

31. *Zacharia Hood, Distributor in Maryland, to Captain Kennedy*

2 September 1765

I have applied to General Gage for a sloop of war to protect the stamps that is coming from England to Maryland as there is no place of safety in the province to secure them. His Excellency returned for answer that he had no command over the ships of war.

That I proposed to his Excellency (if you will please to approve the expedient I think will be the only method to secure them) that you will be pleased to order a sloop of war to lie of [*sic*] the City Annapolis and have them lodged on board of her when they arrive from which I propose to distribute them agreeable to the duty of my office, for its not possible to get a house for mine has been pulled down and I have been obliged to leave the province.

I am under great apprehensions that if the stamps come in merchantmen that they will be destroyed if a ship is not there in time to protect them (as there is no man of war on the Virginia station when I left Maryland being gone to Carolina) the stamps must arrive in a little time as the law takes place 1 Nov. it will not be in my power to receive them if not supported.

If you are please to think that its to Lord Colvill I must apply I beg leave to acquaint you that there is no post to Halifax nor am I capable of proceeding down there having fevers and if able the time would be too long and the stamps might be destroyed. I must beg you would please to show whatever you may think for his Majesty Service in receiving the stamps which I shall be ready to assist all in my power.

I must beg you will please to help my application secret, if it known I shall have my warehouses goods etc destroyed: for there are several that collect all they can to inflame the people. I am informed by agents that is just come from Maryland that if it is known there that I am on the continent everything of mine is to be destroyed.

32.   *Captain Kennedy to Hood*

8 September 1765

I have yours of 2 instant requesting a sloop of war may be ordered from this place to lay of Annapolis in Maryland for the protection and receiving on board of the stamps that you might with safety distribute them. I desire to inform you that the ships stationed at this port and the *Sardoine* at Philadelphia are intended for the protection of the trade security of the provinces of New York Jersey and Delaware rivers. From Delaware to the Capes of Virginia is immediately under the command of Captain Walter Stirling commander of the *Rainbow* application having been made to me by the governor of this province for the aid of his Majesty's ships that are here for the protection of the stamped papers intended for this place, and they being stationed accordingly puts it out of my power to grant you any assistance. If you judge it proper to apply to my Lord Colvill any letter directed to the care of Mr Benjamin Hallowel at Boston will go safe and I make no doubt of his ordering you the necessary assistance as far as the protection of the stamps.

[**33** and **34** not included.]

35.   *Lord Colvill to Captain Kennedy*

13 October 1765

This morning I received a letter from Mr Zacharia Hood, Distributor of Stamps for Maryland, who has fled from the violence of the mob in that Country to New York for protection. After giving me an account of his various difficulties, he proposes as the only method to secure the stamps, that a ship of war should lie off Annapolis to receive them when they arrive and from which he also proposes to distribute them. I have not heard from Captain Stirling since he left this place, the *Diligence* is gone to North Carolina and the *Hornet* is at Hampton in great distress for want of sails etc therefore as this is the situation of the ships on the Virginia station, I would have you send the *Guarland* or *Hawke* to Annapolis (and to continue there whilst it may be necessary) provided either of them can be of more essential service in that Province than in the neighbourhood of New York. I do not mean that a Kings ship should be turned into an office for distributing stamps, but that the Captain should give all possible assistance to Governor Sharp, at a time when the executive power is found too weak to enforce a due obedience to the laws.

[**36.**   No document attached, but summarized within Kennedy's text.]

37.   *Captain Kennedy to Captain Browne*

2 November 1765

In consequence of orders received from Lord Colvill desiring that a ship of war should be sent from this port to lie off Annapolis and Maryland.

You are hereby required and directed without loss of time to proceed with his Majesty's sloop *Hawke* under your command to Newcastle on the Delaware River and there take on board of you from his Majestys sloop *Sardoine* the stamped papers that is intended for Maryland and from thence proceed with all possible despatch to Annapolis in Maryland where you are to remain until you receive further orders or till such times as the present disturbances are settled when you will return to this port, and you are to give all possible assistance to Governor Sharpe of that Province for so doing this shall be your order.

JAMES RAMSAY'S *ESSAY* OF 1780 ON THE DUTY
AND QUALIFICATIONS OF A SEA OFFICER

Edited by Richard Blake

Ramsay's *Essay* originated as a long private letter he wrote when he was a ship's surgeon to an aspiring young officer, a midshipman about to be commissioned in 1760. The same material was given a further airing in 1762 to prepare a petty officer for the life he was hoping for as a commissioned officer. The recipient of this second letter was a seaman whose abilities had attracted the attention of Captain Charles Middleton,[1] who advanced him to the command of a small armed vessel with the local rank of lieutenant. As he was a poorly educated man who might soon be expected to hold his own amongst the more polished lieutenants of the wardroom, Ramsay wanted him to have advice tailored to his situation. He explains he could find no book that gave the kind of advice he felt necessary for any young officer, and he therefore had his original letter of 1760, with the additional material of 1762 as an appendix, published anonymously in book form by a London printer in 1765.

Fifteen years later no comparable work on officer-training had appeared in print, while the need for capable officers had become still more urgent in the face of the dangers threatening Britain from her enemies in arms. Middleton, comptroller of the navy from July 1778, was in anxious correspondence with his friend and former shipmate Richard Kempenfelt, now chief of staff in the Channel fleet, as they considered

---

[1] Charles Middleton (1726–1813), Adm Lord Barham, comptroller of the navy 1778–90, first lord of the admiralty 1805–06, administrator, strategist, reformer. The essential source with extensive biographical introduction is J.K. Laughton (ed.), *Letters and Papers of Charles, Lord Barham, 1758–1813*, 3 vols (NRS vols 32, 38, 39, 1907–11). For modern views, see John E. Talbott, *The Pen and Ink Sailor: Charles Middleton and the King's Navy, 1778–1813* (London and Portland, OR, 1998); and Roger Morriss, 'Charles Middleton, Lord Barham, 1726–1813' in Peter Le Fevre and Richard Harding (eds), *Precursors of Nelson: British Admirals of the Eighteenth Century* (London, 2000), pp. 301–23. Also, I. Lloyd Phillips, 'The Evangelical Administrator: Sir Charles Middleton at the Navy Board, 1778–1790' (DPhil Oxford University, 1978).

ways to strengthen the navy materially, tactically and morally.[1] Middleton sounded out Ramsay's availability to help with his paper work in 1779; and, with danger in the background and reform in the offing, the times seemed to call for a reissue of his treatise on the duties of sea officers. An improved and extended second edition appeared in February 1780, followed by a third later the same year, and others in translation. The time for anonymity had passed, and the author was declared to be the Reverend James Ramsay, chaplain in his Majesty's navy.

Despite its success the book was long lost to view and its significance overlooked. For many years the *Essay* was wrongly attributed to Admiral Sir Charles Knowles since the Bodleian Library's copy of the first anonymous edition bore his name on the cover. The British Library department of rare books holds an example of the first edition available online in its London reading rooms; two copies of the third edition are held in the USA, at the Watkinson Library, Trinity College, Hartford, Connecticut, and at the US Naval Academy's Nimitz Library in Annapolis. The editor is grateful for the assistance of staff at the British and the Watkinson Libraries in allowing copies of the first and third editions to be downloaded, transcribed and compared.[2] Ramsay's first production took the form of a lengthy letter, with paragraphs but no sub-headings. By 1780 he had produced a much improved text, with a table of contents, chapter divisions and headings, and an expanded treatment of some themes, notably signals. The third edition, representing Ramsay's mature reflection on the subject is the text chosen for full display here, with an attempt to show where it departs from the sparse wording of fifteen years before.

The Author's Career and Significance

James Ramsay (1733–89) was born at Fraserburgh in Scotland.[3] A man of piety attracted to the ministry, he lacked the means for the necessary university education. Instead he took up the profession of surgeon, where he could begin to earn his keep while still under training. His skills attracted attention and bursaries, which in turn enabled him to acquire a degree

---

[1]Middleton–Kempenfelt correspondence, *Barham Papers*, I, pp. 288–365.

[2]Digitised version of 1765 *Essay* available on Eighteenth Century Collections Online (ECCO); 1780 edition on Reel 17405 of microfilm series, *The Eighteenth Century*. Information provided by British Library.

[3]Biographical studies: Folarin Shyllon, *James Ramsay, the Unknown Abolitionist* (Edinburgh, 1977); Surgeon Vice-Admiral Sir James Watt, 'James Ramsay, 1733–1789: Naval Surgeon, Naval Chaplain and Morning Star of the Anti-Slavery Movement', *The Mariner's Mirror*, 81 (1995), pp. 156–70; and entry in *Oxford Dictionary of National Biography*.

at Aberdeen University (1753) while completing medical training. After passing the examination of the Company of Surgeons in June 1757 he entered the navy and was appointed to the sixth rate *Arundel*, then engaged in commerce protection in the Caribbean. In waters notorious for illness he achieved high standards of health aboard.[1] From March 1759 her new captain was a fellow Scotsman, Charles Middleton, who had recently adopted the same kind of evangelical convictions as his surgeon. While his successes in intercepting French merchantmen and privateers gained him a small fortune in prize money, his friendship with Ramsay added depth of insight to his faith and boldness in its practical outworking.

In 1759 Ramsay's career drastically altered course. Middleton came upon a distressed merchant vessel, the *Swift* of Bristol, off Barbados. She was a slaver, which had been visited first by fever and then by a French privateer that had taken away the healthy part of her crew and human cargo. Ramsay offered to visit the ship to treat her sick. As he set off in the *Arundel's* boat he was a naval surgeon on operational duty, but he returned an incipient Abolitionist, burning with indignation against the cruelties of the Atlantic slave trade and pledged to expose something of the horrors he had witnessed amongst the filth of blood, vomit and human excrement he had found on the slave deck. Soon afterwards he broke his thigh in a fall aboard ship, and although he recovered he knew his seagoing career was effectively ended, since any tendency to scurvy – still the scourge of deep-water voyaging – would reopen the fractured bones. Instead he went to England seeking Anglican ordination, and then returned to the Caribbean in 1762 as vicar of St John's parish, Capisterre, in the island of St. Christopher (St Kitts), adding Christ Church, Nicola Town, in 1763. He married a planter's daughter, Rebecca Akers, through whom he established a family and a ministry amongst slaves.

For the next sixteen years Ramsay's ministry had three distinct aspects to it: church services for the white plantation owners and their families; pastoral ministrations to the black population – mostly slaves – with prayers and preaching separate from the white congregation; and the use of his medical skills as surgeon, physician and obstetrician. He often had to tend plantation slaves for their illnesses, frequent accidents and wounds inflicted in punishment beatings. But he was also becoming an activist and social reformer who would not shrink from controversy.

His mounting fury against slavery led him first to preach to plantation owners about their Christian duty of fair treatment and humanity. Such

---

[1] In his own ship the *Arundel* he managed to reduce the daily sick list from 21 to never more than nine and frequently none at all; Watt, p. 157.

a stand antagonised a powerful sector of white society, and he inflamed another entrenched group when, to protect the livelihoods of people to whom rich planters owed money, he wrote a pamphlet against an unjust and illegal proposal to reduce interest rates and brought the matter successfully to the notice of the colonial court.[1] In 1770 he warned the British government of incipient disloyalty amongst leading members of society in St Kitts. Ramsay's friends were often those who had no voice but his to speak out for them; his enemies held local sway and they managed to strip him of his magistracy and reduce the scope of his clerical ministry. By 1777 he was ready to return home.

The American War brought another career change for Ramsay, who returned to the Caribbean as chaplain of the flagship *Prince of Wales*. In this capacity he produced a volume of sermons that may well be the first such collection made specifically for seafarers.[2] His detailed knowledge of the theatre of war and his estimate of the loyalty of various merchants and planters made him a valuable source of intelligence to Admirals Barrington and Rodney. Once the war was over the planter community of St Kitts saw him as an informer as well as agitator, and Ramsay recognised that, for the sake of his mental and physical health, he needed to abandon the Leeward Islands for good – but not the cause of Abolition. By now he was convinced that conditions for plantation Negroes would never improve significantly so long as the slave trade continually replaced the lives that were prematurely ended by harsh treatment: ending the trade was the necessary preliminary to the abolition of slavery itself.

By now his friend Middleton was comptroller of the navy, with admiral's rank, baronetcy, seat in the Commons, a substantial estate at Teston in Kent, and the right of appointment to the parish living. Before long Ramsay had become vicar and – surprisingly perhaps – confidential secretary to his important patron, with access to papers of both private and public significance. Early in 1779 Middleton had invited Ramsay to leave the West Indies and join him in England to help with the voluminous paperwork involved in the proposed reform of Navy Board regulations.[3] It is clear from the Barham papers that they worked together on drafts of documents, with originals and amendments appearing in the handwriting of either of them.[4] Ramsay's influence helped persuade Middleton to take the cause of Abolition into parliament, and both of

---

[1] Watt, p. 160, referring to Ramsay, *Essay on Interest* (Basseterre, 1770).
[2] The Rev. James Ramsay, *Sea Sermons, or a Series of Discourses for the Use of the Royal Navy* (London, 1781).
[3] Ramsay's reply, 23 April 1779, *Barham Papers*, I, p. 46.
[4] Watt, p. 162.

them encouraged Wilberforce to become its principal advocate in the Commons. With personal testimony of what he had seen and recorded of the slave trade and of plantation life Ramsay could provide factual evidence to support Wilberforce's skill in oratory. The parliamentary campaign was to a degree planned and organised at Teston – the Runnymede of the Negro's liberation, in Hannah More's phrase.[1] His own pamphlet of 1784 spurred ferocious debate – *An Essay on the Treatment and Conversion of African Slaves in the British Sugar Colonies.*[2]

At last, exhausted by his efforts to advance the cause and at the same time defend himself against the malignity of his detractors, Ramsay collapsed and died on 20 July 1789 in Middleton's London house. But his influence remained – in the eventually successful Abolition movement, in the reforms of naval medicine associated with Sir Gilbert Blane who recorded his indebtedness to Ramsay,[3] in the medical and religious provision made for the First Fleet to Australia, in the developing Christian and evangelical spirit in the navy, in the influence he had over Middleton, and in the development of the ethos of the officer corps which is the substance of the document here reproduced. It amounts to a remarkable life record, surprisingly unnoticed until recently but not inappropriate for a man who shunned wealth and acclaim but not controversy, and who saw himself as an enabler of others.

The Scope and Importance of the *Essay*

While some aspiring officers tried to prepare for naval service by studying mathematics and related subjects at the Portsmouth academy, most learned their profession at sea, picking up the rudiments of a general education from schoolmaster, chaplain or captain, alongside the essential

[1] William Roberts, *Memoirs of the Life and Correspondence of Mrs Hannah More*, 4 vols (1834), II, p. 156.

[2] Op. cit. (1784), countered by Anon., *An Answer to the Rev. James Ramsay's Essay, by Some Gentlemen of St. Christopher* (Basseterre, 1784); J.P. Bateman, *Remarks on a Pamphlet written by J. Ramsay* (1784); and James Tobin ['A Friend to the West India Interest'], *Cursory Remarks upon the Rev. Mr. Ramsay's Essay* (1785).

[3] Watt, p. 165. It can be no coincidence that the navy's surgeons and physicians were becoming more sharply aware of what their profession required, with properly monitored entrance qualifications, general agreement over good practice and necessary equipment of instruments and medicines, and a forum in which surgical advances could be assessed. Ramsay was linked with progressive medical figures such as the anatomist William Hunter, Sir Gilbert Blane, and the London Medical Society. A self-regulating profession was emerging with acknowledged canons of good practice and a context in which new techniques could be exposed to the judgment of peers. In effect Ramsay was suggesting something similar for the officer corps, to develop the thinking which should complement the indispensable practical training provided aboard ship.

skills of seamanship and navigation that could only be mastered practically. Young gentlemen hoping for a commission were inducted into naval ways by the example and oversight of their captains. Often a commanding officer would agree to accept responsibility for a family member, or the son of a friend or colleague, or perhaps a nominee of the admiralty board. Certain captains were known to be particularly good at launching their protégés into the service, and they often took a group of 'followers' with them if they changed ships. As Ramsay noted, these men characteristically adopted the style of their mentors [XV para 2]. Fortunately for the navy, its best commanders were frequently the most sought after patrons and trainers of the rising generation, with beneficial results; but as a system of officer training it had many random and idiosyncratic elements about it. The outcome as Ramsay saw it was a deficient officer corps, competent enough in all branches of ship-handling, but inadequately schooled in the art of command or higher levels of education.

Ramsay explains that he took up his pen simply because he could find no work on the subject already in print. He believed that the navy with its unremitting demand for practical skills, omitted essential elements in the training of officers. He wished to see the commissioned ranks filled with 'complete' men, competent to handle a ship, of course, but also trained to elicit willing obedience from those they led, and accustomed to think critically about the best interests of their profession. Where captains and lieutenants were men like this, ships' companies would prove loyal and manageable, but, as Ramsay observed, 'when men will not obey, it is a strong presumption of the officers themselves being wanting in application' [XVII]. This short book explains his philosophy.

As first printed, the *Essay* retained some of the character of a lengthy discursive letter, full of matter but without an obvious structure or conceptual development. The third edition was a vast improvement, with divisions and chapter headings but not entirely freed from haphazard organisation. Most of the material falls into two main categories: the first dealing with the cultivation of attitudes appropriate to an officer; the remainder offering views of how the navy more widely should strive for improvement. It is important for the light it sheds on the navy of the Seven Years and American Wars as viewed by a detached observer (or 'unconcerned spectator', as Ramsay describes himself on page 1), for as surgeon, chaplain, admiral's secretary and intelligence officer he knew how the navy worked at every level.

The Induction of Aspiring Officers into Appropriate Professional Attitudes

The author assumes that any would-be officer knows how to handle a ship under sail in any wind or sea state, and is a man of courage, cool under fire, able to promote confidence in others and committed to his country's honour. But what are those other qualities which make up a 'complete' officer? He is responsible for the lives and well-being of a body of men [I], and he owes obligations to them. He must respect their need for meals and rest, and they should be sure of considerate treatment from him [VII, VIII, XI]. He will avoid over-much interference with their proper privacy and their leisure time, and he should encourage recreational games and their love of patriotic songs [XII]. At the same time a good officer will be diligent in checking his men for cleanliness and will see that they are properly equipped with clothing and kit [XIII]. He will be quick to enforce discipline, ensuring fairness and justice, and be fully prepared to order punishment where that is due [IX].

As a figure of authority, any commissioned officer should think carefully about the orders he gives, whether they are perfectly clear and appropriate, and about the manner in which they are delivered. He must animate through his brisk demeanour and determination, and he must neither allow himself to handle seamanlike movements in a slipshod way nor put up with a slovenly response from his men [III]. On the other hand he must not be a martinet. More than once Ramsay urges the young officer to take advice from more experienced subordinates [XV], and to treat with respect those who hold responsibility under him – midshipmen, petty officers, leading hands – so that they in turn will be given respect and obedience [IV, XV]. Let him learn to give instructions without larding them in profanity and curses: in this way he will show regard for God above and man below, and he will forfeit neither respect nor obedience so long as his orders are decisive and clear [XLIII].

A junior lieutenant must cultivate the qualities of a seamanlike officer. He will need to develop a propensity for forward thinking and meticulous preparation [II], and he should set himself to understand every aspect of the ship and its workings, especially when she is in harbour and ordinary seagoing duties are suspended [V]. At sea let him master the skills of pilotage by getting to know local waters well [XXVIII], studying the best charts he can find [XXXI], learning the channels and coastal features [XXX], and how to take advantage of the currents – particularly in the intricacies of the Caribbean [XXIX].

To guide him further, the young officer requires a mind which is trained to reason from principles of thought to practical remedies in situations where he has no experience to rely on [II]. He needs to acquire the breadth of understanding which comes from a good education, but he has forfeited much schooling by leaving home so young. During spells of time ashore, let him hire a tutor to teach him the first six books of Euclid, as a prelude to further studies in algebra, geometry, trigonometry and logarithms. In default of formal instruction self-tuition has to make good, and Ramsay offered a rather daunting home curriculum. Trained as he had been for the exacting Master of Arts degree at Aberdeen University, and subsequently taken in hand by Thomas Reid, an eminent Scots mathematician and philosopher, Ramsay had a high view of human capacity for mental improvement; he would have his young officer find time to acquire a knowledge of astronomy, geography and mechanics as well as two subjects of pressing relevance to a sea officer – navigation and gunnery. And there were other 'ornamental accomplishments', as Ramsay rather quaintly called them, the ability to write, reason and converse, skills acquired through reading periodicals of quality such as the *Tatler*, *Spectator*, *Guardian* and *Connoisseur* [XLV], and of course the Bible, which would be an education in itself [XLI]. He would be well advised to read plenty of history, ancient and more recent, not least because of its value in conversation [XLVI]. And any accomplished naval officer would need a knowledge of modern languages, certainly French and preferably Spanish as well, and he should pay for a tutor to help him with grammar [Appendix]. This course of study Ramsay recommended as a source of delight, and a way of training the intellect to welcome new thinking and value innovation.

Particularly in the case of 'Mr. L——, commander of the armed vessel ——', Ramsay was anxious to see him kitted out with social accomplishments that would aid acceptance by his new wardroom colleagues. It was a bit too late for him to adopt the full curriculum of self-improvement, but he should certainly make a stab at learning decent English with proper grammar and spelling; he must know about keeping accounts, and both mathematics and languages were necessary pursuits. There were other pieces of advice he wanted him to heed, like avoiding unnecessary controversy, and making sure he never sounded like a Billingsgate fish porter when roused to anger [Appendix]. To all his readers Ramsay urged the need to avoid conceit and self-advertisement, and the envy which begrudged others the credit they deserved [XLVIII]. Every officer after all was one amongst colleagues, and learning to live agreeably among fellow members of the wardroom was a proper professional accomplishment.

So much for the officer-induction part of his manual, but with his acute powers of observation and his liking for analytical reflection, honed by discussions with his well-matched captain, Ramsay had much to add about other aspects of the naval service.

Improving the Quality of Naval Manpower
First, he was keen to improve the officer corps, and not just through the advice he was giving to new entrants. He wanted to see the passing

examination for lieutenants expanded to include much more than sea-manship: a man might know all he needed about making sail, mooring or handling a ship in a gale, but what did he know about handling a crew of six hundred men? What had he learned about the art of command [XL]? At a more senior level, he suggested that a new appointment should be introduced, the rank of second captain – not unlike the later post of com-mander as second-in-command in a capital ship [VI]. This would offer training in high responsibility to prepare an officer for command, and it would be a proper ambition for any lieutenant who could never expect to be made post. At a more exalted level still, he alleged that admirals were often too aged for their senior responsibilities, and there should be some way to raise capable officers to flag rank while still in their prime [VI].

Another of Ramsay's concerns was how to improve the human resource of the fleet. In an emergency the navy increased to several times its peacetime establishment, bringing a perpetual worry over how it could be manned by competent seamen. Impressment was the time-honoured way, but it had many drawbacks. Ramsay proposed a system of registration for merchant seamen and a period of limited service, like the French *Inscription Maritime*, and he had other ideas to ensure an adequate supply of the petty officers who formed the corps of the trained lower deck [XVI]. On surer ground, he suggested measures to secure adequate numbers of qualified sea surgeons, so essential for the day-to-day health of the navy as well as the treatment of accidental and combat injuries [ibid.]. He was a strong believer in the need for hygiene and cleanliness: the idea then coming into vogue, of dividing a ship's com-pany into bodies of men under the oversight of a lieutenant, provided the ideal unit for frequent inspection of sailors' kit and health, and Ram-say became an advocate for the adoption of the divisional system, as it came to be called [XIII]. With successful experience of his own and links with progressive medical developments, Ramsay offered comments on health issues which were relevant to his theme, including how to secure adequate sleeping space for the watch below decks [XIV], the risks to health if hammocks became soaked while being used as an improvised barricade on deck [XXII], the need for the rum ration [VIII], and the necessity for keeping living space and holds clean and sweet [XIII].

He had much to say about morale and discipline, besides promoting the kind of considerate attitude towards the lower deck which would do much to obviate any spirit of indiscipline [XI]. He saw the importance of finding ways to reinforce loyalty to service and ship, with dress to distin-guish the Royal Navy and a badge to link a man with his crew [XVIII] – foreshadowing the later bluejacket's uniform and cap tally. In the cause of discipline he urged humanity, indeed every appropriate kindness, but

had no qualms about corporal punishment when justly applied [IX]. One
of his more original suggestions, and one that never commended itself
to the navy, was his idea for a 'court of equity' in every ship, composed
of the captain with all commissioned and warrant officers, with powers
beyond a commanding officer's summary jurisdiction – often exceeded
in practice – but less than a full court martial [X].

Improving Warlike Effectiveness
A surgeon-turned-chaplain might reasonably express opinions on personnel issues, but rather unexpectedly he had much to say about the navy
as a fighting service. Aware of the ever-present dangers of fire in peace
or war, he wrote about closed lanterns and hooped iron candlesticks,
and he gave a detailed description of precautions taken in his ship the
Prince of Wales to guard the magazine in action from the risks of explosion [XXIII]. He was appalled to note that some ships were lax in gunnery training: instead men should be well drilled at the great guns and
with small arms, so that they could deploy as required in action; those
stationed in the fighting tops or told off for boarding parties should be
properly trained and equipped [XIX]. Crews must be disciplined to hold
their fire until ordered and to keep silent when necessary [XX].

Always keen to preserve the safety of his fellow countrymen, Ramsay
criticised the reckless courage that scorned to fight at advantage, even
when overwhelming help was at hand, and so needlessly imperilled life
and limb – and he had some examples to quote where a commander's
thirst for renown and promotion had been satisfied at avoidable cost. 'In
reality, whenever you run into any unnecessary hazard, you are unjust
to your country and cruel to your men, by omitting to take an advantage which offered to secure an easy victory' [XXI]. In similar spirit
he recommended having defensive barricades semi-permanently rigged
on poop or quarter-deck to protect commander and boarding party from
small-arms fire: he discounted the idea that this might either slow the
ship by masking her sails or show any lack of courage [XXII]. This is
typical of Ramsay: he had no patience with empty displays of bravery
for the sake of personal glory instead of national gain. Let the admiral
direct an engagement from where he can best see what is happening, and
if that meant flying his flag in a frigate behind the line of battle, so be
it: his task was to secure a victory, not enhance his reputation for valour
[XXVIII].

He had views on convoy discipline [XXXIII], on preserving the effectiveness of gunpowder [XXIV], on the proper way to counter the effect
of calms and currents in the Caribbean [XXIX], and on the value of
surprise in battle tactics [XXI]. Drawing on the record of the past, he

was confident that English seamen with their notions of liberty, and led by brave commanders, could always be relied on to fight courageously against all odds: 'valour, and the persuasion prevailing among our seamen, that each man fought for himself and his country against the slavish instruments of a tyrant, were superior to numbers and discipline. Whenever a few men more, or a few ounces of metal, become a reason for declining or yielding the battle, the naval glory of Britain is set in obscurity' [XLVI].

Developing Naval Signalling

If that sounds like bravado as a way to success, it is offset by other parts of the *Essay* where Ramsay appeals for the rigorous application of disciplined thinking. He knew that successful deployment of maritime strength depended on cohesion and direction, on the ability of a commander to combine individual ships into a united force under his control. An admiral who could communicate rapidly and clearly with his captains had the potential to secure tactical advantages before or during an action. For this reason, developing a reliable code of signals was a quest of major significance in the eighteenth century, with the French generally ahead of their British rivals. While aware of the schemes introduced to their fleets by Admirals Keppel and Howe, Ramsay believed he could offer improvements [XXV, XXVI]. He was concerned that the meaning of flag hoists depended on the mast or the height at which they were flown: what happened if masts had been shot away or flags were obscured? Furthermore he was troubled by the arbitrary nature of existing codes, where the meaning could only be discerned by reference to a key. Would it not be possible to build up a language of signals, where one flag would show the type of order, and successive hoists the numerical designation of the instruction under that heading? In this way, once a single code had been issued for the whole navy, officers might learn to read the message without laborious reference to the signal book, and fleet commanders would have their powers of direction much enhanced. In the 1780 editions Ramsay included a detailed description of his proposal with illustrations, and expressed the view that if the Admiralty would give attention to his ideas he would feel well rewarded for his injuries suffered in naval service [Advertisement to the Second Edition, p. vii].[1]

---

[1] The 'language of signals' became a particular concern of two notable admirals who shared his evangelical convictions – Kempenfelt and Gambier. Gambier's handbook, which owed much to Howe's, was the first standardised signal book issued by Admiralty in place of the schemes devised by individual commanders for their own fleets – the cause of

Towards a Better System of Ship Construction
Given his own understanding of mathematics, Ramsay highlighted the
lack of theoretical insight in the designing of warships. British ship-
wrights were perhaps the best practical builders, but while the French
employed their ablest mathematicians to direct the carpenters, ours were
'just handy mechanics, fit to execute but not to plan'. He proposed measures to develop a corps of naval constructors, well versed in the theory
of design, with principles for evaluating hull shape and sailing trim, and
he suggested the value of building whole classes of vessels on proven
lines [XXXV–XXXIX].

Improving Admiralty Oversight
A final clutch of ideas concerned the central direction of the navy. Not
only should the Admiralty enforce a uniform signal code and apply
cogent principles to ship construction: they should also revise the whole
unwieldy set of regulations that governed the sea service – 'that heap
of contradictory instructions by which the navy is pretended to be regulated' [XXXIV]. And why leave so much of importance to private initiative when state provision could be a more efficient supply-master?
Let the Admiralty see that every warship is equipped with a set of up-to-
date charts, regularly checked for their accuracy, and supplied with telescopes at public expense [XXXI, XXXII]. It was all too risky to leave
essentials for masters and captains to purchase out of their own purses –
and, it might be added, for naval surgeons to be expected to buy their
own instruments and medicines, another absurdity in Ramsay's eyes.[1]
In these instances Ramsay was applying the methods of Enlightenment
thinking, familiar to him from his Scottish academic training, to issues
of the day, calling on the resources of reason rather than tradition or
sentiment. But reason, in his mind, was by no means incompatible with
private piety or public religious observance.

Encouraging Religion
Ramsay devotes a page or so of the original edition to religion. The book
reflected the religious outlook of both Ramsay and Middleton, particularly when it recommended Bible reading and personal piety, but it
was not written as a tract and could be read without offence by secular-
minded officers. The *Essay* was true to its theme of a sea officer's duty

much confusion. Gambier's scheme supplemented by Home Popham's additions was used
by Nelson at Trafalgar [see *SIG/B/76 DUP* in NMM collection].
    [1]*Barham Papers*, I, p.48.

and the attributes he would need. Amongst these qualities was 'one particular, not generally regarded indeed; but . . . more essential than all the rest; this is religion, revealed religion, not the religion of deists' [XLI]. When Ramsay wanted to commend biblical faith to 'a man, an accountable creature' and particularly to someone carrying responsibility, he used terminology that was neither pietistic nor overtly evangelical but would be acceptable to a wider range of thought: personal piety would strengthen character and provide inner resources for testing times. Studying the Bible would be educationally beneficial, and would give insight into the will of God.

When it comes to public worship, there is a noticeable difference between the first and third editions. In 1765 when, in spite of the requirement in the *Regulations and Instructions*, divine service was rarely held outside a flagship, he recommended 'the usefulness of keeping up the appearances of religion'. Although sailors are 'reckoned the most profligate of mankind' he was sure that they would become better men for being exposed to religious practice – 'more obedient, more sober, more diligent, and of consequence more healthy, serviceable and more to be depended on'.[1] Fifteen years later Ramsay writes with some knowledge of the beneficial results of a growing religious movement in the navy: 'there never yet was a well regulated orderly ship's company, but where a respect for religion was kept up in public. Religion carries its influence into all the various circumstances of a man's behaviour. It makes him regard himself and every being around him. Where officers promote decency among the men, these become also more obedient, more sober, more diligent, and of consequence more healthy, more serviceable, more to be depended on' [XLII]. In the light of the Seven Years' War Ramsay believed religious observance would have good effects on a ship's company, but in the American War he was sure of it.

Influencing Middleton

At several points the *Essay* shines a light on Middleton (referred to as 'Captain M——') as the example any aspiring young officer should follow. He is commended for the way he gives orders – with clarity and firmness, but never needing to be reinforced by profanity – for his skills in pilotage and his knowledge of the intricacies of Caribbean currents

---

[1]This was also Kempenfelt's opinion, as he explained to Middleton: 'with order and discipline you would increase your force; cleanliness and sobriety would keep your men healthy; and punishments would be seldom, as crimes would be rare'. *Barham Papers*, I, p. 309.

and channels, for his alertness to the moves of the enemy (and his skill in netting prizes for the advantage of himself, his crew and his country), and for the extraordinary breadth of his mind [Conclusion]. Middleton then can safely be taken as the beau ideal of the complete officer, skilled in both seamanship and the arts of command. 'Follow the example of your commander; copy his assiduity, his application to his profession, his attention to every branch of knowledge . . . humanity and goodness of heart . . . regard for virtue and religion' [I, para. 3].

If Ramsay thought highly of his former captain, it is safe to infer that Middleton was no less indebted to him for spiritual guidance – but not for his initial induction into 'vital religion' (as evangelicals were apt to express it). In later years Middleton wrote 'it was to my dear wife's perseverance, as a means, that I owe all I possess of religion'.[1] Thanks to Margaret Gambier, he experienced a religious conversion while ashore sometime before 1753, but thereafter he was much at sea and removed from her direct influence until 1761 when they were married. During these years he obtained his first command in 1757 and began to hold the once-traditional Sunday prayers that had long become rare in private ships. When as a young post captain of less than a year's standing he took command of the *Arundel* in March 1759 he found himself with Ramsay as the ship's surgeon, a man of established Christian conviction who if gifted with ampler means would have become a clergyman. A lifelong friendship developed, which would eventually bear fruit in their collaboration over the movement against slavery, the fitting out of the first convict fleet to Australia, the revision of naval regulations, and Ramsay moving into the parish church of Teston for which Middleton held the right of appointment (advowson). As they served together in the *Arundel* Ramsay devised the idea behind the *Essay*, of urging potential officers to adopt the attitudes he described there, taking none other than Middleton as their exemplar. By the second edition Ramsay would have liked to demonstrate how the mature and experienced Middleton regulated his ship's company – as in the Captain's Order Book in the *Ardent* (1779) with its moral and religious stipulations – but he had no permission to use it.[2]

Nevertheless, it is possible to discern in their collaboration the genesis of a movement of low-church piety operating inside the navy, reviving religious practices once vibrant but by mid-century gravely neglected. The *Admiralty Regulations*, introduced in 1731 and regularly reissued,

[1]Middleton to Rev. C.I. Latrobe, 17 Dec 1792; NMM MID/2/28 (2).
[2]Advertisement to the Second Edition, reprinted 3rd edn, p. vii.

required daily prayers and Sunday service with a sermon, but divine worship was effectively restricted to ships with a clergyman – and far from frequent even then. The quality of chaplains' ministry was variable and rarely even adequate. Although the SPCK would give literature for public worship on request, they were rarely asked. Yet all this inertia slowly gave way to rekindled fervour in the later eighteenth century. Change developed from three men of vision – Middleton the central figure, Kempenfelt and Ramsay perhaps the most original of the three.[1]

It is worth constructing a chronology to demonstrate how interwoven their thinking became. First came Middleton's efforts, tentative at first but growing in boldness, to hold Sunday service and to read a sermon for his crew (1757).[2] Then there was Ramsay's originally anonymous advice, that the aspiring officer should give attention to personal religion and public observance, and that he might well seek the will of God from reading the Bible (1765). In 1775, Middleton drew up his standing orders for the guard ship he commanded, insisting on divine worship every Sunday and taking disciplinary steps to curb drunkenness and moral measures to exclude loose women. In 1779, Ramsay published a collection of sermons that were especially suitable for reading to sailors. Independently of such initiatives, a pair of Methodist laymen were setting up the Naval and Military Bible Society to make personal copies of the Scriptures available to sailors: the first consignment put aboard a man-of-war were 600 Bibles supplied to Kempenfelt's flagship in 1782.[3]

Around the same period Middleton and Kempenfelt were exchanging letters about the state of the fleet and what could be done to improve its moral and fighting qualities. They came to a similar conclusion – that religious observance was beneficial to the men and, by making them more responsive to discipline, would make them better seamen. Here was a key to maximising strength by improving the quality of the human resource. This programme is some distance away from the life-changing

[1]See Richard Blake, *Evangelicals in the Royal Navy, 1775–1815: Blue Lights and Psalm-singers* (Woodbridge, 2008), *passim.*

[2]'I was 16 years in the sea service before I was made a captain, and never, during that time, heard prayers or divine service performed a-board of ship . . . As soon as I became a captain I began reading prayers myself to the ship's company of a Sunday, and also a sermon . . . I did not venture to carry it further than Sundays because the practice was confined to those days by the ships who had chaplains, when followed at all.' *Barham Papers,* II, p. 163.

[3]Middleton's Order Book, HMS *Ardent,* Aug 1775, *Barham Papers,* I, pp. 39–45; Roald Kverndal, 'The 200th Anniversary of Organized Seamen's Missions, 1779–1979', *Mariner's Mirror,* 65 (1979), pp. 255–63; *NMBS Report of Proceedings,* 1804, p. 12; 1847, p. 19.

doctrines of repentance and faith – 'conversion' – so characteristic of Methodist and evangelical piety, but it provided a public space for prayers and even preaching. Once the long-standing instruction to hold divine service according to the Anglican liturgy every Sunday was acted upon, the accompanying requirement for a sermon would have to be met as well. Chaplains might preach their own sermons; captains, if they saw the need for a homily at all, would most likely borrow an address from a published collection of sermons – Ramsay's perhaps, or Stanier Clarke's, or for the more evangelically inclined, Burder's *Cottage Sermons*.[1] And so the opportunity was given for persuasive preaching to do what it might for the souls of His Majesty's sailors.

The religious programme was part of a scheme to transform discipline afloat. Like Ramsay, Kempenfelt was an advocate of cleanliness of persons, uniform clothing and living space, and his wording suggests familiarity with parts of the *Essay*. As chief of staff in the Channel fleet he was well acquainted with the ways in which some ships' companies had been divided into groups of men each under the supervision of a lieutenant – as indeed Middleton had done in the *Ardent* – and he wanted to see such shipboard organisation along with reforms of cleanliness and religion enforced throughout the fleet by order of the admiralty.[2] In 1782, Kempenfelt's death in the loss of the *Royal George* deprived the would-be reformers of their most celebrated figure, but the concept of religious renewal as a way to maximise naval strength was not forgotten by the remaining two.

When Ramsay was his confidential secretary, Middleton compiled a memorandum on the duty of captains, showing his intention of recruiting the awesome authority of commanding officers to serve a programme of moral and spiritual regeneration for the navy.[3] The whole scheme took time to develop, and it was not until 1805, with Middleton in power as First Lord, that he had the undoubted authority to press his ideas on the navy. The revised *Regulations* published the next year set the imprint of Middleton's values on the ruling principles of the fleet for the next seventy years or more. It seems reasonable to infer that he derived the idea of influencing the ethos of the service from the example of his friend Ramsay, who showed how the printed page might be used to shape

---

[1] The Rev. James Stanier Clarke, *Naval Sermons Preached on Board His Majesty's Ship the Impetueux, in the Western Squadron, during its Service off Brest,* 1798; the Rev. George Burder (1752–1832), eventually published 100 *Village Sermons* in 8 vols.

[2] Kempenfelt to Middleton, *Barham Papers,* I, pp. 306–9.

[3] 'Duty of Captains in the Navy', *Barham Papers,* II, pp. 161–5.

thinking and conduct, to mould the values – the soul – of the sea-going service. Ramsay's thinking surfaces in the revised *Regulations*, with ground-breaking *Instructions for the Chaplain*, and directions for the surgeon to use 'consolatory kindness' in treating the sick, and in efforts to give public religious observance a high profile at sea.[1] As one contemporary expressed it, Ramsay had 'done everything in his power, by his writings, to suggest and introduce method, manners and religion into the royal navy', and had 'been the means of awakening the public attention to that reproach to humanity, West Indian slavery'.[2] He left a mark not only on his own age but on decades to come.

Editorial Note

In the text of the Third Edition that follows, ship names have been italicised. Ramsay's footnotes appear in square brackets. Extracts from the First Edition are given where they are of particular interest: they are shown in italics within round brackets.

---

[1] *Regulations and Instructions relating to His Majesty's Service at Sea*, 1806: Sect. 8, chap.1, 'For the Chaplain', pp. 247–9; 'Surgeon', p. 284.
[2] *Barham Papers*, II, p. 254.

The Reverend James Ramsay

AN ESSAY ON
THE DUTY AND QUALIFICATIONS OF
A SEA OFFICER

Third Edition
London
1780

AN ESSAY ON THE DUTY AND QUALIFICATIONS OF A SEA OFFICER

Written originally, Anno 1760, for the Use of two Young Officers

By the Reverend JAMES RAMSAY, Chaplain in his Majesty's Navy.

Tum demum periculo atque negotiis compertum est, in bello plurimum ingenium posse.

SALLUST

THE THIRD EDITION, IMPROVED
LONDON

Printed for G. Robinson, in Pater-noster Row.
MDCCLX

CONTENTS

[Page iv]

SUBSCRIBERS to the Second Edition
[102 names including:]
His Excellency General Vaughan; Right Hon. Earl of Winchelsea;
Hon. Major Damer; His Excellency William Matthew Burt,
Esq. Capt. General
Gentlemen of the Navy
Admiral H. Parker; Commodore Hotham; 22 Captains
Inhabitants of St. Christopher
His Honour the President, Hon. John Fahie, Esq.
72 individual names, and Philo Nauticus[1]

---

[1]Believed to be a pseudonym for Adm Sir Charles Knowles (1754–1828), a capable sea officer interested in signalling, shipbuilding and scientific matters.

[Page v]

N.B. The profits of the first edition, which was published anno 1765, were appropriated to the Magdalen and British Lying-Inn Hospital.
The profits of the second and third editions are intended for the benefit of the Maritime School; or, in case of its failure, the Marine Society.[1]

Preparing for the Press, and intended for the benefit of the same Charity, A Series of Sermons, adapted to the Royal Navy.[2] Those officers who wish to encourage it, or to contribute to the Maritime School by means of it, are requested to give in their names and contributions to the author; or to Messrs. Thomas and William Maud, Downing-street, Westminster; or to the Secretary of the Maritime School.

[Page vi]

TO THE RIGHT HONOURABLE THE LORDS COMMISSIONERS FOR EXECUTING THE OFFICE OF LORD HIGH ADMIRAL, THE FOLLOWING ESSAY IS RESPECTFULLY INSCRIBED, BY THEIR LORDSHIPS
Most obedient and most humble servant,
JAMES RAMSAY

[Page vii]

ADVERTISEMENT TO THE SECOND EDITION

The present edition is offered to the public with considerable corrections and additions. When the essay was first published, the author entertained hopes, that he had led the way to some better pen, in a matter new, and of importance to the public. Fifteen years have elapsed, and

---

[1]The Maritime School was founded in 1777 by Jonas Hanway, merchant and philanthropist, in Chelsea to educate boys for the sea, but it failed to thrive. The Marine Society of 1756 was also founded by Hanway, in conjunction with a magistrate Sir John Fielding, as a charity to take poor boys off London's streets and prepare them for entry into the navy or a career at sea. It recruited thousands for service on the lower deck.
[2]The Rev. James Ramsay, *Sea Sermons, or a Series of Discourses for the Use of the Royal Navy* (1781).

the subject remains as he left it. He has therefore resumed it, at a period when the being of the state depends on the exertion of those, to whose improvement the Essay looks forward. Could he have made free with the regulations drawn up for the use of a particular ship, by the person here proposed as the pattern of his young officers, it would have been more worthy of notice. The diffidence attendant on true modesty withholds that gift from the public. Till it can be overcome, he hopes what is here offered will be favourably received. Though it exceeds the first but little in bulk, it contains several new important articles: that on the language of signals is an attempt to improve on our and the French plan. The author flatters himself it will bear a scrutiny, and may be made to contribute towards completing this branch of the service. Above fifty flags and pendants, many not to be distinguished at any considerable distance, are used in the navy, to express a few unconnected signals. On our plan, 600 signals, which are three times as many as are used, may be made with twenty-four flags, all of them distinct, none of them depending on place for their signification. Did the admiralty-board pay an attention to this alone, the author would think his labour had been well bestowed. His heart is with the service, and the reflection of his having contributed to its advancement, in any part, would be a recompence for hurts received in it, that have met with little other reward.

St. Christopher,

February 22nd, 1780

[Pages vii, viii]

ADDRESS
PREFIXED TO THE FIRST EDITION

To ——— of his Majesty's Navy
SIR,

Had I reckoned myself able to do justice to your merit, your name would have appeared at full length before this Essay. Indeed, I had not the vanity to think that your reputation stood in need of such a herald as I am. The only design of this, if it may be called a dedication, is to make an apology to you for having so often mentioned you in my performance; should you, from circumstances, find out that you are the person intended for the pattern of my two young officers. Both were brought up under you: the last you discovered to have merit, when he acted in a very low character; and you trained him up to do, as a petty officer, more essential service to his country than, in the late extensive war, has fallen to the share of almost any one lieutenant. Therefore your relation to them, as well as your abilities, pointed you out to me as an example fit to be set before them. In truth, if there be any proper advice given to them, it was collected from your conversation, or copied from your behaviour.

Should this Essay be read, and your person be discovered, my wish is, that the world would hear your abilities and virtues mentioned with a candour equal to the modesty with which you carry them. Yet, indeed, for the good of our country, and the indulgence of your modesty, I rather desire, that every good thing, which I have been obliged to say of you, were equally applicable to thousands.

May you long live an ornament to the service, and a blessing to your family and friends.

[Page ix]

ADVERTISEMENT,
PREFIXED TO THE FIRST EDITION.

The following Essay was originally intended for the benefit of two young officers, to whom the author wished well. The first copy was given in 1760, the other in 1762. Had he since seen any thing on the subject in print, he would not have ventured the publication of this. As the subject is important, and, hitherto, has been overlooked, he hopes he has only led the way in it.

It may, perhaps, be supposed, that some things mentioned here are too trifling to be presented to an officer of the rank of a lieutenant; but men acquainted with the navy know, that the meanest article of advice in it, is not beneath the attention of many in that important station. To suppose that all, or the greater part, needed to be so dealt with, would be doing injustice to many accomplished young men of the author's acquaintance.

It was first written in form of a letter; and, though it be now considerably enlarged, yet the author was of opinion, that this form would still be proper for advice of such a familiar sort, and therefore he has continued it.

The latter part was addressed to a young man, who, after being long a common seaman, was distinguished so much by the officer commanding on the station, as to have the separate command of an armed vessel, with the promise of a commission; a reward which every body thought due to his merit, so many brave things, and such important service had been performed by him. When the war was finished, there was no occasion for one of his active turn, and no commission was made out for him. Indeed his total want of education made it necessary to provide for him in another line. But as there are in it hints that may be useful to some young man of merit, who may, like him, want education, and be more persevering in the attainment of it, it is offered, with the rest, to the public.

I once thought of making an apology for the freedom of my remarks. But having had one of the most complete, and one of the worst formed, officers in the navy, to draw my observations from, were I to mention their names, modest good officers would readily allow of my partiality to the first; those who are blame-worthy may easily prefer themselves to the second: so that I might hope to pass uncensured by both.

I have an excuse to offer for the remarks made on the defects of the service. I thought it might be useful to point them out, because, though they cannot be entirely obviated, yet, in the unlimited command which a captain has in his ship, sagacity may always find out little expedients, to make the service suffer less by them; and it is right to make a young officer look up to the higher stations, because opinions, formed early in the service influence the conduct in every successive rank.

[Page 1]

ADDRESS to LIEUTENANT J—— D——on the Charibbean (*sic*) Station[1]

Dear Sir,

I was insensibly drawn into the conversation which gave rise to the promise that I am now attempting to execute, by several openings which you yourself gave me. A fixed esteem for the person who was the subject of our discourse, and a desire to see Mr. D. imitate his example, and rise by his steps, made me pursue it farther than I should have ventured with

---

[1]Of names listed in David Syret and R.L. DiNardo (eds), *The Commissioned Sea Officers of the Royal Navy, 1660–1815* (NRS Occasional Publication 1, 1994), the most likely is John Leigh Douglas, a Lt of 17 June 1760. He was promoted Cdr, 17 Sept 1777; Capt, 5 May 1779; RA of the blue, 1 June 1799; and eventually became Adm of the white, 21 July 1810 shortly before his death on 13 Nov 1810. Capt J. Douglas was a subscriber to Second Edition.

one of less sense and less good-nature than yourself. You can indulge the impertinence of a friend, when you know it proceeds from a concern for your reputation and success. You observed how fortunate it was for you to serve with Captain *** in a station where you could remark his actions, and form yourself, as an officer, on his plan. A pleasure which I had in observing the method and consistency of captain *****'s conduct, and a desire to inform myself of the nature and extent of the service, which, since I have been in the navy, I have ever indulged, encouraged me, at that time, to mention some particular things, which I judged worthy of your attention, as an officer, who, following so excellent an example, had the ambition to hope to rise to an extensive command in the service of your country.

Far be it from me to assume the appearance of a knowledge superior to you, in a profession in which you are bound, both by duty and honour, to be well skilled. I beg Mr. D. may do me the justice to believe, that, whatever air of an adviser I might unwittingly put on, I wished in it to express the anxiety of a friend, uneasy lest any thing that could contribute to complete you should be neglected by you. In respect to the duty of an officer, I am, in my station, an unconcerned spectator; as such, it lies more in my way to observe little failures and defects in the management of persons in that active station than they can be supposed to do themselves, while employed in matters of greater importance. Of these I endeavoured to remind you, and in the warmth of a friendship, which you kindly acknowledged, promised to put in writing my sentiments concerning them. To pretend farther would be beyond my province, and might be deemed an affront. Interpret my endeavours with candour, and receive them with kindness, and I shall think myself obliged.

[Page 3]

I. Extensive Knowledge necessary in a Sea Officer.

It is too general an opinion in the sea service, to suppose few qualifications necessary to complete an officer. If he be able to direct the boatswain in strapping a block, or stowing an anchor; if he can bustle, and make work appear to go briskly on in the ship; if in battle he shows insensibility amidst fire and smoke, he is pronounced a brave experienced officer. But if we consider a navy commander (and all lieutenants ought to know as much as they) in the view of a person to whose care his country has committed a considerable number of fellow-citizens, to distribute impartial justice among them, to protect them from injury, to find out the particular genius of each individual (*particular qualifications of each man under him)*, that he may be put in that station where he can do the public best service; if we consider him as a person to whom are committed the honour and safety of his country, which may suffer either through his indiscretion in transacting affairs with foreigners, or want of courage and conduct in fight; if we consider him by his rank, by the respect which he owes himself, by what is paid him by the public; as obliged to shew himself the gentleman, in strictness of manners, politeness, useful learning, and nice honour; our notions of a complete officer will be greatly enlarged, and many endowments added to that necessary one, of being a practical seaman.

Indeed, even in this branch, which the tar so confidently appropriates to himself, he is deficient. He can waer [*sic* – wear] and stay a ship, he can manage her in the most violent gale, and you are safe in almost every circumstance, when he is on deck: but he knows nothing of the principles of his art; and if any difficulty arises, in which experience has not before suggested a remedy, he can draw none from his store of general knowledge; nor at once apply the fundamental rules of his profession to circumstance or contingency. He does everything by rote; and so wedded is he to his own particular manner, and so far from being able to discover anything useful in practice, by the application of general principles, or to make an advantage of the discoveries of others, that every improvement must literally be beat into his head before he can be brought to use it. To be convinced of the truth of this, only recollect the reception which Hadley's quadrant at first met with amongst mere seamen, and the contempt with which they treat every endeavour towards ascertaining the longitude.[1] What a seaman knows, or will allow of, is confined within his own narrow experience. He would laugh at your ignorance, should you call his ship a machine, or assert that her motions may be explained from the properties of a simple lever. How much more satisfactory to such a man would it have been, how much farther might he have carried his experience, had he laid a proper foundation in mathematics, had he known the principles of mechanics and geometry.

---

[1]John Hadley (1682–1744) in 1731 devised a double-reflecting octant (which was termed a quadrant), enabling much more accurate navigational sights to be taken. The Board of Longitude was set up in 1714 to encourage by grants of money the discovery of a sure way of measuring longitude at sea. Lunar and other astronomical observations provided a possible solution after complex mathematical calculation. The problem was largely solved once John Harrison had invented a timepiece so accurate that the time lapse between the Greenwich meridian and local noon anywhere in the world could be reliably measured. Harrison constructed four chronometers of revolutionary accuracy between 1735 and 1760. His fourth, the size of a large pocket watch, earned him a £10,000 prize from the Board in 1765.

Be persuaded, nothing can enter into the character of a good, a brave, an accomplished, skilful, learned or a public-spirited man, that would not shine with lustre in the person of a sea officer, while rendering happy his fellow-citizens committed to his care; and conducting, to that noblest purpose, the safety and glory of his country, one of the proper bulwarks of the state. Follow the example of your commander; copy his assiduity, his application to his profession, his attention to every branch of knowledge that can better the man, or add skill to the officer. Imitate that humanity, and goodness of heart, that never left a generous or friendly action undone for the man of merit or misfortune, that was under his care, or known to him. Transcribe into your own practice that sincere regard for virtue and religion, which, in him, doubles the value of every other qualification. Then will you have formed yourself a pattern for future young officers: then will you have done your part towards wiping off the reproach that is too generally thrown on the profession.

II.   Necessity of Method

In every piece of duty which you carry on, consider if your commander were spectator, would your manner please him; will he approve of it when finished. In all sea duty, the preparation for the thing takes up more than double the time necessary for the execution, and gives twice the trouble. It is in foreseeing, and making the necessary preparation, and so rendering the execution easy, that he shews a peculiar address and skill. Recollect how, in one fourth part of the time spent on other frigates, his ship was careened in the same unhealthy place, and, amidst several obstacles, got ready for sea; by which he saved the health of his people, and was in the way of enriching himself and them, by annoying the enemy. But remember what preparation was made for it; how every thing that could be done beforehand was completed, how every thing that could be carried on at sea was postponed, till we quitted that sickly spot; and in what exact order all was pushed forward under his own eye. Endeavour to acquire his method. Before execution, run every part over in your mind, weigh each well, and observe the order in which it will naturally fall. But to do this requires you to be a complete master of what you are going to execute.

III.   Accuracy of Manner

You will irrevocably lose yourself, if you ever accustom yourself to slobber over the most trifling part of your duty. Do everything with the same exactness and briskness, as if the lord high-admiral was present, and with the same care as if the safety of the ship depended on it: for indolence, if indulged, will grow on you, and a habit of slothfulness and indifference, which you can never shake off. You will come to look with the same unconcern on the most important, as on the most trifling parts of your duty; your commander will place no confidence in you; you will become an encumbrance to the service. Take the following example:

When a ship is in her usual trim, the wind moderately brisk, and the men properly stationed, if the officer on deck pays due attention to her, orders the helm down when the sails are full, seizes the critical moment just before the wind comes right a-head, to hawl [sic] the mainsail; is careful to have the head-sails duly tended, the tacks hawled briskly down, and the yards braced up, the ship will never miss stays, or lose much head-way in the manoeuvre. But if the ship be on her station, and the officer think it of no consequence whether she stays or waers; without being at much pains to station the people, he orders the helm down when the sails are shivering, and the ship has already lost her way; the head sails are neglected, or he hawls the main-sail too soon; or he suffers the ship to fall too much off; the consequence is, he either is disappointed in his intention of staying the ship, and so loses both time and ground; or she drives too leeward before she can be brought to the wind. By doing this usually with an air of indifference, he becomes incapable of doing it briskly when necessary in chace [sic]. And you are sensible, that, on this station particularly, the enemy is so very expert in managing his small vessels (*their sloop privateers*), that many a capture has been missed by no greater distance than has been lost in being obliged to waer, after being baulked in an attempt to stay the ship. – Besides, this spirit of indolence spreads wide among the people: they catch the infection, and never obey with briskness a sleepy officer. And if they be once taught this lifeless manner of doing things, it will cost many a blow, many a punishment, to restore them to vigour and alacrity.

IV.   Of forwarding the Duty of Warrant Officers

I have observed lieutenants, who are brisk in carrying on that branch of duty which they take under their own inspection; but if a warrant officer, a carpenter, or a gunner, comes to ask a few men, to do something fully as necessary, often he is sent off with this answer, not delivered in the most gracious terms, 'I can't spare them from the duty of the ship:' as if their province was not indeed the duty of the ship equally with what is carrying on under his own eye, which generally is in the boatswain's or the master's department: for such men take pleasure in usurping the office of these last; and their talents were mistaken, when they were advanced to a station, which gives them the command over them.

This is to have a confined notion of an officer's duty; and, in truth, it occasions many clogs to the service. A lieutenant ought to consider himself as the protector and patron (*encourager*) of every officer under him, and should promote the duty of each equally. From his rank and command in the ship, he can do the same work with fewer hands than an inferior officer, and therefore should never starve their part, to get his own finished quickly. It looks something like the low ambition of a schoolboy, in getting first done with his task. Instead of fixing himself in the boatswain's place, on the gangway, to see the cask hoisted in, a lieutenant should be, by turns, in every place, to keep the people at work on their guard, and to encourage them by his presence: for every particular branch of ship duty is assigned to a particular warrant officer, who must see it done, and be answerable for it. A lieutenant properly speaking, has no particular duty, but, under the captain, has the controul (*sic*) and direction of the whole.

V.   Of Harbour Duty.

Custom has thrown great part of the harbour duty of the ship on the first lieutenant, so that the other lieutenants have little else to do but to go and saunter their time away on shore, in the sea-port towns. There they often form very low connections, that check their ambition, and for ever prevent their rise. But the chief reason for mentioning this absurdity in the service is, that, by being frequently absent from their duty, they are ignorant of what is going on in the ship; and if, at any time they meddle with the work, they confuse rather than promote it: hence, when the first lieutenant, on any occasion, leaves the ship to them, the duty is at a stand till he returns. This custom you ought carefully to avoid, lest you acquire a habit of sauntering, and, which is a possible case, lest you forget your duty.

Though, as second lieutenant, you will seldom have the direction of the work, or the employing of the people, yet, to carry on the duty should be your chief business and pleasure. Inform yourself of what is doing, and is to be done: observe how any thing in hand might have been better executed; and foresee every thing before it be necessary to set about it. If you take this care you will never be at a loss, when the direction and command devolves on you. The work will go equally on; and, in a manner that cannot give offence, you will have an opportunity of correcting any little mistake that may have escaped the first officer.

VI. Of Second Captains

This customary duty of a first officer, naturally suggests a necessity of establishing in the navy an intermediate rank between the lieutenant and captain. Such an officer is the second captain in the French navy. His duty should be to superintend the other officers, and be answerable for the state and condition of the ship. He should be an experienced officer, and thoroughbred seaman. The rank of master and commander should be done away. All lieutenants of a certain standing should be advanced to this rank by seniority; no young officer should ever be brought forward into it.

All twenty-gun ships and under should be commanded by second captains. Lieutenants of any standing may be advanced at one step to the rank of post-captain in frigates or line of battle ships; but each such ship should have a second captain, an experienced man. The step from second to post captain should also be open, but not be necessary. By this regulation every ship would have an experienced officer in the first or second post: old lieutenants would be raised to a respectable station, without interest or solicitation; the duty of lieutenant would be confined to young men capable of enduring the fatigue; and advancement to the rank of post captain, without passing through that of second, being open to young men of merit or influence, the rank of admiral would more frequently than at present fall to the share of men in the vigour of life. Our navy officers are in general too old before they rise to be admirals: hence the difficulty of selecting a sufficient number to command our numerous squadrons. And it has also happened, by the present constitution of the navy, that a ship has not had an experienced officer either in her captain or among her lieutenants. Both these inconveniencies might be avoided by the arrangement above.* And that it might be less expensive to the public, let the present senior lieutenants continue to serve till there were vacancies to receive them.

[* This was particularly felt in the beginning of 1778. There were instances where the captain and his officers were almost all minors. Yet, though there had just been a numerous promotion of admirals, it was found necessary, on the fitting out of Byron's squadron,[1] to raise a captain

---

[1]John Byron (1723–86) survived the loss of the *Wager* off the coast of Chile in 1740. In 1764 he commanded the *Dolphin* on an exploration voyage in the Pacific. As a vice-admiral during the American War he took command in the West Indies from the highly capable Adm Barrington early in 1779, fought indecisive battles against d'Estaing's force off

to the rank of commodore in it, for want of admirals fit for service. Second captains in frigates and line of battle ships might have the pay of masters and commanders, without the privilege of their usual number of servants.]

VII.   Of encroaching on the Men's own Time

Never use yourself to that inhuman and inconsiderate custom of calling all hands, on every trifling accident. Avoid it especially by night. If you expect the men to behave briskly, allow them their hours of rest and meals; and never without the strongest necessity break in upon them.

VIII.   Of searching into their Behaviour.

It is derogating from the character of an officer, to be peeping and prying into the little actions of the people, in order to cavil and find fault; but he seldom ought to overlook a fault committed in his sight, or complained of to him. He should never punish till he has made the criminal, or at least the by-standers sensible of the fault. The stopping of grog in the West Indies is a very common punishment, and often abused. It is part of the men's provisions, and essential to their health; it, therefore, should seldom be taken from them, unless to punish drunkenness or nastiness, and not above a day or two at one time.

IX.   Of correcting Seamen.

It is unbecoming an officer himself to beat the people. In faults that require immediate redress, the boatswain's mate should be ordered to correct them. They dread to fall into his hands, and it prevents the appearance of passion in you, than which nothing hurts an officer's authority more among the people.

In their mutual complaints never grudge the trouble of finding out the guilty person that he alone may be punished. But if both, as frequently is the case, be equally in fault, send them not away without correction, lest each think himself right, and repeat the crime. Punish both. They will be peaceable, and will take care not to offend.

Grenada and St Kitts in July, found no way to blockade Martinique effectively, and did not manage to relieve the pressure on the British in North America. Ramsay was highly critical of his performance – 'never was so mighty a force kept doing so little'. *Barham Papers*, I, p. 47.

X.   Of private Courts Martial

I have long thought, that constituting a court of justice (*equity*) on board ship would be attended with good effects. The bench might consist of the commission and warrant officers: the jury might be taken from among the petty officers, with an exception to young lads, midshipmen. The captain should summon them (*preside, and have a negative*), and his authority should be necessary for the execution of the sentence. Their power to punish should be enlarged beyond what is at present allowed the captain, but should not extend to life, limb, or any dangerous number of lashes (*beyond an hundred lashes*). It should have no power over a commission or warrant officer: but, at the requisition of the officer censured or confined, may be assembled, to establish the matter of fact respecting him; and its decision shall be sufficient ground for a court martial to proceed immediately to judgment, without any new enquiry into the merits of the cause. Every sentence should be recorded.

The court should be regulated by act of parliament: thus the punishment would be more awful, and strike a greater terror into the minds of the people. By the present constitution of the navy, the captain cannot effectually punish many crimes, that are not proper or convenient to be brought before a court martial: or, if he exceeds his power (*a little to punish properly*), he is in danger to be called to, not always, a fair account. On the other hand, such a court would be a check on officers of a tyrannical disposition, without injuring their just authority.

XI.   Of Attention due to the Men.

It is often matter of complaint in the navy, that officers value themselves and their concerns too highly, and despise those under them more than humanity allows of. I cannot help saying, I have seen too much of this unfeeling behaviour. Their most trifling matters are generally preferred to the most important interests of people beneath them. Such officers appropriate every indulgence to themselves, and will not permit others to enjoy even what is compatible with the service. For instance: a poor fellow, lately pressed, informs them, that he observes a ship, which owes him six months wages, just getting under way from the road. He is answered, 'There is no boat to spare;' and perhaps is damned into the bargain for his impertinence in troubling them. In a few minutes after this, the steward is sent ashore to buy a few greens for the officer's dinner, and the boat is ordered to attend and bring him off. – Give not the men occasion of saying this of you. When a person, especially one under your command, solicits a good office from you, suppose yourself in his place, consider the consequence of the thing desired, and how ill you could bear a refusal. I need not make the inference. To have the power to oblige, and to embrace the opportunity, is god-like. Be not, like some men, glad of an occasion of refusing a common civility, that may be performed without expence or trouble. If you value yourself, shew it in being above a mean or a selfish action, in making all around you happy, not, in taking advantage of your station, to be insensible of the interest of your people, fellow-creatures committed to your care, and looking up for happiness from you. Indeed, if you make a conscience of your duty, you are not left at liberty to use them otherwise than well. They have a right to your attention, and to every indulgence, not encroaching on the good of the service.

XII.   Of the People's Amusements

During a voyage, or cruise, seamen amuse themselves with various rude diversions, at leisure hours, especially in the afternoon. They should be encouraged in them, and little rewards be proposed for him that excelled in agility and address. The play is generally rough, and many a hard blow is given and received in pure sport, which enures them to pain and perseverance. It is therefore particularly useful for boys, and growing-up lads, for making them hardy, and capable of enduring the buffetings that they must meet with in the service.

Again, in the night-watches, they are fond of singing. The songs generally turn on the honour of the service, and the sailors' attachment to the other sex. From what circumstance it has happened I cannot say, but the music, in general, is plaintive and slow. I would propose a collection of sea-songs to be made, and printed at the public charge, and distributed among our ships of war. Premiums should be offered for the best odes, or ballads, on our several celebrated sea actions. For example, the late fate of the *Quebec* [1] would be a good subject.

---

[1] On 6 Oct 1779, the 32-gun frigate *Quebec* (Capt George Farmer) engaged the more powerfully armed French frigate *Surveillante* (40) off Brest. The *Quebec* caught fire when her mizzen fell and a sail was set alight by her own muzzle-flashes. Farmer died and 150 lives were lost when she blew up after what was regarded as a most creditable fight. *Surveillante*, badly mauled, reached safety in port.

I see not why our poet laureate might not be employed in collecting and composing ballads for the use of our seamen. As our sovereign, I hope, will always have a claim to the title of King of Ships, may not the annual birth-day odes consider him in that light, and be adapted to seamen, a loyal and most useful part of his subjects. In every thing that concerns the public, sentiment should be interested. It is by considering themselves as participating in the glory of old England, that our seamen have effected incredible things. By falling in with their customs, and feelings, this sentiment may be wrought up into a professional habit.

XIII.   Of Attention to Cleanliness and Cloathing.

It is a very important branch of attention to the men, to keep the ship clean and sweet, the people neat, and well clothed: thus only can you have an healthy vigorous ship's company. Indeed, this is a matter of such general consequence in the navy, that it should not be left, as at present, to the good sense of the officers (*with your present commander you will see that so properly attended to, that you will naturally ever after take care of it*). It ought to be subjected to one fixed general rule, every breach of which should be marked in the log-book, with the reason added; that the state of the crew may be compared with the obedience paid to the regulation. To keep the ship healthy, or, when sickly, to make her so, is much more in the (*captain and*) officers than in the surgeon's power.

(*To guard effectually against nastiness*) The times of cleaning the ship, which should respect the hold and orlop equally with the lower deck, should come in rotation (*at least twice a week*). Every officer, both commission and petty, should take care of the cleanliness and cloathing of some one part of the ship's company. For there can no reason be given why seamen should not, equally with soldiers, be made answerable for their slops; and if it were once a regulation to take account of them every month, it would give little trouble, and would prevent many a dangerous disorder, arising from colds caught, through want of cloaths, and the use of those fiery spirits for which they are bartered.

XIV.   Of Berthing the Seamen.

Here we must take notice of that improper custom of berthing the people by larboard and starboard watch. Hence, in a large ship, there may be three hundred men on one side, lying as close together asleep, as if stowed in one bed. It is impossible for them to get one mouthful of fresh air in this situation. They are surrounded with, and breathe an atmosphere of, highly volatilized perspired matter, which proves no small cause of the scurvy, and helps to produce those infectious fevers so frequent in the navy. Besides this injury to the seamen's health, the ship's going on a wind is injured, as often as the watch turns in on the lee side; for then the weight of half the ship's company presses her to leeward, and impedes her way. I have known officers observe, in this case, that the ship went worse, but not allow it to arise from the windward watch's being on deck (*because the people were in their hammocks on the lee side*). Now, if the watches were berthed alternately, every single man would have the room of two to breathe and sleep in; and the ship's way would be equal on both tacks. This was the method on board the *Swiftsure*,[1] in the beginning of the war of 1756; and, compared with other ships on the same service, she was remarkably healthy. The only objection is the difficulty of turning up the watch; but, if a rule be made, that the man who turns in shall see the hammock on each side clear, there will be little trouble left to the officer.

XV.   Of Inferior Officers.

Inferior officers of long standing brook ill the command of young officers: building on their experience, they are apt to raise difficulties in the execution of orders. You, therefore, must be careful to weigh every objection before-hand that can be started, and to deliver your commands in so clear a manner, as that no reasonable difficulty may be found in them. If they begin to raise obstacles, you may easily perceive if they do it with a design to puzzle. In this case, without giving a reason, insist on the performance: nay, rather than make your authority cheap, allow some small irregularities to pass uncorrected, even after you are sensible of them, till your command be firmly established among them. For think not that you always deal with reasonable men, who can suppose a man to be skilful, though guilty of an oversight.

On the other hand, do not, through obstinacy or positiveness, hurt the service or bring yourself into difficulties, to get out of which you must have recourse to the assistance of those whose counsel you before despised. When proceeding neither from irresolution nor easiness of temper there is a greatness of mind in condescending to the advice of others. In the storm off Louisburg, September 1757, admiral Holbourn[2] ordered

---

[1]*Swiftsure* – a 3rd rate of 1750.
[2]Francis Holburne, Capt, Feb 1740; RA, 1755 (d. 1771). *Newark* – a 3rd rate of 1695, finally broken up in 1787. Attempting to draw De la Motte and his force out of Louisburg,

the *Newark*'s main-tacks and sheets to be cut away: the mate, stationed at them, ordered them to be kept fast, till he had spoken to the admiral; he represented the consequence to be the rolling away of the ship's masts: the admiral saw it, kept all fast, and thanked and advanced his adviser. Perhaps it would be difficult to find in the life of that experienced officer a more praise-worthy action. Hardly inferior to the wisdom which can advise, is that which enables us to know what advice it is expedient to take. And, as a duty which you owe to your humanity, and as a respect due to their service, be careful to shew every possible regard to the advice of such experienced men, and to allow them every indulgence that circumstances will admit of.

Preserve a respect to every one who acts in any office under you. If you wish them to support any authority among the people, regard them yourself: in obeying petty officers, seamen are directed by the esteem such are in among the officers. Particularly regard midshipmen; lately you were one yourself: they will one day be officers, and ought not to be accustomed to a slavish submission. Those who have been treated haughtily become tyrants in their turn: generous treatment inspires generosity. I have often amused myself in tracing, in their pupils, the manners of our great naval officers. The faults of midshipmen ought not to be overlooked; but they are not to be punished as common seamen. To beat a midshipman, if he takes it patiently, renders him unworthy of being made an officer.

XVI.   Of supplying the Navy with Petty and Warrant Officers.

The difference between our peace and our war establishment is so great, that, when an armament is to be suddenly fitted out, trade is distressed, and our ships of war are filled with men raw and unacquainted with the service. This was found a very serious circumstance when we began to arm in 1778. I would propose, that a statute should be enacted, by which every man's age, on his going to sea, should be registered in the port from which he sailed; and that none under the age of twenty, at the time of passing the act, should be advanced to the rank of master, or mate, of

---

Holburne's squadron was operating off the North American coast on 24 Sept 1757 when it was beset by a sudden and unexpected hurricane which threatened to wreck his ships on a lee shore. When all seemed lost, the wind veered and Holburne's force was saved. Six ships were dismasted, his squadron shattered, and it was reckoned a feat of seamanship that they made it back to Halifax. Julian Corbett, *England in the Seven Years' War* (1907; Folio Soc edn 2001), pp. 131–2.

a merchant-ship, until he had served a determined time in the navy. The service should be open to such men, and they should have their discharge freely, when the time was expired. While in the navy they should be made conversant with every branch of the service, particularly sea-gunnery, and the language of signals. This would enable them to defend themselves, and behave well when under convoy.

Merchant ships, above a certain tonnage, should be obliged to carry artillery in time of peace. Some discreet half-pay officer should be settled, with a small additional salary, at each of our principal ports, to examine into the warlike state of the ship, and to see that the crews be properly trained. Each merchant ship, in proportion to her tonnage, should be obliged to carry a certain number of supernumeraries, for whom the public should, in all branches of trade, where there is danger of rivalship, allow a small bounty.*

[* This is the suggestion of that true friend to mankind and his country, Mr.Hanway.[1]]

In time of peace ships of war should carry double the usual establishment of petty officers. Every petty officer should be brought forward in navigation, piloting, gunnery, and the language of signals. Ships should be continually going round our several stations. Officers, out of employment, that wished to visit any particular station, should be received as passengers, only being obliged to communicate their observations to the admiralty-board at their return. Ships, while on their stations, should be employed in taking soundings, ascertaining channels, making observations. Stations, which have been studied by particular officers, should be registered at the admiralty, that, in time of actual service, they may be supplied with proper commanders. A want of this caution has often produced untoward consequences.

Merchant ships, of a certain tonnage, in all distant voyages, should be obliged to carry surgeons, who have passed an examination.[2] The want

---

[1]Jonas Hanway (1712–86), founder of the Marine Society, became a commissioner for victualling the navy 1762–83 and was a friend of Middleton. Although not quite an evangelical, he was deeply concerned for religion amongst the seafaring community. James Stephen Taylor, *Jonas Hanway: Founder of the Marine Society* (London and Berkeley, 1985).
[2]Eighteenth century surgeons entered their profession by one of two routes. Some undertook the seven-year apprenticeship and examination of the Company of Barber-Surgeons; others came through a university and hospital teaching school. Until 1745 all entrants to the navy

of proper men in this branch has been severely felt in this war of 1778. Indeed, though one of the most necessary officers, a surgeon is the least regarded, being at the end of every war, turned a-drift to starve, without friends, without a settlement, without employment.*

[* In the war of 1756, there was such a proportion of experienced lieu-tenants, that masters were not then greatly accounted of. But in this of 1778, so many raw lads have been made lieutenants, that in too many ships, the master is an officer of the first importance: yet he, as well as the surgeon, is left to be supplied by chance, and equally with him is turned a-drift to starve when the war is over. The small number of each on the half pay list is not to be taken into account; the provision being confined and inadequate.

The sinecure places of two tellers of the exchequer would provide for both these useful ranks of officers.]

Did we resolve on such measures as these, an enemy could never take us unprepared. At a very small expense, we should secure peace and respect among our neighbours.

XVII.   Of the Character of the Ship's Company.

Officers are apt to complain, that they have a bad ship's company, and that they cannot carry on the service with them. A ship may contain a greater or less number of thorough-bred seamen; but otherwise, when men will not obey, it is a strong presumption of the officers themselves being wanting in application, and that they have not done their duty in training them to obedience. All bodies of men have like passions, like affections, and generally are pretty equally mixed as to good and bad. What one mixed number can be brought to perform, all other such may be rendered capable of. The ship's company is good where the officers are good: where they want application, the crew is mutinous and lazy. It is indeed more in the lieutenants than in the captain's power to form the men: they are constantly among the people, and see their behaviour. He, to preserve his authority for emergencies, must seldom interpose. He can only give orders to his officers; and, if they be not actuated by the like

were assessed by examination at Barber-Surgeons' Hall, and thereafter by the Company of Surgeons. Successful applicants were recommended to the Navy Board who would issue a warrant as surgeon or surgeon's mate appointed to a particular ship. Naval service often opened the way to a private practice later ashore.

spirit, he must repeat every order as often as he means it to be complied with; even then there will be neglect and carelessness.

XVIII.   Of the utility of forms

Many advantages are lost to the navy for want of an attention to form. In their own hours, the people should be left to themselves; officers should not meddle with, or interrupt them. They will fancy themselves free, and exert the vigour of free men when the service calls on them. But certain forms, or ceremonies, should mark their union as a body, in carrying on the public service that solemnity, order, and combination of force may accompany every act of duty. Society aims at giving one heart and one hand to many; forms, therefore, which attain this, may be called the life of society. That society is most perfect, which adheres most strictly to them. It is form or habit, that distinguishes regular forces from a mob. The fifer, drummer, or trumpeter, is therefore, a necessary man in the execution of every piece of service.

Every seaman should wear an uniform; one fitted for work, another for parade. Their days of exercise, or parade, should come in rotation. Caps, linen, in short, every article of dress, should have some mark interwoven, or impressed, on its substance; to shew that he who wears it is of the navy. An anchor on the button, and a blue colour, should be general. Caps, cuffs, and collars, should distinguish ships and commanders. Thus might seamen be attached to the character of their ship, and her commander, and be made to value themselves as composing too respectable a body to behave ill or desert the service. Desertion indeed, would be more difficult than at present if every article of his dress discovered the man who wore it to belong to the navy.

XIX.   Of Discipline.

It has been frequently matter of admiration to me, how officers, who are esteemed in proportion to their martial qualifications, and whose characters depend on the effort which their ships are able to make in fight, can excuse themselves for paying so little attention to the discipline of their men, as one may generally observe in the navy. Our countrymen possess a large share of natural courage, and we out-number our present enemy (1760) greatly in ships. But should the time come, that brings us nearer to an equality, they pay so much attention to arms, that we may well dread the consequence, unless the teaching of our people the use of great guns and small-arms becomes also more general. At present, this part of the service depends wholly on the good sense of the captain and his officers. Yet surely it may be the object of a general regulation, and be subjected to certain rules. After all, the exertion of the ship's company will sufficiently depend on the attention which the officers pay to discipline.* It will hardly be believed, that ever a King's ship should be nine months in commission, in time of war, before an ounce of powder had been expended in exercising; yet to two such have I belonged, where the people also were raw and inexperienced, but the officers some of the oldest in the navy.

[* An officer, answering to the rank of adjutant-general, and having a similar power, might be usefully employed in each naval port. He might be taken from the list of admirals, that he may command all private captains, and should have a power of enquiring into the state of discipline in each ship, and of correcting abuses in it. While the ship is fitting out in the several ports, all the petty officers and captains of the guns should, in rotation, be exercised ashore, by some experienced artillery officer, acting under the adjutant-general.]

From your captain's practice, when he commanded us, I know the orders for exercising will be strict in your ship: and it is your province, as lieutenant at arms, to see them carried into execution. As there may be accidents that will turn small-arm men to great guns, and those at great guns to small-arms, you ought, as fast in rotation as possible, to make the whole ship's company expert at both. Particularly, you should teach the use of the firelock to those quartered in the tops (who should be the smartest and most active little fellows in the ship), to those on the fore-castle, to the boats crews (*who will be frequently called to such duty*); and to those armed with a musket, or pistols, at the great guns. It is also necessary to have a proper number of the stoutest men in the ship selected for boarding, who ought to have the arms fit for that service at their other quarters, ready, should an occasion offer. A neglect of this last precaution has often deprived officers of the fairest opportunities of doing their country and the service honour.

XX.   Of Obedience in Time of Action.

Seamen are apt to throw away their fire, without regard to orders; and it is excused with saying, it is impossible to prevent it. But, why should not the same attention to orders be paid in the sea, as in the land service? I am sure at sea it is much more necessary; and as seamen are more under the eye of their officers than soldiers, it might be expected that they should be more under command. The very cause of giving power to officers is, that the body of men, under their direction, may act with one heart and one hand. Be distinct and methodical in your orders; and in every thing that is carried on enforce silence. Whooping and hollooing ought to be punished as severely as the passing an earing wrong. I always remarked with pleasure the exact order, deep silence, and strict attention, that reigned throughout the ship, when your captain gave command on going into English harbour. If you and his other officers assist him, the same will be practised in an engagement; and if so, what is it such a ship's company, as he has now formed, may not perform?

XXI.   Of Bringing the Ship into Action

To insure success, it is not only necessary that your men be properly trained, and quartered, but also that the ship be brought into action in such a manner as may annoy the enemy most, with the least hazard and loss to your own ship and men: for though you may acquire the character of intrepid, by running down to engage at a disadvantage, and, if you succeed, may add to your fame, by the shattered condition of your ship, and the number of your killed and wounded; yet, (*in reality,*) when you run into any unnecessary hazard, by omitting to take an advantage which occasion, or skill, offers, to secure an easy victory, you are unjust to your country, and cruel to your men. (*It is said to have been a punctilio of this sort that occasioned the* Marlborough *to be shattered in the manner she was in Matthews's engagement:*[1] *and in this war the* Thunderer *when she took the* Achilles.[2])

In bringing the ship into action, where circumstance points out no particular mode, the best general rule is to take the lead from the enemy, and

---

[1]Thomas Mathews (1676–1751) was C-in-C Mediterranean in 1744 when his fleet encountered an inferior force of French and Spanish ships off Toulon. Without waiting to form line Mathews engaged bravely, but without support from his second-in-command Richard Lestock he failed to achieve a victory. Relying on the Fighting Instructions, which required that a fleet form line of battle, Lestock escaped blame, while Mathews was cashiered.

In the action Mathews in the *Namur*, flanked by *Marlborough* (90) and three others, engaged the Spanish flagship *Real Felipe* (114) and her supporters, but *Namur* and *Marlborough* both suffered much damage and casualties.

[2]In July 1761 HMS *Thunderer* (74) under Capt Charles Proby pursued the French 64-gun *Achille* and a 32-gun frigate off Cadiz. Proby had superior forces with him but suffered heavy casualties (17 killed, 17 mortally wounded, 86 wounded) when he engaged the *Achille*. Much of the loss was caused when a quarter-deck gun exploded.

to make the attack where least expected. For example, the *Eagle* bore
down on the *Duc d'Aquitain*, and made a feint of engaging her on the
weather-side:[1] but while the enemy was busy in getting ready to receive
her there, she suddenly bore under her stern, and gave her whole fire,
before a shot could be returned (*from the lee-side*). How to act in particular situations will be best learned by conversing, on your profession,
with experienced officers, and by observing, in your reading, through
what address such a particular action was successful; through what error
such another failed. Indeed, to the honour of the service, there have not
been more than two or three unsuccessful single actions, this war, where
the enemy excelled (*us*) in seamanship.*

[* It is remarkable that the actions of 1778 and 1779, under Vernon,
Keppel and Byron, were all between squadrons on different tacks.[2] As
our ships are usually disabled early in battle, if this mode becomes general, the battle must always be indecisive, and, at least apparently, in
favour of the enemy. Could we, by the bow and quarter line, contrive
with our best going ships to take up, each in succession, the enemy's
bad going ships on the same tack, we should effect something of consequence, and oblige the enemy to come to close fight, or abandon their
rear. In entering on action it is a rule to keep the ship under command, or
under sail, that she may not be engaged to a disadvantage. If the inferior
ship be chaced, it is generally prudent to get on the tack opposite to her
enemy, that she may rake or keep on her quarter. The chacing ship generally engages on the quarter, and if she can get near enough to leeward.
When a squadron chaces, it would seem to be necessary, where possible,
to take the weather-gage.]

[1]On 30 May 1757, the *Duc d'Aquitain* French East Indiaman, powerfully armed, was
captured after an hour's defence by two British 64s acting together, the *Eagle* (Capt
Hugh Palliser) and *Medway* (Capt Charles Proby). British casualties were ten dead and
ten wounded.
[2]On 27 July 1778, Adm Keppel engaged a French fleet of similar strength under the Comte
d'Orvilliers in the indecisive battle of Ushant – notorious for the Keppel-Palliser court
martial which followed. On 10 Aug 1778, Cdre Sir Edward Vernon with four sail was
pitted against a French squadron of five vessels under Commodore Tronjolli off Pondi-
cherry; Vernon's ships, crippled aloft, were unable to pursue their opponents. On 6 July
1779, VA the Hon John Byron engaged a larger French fleet commanded by the Comte
d'Estaing off Grenada. Although he signalled closer action, Byron did not manage to
form his scattered ships into an effective line of battle, and the French withdrew in good
formation. In all three instances the fleets passed each other on opposite tacks and no
decisive result was obtained.

XXII.   Of Barricadoes.[1]

There are commanders who, afraid of appearing too careful of their own persons, (*in avoiding danger*), or of hurting the ship's way by binding her up, or by making what they call a back-sail, despise a fixed defence on the quarters. (*I have no objection to the common doctrine of predestination, in particular persons, who have no other principle of courage*) The notion of predestination may be allowed in persons who have no other principle of courage, though, considered in its consequences, it be but a poor incitement to brave actions; but a commander should reflect, that the ship's company is committed to his care, and that the defence, which secures him, contributes to the safety of men, whose preservation he is obliged to consult.

That a fixed barricadoe binds up a ship (*hinders her going*) is a position not yet proved, and obtains chiefly among practical seamen. Could a ship be made flush on the quarter-deck, might quarter-cloths, rails, timber-heads, mizen-mast, binnacles, wheels, hen-coops, arm-chests, after-part of the poop, etc., be done away, her sailing would be improved. But as these are necessary, and, on trial, will be found to resist almost the whole wind that would strike on the barricadoe, and, when the ship is close hawled, must receive it in a worse direction, the objection to a fixed breastwork cannot be great: or it may be entirely done away by fitting it for the quarters in moveable pannels [*sic*], to be fixed occasionally. On the other hand, a ship barricadoed, particularly a frigate, which every day may meet with her match, is always ready to bear down on the chace, especially in the night-time. The people, when entering on action, have no disagreeable notions of wounds, and broken limbs, which they must entertain, if, instead of preparing arms and engines to annoy their enemy, every one be busied in securing themselves. On board the *Hussar*, this was carried so far in 1757, that the ship was kept constantly clear for action, the captain sleeping between decks, that the main deck might be free of whatever could hinder the immediate working of the guns. It was owing to this readiness, that, in company with the *Dolphin*, she was able,

---

[1] A barricade of posts and rails was normally placed across the quarterdeck or poop, and packed with rope and canvas as a protection against small arms fire. Nettings were often rigged above this barrier to provide extra cover when packed with rolled up hammocks. Ramsay advocated keeping a barricade in position at all times.

in the night-time, to send to the bottom a French two-decked ship, in a very short engagement.[1]

To make a defence with the people's bedding in long chaces, and rainy weather, proves injurious to their health, by occasioning fevers and scorbutic complaints (*many a dangerous cold, and becoming no small cause of the scurvy*). In your present station, therefore, and when you rise to a command, take every prudent measure in your power to secure yourself and your people (*the people under [your] care*), that there may be the less preparation necessary, when entering on action, and, if possible, only of weapons of offence. The people then will think not of maims but of victory; the enemy will be intimidated at the quickness and violence of the attack, and be taken unprepared.

XXIII.   Of preventing Accidents from Fire.

The regulations of the navy, if enforced, would be sufficient to guard against fire: but the master at arms has not always sufficient weight in the execution of his duty. Candles are often put in bottles, or stuck up against beams over cables, and the person who put them up, being suddenly called away, they are left to the care of any chance person that may come after him. Iron candlesticks, hooped, in form of a lantern, with strong iron wire, should be provided in every berth; and, to make the men careful of them, if lost they should be an impress against the wages of the man who receives them.

Frequent accidents happen in stowing, or drawing off spirits. Close lanterns, if any light be allowed, should only be used: even they should be kept at a careful distance, while the cask is in the slings.

The following method to prevent accidents in action was successfully used in the *Prince of Wales*.[2] The cockpit ladder was removed; the hatchway

---

[1]On 23 Nov 1758, the 28-gun *Hussar* (Capt John Elliot) and 24-gun *Dolphin* (Capt Benjamin Marlow) engaged a large French ship, probably the 50-gun *Alcyon*. She was dismasted and sank during the night. The *Hussar* was damaged and had no boat to send for survivors; the *Dolphin* sent hers but managed to rescue no one.

[2]Third-rate line of battle ship, built 1765; broken up 1783. Flagship of Adm the Hon Samuel Barrington in the West Indies. Ramsay was appointed chaplain, and in this capacity gathered material for his collection of sermons for sailors. In the *Prince of Wales* Ramsay had been under fire at the capture of St Lucia by Barrington in Dec 1778, as well as Byron's actions against d'Estaing in July 1779.

was hung round with wet canvas. A small scuttle, with an easy-moveable valve, was made in the after-grating; a tarpawling [sic] covered the gratings; the valve had a particular cover. A trough, filled with water, was placed before the magazine door. The orlop-deck was covered with wet swabs; no light was admitted. The man who handed the powder, pushed up the case through the scuttle, to one ready to receive it, and the valve shut of itself. In two severe actions no accident happened in this ship from powder.

XXIV.   Of the care of powder.

It has been a general complaint, on this station, that our powder is bad. The ordnance office charge this on the climate, and want of care in the gunners to keep it dry, turn it, sift it, and air it. I have known ships, where this care has been taken, continue on this station without complaining of their powder, and it is certain that this care is not so general as the importance of the thing requires. The following method would effectually remedy the complaint. Let proper places on the several stations, as Bridge-Town, Barbadoes; English-Harbour, Antigua; Port-Royal, Jamaica, be furnished with magazines filled with powder sufficient for four or five ships, and conducted by one or two men skilled in the art of making and recovering powder. Let their powder be kept constantly in good order. When a ship's powder wants airing or manufacturing, let it be sent ashore to these magazines, and replaced by the like quantity of good powder; and let that powder be immediately manufactured and recovered to be ready to exchange with the next ship that needed. Thus no time would be lost; and the ship would not be endangered by frequent working about powder. A certain number of cartridges might be sent on board ready filled and prepared for service, and put up in such a manner as to allow of the frequent changing of it upside down. Till this regulation can be brought to bear, it will be necessary to keep a strict eye over the gunner's department.

XXV.   Of Signals in general.

The knowledge of the language of signals is an important branch of an officer's duty, too generally neglected. The fate of whole fleets, nay, of your country, may depend on your right apprehension of a signal.* Let me therefore, intreat you to pay a particular attention to this part. Without being familiarly acquainted with signals, you cannot look on yourself as a good officer. Commanders are generally made out of admiral's ships; but how would it look, if you were on board a flag- ship for preferment, and could not direct the making of a signal? A young officer needs not think it a childish amusement, to have the different signal flags and pendants painted on slips of paper, to instruct himself in making and answering signals, between two small models of ships properly rigged.

[* This was fatefully the case on that important day, April 17th 1780.[1]]

Indeed, this part of the service is very imperfect, though no branch so capable of being made complete. The colours are often badly chosen, and indistinct; and every commanding officer of the squadron has his peculiar language in signals, which he prefers to all others. Every captain makes a collection of the signals of all those under whom he has served, and when he becomes commodore of one or two private ships, retails them out, not always properly mixed. Thus every officer has a new language to learn from every admiral and commodore under whom he serves; and, except in a few common signals, must, on every occasion, run to consult his signal book: even then he cannot always comprehend clearly what is meant. Thus confusion arises, and time is lost.

Now all, except signals for knowing friends, should be fixed by one standard, and enforced by authority. At present Keppel's and Howe's are used together with the printed general instructions.[2] The first of these two is delivered out as a supplement to the third. The signals appear to

---

[1]On 16 April 1780, Adm Sir George Rodney was blockading Martinique with 20 ships made the signal for general chase when he sighted French Adm de Guichen at sea with 23. When the fleets drew near each other Rodney formed line of battle on 17 April and manoeuvred to gain an advantageous position. Judging that he might envelop the French rear, he attempted to make his fleet bear up in line abreast and engage the enemy. However, the signal book proved inadequate to the task: several of the leading British ships maintained their course and tried to reach the van of the French line. Deprived of their help at the critical time, Rodney lost the advantage of local superiority, suffered considerable damage and casualties, and had to watch his quarry escape. Two captains were particularly blamed for failing to obey the admiral's intentions and thus for the inconclusive outcome.

[2]Augustus, 1st Viscount Keppel (1725–86), served under Anson, commanded a 74 under Hawke at the battle of Quiberon Bay in 1759, led the expedition which took Belleisle, was the second senior officer at the taking of Havana in 1762, and commanded the Channel fleet in 1778. In June he drew up a set of signals for the use of his fleet, taking what he considered most suitable from earlier codes. An inconclusive action off Ushant in July 1778 (where he was poorly supported by his second-in-command Sir Hugh Palliser) left his reputation unharmed, and he became first lord of the Admiralty 1782–83. Richard, Earl Howe, AoF (1726–99); when C-in-C on the North America station in 1776, issued a Signal Book for the Ships of War under his command, utilising 23 flags and seven triangular flags. His system when considerably modified was the basis for the 1799 Admiralty publication with the same title.

be judiciously selected; but each stands unconnected with the preceding and following, and no general knowledge of signals, no attention to the circumstances of the fleet, can lead an officer to the signification. The second set is still more comprehensive, and shews great knowledge of the service. The several signal flags are carried on through all their varieties; but, as in the preceding, no analogy is preserved in the signification; the whole depends on memory, unassisted by method or derivation. The confusion of each may be accounted for by the breaks made in each series, by the general instructions. The French signals are strictly analogical in their construction; but, like all our's, particular and unconnected in signification. Could analogy be preserved in construction and signification the art would be complete. The following is an attempt.

[The 1765 edition contained only four paragraphs on signals. XXV paras, 1 and 2 and the first sentence of para. 3 are substantially the same. In the first edition Ramsay had just this to add – material greatly expanded for his later publication:

Let all the actions to be commanded or communicated by signals be clearly enumerated. Let particular distinct flags of the most different colours be assigned to each: and the circumstances of each particular action might be accurately marked out, by joining pendants, shifting the place of the original flags, and firing of guns.

To explain this farther. The principal actions to be signified are anchoring, chacing, fighting, intelligence: making of sail may be comprehended under that of chacing. Four original flags, of the sorts most distinct from one another, might be made to signify these actions separately; and when any of them were to extend to the whole fleet in their highest sense, that flag by itself in the most conspicuous place should signify it. Thus the whole fleet to moor, which is the highest act of anchoring, might be expressed by the anchoring flag at the main-top-mast-head: a general chace or a general engagement by its peculiar flag in the same place; and so of the rest. The particular circumstances of each might be easily ascertained by shifting the flag to particular places, adding the private signal of the ship to be ordered to act etc. Thus in anchoring, besides mooring, there must be distinguished single anchor, unmooring, heaving short, slipping, cutting, getting under way. Indeed, when the fleet is moored, the same signal appointed for coming to a single anchor, will serve clearly to unmoor: and the like oeconomy might be used in many other parts of the service, which would make the signals fewer in number, and therefore more distinct. In chacing we must distinguish the ships to chace, the quarter towards which the chace lies, the distance from the fleet to which they are to chace before they return. In fighting, there must be distinguished, whether all are to come to an engagement, as they can come up, or in a line a-head, or a-breast; at what distance they are to bring up, I mean from each other, not from the enemy; what ships are to leave the line; what ships are to chace such of the enemy as fly, etc. But in every particular case it must be remembered, that the original flag be not omitted.]

XXVI.   Signals formed into a Language.

The actions to be signified by signals, may easily be comprehended under six classes, each to be expressed by a flag or broad pendant of one of the three simple colours, red, white, and blue, used in the navy.

I.	Fighting —	Flag,	Red
II.	Chacing, discovering strange sails,		White
III.	Anchoring, getting under way, tacking,		Blue
IV.	Discovery of land, sounding, danger, distress,	Broad pendant,	Red
V.	To know a friend, rendezvous,		White
VI.	Particular ships, and officers signals		Blue

A pendant or flag of one colour may be red, white, blue. Each flag may be pierced, have a cross, a stripe of different colour, perpendicular, horizontal, diagonal.*

[*Each stripe or piercing should be nearly equal to one third of the flag, that it may be distinguished at the utmost possible distance.]

The diagonal stripe may depend, as [**A** below] or project, as [**B** below].

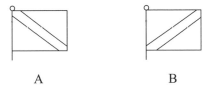

A   B

Two colours may be arranged perpendicular, horizontal, diagonal: three colours may be perpendicular, horizontal. We must remember, that the first colour mentioned is uppermost, innermost, or the ground: the whole gives twelve divisions, each containing six flags. We have hence, as in the scheme annexed, 72 flags, which may be combined into an infinite number of signals; our present collection needs not so many. Fighting, the most numerous class, exceeds not 50 in number in all the three books before mentioned: chacing contains about twenty-three. We can allow each class a century of signals, which will leave ample room to every admiral for improvement and variation. Let then a simple flag, or broad pendant, stand each for a class, and in a series according to their rank, express in the instructions, 100, 200, 300, 400, 500, 600 the signals of each class proceeding from their respective centuries on to the next class, or century, in succession. Suppose nine of the next most distinct simple flags to stand each in a series for 10, 20, 30, 40, 50, 60, 70, 80, 90, and the next nine in the place of units. We shall make 600 signals, (which are three times the number used in the navy), with twenty-four flags and pendants. To make the greater uniformity, as we have so many spare signals, each century may begin 111, 211, 311, 411, 511, 611. As no class has sixty signals at present, the tens need not to be carried higher than six, which will reduce the number of flags to twenty-one.

By this arrangement each signal requires the flag or pendant of its class, and a ten and a unit flag. The first denotes its meaning, the second and third the circumstances. The three may be hoisted in any order, and placed where most conspicuous. Suppose a red flag, a red with a perpendicular white stripe, and a blue with a horizontal white stripe hoisted; the first is 100, the second 30, and the third 4; the whole 134. This is the 34th or, as it is expressed, the 134th fighting instruction. Suppose the two last, with a white flag, it is the 234th, or 34th chacing signal. Suppose the two last, with a blue broad pendant, it is the 634th, or 34th particular ship or officer's signal.

Preparatory to the making of a signal, a flag signifying the class, and, if it be for a particular ship to act, her particular signal, should both be thrown out, and be first answered by hoisting, or hauling down the ensign.* Then the particular ship's signal, if out, should be taken in, and the ten and unit flags be added to that for the class already hoisted, which should be answered as before.

[* To prevent the possibility of mistake, each ship should have a complete set of signal flags, and should repeat every signal. They should be able to signify by signal, that they cannot comply with it, and also that they do not understand it.]

We may remark, that the ten and unit flags, being common to all the classes, signify nothing of themselves, without the flag, or pendant, of a particular class to give meaning and number to the signal. In the flags selected for our series of signals, it may be observed, that red and blue are not brought together, it being difficult to distinguish them at a distance. In tens the field is red, and the distinction white. In units the field is blue, and the distinction white. In short, though a few particular flags may mark a few signals more simply, a plainer method cannot be suggested for the whole language; and the liberty of placing them in any order where they can be best seen is an important advantage.

The only difficulty is, when particular ships are to execute any thing by signal. The signal for the service may require the flags that express the ships. This may be obviated by reckoning the ships backward in alphabetical order. Thus the *Albion* would be 699, the *Britannia* 698: as no class contains above 50 signals, this would leave room for fifty ships. But this method would require six flags and pendants for a particular division or ship, to act. This may be avoided by first making, as above, the division or ship's signal. When answered, by hoisting or lowering the ensign, or by being repeated, the service-signal may be thrown out. At present a ship may be in a situation that she cannot distinguish her signal. Here it may be hoisted where it can be best seen, and the distinctness of the method more than compensates for the seeming delay. The whole may be finished within five minutes.

Service to be executed by night may be signified by signals thrown out before dark, and the hour of execution may be marked by a gun without a consequent signal, or by a sky- rocket: or the following plan is simple and distinct.

The night-signals at present are under sixty in number. Let guns make the tens, and lights and false fires the units. By beginning to reckon from ten, the gun, or guns, will both be preparative and mark the tens. The consequent lights and false fires will mark the units. Thus:

1 Gun is	10
2 Guns, slow,	20
3 Guns, slow,	30
2 Guns, quick,	40
2 Guns, quick, & 1 slow	50
3 Guns, quick,	60
1 Light is	1
2 Lights	2
3 Lights	3

1 False fire,	4
1 Ditto, and one light,	5
1 Ditto, and two lights,	6
1 Ditto, and three lights	7
2 Ditto,	8
2 Ditto, and one light,	9

Thus 1 gun, 2 false fires, and one light, is signal 19. Two guns quick, one false fire, and one light, is signal 45. Three guns quick and three lights is signal 63.

Hence it is only necessary to number the night-signals, and apply the above scheme to them. Nothing can be more simple, or easy of execution. The small number of guns necessary on this scheme and the liberty of placing the lights where most conspicuous, are great advantages.

[In the Third Edition, pages 45–7 follow, as reproduced here on pp. 181–3. Courtesy of the Watkinson Library at Trinity College (Hartford, CT.)]

XXVII.   Of the Admiral's Station in Battle.

This necessary branch of naval skill, the language of signals, can never be brought to perfection till it becomes a general rule for our admirals to station themselves in battle in a frigate (*in the rear*), to observe circumstances, and give the necessary orders. For how can he manage his fleet, when involved in a cloud of smoak [*sic* – smoke], which hinders him from seeing or being seen? Or, if this be not the case, how can he throw out signals, which on the present prevailing mode, must be made from a particular mast, when perhaps that mast is carried away. This must often happen to a brave commander from his exposing himself, and the enemy aiming particularly at him. It is a pity that, among so many brave officers, we should ever have an admiral whose courage is doubtful: and if he has signalized himself (*his courage*) as a private captain, it is not necessary to put his personal bravery to the test, when he might be doing his country far better service by his skill and conduct. This is an evil arising from a regard to seniority in the service. Yet if an actual display of courage be thus necessary in an admiral, an indifferent person might be apt to think, that where so many brave men fail of such promotion, the rank of post captain in the navy may satisfy the ambition of men, who having had no opportunity of shewing their merit, leave it doubtful how far they deserve the honour and interest of their country entrusted

S I G N A L   F L A G S.

I. II. III. IV. V. VI. VII. VIII. IX. X. XI. XII.

Flags of 3 Colours.
IV.

Red perp. ftripe	White	Perpendic. Red & White
	Blue	Blue
	Red	Red
	Blue	Blue
White	Blue	Red
	Red	White
Blue	White	

Flags of two Colours.
III.

Red croffed with	White	Red proj. diag. ftr.	White
	Blue		Blue
	Red		Red
White	Blue	White	Blue
	Red		Red
Blue	White	Blue	White

VIII.

VII.

Flags of one Colour, pierced, &c.
II.

Red pierced with	White	Red dep. diag. ftr.	White
	Blue		Blue
	Red		Red
White	Blue	White	Blue
	Red		Red
Blue	White	Blue	White

VI.

Flags. Pendant.
I.

Flag	Red	Red horizont. ftr.	White
	White		Blue
	Blue		Red
Broad Pendant	Red	White	Blue
	White		Red
	Blue	Blue	White

V.

White
Blue

IX.

IX.
Horizontal Red & White
Blue
White, Red
Blue
Blue, Red
White

X.
Diagonal Red & White
Blue
White, Red
Blue
Blue, Red
White

XI.
Perpen. Red, White, Blue
Blue, White
White, Red, Blue
Blue, Red
Blue, Red, White
White, Red

XII.
Horiz. Red, White, Blue
Blue, White
White, Red, Blue
Blue, Red
Blue, Red, White
White, Red

Tens and Units combined.

1,	2,	3,	4,	5,	6,	7,	8,	9.	
10,	11,	12,	13,	14,	15,	16,	17,	18,	19.
20,	21,	22,	23,	24,	25,	26,	27,	28,	29.
30,	31,	32,	33,	34,	35,	36,	37,	38,	39.
40,	41,	42,	43,	44,	45,	46,	47,	48,	49.
50,	51,	52,	53,	54,	55,	56,	57,	58,	59.
60,	61,	62,	63,	64,	65,	66,	67,	68,	69.
70,	71,	72,	73,	74,	75,	76,	77,	78,	79.
80,	81,	82,	83,	84,	85,	86,	87,	88,	89.
90,	91,	92,	93,	94,	95,	96,	97,	98,	99.

I. Class numbered, 111, 112, 113, &c. to 200.
II. 211, 212, 213, &c. to 300.
III. 311, 312, 313, &c. to 400.
IV. 411, 412, 413, &c. to 500.
V. 511, 512, 513, &c. to 600.
VI. 611, 612, 613, &c. to 700.

SIGNALS

SIGNALS by CLASSES and CENTURIES.

Class	Centuries.	Tens.	Units.
I. Fighting,	Flag Red 100	Red pierced with White, 10	Blue pierced with White, 1
II. Chacing, ftrange fails,	White, 200	crofled with White, 20	Crofled with White, 2
III. Anchor, getting under way, tacking	} Blue, 300	Perp. ftripe White, 30	Perpen. ftr. White, 3
		Hor. ftripe White, 40	Horizon. ftr. White, 4
IV. Difcoveries, danger, diftrefs, foundings,	Broad Pend. Red, 400	Diag. dep. ftr. White, 50	Diag. dep. ftr. White, 5
		proj. ftr. White, 60	proj. ftr. White, 6
V. To know friends, rendezvous,	White, 500	Perpendic. Red & White, 70	Perpendic. Blue & White, 7
VI. Particular fhips, officers,	Blue, 600	Horizon. Red and White, 80	Horizont. Blue & White, 8
		Diagonal Red and White, 90	Diagonal Blue & White, 9

Abbreviations.—Perp. perpend. perpendic. *Perpendicular.*—Hor. horizont. *horizontal.*—diag. *diagonal.*—dep. *depending.*—proj. *projecting.*—ftr. *ftripe.*

Note, The Tens are the firft, and the Units the laft, in each table between the firft and eleventh.

XXVI. *Of*

to them in the command of a squadron. Sir J. Moore had the good sense to break through this custom, at the attack on Guadeloupe, in 1759.[1] Lord Howe, in opposing d'Estaing, in 1778, broke through the custom, to serve his country.[2] The direction should be general, except in the case of a flying squadron: but it should be confined to the very moment of action; the admiral's ship being for every other purpose best adapted for conducting the squadron.

XXVIII.   Of Skill in Piloting.

Another thing necessary to complete an officer, yet frequently under-valued, is a skill in piloting. What should be thought of a king's ship, with the wind off the land not daring to stand on within three miles of her port, to receive a pilot? though the captain and lieutenant had formerly spent some considerable time in it; and used to express the boldness of the coast, by saying, the ship might run her bow-sprit on the rocks; and though one of her convoy run in without having a person on board that had seen the place before, or having any directions but from a small draught in a monthly Magazine, which was a help they had likewise in the man of war.

Your captain is as well acquainted with these islands as any professed pilot. He knows through what channels to push, how near the coast to keep, in pursuit of interest or honour. He is never uneasy, or at a loss, for

---

[1]Adm Sir John Moore (d. 1779): Lt, 1738; Capt, 1743; flag 1762. As a Cdre he was sent to cooperate with military forces in an attack on Martinique 1759. When in the theatre of war, he judged Martinique beyond the resources available, but proposed instead an attack on Guadeloupe, another of the prosperous French Antilles. Disdaining to capture merchant prizes when there were higher strategic interests at stake, he placed his force in Prince Rupert's Bay in the north of Dominica, from where he believed he was best placed to protect the British forces ashore in Guadeloupe from a French naval counter-attack. In the end a powerful French squadron under Adm Bompart eluded Moore, helped military forces recover the main island of Guadeloupe, and returned in safety to Martinique. In the longer term Moore's strategy was vindicated: he regained control at sea, suppressed French commerce, escorted a huge convoy of British merchant ships taking sugar to England, and supported the British land forces which eventually did succeed in taking Guadeloupe. He won no battle at sea but he helped Pitt to win the war in the West Indies. Corbett, *Seven Years' War*, pp. 284–99.

[2]When the French government openly intervened in the American War of Independence the Comte d'Estaing with 12 two-decked warships was sent to North American waters, outnumbering Howe and his fleet in ships, guns and men immediately available. Howe skilfully adopted a defensive position in the Delaware river and saw off the immediate threat from d'Estaing. On 10 and 11 Aug the two fleets manoeuvred against each other off Rhode Island, and to help him direct his force more effectively Howe shifted his flag from the 64-gun *Eagle* to the frigate *Apollo*. In the night that followed, bad weather separated the hostile fleets – and damaged the topmasts and rigging of the *Apollo*.

want of a pilot: his orders for working in with a port by night, are safe, full, and distinct. He is not to be biassed by the fears of such ignorant men as pilots in general are.

Officers, in common, leave this business to the master and pilot; as if it were not their duty. But that commander who is himself acquainted with the ground, will push more boldly through, to aim at some noble stroke, than when his activity depends on the will of an old driveller, whose only wishes are to bring back the ship safe into port. When Sir James Wallace laid his ship a-ground, to accomplish the destruction of an armament fitted out against Jersey, he consulted not with his pilot on the propriety of the measure.[1]

Every young man, who receives a commission, ought to cherish the ambition of being one day at the head of a squadron. If in that station, how necessary for him to know the proper head-lands for placing his cruisers, the channels though which the enemy carry on their trade, the nature, the defence, the exposure, the depth of water, and capacity of their ports: you might have observed, how an ignorance in this necessary branch, exposed an officer, in a very extensive command on this station, to unpardonable blunders, and a load of censure. As this must ever be an important station in time of war, from the circumstance of the French colonies being intermixed with our's, I shall make no apology for attempting to fix the just observations of your commander on the subject.

XXIX.   Of Cruising on the Charibbean [sic] Station

In the war of 1743, Sir George Pococke, by keeping among the French islands, and intercepting their supplies from Dutch and American smugglers, reduced them, particularly Martinico, the principal island, to a state of famine.[2] Since his time the dread of calms and lee-currents, in this war of 1756, has kept more numerous squadrons from doing much

---

[1] In May 1779, Capt Sir James Wallace in the *Experiment* (50) with frigates and lighter vessels in company was ordered to intercept a French force preparing to attack the Channel Islands. The British squadron split up during their search, but when Wallace located enemy ships in the Bay of Mont-St. Michel he went in to attack, despite the risk of running ashore under enemy gun batteries. For a while the *Experiment* took the ground, but succeeded in silencing the guns ashore. Several French vessels were destroyed in the attack, and the frigate *Danae* (34) was brought off as a prize.

[2] Adm Sir George Pocock (1706–92); Lt, 1726; Capt, 1738; flag 1755. Best known for his three hard-fought actions against a French fleet in East Indian waters 1758–59, and for commanding the naval force at the taking of Havana in 1762.

essential service: continued calms are chiefly to be found about eight or ten leagues to leeward of the islands. In with the land they seldom exceed an hour or two. The frequent flaws from the vallies[1] soon carry a ship along shore under the lee of the several islands: but whatever the calms be, they equally affect the enemy and our squadron; and will never keep a man, acquainted with the station, from attempting and executing any piece of service. Currents often run strong to leeward in mid-channel, while they set to windward along the islands; but under the lee of the islands they are not felt. Generally when they run to leeward on one side, they run to windward on the other: in the north St. Lucia channel, a ship may always get to windward by making short tacks under that island, and around Gros-islet, carefully avoiding mid-channel and the Martinico shore.[2]

In beating to windward, make it a rule to keep hold of one island, by working close in shore, and depending for your progress on the flaws from the vallies, till you can take hold of the next island, by stretching across the channel. In the large bay of Fort Royal, Martinico, which may be considered as extending from the Pearl to the Diamond, on account of the lowness of the land to windward, the trade-wind is more constant than in any other leeward bay on the station. It is, therefore, safe cruising-ground, as Sir George Pococke found it*; and being the enemy's chief port, and only to be effectually watched to leeward, it demands particular attention. Consider the whole station, as forming a large arch, of which Martinico is the vertex, or chief point, and Barbadoes an out-work; and the reasoning used here may be applied to each particular island, and the several channels.

[* Sir George Rodney also freely used it in this year, 1780.[3]]

[1]Gusts of wind sweeping down the valleys from the hilly interior of several islands.

[2]Ramsay was critical of Adm Byron's operations off Martinique, where lee currents were held to blame for his inability to stop French reinforcements reaching the island. Ramsay quoted maritime opinion that a squadron stationed to windward might have been a more seamanlike response. *Barham Papers*, I, p. 47.

[3]After successfully relieving Gibraltar, Rodney sailed to the West Indies and linked up with the battle squadron already off St Lucia. His force of 21 of the line manoeuvred against de Guichen's fleet of 23 ships off Martinique, leading to three inconclusive actions in April and May. Lack of wind or changes of direction, combined with lee currents and some confusion over signals, made it easier for a reluctant de Guichen to avoid battle on unfavourable terms.

XXX.   Of making Drawings

To fix this knowledge of piloting firmly in your mind, observe the bearings, and marks for going into every bay, or road which you have an opportunity of seeing. Write down every thing worthy of notice, and make sketches of every place which you coast along, or touch at. Compare your observations with the printed charts, and this will settle it ever after in your memory.

XXXI.   Of Sea Charts

Here let me observe, that the greatest benefit would accrue to the service, if a general collection of the best sea charts were printed at the public charge, corrected by the observations made in this war by our officers; for our operations by sea have been so general, and we have made so free with our enemies coast and ports, that the improvements to be made by these means, are very great. But if these observations be not collected, and preserved by the public, this advantage will be lost, as the observers die off, and their sketches wear out. The collection might easily be made, as the copies of the drawings have generally been presented to the officer commanding on the station. Each ship should have a complete set for her station, put up carefully in a chest, and committed to the charge of the captain. Every officer should be allowed to consult them at pleasure: at the return from the station, a report should be made how far the observations of the officers agree with the printed charts.

The admiralty have been at the expence of printing a set of charts of the French coast, found on board a French man of war. These have been distributed to our channel cruisers. The plan should be extended generally, and not continue as at present, submitted without control, to the master's ignorance or poverty.*

[* The master is ordered to supply himself with charts, but no body is appointed to examine his collection. To do it properly would in truth be too expensive to most masters.]

 (*At present all the care that is taken to provide the ship in sea-charts, is an injunction laid on the master to furnish himself; but no body is appointed as a judge of his having done or not done it properly; at least, I never heard of such a power having been exercised: and often through poverty, often through ignorance, he is very badly provided.*

The admiralty, I think, have been at the charge of printing a set of draughts of the French coast, originally found on board a French man of war, and published by authority. These have been distributed to some of our channel cruisers; at least, I was informed by a captain, who had a copy of them, that he had them from the admiralty. I speak thus doubtfully of them, because it was in the beginning of the war that I saw this copy, and I have never met with any since.)

XXXII.   Of Telescopes.

Telescopes are intimately connected with what we have advanced concerning signals and piloting. At present they are left to the captain and officers discretion; and though many important pieces of service, as the safety of the ship, or capture of an enemy, depend on the choice made of them, they often prove ill adapted to the purpose. Good telescopes will never be general in the navy, till the public supply them. Each ship should have a case with the telescope for the captain's private use, one for the officer of the watch, one for the mast-head, and two night-glasses.

XXXIII.   Of Convoys

To conduct our fleets of merchant-ships safely from our distant settlements, requires great address, much patience, and more authority than is lodged with our navy commanders. I have frequently been with convoys, and, without an exception, I can affirm, that in every fleet there were masters of merchant-ships who behaved with insolence that deserved to be chastised, and disobedience that called aloud for punishment.

The following method has been attended with success. A stout merchant-ship, commanded by a discreet man, who has served in the navy, is appointed to lead with a broad pendant. The ships of war have no fixed station, but change their places to the skirts and rear of the fleet, to keep the ships together, and guard against danger.

The merchant-ships wear distinguishing vanes*, by which the conduct of each is easily known, and marked down. This only needs to be added; let the complaints against any particular master be authenticated from the commodore's log-book, and at the end of the voyage, sent down to his owners, that he may be removed, if undeserving, and let him be rendered incapable of ever taking orders again in a fleet. Let every shot that has been fired at him, to bring him into his station, be an impress against his wages of twenty shillings, to be paid into the ordnance office.

The French commodores have a power of taking out a refractory master of a merchant-man, and giving the command to his mate, or some other proper person, during the voyage. I see no ill consequences that could arise from giving our officers the like power. The dread of it would keep the masters to their duty, and it never would be necessary to exercise it **.

[* This practice begins to take place in our squadrons: but the vanes are in general too narrow. They should not be less in breadth than a yard; and the colour of their division should be the field or chief colour of their vane.

** In all convoys of merchantmen, there should be a general instruction to prohibit visiting. Many dangers and inconveniences attend it; many opportunities are lost, and not unfrequently damage is the consequence. Sometimes gales of wind arise, and the visitant cannot regain his ship. Sometimes the visit and drinking are protracted till dark night. The people are unnecessarily fatigued; there is a chance of ships falling on board such as have brought to, to hoist their boats in; or of the boats being run down, in crossing undiscovered to her proper ship.

If a ships wants [sic] any necessary, or a surgeon, from, or wishes to send a joint of fresh meat to another ship, let both run a little a-head with wefts in their ensigns, and bring to, to hoist the boat out; and after using all possible speed to expedite their business, return to their proper stations in the fleet.

Visiting in our squadrons is also of bad consequence. Often a sail is discovered while the captain of the ship most convenient or best adapted for chacing is at dinner with his admiral.

XXXIV.   Of Admiralty or Naval Instructions.[1]

While observing defects, which parliament, or the admiralty-board, alone can remedy, we will suggest the propriety of calling in that heap

---

[1]The Commonwealth navy attempted to codify crimes and punishments in the Articles of War 1653, a document itself distantly related to the Black Book of the Admiralty 1336 and the ancient Laws of Oleron. The Restoration Navy accepted them in revised form as the (first) Naval Discipline Act of 1661. Subsequent additions and modifications led to the publication of Regulations and Instruction relating to His Majesty's Service at Sea by the Admiralty in 1731, the handbook of discipline, organisation and practice which remained substantially unchanged until Middleton's monumental revision of 1806.

of contradictory instructions by which the navy is pretended to be regulated, to abrogate such as are obsolete, to add such as are wanting, and
range them in such a method, that officers may know how, and what to
obey. This would be an important improvement in the service; and as
the present regulations have been gradually heaped together, from the
time of James Duke of York,[1] as necessity or circumstance required; (*and
some of them, it must be acknowledged, from very slight and partial considerations*); it would be proper to encourage every officer to send in, to
those appointed to revise them, his objections to the present rules, and
the improvement in the constitution of the navy which his experience has
enabled him to make. This might produce a complete system of laws for
the government of the navy.

XXXV.   Of Ship Building.

One thing is still wanting to bring the navy to perfection, (*which I dare
say the admiralty-board, by its influence, might accomplish, were the
usefulness and necessity of it once apparent:*) the establishing the art
of ship-building on mathematical principles. In ship-wrights that can
follow directions we excel; and we can copy models, if we please: but
so confined has been the education of those who have generally risen
to be head-builders, and surveyors of our navy, that there needs little
apology for saying that we have had few who understood the principles
of the art.

Ship-building depends on the most abstruse parts of mathematics, and
no man is capable of constructing perfectly, such a machine as a ship for
burden and motion, without a thorough knowledge of geometry, conic
sections, algebra, logarithms, fluxions, mechanics, or an acquaintance
with the rules, which masters in these sciences have established to direct
the art. Were we to enquire into the advancement of those, to whom the
construction of our navy has been entrusted, we shall find that often
they have risen insensibly (*from the lowest rank*) in the dock-yard, by an
address in their business superior to their fellow workmen, or by means

---

[1]James, Duke of York (1633–1701), was second son of Charles I and younger brother of
Charles II. At the Restoration he was appointed Lord High Adm and proved himself an able
administrator and brave commander in battles against the Dutch (Lowestoft 1665 and Sole-
bay 1673). As King (1685–88) he continued his strong interest in the navy and its reform
under Samuel Pepys, the secretary to the Admiralty. James's religious policies contributed
to growing unpopularity and the transfer of the crown to William of Orange and his wife,
James's daughter Mary. He died in exile in France.

less honourable; that few apply to the art of ship-building with the hopes of being one day surveyors of the navy, and of consequence few begin with an education proper for it.

Farther, we have had some good going ships in the navy, that might be esteemed lucky hits: though their models be preserved, though the stepping and distance of their masts, their best sailing draught of water, and staying of their masts (which last is the index of their trim by head or stern), be known, yet they have not been made general models, but we have kept on in the same rule-of-thumb-road as before.

XXXVI. Of French Bottoms.

In the present war of 1756, we have been so wise as to copy French bottoms in the construction of some capital ships, and we have generally imitated them in our frigates, with this absurd difference, that their extreme breadth is made properly (*where it should be made*) in the water line, when the ship is fitted and victualled for a three months cruise, and our extreme breadth is carried up to the main deck. Hence our frigates are in their best, though not best possible, trim, when fully stored, and go badly when light.

The French have applied theory to ship-building. Their best mathematicians, the Jesuits, have been employed in directing their carpenters; while the directors in the construction of our ships are just handy mechanics, fit to execute, but not to plan. Yet it is said the French bottoms were copied from us, about a century ago. If so, we have not only lost our property but the knowledge of it; for all our publications on ship-building are copies from French performances (*even Martin's late performance is properly speaking a translation from it*).[1] Yet it may be supposed, had we joined theory to our practice, we might have excelled them as much in the art of modelling as in executing.

XXXVII. Of Premiums for Models.

The present remedy for this defect is to propose rewards to ingenious men (*at the universities*), for examining the models of our best going

---

[1]Possibly an error: could Ramsay have meant Murray instead? *The Elements of Naval Architecture; or A Practical Treatise on Ship-Building* . . . by M. Duhamel du Monceau, carefully abridged by Mungo Murray (London, 1754). Duhamel (1700–82) published his treatise on naval architecture in Paris earlier in 1754. See www.archive.org/details/treatis eonshipbu00murr Independence Seaport Museum.

ships, to compare them with the models which theory would suggest; to compare models of our best sailing frigates with those of our best sailing capital ships, to observe if any difference besides that of the scale, obtains; to compare models of the best sailing of those ships who are trimmed most by the head, with models of the best sailing of those who go trimmed most by the stern, to determine the preference. From all these taken together, they might ascertain the extreme breadth, from the stem aft, and from the keel to the gunwale, the steps of the masts, the breadth of the rudder, the depth of the cutwater (*or gripe*), the form of the bows, and run aft, and draw out models for each rate.

XXXVIII.   Of Training up young Artists.

In time to join together theory and practice, (*to chuse out, at Christ's Hospital,*[1] *or wherever they offer*) boys, shewing ingenuity, and a turn to mechanics, should be selected from the public hospitals, or where they offer, (*to give them a liberal education at the university*), to be liberally educated, and have their studies directed to those branches of mathematics, that are useful in ship-building. When properly instructed, they should be entered in the dock-yard, and rise by their merit; or, if masters, properly qualified, were added to Portsmouth academy,[2] the boys might be entered young in the yard, and learn the theory and practice together. Every ingenious young man among the (*common*) ship-wrights should be allowed to attend the masters without expence. Thus the art of ship-building would be reduced to a science. The best invented plans should be sent to the several dock-yards, and a reward should be proposed for the best execution.

When experiments are to be made with such ships, they should be put under the command of ingenious officers, favourers of improvements;

[1]Christ's Hospital at Newgate, London, was granted a royal charter by Edward VI in 1553. Samuel Pepys secured the support of Charles II for a new mathematical school at Christ's Hospital in 1673 to encourage 'the art of navigation and the whole science of arithmetic'. It was particularly designed to educate future navigators, masters and naval officers. Pepys became a governor in 1676. Similar institutions were established at Greenwich in 1685 and Rochester in 1701.

[2]While most aspiring young officers learned their skills through practical on-the-job training aboard ship, some preferred to acquire a shore-based education first, combined with elements of professional instruction, at the Portsmouth Naval Academy, founded in 1729. It became the Royal Navy Academy in 1773 and the Royal Naval College in 1806.

not be given to men (*to mere tars*), who have neither skill to make experiments, nor candour to acknowledge the benefit of a new invention.

XXXIX.   Of the Sailing Trim of Ships.

Now, besides the public benefit arising from a well-built navy, the advantage of such ships to their officers, which is the reason for mentioning it here, is considerable. The builder, from her construction, can tell whether she is to be trimmed by the head or stern. All the trouble an officer has, is in changing a few inches, more or less, to find the medium. At present a commander knows not how to trim his ship. Perhaps one or two years are spent in fruitless trials, during which noble opportunities are lost of doing himself and his country honour. Often her best trim is never found, or if found, she is so badly constructed, as to continue, in the seaman's phrase, a mere tub. Or, if one commander lights on her sailing trim, it is lost when he is removed to another ship; for his trials not being directed by method, are not trusted by his successor, who hopes to excel him by undoing his plan. Instances of this may often be met with. I, indeed, knew a commander, who, having first sailed in a ship, to make observations on seeing her bottom, in dock, or on a careen, could at once determine, whether she would go best trimmed by the head or stern; whether to increase or lessen her ballast. By these means, he considerably improved several bad sailing ships; but his successors, not comprehending his principles, though good practical seamen, usually undid all his work.

XL.   Of an Officer's Examination.

I have now completed my idea of the general duty of a sea-officer, as, however different from common opinion, and common practice, it arises from the nature of his office. Nothing gives officers so narrow and confined a notion of their duty, as their absurd examination at the navy board, before they are commissioned. They are examined about knotting and splicing: they are made to run over by rote a few canons (of which they know not the reasoning), in astronomy and navigation: they are required to get the ship under way from, or bring her to anchor at, Spithead. If strictly examined, indeed, they work her according to art in a storm, and – that is all. – Not a word is said of discipline. No enquiry is made if the man can manage six or seven hundred men in his country's service: they ask not of the service he has seen, nor of his observations on it. I hope our officers will ever continue good practical seamen; but, in truth, there are many more other things equally necessary to fit them for their station.

XLI.   Of Piety.[1]

I have drawn you on, thus far, insensibly, before I dared to mention one particular, not, indeed, generally regarded, but respecting you as a man, an accountable creature, essential to your happiness, and, even as an officer, necessary for carrying your duty its full length; this is religion, the religion of revelation, not that of deists, formed by each man, to suit his particular passion or folly. The jest may probably be on your side, did you laugh out at seeing religion mentioned as a necessary qualification in a sea-officer: but I am vindicated in my exhortation by having remarked, that every good officer within my acquaintance pays an attention to the appearance of religion; and if to preserve appearances be a good thing, to possess the substance must be truly valuable. [*NOTE: The section from 'I am vindicated' is added since 1765.*] I hope you have learned none of that subtle wisdom, which, hurried on by youthful vigour, or fascinated by the love of paradox, to draw every enjoyment within the vortex of the man's own inflamed desires, and colour reasoning after his own folly, despises things sacred, and looks on heaven and hell as the bugbear of the vulgar. Agreeably to the experience of the sober part of mankind, be assured that an humble dependence on the God of Heaven can alone give a relish to prosperity, can support you under misfortunes, can give courage in the day of battle, or comfort on a death-bed. The man whom conscience approves, who is confident that Heaven is on his side, can do things that human strength cannot of itself perform.

In every action, consider that God is present with you, that your conduct in every instance, that even your most secret thoughts, lie open before him (*that he sees, and approves or disapproves your smallest actions, nay even your most secret thoughts*). If you desire to know the sacred will (*the will of God*), consult the Bible. It is a book which I can recommend to you: it alone gives a rational account of man, and the globe which he inherits. It will improve your understanding in things not immediately concerning religion; and the simplicity, the propriety, and authority of its precepts, will influence your life and conversation.

---

[1] As well as public observance of religion (as enjoined by *Regulations*, for instance) Ramsay was advocating personal piety based on Bible reading and private conviction. Although he can be described as evangelical, he writes in strictly non-partisan terms.

I am sorry that the fashionable manners of the age will bear me out in supposing you so ignorant of the book, as to reckon it necessary to give its character, without running the hazard of affronting you. But if you wish to get at the head of your profession, you will get above these narrow prejudices, and take the extensive law of God for the rule of your conduct.

XLII.   Of public Respect for Religion.[1]

(First edition: *If you once try it, you will find the usefulness of keeping up the appearances of religion, even among those who are reckoned the most profligate of mankind, seamen. They will be more obedient, more sober, more diligent, and, of consequence, more healthy, serviceable, and more to be depended on.* Significant changes in Third Edition:)

There never yet was a well regulated orderly ship's company, but where a respect for religion was kept up in public. Religion carries its influence into all the various circumstances of a man's behaviour. It makes him regard himself, and every being around him. Where officers promote decency among the men, these become also more obedient, more sober, more diligent, and of consequence more healthy, more serviceable, more to be depended on. The old Romans were in their days the most devout people on earth; and they were the most valiant, flourishing and prosperous: and their prosperity continued till they became so wise as to despise their religion.

XLIII.   Of common Swearing

I would fain see an exact, active young officer, who did not hector and swear like a common bully. Cannot you be the person? I am sure the custom (*as it universally prevails,*) is so ungenteel, so mean and vulgar, that it may well be matter of surprise to find a person, who reckons himself better than the very refuse of the people, guilty of it.

---

[1]When Middleton began holding services at sea on Sundays in the Seven Years' War he knew this was unusual – at least for ships without a chaplain – and a sample of ships' logs confirms his opinion. During the American War the practice became a little more frequent, as Ramsay roundly declares. In the French Revolutionary War, when monarchical Anglicanism was one way of defining the ideology that separated Britain from atheistic republicanism, public religious observance became more regular, particularly when Earl St Vincent was C-in-C. The process gathered pace during the Napoleonic War, in parallel with a movement of both lower-deck and officer-led piety, often evangelical in origin and keen to win new adherents.

When fashions are profaned by vulgar use, people of taste lay them aside. I wish gentlemen would carry this attention to their rank so far as to leave this odious, horrid, unprofitable, and contemptible custom to the scum of mankind, who have taken it up, and who, from their thorough want of shame, will allow the politer part to hold only the second place in it as a fashion. But if we consider ourselves as accountable creatures, objects of rewards and punishments in a future state, such swearing is a flagrant act of insolence and impiety, committed against the Majesty of Heaven. It is related of (*the great*) Mr. Boyle,[1] that he never mentioned the awful name (*of God*), without making a sensible pause in his discourse, as if performing an act of adoration (*surely we all owe the same respect to our bountiful Creator and Preserver*). Is this recorded of this valuable man to his honour, and would the like pious custom not be to the credit of men in common?

In the navy, the common plea is, 'it is impossible to get duty done without swearing'. If this were really the case, the service would be very pitiful, and inconsistent with the character of a conscientious man. But there are officers who carry on the service, and execute it well, without swearing. You may observe, that the method of your own commander requires no swearing. He secures obedience to his orders, by delivering them in a distinct, determined manner, and method, without calling in this vulgar custom. To have duty briskly done, it is only necessary to shew your people, that you yourself are steady, resolute, in earnest, and determined in your orders. A brisk carriage, with a few well dispensed punishments, will do more service, and have a more sensible effect, than thousands of imprecations. We have both known officers, whose orders were trifled with, and their persons despised, for the promiscuous use of certain odd imprecations.

XLIV.   Of Conceit

Young men, when lucky enough to get a commission, are apt to fancy there is no occasion to learn any thing afterwards. In an instant they commence gentlemen, and often suppose, that an uniform alone can equip

---

[1]Robert Boyle (1627–91), natural philosopher and one of the founding members of the Royal Society; the framer of 'Boyle's law' he is widely regarded as 'the father of chemistry'. A man of great personal piety, he wrote a classic of Christian devotion (*Seraphic Love*, 1660).

them for the title. Good sense, and a knowledge of mankind, must be silent before their sword and cockade. But be assured that a commission sets a clown, or a blockhead, in a more conspicuous, and, consequently, only in a more ridiculous light. It makes a man's folly and ignorance more apparent, and affords the man more frequent opportunities of publishing his emptiness. This conceit should be guarded against, in proportion as a man values a good name, or desires to be esteemed in his profession.

XLV.   Of Ornamental Accomplishments

To grace a commission, the mind should be adorned with the knowledge of men and manners. The officer ought to know what is due to every person around him, what he owes his station, what to the dignity of human nature. He should have such a general acquaintance with arts and sciences, as polished conversation supposeth. But these accomplishments can only be acquired by diligent observation, by unwearied study, and application (*reading*). Persons intended for the navy generally leave school too soon to bring a settled taste for such things into the service with them. What they can afterwards acquire, must be from books that treat of them, in the most agreeable plain manner.

Among the books that contribute in the easiest manner, to a polished way of thinking (*a humane polite way of thinking*), are our several periodical publications, the Tatlers, Spectators, Guardians, Ramblers, the Idler, Adventurer, Connoisseur, World.[1] (*They were written by persons who were acquainted with human nature, who were themselves benevolent and polite.*) They are addressed to humanity, they exhort to benevolence; while they improve, they entertain the mind: they give a taste for history; (*If you like romances, some of them abound with the most entertaining, improving stories.*) they are full of excellent maxims, and directions for the various circumstances of life; in a pleasing manner, they teach the respect due to one-self, and that expected by

---

[1] *The Tatler, The Spectator* and *The Guardian* were periodicals edited by Richard Steele and Joseph Addison, begun in 1709, 1711 and 1713 respectively. *The Rambler* (from 1750) and *The Idler* (1758–60) were vehicles for Samuel Johnson's writings, mainly covering matters of religion, politics, ethics and literature. *The Adventurer* was a London newspaper published twice a week 1752–54, associated with John Hawkesworth, with Johnson again a contributor. *The Connoisseur* was another London weekly, and *The World* a periodical issued by John Moore, both in the 1750s.

society: but above all, they set religion and virtue in so amiable a light, as to force the love and approbation of those who seriously peruse them.

XLVI.   Of History

History, particularly that of your own country, claims your close attention. In a critical knowledge of naval affairs, it would be a shame for you to be wanting. In acquiring it you will see by what contrivance, by what efforts, the most desperate attempts have succeeded; by what blunders the best-laid schemes have been disappointed, and the most powerful armaments brought to nothing. You will there find intrepidity an overmatch for numbers, and address subduing strength. In short, after having done every thing to prepare for the combat, you will thence conclude to fear nothing, to hope every thing, and to expect, as much from the blunders of your enemy, and his want of perseverance, as from your own skill and management. The Spartan discipline forbad a man to flee, or kill a flying enemy. Our English seamen have much of the Spartan in them; in the sea-phrase, they bear cutting up; and, if they be properly trained, will never abandon a brave commander. They are excellently fitted for persevering even to extremity, and may easily be brought to resolve not to give up a ship, while capable of obeying the helm. There are periods of our history, in which we did not calculate the crews of our enemies ships, nor estimate their weight of metal. Valour, and the persuasion prevailing among our seamen, that each man fought for himself and his country against the slavish instruments of a tyrant, were superior to numbers and discipline. Whenever a few men more, or a few ounces of metal, become a reason for declining, or yielding the battle, the naval glory of Britain is set in obscurity.

By studying our naval history, to your own experience you may join the cool resolution of Blake,[1] the thunder (*intrepidity*) of Bembo,[2] the skill

---

[1] Robert Blake (1598–1657), General at Sea of the Commonwealth navy, renowned for his part in the organisation of a national sea force and for his combat successes in the First Dutch War (1652–54), in the Mediterranean and against the Spanish (1657).

[2] John Benbow (1653–1702) had a colourful career at sea in merchant and royal navies. He was master of the fleet at the battles of Beachy Head (1690) and La Hogue (1692). As C-in-C West Indies he fought against a French squadron, was left unsupported by some of his captains and had to break off the battle, but earned an undying reputation for courage: his leg shattered by a shot, he continued to direct the action with his injured limb held up by an improvised sling; he died of his wounds soon afterwards.

of Herbert,[1] the perseverance of Anson.[2] From Barnet[3] you may learn a humane attention to every one under your command, and may know, from what he effected, what great purposes may be accomplished with a small force, properly directed. From him you may learn, what great advantage a commanding officer reaps from an intimate knowledge of his station, and the happy effects of prudent foresight. His method will inform you how to support your authority, and yet preserve a deference and respect for your officers. Be ashamed of reading romances, when you have things to study, that not only please in the reading, but form your mind to future fame.

When you have acquired a familiarity with our own affairs and great men, get acquainted with those nations, with which our situation invites us to an alliance, or renders us obnoxious to a war. Read the histories of Holland, France, Spain, Portugal, Denmark; and, as the conversation turns often on ancient history, and the affairs of remote nations, by degrees extend your knowledge to them: for a gentleman, which every sea-officer is (*or ought to be*), should have some knowledge of whatever can be properly introduced into the conversation of polite people.

[1]Arthur Herbert, 1st Earl of Torrington (1647–1716), AoF. After service against the Dutch and Barbary corsairs, he was dismissed by James II from his flag rank for opposition to the King's religious policies. He joined Prince William of Orange in the Netherlands and was appointed by him to command the invasion fleet that brought William to England and the throne, and led to James's flight. As first lord of the admiralty he commanded the fleet against the French in operations off Ireland in 1689 and off Beachy Head in 1690. Outmanoeuvred and outfought, he considered it essential to keep his fleet in being as a protection against invasion, and withdrew his forces safely into the Thames. A court martial judged that he had acted properly.

[2]George, Lord Anson (1697–1762), AoF, strategist and administrator. As Cdre of a small squadron in 1740 he was despatched to the Pacific to attack Spanish possessions. Disease, storms and shipwreck reduced his force to one ship, the *Centurion*, and in her he achieved remarkable success, most notably the capture of a treasure ship that made Anson a rich man for life. He returned home in 1744 after circumnavigating the globe. Made Adm in 1745, his fleet gained a victory over the French off Finisterre in 1747; Anson became a peer and first lord of the admiralty. He proved himself a far-sighted reformer who did much to develop the values and training of the officer corps, the way that ships were rated, the efficiency of the dockyards, and – bearing in mind the fearful experience of his *Centurion* voyage when he lost over 1,300 men from disease – the effectiveness of naval medicine.

[3]Cdre Curtis Barnett (d. 1746); Post Capt, 26 Jan 1731; during War of Austrian Succession when commanding the *Deptford* (50) he was appointed commodore of a squadron sent to the East Indies in 1744. He divided the force to increase its range of operations. With the *Preston* (50) in company, he sailed on to Batavia and beyond, intercepted three French East Indiamen with a valuable cargo in Jan 1745 and shared prize money amongst the ships' companies. Thereafter British control of the Bay of Bengal was uncontested for many months. After a short illness he died aboard the *Harwich* at Fort St David, Cuddalore, on 2 May 1746.

In reading, it would be of advantage to you to have a friend, of whose knowledge and parts you think well, with whom to talk over your observations; who could help you to form characters of men and times, and direct your judgment what chiefly to remark in every book.

You must not consider what is here proposed as a task, but as a mine of pleasure and profit in your possession, not yet opened. Trust me, the pleasures for which these are too frequently abandoned, are not half so poignant or full of lasting delight. But I mean not, that you should, for books, abstract yourself from the world. No – What you read you are to practise (*in the world*). When you retire to study, it is to form yourself to be an agreeable companion, and an useful man.

XLVII.   Of Mathematics

There is a particular branch of learning, which I recommend to you for the improvement of your mind, and strengthening of your judgment, independent of its being necessary for you as a seaman: this is the study of mathematics. When peace is made, you may expect to be put out of employment. When this happens, apply to some teacher of mathematics: with him make yourself master of the first six books of Euclid, as a foundation. Then learn trigonometry, plain and spherical; practical geometry; the principles of astronomy, geography, mechanics, navigation, gunnery, algebra, and the construction of logarithms.

This study may appear dry at first; but the advantage arising from, and after you are advanced in it, the pleasure accompanying the pursuit of mathematical truth, and the gradual enlargement of your mind, will soon overbalance the first disagreeableness. Nor need the time necessary for the acquisition be grudged: six months ordinary application has made a much greater progress than is here suggested. (*I know a person who got some knowledge in all these branches of mathematics, and in most other branches of them, who did not spend much above six months in the acquisition.*)

When you have made this progress, you will then have the satisfaction of understanding the principles of your profession, and the manner in which things operate, that now you only know by experience, or by their effects. In any emergency you will be ready at finding out expedients; and when a case is referred to you, you can, with assurance and ease, propose your opinion.

XLVIII.   Of talking of yourself and others

An officer, of the general knowledge here recommended, will never be under the disagreeable necessity of talking in company, of himself and his exploits; a fault which mere seamen are apt to fall into, from their confined ideas and views. Indeed this habit is always esteemed the production of emptiness, and is sure to put people on prying into the truth of the stories related: and that man must have acted properly and prudently in life, in whom ill-nature, scandal, or a love of raillery will not, on search, find something to reprehend, something to laugh at.

Of a still worse tendency is a spirit of detraction in speaking of others. It is not every officer, it is not a majority of officers, that can expect opportunities of doing brilliant acts of service to their country. Yet the ordinary discharge of their duty, though not surrounded with glare, though unattended with honour, requires an unremitting assiduity, and painful perseverance. This unavoidable distinction between brilliancy and application, has often improper consequences among officers. He who has signalized himself, is apt to look down on a less lucky man, though perhaps of double his merit; and this is too ready to return it, by lessening his real credit: and it must be confessed that this last is most frequently in fault. If a man celebrated for performing, by his courage or his conduct, some material service to his country, 'there was some extraordinary good luck in the affair;' as if good fortune were not a sign of Heaven's regard: or, 'he took the glory out of the hands of another, who deserved it better:' or anything but his merit. In forming of characters, let not conceit blind you, nor envy or prejudice mislead you. Allow merit wherever it be found: let it excite emulation in you to excel, not malice to pull it down to your own level.

Conclusion

These hints on the duty and qualifications of a sea officer, are such as my service in the navy has enabled me to make; and which my concern for your character, both as an officer, and the pupil of a man whom I admire (*captain M——*),[1] has made me bold to offer to your attention. You are now in the most dangerous period of life. According as you take a turn

---

[1] 'Capt ——' (1780) and 'Capt M——' (1765): Charles Middleton.

to thoughtlessness (*and dissipation*), or to a manly rational conduct, so will it fare with you in every future step. You are at present with a person, whom, without reserve, I can recommend to your imitation. Copy after him, and be a second Capt. —— (*M*——). He continues to learn and improve himself; and, though already among the completest in his profession, adds every day to his knowledge, either from books, conversation, or his own observations and experience.

....

APPENDIX
To Mr. —— (*Mr. L.*), Commander of the armed Vessel ——

The substance of the foregoing was presented to a young gentleman, of whose parts and disposition I had formed a good opinion, and whose improvement and success I earnestly wished. I have copied it, and offer it to you with the same good intention, and with equal earnestness, not so much by way of advice, as to set you on thinking and reflecting on what should be your conduct and employment as an officer, of which rank you have so near a prospect, and so just an expectation. It was your activity, your accurate execution of orders, that first induced Capt. —— (*M*——) to take notice of you. Your application, your steady cool resolution and courage, confirmed you in his favour, made his friends your's, and gained you the good will of those who knew or heard of you; and your modest carriage, and equal bearing of your good fortune, have, in a great measure blunted the edge of envy itself.

But you must not think, that when you have attained your wishes, and got confirmed in the rank at which you aim, that these things are to be cast aside, as of no more use; or that good qualities, and the favourable opinion of your friends, are to be used only as a stalking horse to preferment. To fill that station with honour to yourself, you must continue to exert every nerve, and exercise every worthy qualification. You must still lie open to the advice of those who are really your friends. You must double your application; you must increase your diligence. You must persevere in shewing the same intrepidity in action; the same unconditional obedience to the orders of superiors. If ever you cast off your modesty of carriage, or become conceited, and put on an overweening opinion of yourself, you are lost for ever. Modesty forceth esteem; conceit, pride, haughtiness, disappoint their aim of procuring respect. On the other hand, I need not caution you against a mean flattery (*and adulation*) of people: against that your own natural sense of honour will sufficiently secure you. Nor have I mentioned this fault of your thinking too highly of yourself, and growing on your good fortune, from anything that I have observed in your carriage. It gave me pleasure to find in you a different behaviour. But it is, in general, so difficult for a man to bear good fortune as he ought, that I chose to leave the interpretation of the sincerity of my intentions to your good sense, rather than, at this time, when your character for life must be determined, that you should go unwarned in this important point.

I only fear, lest the things proposed as necessary to complete an officer appear too hard and difficult in the attainment, at your time of life (*especially as it is so late in life, now, that you should turn your thoughts to them*). There are, indeed, things mentioned, which you cannot think of acquiring soon, if ever; but difficulty, in general, must only be a spur to industry. Many of the things required of you may be learned by way of amusement; and valuing them only as such, you cannot spend your leisure time more pleasantly.

But you must attend to the most necessary parts first; writing, accounts, navigation. Accustom yourself, every day, to read in some useful book. Though, at first, you may not apprehend it clearly, yet a second or third perusal will bring you to the meaning. When you come to a passage in a book that pleaseth you, transcribe it; not to keep by you, but to make it more firmly your own, and to improve your writing and spelling. This custom will, in time, make writing of letters easy to you.

I especially recommend writing and accounts, because I have long entertained an opinion (*a very odd notion*), that nine out of ten of the spendthrifts among us are such, from their not knowing, that there can only be a hundred units in a hundred. For if you will not indulge a prodigal, who, with an income of one hundred pounds, spends at the rate of four hundred, with the credit of being ignorant of the single pounds that go to make up his income, you must conclude him to be a cheat and a deceiver. Yet there are many extravagant young men in the navy, who seem too thoughtless to lay any deep schemes to defraud the friend who trusts them with his money.

I mentioned to you, in conversation, the advantage of learning French; I would recommend the Spanish also. Those are the only powers that can ever engage the attention, or call forth the exertions, of a British navy officer. As an officer, those languages are an indispensible qualification; therefore try, and find some one on board that can teach you; but, as soon as you are out of employment, you must learn them by grammar (*from a master*). This will, in some measure, make up your want of education (*at school*), before you came to sea. It will teach you your own language, and make you more correct in speaking and writing your thoughts (*good sense*).

I, at present, think only of one more necessary caution. The malice and the low confined turn of many of those, with whom you expect now to be on a footing of equality, will be apt to lay you open to disputes (*they will think it hard to rank with you*); because the ambition, the borough-interest, perhaps the vices of their parents, without pretension to merit in the service, enabled them to set out with the hopes of being officers, they will think it hard to rank with you, who had no other claim to promotion but hard service, and thought not of the station (*the rank*), till your actions, in the opinion of every person, had shewn you more than deserving of it. I am not afraid of your exerting a proper spirit, when occasion calls for it; but avoid disputes. Make your superior knowledge of service as easy to every body about you as you can. But if a dispute be unavoidable, in altercation with your adversary remember what you owe to your own character, and defile not your lips with language that would be scandalous at Billingsgate.[1] Your adversary may deserve foul language; but the respect due to yourself and to your station requires ignorance of such vulgar endowments (*you in this owe a respect to yourself, and to the rank of a gentleman, whose glory it is to be ignorant of such vulgar endowments*). I heartily wish you success, and, with the most friendly regard,

I am, etc.

---

[1]London's fish market from the sixteenth century, well known for the crude language of its fishmongers, and thus a byword for coarseness and profanity.

SIR JOHN BORLASE WARREN AND THE ROYAL NAVY'S BLOCKADES OF THE UNITED STATES IN THE WAR OF 1812

Edited by Brian Arthur

The Descent into War

The origins of the changed relationship between Britain and the United States, from interdependent trading partners to enemies in the War of 1812, can be found in the Treaty of Paris of 1783, which had ended the previous Anglo-American War. Heated debate in Britain over future trade with its former American colonies often focused on the extent of American trade with the British West Indian 'sugar islands', as did the influential writer Lord Sheffield.[1] Nevertheless, in time, a mutually beneficial 'Atlantic economy' had reasserted itself – each country became the other's major customer and source of supply. American wheat, flour, rice, timber, tobacco and raw cotton found outlets in Britain and its overseas territories, while the United States, as a predominantly agrarian economy and growing market for British manufactures and re-exports, became crucially important to Britain's economic development. By 1810, although America had an adverse balance of *trade* with Britain, often resented by contemporary American commentators, its merchant navy of over a million tons carried over 90 per cent of its overseas trade, and earned more than enough to produce a favourable balance of *payments* for the United States.[2]

However, a French declaration of war on Britain in 1793 meant more frequent contact between American merchant vessels and warships of

[1] J. Holroyd, 1st Earl Sheffield, *Observations on the Commerce of the American States* (London, 1783, reprint 1784), advocating maintenance of British trading rights.

[2] For expression 'Atlantic economy', see: F. Thistlethwaite, *America and the Atlantic Community: Anglo-American Aspects, 1790–1850* (Philadelphia, 1959), p. 5. For details of Anglo-American economic interdependence, see: B. Arthur, *How Britain Won the War of 1812: The Royal Navy's Blockades of the United States, 1812–1815* (Woodstock, 2011), pp. 46–50, and C. Nettels, *The Emergence of a National Economy 1775–1815* (New York and London, 1969), p. 49.

the Royal Navy, as Britain imposed maritime blockades on France, and neutral American vessels sought to gain the trade denied to French shipping. American shippers increasingly maintained that 'Free Ships' meant 'Free Goods' which were not subject to British 'stop and search', or confiscation of cargoes as broadly defined contraband. Furthermore, the Royal Navy would soon seek to ease its perpetual manpower shortage by impressing apparently British seamen – but often, in fact, American citizens – from American merchant vessels, sufficiently often to strain diplomatic relations. By 1807, of the 55,000 seamen engaged in American overseas trade, no less than 40 per cent were British born. Between 1803 and 1812, the Royal Navy may have impressed as many as 6,000 Americans.[1] Neither nation could afford the loss of so many trained seamen. The forcible British seizure of four men from USS *Chesapeake*, a United States warship leaving an American port in June 1807, brought war very close.

Nor, despite the Anglo-American Jay Treaty of 1794, which had sought to define neutral rights in wartime, had the problems raised by American vessels trading with and between the islands of the West Indies been resolved. The American Senate would ratify the treaty only without Article XII, which had specified that, while British or American vessels could import livestock, timber, grain and flour into the islands without increased duties, American vessels could only legally export molasses, sugar, coffee or cotton from them to the United States and not directly to any European market, despite the opportunity for abnormal profits. In Britain, some thought that American trade in contravention of Article XII would undermine Britain's own trade.

Britain's position was summarised by the 'Rule of 1756' which held that a neutral could not conduct in wartime any trade that had been closed to it in peacetime. When France declared war on Britain in 1793, neutral American trade increasingly carried sugar and coffee from the French West Indies to France, circumventing the 'rule' by the use of 'discontinuous voyages' in which such cargoes were offloaded at an American port then, with import duties paid and reimbursed less costs, the cargo was reloaded and 're-exported' to Europe. The practice appeared to be condoned in 1800 by a British Admiralty Court verdict on the American ship *Polly*. The value of American re-exports almost quadrupled in two years,

---

[1] J. Gwyn, *Frigates and Foremasts: The North America Squadron in Nova Scotia Waters, 1745–1815* (Vancouver and Toronto, 2003), p. 131, citing S. Jackson, 'Impressment and Anglo-American Discord, 1787–1818' (unpublished PhD dissertation, University of Michigan, 1976), p. 52. D. Hickey, *The War of 1812: A Forgotten Conflict* (Urbana,1989), p. 11.

reaching $53m by 1805. As Anglo-French war resumed after the Peace of Amiens, these 'fraudulently circuitous voyages' were outlawed by the *Essex* ruling, in May 1805, that, unless the shipper could prove that re-exportation had not been the original intention, such voyages were illegal.[1] Vessels and cargoes engaged in such trade would be legal prize. As a result, the Royal Navy was called upon to monitor foreign shipping movements in the Caribbean and Atlantic, which meant that American vessels were listed among British prizes [1].

Although far from universally held, the view of many in Britain, such as James Stephen, was that uncontrolled neutral trade weakened the British maritime blockade of France, thereby supporting a tyrannical regime with which Britain had long been at war.[2] In November 1806, Napoleon's Berlin Decree closed Continental ports to British trade, and the following year, his Milan Decree sought the detention of neutral vessels, often American, known to have traded with Britain. Retaliatory British Orders in Council required neutral ships trading with the Continent to pass through British ports. Conciliatory British measures such as reduced transit fees were ineffective as an American Non-Importation Act against British manufactured exports took effect.[3] By 1807, many British goods were banned from the United States, as well as British warships from American waters.

In May 1811, an uneven encounter between the heavy frigate USS *President* and the sloop-of-war HMS *Little Belt* off Cape Henry, Virginia, resulted in nine British deaths and mutual recrimination. Feeling was further heightened in February 1812 by the accidental revelation of an unsuccessful British attempt to convert government bills into specie, at exchange rates for the pound against the dollar artificially raised by rumours spread by British agents. Totalling £600,000, and brought especially to America aboard HMS *Macedonian*, the bills had been intended to obtain specie from American banks with which to pay American

[1]W. Dudley, *The Naval War of 1812: A Documentary History*, 2 vols (Washington D.C., 1985), 'Sentence of the Vice Admiralty Court of Nassau, New Providence, in the case of the Brig Essex, Joseph Orne Master', vol. 1, pp. 19–20.

[2]Whig opponents such as Henry Brougham, Samuel Whitbread and Alexander Baring felt that in the long term all trade was beneficial, and anti-American sentiment unnecessary, while James Stephen, author of *War in Disguise or the Frauds of the Neutral Flags* (London, 1806), and George Rose, Vice-President of Britain's Board of Trade, advocated war with the United States.

[3]Annals of Congress, 9th Congress, 1st session (hereafter AC: 9–1 etc.), 1259–62. Although passed by Congress in December 1806, America's first Non-Importation Act was suspended, not to come into effect until Dec 1807. Macon's No. 2 Bill of April 1810, became what is referred to as the Non-Importation Act of 1811.

exporters of grain and flour to the British Army in Spain. Rather than as an admittedly covert but expedient solution to a critical shortage of specie in Britain, it was seen in America as typically devious and hostile.[1]

By April 1812, Anglo-American relations had deteriorated seriously [2]. Caution by British commanders on the North America station was called for in a Foreign Office letter to the Admiralty, dated 9 May 1812. While commanders were to have 'Instructions and Authority to repel any hostile aggression' once a declaration of war had been authoritatively confirmed, they were, as far as possible, 'at the same time to take especial care' to avoid confrontation [3].

That such a confrontation was likely is illustrated by a letter of 8 June 1812 from William Hamilton of the British Foreign Office to the First Secretary of the Admiralty. On 4 April 1812, Congress had supplemented its ban on British imports with a Non-Exportation Act, forbidding American ships to leave any American port for abroad, and the export of goods or specie by any means. Despite the serious damage to the American economy caused by Jefferson's Embargo, widely remembered from only four years before, this 'restrictive system' of legislation was reinforced by President James Madison's own 90-day Embargo, in force until July, which one Congressman called 'a direct precursor to war'.[2] Familiar with the consequences of the Republican party's earlier economic sanctions against Britain, exporting shippers, many with Federalist political sympathies and threatened livelihoods, did all they could to evade them [4].

On the same day, William Hamilton sent Croker a copy of Despatch No. 30, dated 24 April 1812, received by the Foreign Office from Augustus Foster, the British Minister in Washington, which reported a growing American mood in favour of war in which impressment was becoming a major issue [5].

That, in the event of war, British maritime blockade of the United States was widely considered feasible – by Augustus Foster, British Minister in Washington, amongst others – is shown by his report to Secretary of State for Foreign Affairs, Lord Castlereagh. This was the final copied despatch in a group sent by William Hamilton to First Secretary of the Admiralty John Wilson Croker, on 8 June 1812 [6].

---

[1]T. de Kay, *Chronicles of the Frigate Macedonian, 1809–1922* (New York, 1995), pp. 54–61, and S. Budiansky, *Perilous Fight: America's Intrepid War with Britain on the High Seas, 1812–1815* (New York, 2011), pp. 103–6.

[2]AC: 12–1, 203, 1622–23, 2269–70, 1–4 April 1812, and AC: 12–1, 1588, speech of Henry Clay, 1 April 1812.

In the United States, according to the British lawyer-turned-historian William James, 'the ablest politicians in the republic were engaged to prepare a specious manifesto, representing the United States as the aggrieved, and Great Britain as the aggressive party'.[1] President Madison addressed a combined Congress on 1 June 1812, complaining particularly about continued impressment, and the legality of British maritime blockades, including their alleged use for the protection of Britain's comparative advantage in maritime trade [7].[2]

In Britain, concern grew that deteriorating relations with the United States, often seen as co-operating with France, might lead to war. The British Government seemed anxious to avert war, but also took the first steps to prepare for it.

On 17 June 1812, Foreign Secretary Lord Castlereagh sent Augustus Foster, the British Minister in Washington, his view of the current situation. A copy was also sent to Admiral Sir John Borlase Warren, known for both his previous professional distinctions and diplomatic experience, and almost certain to be chosen as Commander-in-Chief of a new 'United Command of the West Indies and North America' station.

Prevailing winds, ocean currents and resultant trade routes meant that any maritime war between Britain and the United States was almost certain to include the Caribbean, where owners and operators of American privateers would be hopeful of rich pickings amongst British merchant vessels trading with and between the West Indian islands. Consequently, Warren's responsibilities would include safeguarding Britain's financially vital and politically influential West Indian interests. He would therefore have to supersede not only Admiral Sir John Duckworth at St John's, Newfoundland, and Rear-Admiral Herbert Sawyer at Halifax, Nova Scotia, but also Rear-Admiral Sir Francis Laforey in the Leeward Islands as well as Vice-Admiral Charles Stirling at Port Royal, Jamaica. In the event of war, Augustus Foster would leave Washington, and any negotiations would have to be conducted by Warren. It was crucial that from now on he was kept fully informed [8].

Declaration of War

Rumours in Washington of the Parliamentary revocation on 23 June 1812, of the British Orders in Council as far as they applied to Americans, were

---

[1]W. James, *A Full and Correct Account of the Military Occurrences of the Late War between Great Britain and the United States of America*, 2 vols (London, 1818), vol. 1, pp. 1–2.

[2]Ibid., pp. 2–15; also in Dudley, *The Naval War of 1812*, vol.1, pp. 73–81.

too late to prevent a declaration of war being passed by Congress and signed by President Madison, on 18 June 1812. Voting in the Senate had been relatively close.[1]

Misgivings over war with Britain continued in America, particularly in New England, where opposition remained remarkably forthright. In Providence, Rhode Island, flags were flown at half mast and church bells tolled in protest at the apparently inevitable commercial disaster implied by war with the United States' major trading partner, and the world's economic, financial and maritime superpower, also currently enjoying a period of diplomatic and military success.[2] Editorials in New England newspapers often remained extremely outspoken, as exemplified by *The Repertory* of Boston [9].

Having declared war, the United States had a degree of initiative at sea, and a brief advantage until Britain could send naval reinforcements. On 23 June, a powerful American squadron commanded by Commodore John Rodgers encountered and sought to capture the British frigate *Belvidera*, which narrowly escaped. The episode was described from Halifax, Nova Scotia, in a father's only occasionally inaccurate letter to his son, on 20 July 1812, ten days before war was confirmed in Britain [10].

Confirmation of the American declaration of war did not reach London until 30 July 1812. On 1 August, the *London Gazette* announced the Admiralty's revocation of 'all licences granted by us to any ship or vessel to sail without convoy to any port or place in North America, Newfoundland, the West Indies or the Gulph of Mexico'. Initially, the British government hoped that excluding the largely Federalist New England states from the Royal Navy's commercial blockade of the United States would heighten the political differences between them and the rest of the Union, perhaps even to the point of their secession from it and the conclusion of a separate peace with Britain.

On 30 July, Lord Melville, First Lord of the Admiralty, wrote to Warren, about his selection for overall command in North America, and arranging a discussion of his imminent orders to offer the American government an armistice, on confirmation of Britain's revocation of the Orders in Council concerning American shipping, and on condition that the Americans 'instantly recalled their Letters of Marque and Reprisal' against British shipping. Originally intended for Foster in Washington, modified Foreign Office guidelines would now be for Warren. Augustus

---

[1]AC: 12–1, Supplement 1637–8, and 2322–3, House of Representatives, 4 June 1812, voted for, 79 to 49; Senate, 17 June 1812, voted for, 19 to 13.

[2]Dudley, *The Naval War of 1812.*, vol. 1, p. 69.

Foster had left Washington on 25 June, and America on 14 July 1812. On 8 August, Warren received the Foreign Office guidelines [11].

On receipt of Melville's letter, Warren began framing a reply, confessing his need for some clarification of his instructions in the event of potential changes in an already complex situation in North America. Warren's much-revised letter to the Admiralty was not ready for despatch until 8 August [12].

The importance of Warren's questions may be reflected in the speed with which they were answered, as shown by his acknowledgement to Melville [13].

Warren's appointment was confirmed on 3 August, and carrying both Foreign Office and Admiralty orders, he left Portsmouth on 14 August 1812, reaching Halifax, Nova Scotia, on 26 September, after a 'boisterous' crossing during which the sloop *Magnet* was lost with all hands. On 30 September, Warren wrote to Madison's Secretary of State, James Monroe, along the lines provided by the Foreign Office, offering the American Government an armistice in the light of the British revocation of the Orders in Council as far as American merchant vessels were concerned, and upon American withdrawal of their Letters of Marque and Reprisal.

On 16 November 1812, Warren at last received Monroe's reply to the British armistice proposal, dated 27 October 1812, containing the unacceptable precondition that Britain suspend impressment during any armistice. Monroe's answer was not to reach London until 25 December. On 21 November, in anticipation of an unacceptable American reply, Lord Bathhurst, Secretary of State for War and the Colonies, issued orders for the Admiralty to begin the commercial blockade of the United States.[1] On 13 October 1812, the Privy Council had also ordered General Reprisals 'against the ships, goods and citizens of the United States', a de facto British declaration of war, not to be fully implemented until an American reply [14].

Warren and Melville initially maintained a fairly regular correspondence which shows the progress, problems and tensions of Warren's United Command and of London's political environment. Melville's later occasionally patronising and critical tone suggests his incomplete appreciation of the prodigious length of the American eastern seaboard, and the severe practical and operational problems that Warren was to encounter [15].

---

[1]The National Archives, Kew (TNA): CO 43/49, Copy of letter from Lord Bathhurst, Secretary of State for War, to the Admiralty, dated 'Downing Street, 21 November 1812'.

Meanwhile, some letters written in the United States, in New Bedford, Massachusetts, by shipowner and whale-oil merchant Samuel Rodman, to his son-in-law William Logan Fisher of Philadelphia, illustrate the unpopularity of both Madison and his Republican government amongst New England Quakers, and the administration's increasingly urgent need for money and credit [16].

Although in March 1813 Warren was ordered to establish his permanent headquarters in Bermuda, as 'more centrical' for his United Command, a serious and lasting problem remained unsolved. Wear and tear from Atlantic weather, and the arrival of reinforcements in need of repair, highlighted the persistent shortage of skilled manpower and basic naval stores in both Bermuda and Halifax. Vessels on blockade duty would often trade with fishing boats, or with co-operative Americans ashore, relieving the need for water and fresh provisions, but the lack of stores and dry dock facilities, even in Halifax, meant that vessels in need of major repair had to return to Britain, which, while it was sometimes possible to combine with the frequent need for homeward bound convoy escorts, implied a constant shortage of vessels. Warren complained once more to Secretary of the Admiralty Croker [17].

In addition to acute shortages of vessels, men, stores, provisions and straightforward instructions, Warren was troubled by persistent complaints in London of inadequate protection from enemy action by the West India Committee, a pressure group representing the interests of influential owners and shippers of the islands' sugar-producing businesses. Furthermore, Warren felt that he needed to seek Melville's help over the conduct of Admiral Stirling in Jamaica, which was to lead eventually to Stirling's court-martial [18].

Notwithstanding difficulties, before the end of 1812, Warren's United Command had sent 120 merchant vessels into Halifax as prizes, of which 55 were re-captures, 54 more into Bermuda, 40 into the Leeward Islands, and 30 into Jamaica.[1] Four small prizes had also been taken from the United States Navy.[2] Despite prolonged armistice negotiations,

---

[1] F. Kert, *Prize and Prejudice: Privateering & Naval Prize in Atlantic Canada in the War of 1812* (International Maritime Economic History Ass., St John's Newfoundland, 1997), pp. 160–203, adapted in Arthur, *How Britain Won*, Table A1, pp. 210–13; see also National Maritime Museum (NMM): WAR/37, 'Vessels Captured & Detained'; and NMM: HUL/18, 'A List of Vessels Brought into Bermuda from the Commencement of the American War'.

[2] Arthur, *How Britain Won*, Table A2, pp. 221–2: USS *Nautilus* (14), captured by HMS *Shannon* on 16 July 1812; *Wasp* (18), by *Poictiers* on 18 Oct 1812; *Vixen* (14), by *Southampton* on 22 Nov, and lost on 27 Nov 1812; and *Vixen* (18), by *Belvidera* on 25 Dec 1812.

inadequate reinforcements, desertions, limited dockyard facilities, active American privateers and apparently innumerable British Licences to Trade, Warren initiated British maritime blockades of the United States. By 16 November, a blockade of the southern coasts of South Carolina and Georgia was in place, interfering with the export of American raw cotton from Savannah and with supplies of live oak and pine needed for construction and repair by the United States Navy.[1]

After February 1813, once Sawyer had been replaced as Warren's second in command by Rear Admiral George Cockburn, an energetic blockade of the Chesapeake and Delaware was conducted. As soon as March 1813, Cockburn was reporting to Warren at length on its impact.[2] He described the incarceration of USS *Constellation* in the upper reaches of the Elizabeth River beyond reach of a cutting-out party [19].

By coincidence, on precisely the same day, Samuel Rodman's next letter from New Bedford continued his earlier theme, as well as Cockburn's, of the unpopularity of the war and its advocates, and the American government's increasingly urgent need for money [20].

Before Warren can have received Cockburn's report of successful blockade in Chesapeake Bay, Lord Melville wrote Warren a private letter, confiding that Admiralty orders to extend the British blockade were on their way. Since the duties paid on imports and shipping tonnage in New York alone made up a quarter of United States customs revenue, any successful British commercial blockade would have to include America's biggest port, with a population of more than 83,000 since 1808. If British blockade was to be effective in reducing American government income, New York's enormous commercial and fiscal role had to be curtailed. In the event, when allowance is made for Congress having doubled custom duty rates from 1 July 1812, the *real* decrease in net customs duty collected in New York State between 1812 and 1813, is over 68 per cent.[3] Melville's letter to Warren, dated 26 March 1813, again attempts to forestall any complaint of inadequate resources [21].

[1]British Library (BL): C. Lyne, *A Letter to Lord Castlereagh on the North American Export Trade During the War* . . . (London, 1813), assured the British government that stocks and alternative sources would allow the blockade of American raw cotton exports without incapacitating Britain's cotton manufacturing industry. Georgian 'live oak' was a particularly dense timber, preferred for hulls by American shipbuilders.

[2]Dudley, *The Naval War of 1812*, vol. 2, pp. 326–8, letter from RA George Cockburn to Adm Warren, HMS *Marlborough*, Hampton Road, 23 March 1813.

[3]Raw data in A. Seyburt, *Statistical Annals* (Philadelphia, 1818), pp. 434–7. Real decrease in net customs duty revenue calculated in Arthur, *How Britain Won*, pp. 146–7.

By the same post, Warren received the rather more specific Admiralty instructions that Melville had mentioned ordering the blockade of the American coast from north to south and of the Mississippi River [22].

The degree to which Warren was aware of the financial and fiscal effects of the British blockades on the American government are shown by extracts from a letter he wrote to Melville while London's letters about extending them were on their way to him [23].

Beside his shortage of available vessels, Warren had already been blockading the northern approaches to New York before the orders to extend his blockades were sent. These orders legitimised what he had been doing, and sanctioned his blockading the more difficult southerly approaches to New York. This extension passed into British law with an Order in Council dated 30 March 1813, with neutrals given their customary warning in that day's *London Gazette*. Warren's proclamation from Bermuda on 26 May, and a letter to the Russian Vice Consul in New York, specifically warned of the blockade's application to neutrals. The effects were soon felt. By December 1813, New York's registered merchant tonnage had already fallen by 10 per cent, and wholesale commodity prices had risen by more than 21 per cent since June.[1] In the House of Representatives in June 1813, Jonathan Fisk of New York referred a second time to the impact of the blockades and the need for maritime defensive measures [24].

Some redistribution of Warren's blockading vessels appears to have occurred, as reported by the local press of Norfolk, Virginia [25].

The United States' vulnerability to economic and fiscal damage by British maritime blockade had been foreseen by those who had advised against an American declaration of war, especially without the necessary tax reform. A year into the war, Fisk's suggested countermeasures were basically the gunboats Jefferson had advocated so long before, and which had since been found unweatherly in all but the most sheltered waters, unpopular and difficult to man.

While extending his blockades, Warren also sought to hunt the American privateers using the eastern seaboard's innumerable coastal inlets. On 28 March 1813, Warren stationed HMS's *Aeolus* and *Sophie* off Charleston, North Carolina, in order to blockade Beaufort, Ocracoke and Roanoke, south-west of Cape Hatteras, although it was not until September 1813 that he added the names of these places to his earlier

---

[1]*American State Papers: Commerce & Navigation*, vol. I, pp. 998, 1018, and A. Cole, *Wholesale Commodity Prices in the United States 1700–1861* (Cambridge, MA, 1938), App. B, Table 46, p. 136.

proclamations [26]. Despite this, on 12 July 1813, Warren had ordered Cockburn to attack Ocracoke with his marines reinforced by other troops, whose boats captured the privateering brig *Anaconda*, and the schooner *Atlas* with its letters of marque.[1]

Warren's next extension of his blockades was explained in a letter to Croker on 20 November 1813, enclosing a copy of his proclamation of 16 November 1813 [27].

Meanwhile in New Bedford, Samuel Rodman speculated in a letter to his son-in-law, how far the inflation caused primarily by the British blockades might damage the American economy, concluding that it might prove lasting. He vilifies those New England Federalists found lending to Madison's Republican administration in pursuit of profit [28].

The American government's efforts to finance the war by obtaining successive loans met with increasing difficulties. The first attempt to borrow had, after a promising start, proved unsuccessful: of the $11m sought, only $8.1m was ever raised. A second loan, sanctioned by Congress in February 1813 succeeded, although at a cost. Eventually, all $16m was raised, but only after reopening subscriber lists, itself unprecedented, and at a 12 per cent discount, with only $88 paid in cash and Treasury notes for each $100 bond issued. As part of an unrepeatable effort to raise the loan, Secretary of the Treasury Albert Gallatin had called in favours from three prosperous merchants he had previously obliged.[2] In March 1813, he effectively resigned. Offering himself as one of the United States Peace Commissioners, he left America for St Petersburg, to take part in peace negotiations later transferred to Ghent.

Despite the impact of British blockades on American efforts to finance the war, including that on the morale of prosperous Americans deciding to withhold loanable funds, the continued machinations of the West India Committee in London had synchronised with Melville's growing dissatisfaction with the Royal Navy's apparent lack of immediate and politically useful success. This resulted in what was, in effect, a letter for Warren's recall [29].

Warren's reply was a model of restraint [30].

At a Cabinet meeting on 27 June 1814, it was agreed that the American Peace Commissioners could, if it appeared unavoidable, proceed to a treaty which made no mention of British impressment, which only nineteen months before, Madison and Monroe had made their major war aim.

---

[1]Dudley, *The Naval War of 1812*, vol. 2, p. 184, letter from Cockburn to Warren, dated HMS '*Sceptre* off Ocracoke Bar, 12th July 1813'.
[2]Arthur, *How Britain Won*, p. 149 and n. 121, p. 286.

Extraordinarily, two days later, in a Presidential Proclamation dated 29 June, Madison was still protesting that British maritime blockades were impracticable over such an extensive coastline as the United States eastern seaboard and being therefore illegal, should, presumably, cease [31].[1]

Since by this time, the British commercial blockades had been sufficiently prolonged and effective to have curtailed American overseas trade and its tax revenues, while the British naval blockade had rendered impracticable any American attempt to lift them, Madison's proclamation was merely legalistic nonsense, no more realistic than American government attempts to borrow sufficient funds to continue the war, especially from those whose livelihoods had been most damaged by it.

On 1 April 1814, while in Europe Napoleon considered his first abdication, Warren was replaced as Commander in Chief North America by Vice Admiral Sir Alexander Cochrane, a fellow Scot and family friend of the Melville's. Warren's 'United Command' of North America and the West Indies was to be dismantled, exactly as he had unsuccessfully suggested to the Admiralty only nine months before. As Warren's retention of only the Halifax station, with other officers allocated to the re-separated West Indies stations, would have constituted an unacceptable demotion, he was recalled to Britain, Melville giving the now apparently urgent need for re-separating the New World stations as the ostensible justification for a politically expedient, but essentially unjust decision. Only on 30 December, just before receiving Melville's letter of recall, Warren had again requested Croker for reinforcements [32].

In a private letter to Melville, after confessing that adverse weather conditions made it impossible to guarantee any complete blockade, Warren again referred to Jamaica and his unmet need for sufficient reinforcements [33].

Warren relinquished command on 1 April 1814. As early as 25 April 1814 Cochrane was to implement a maritime blockade of the ports of New England, including their use by neutral vessels, since even their limited imports had been bringing some tax revenue to the American government. With the pressures of the European war temporarily abated, Cochrane was able to employ more vessels of every size than Warren had ever had at his disposal to complete the economic and diplomatic isolation of the United States. Between 24 and 25 August 1814, the Royal Navy's control of Chesapeake Bay facilitated the capture, almost unopposed, of the American capital Washington, with the destruction

---

[1] Arthur, *How Britain Won*, pp. 191–2; see also James, *A Full and Correct Account*, vol. 2, text of Treaty of Ghent, Appendix No. 116, pp. 575–82.

of most of its public buildings. This brought about a run on American state and private banks, causing a chronic shortage of specie, resulting by early November 1814, in the American government's insolvency, and its consequent inability to continue the war. Cochrane's inclusion of the ports of New England in the British blockade led to real anxiety over the possibility of a British attack on its ports, as shown by Samuel Rodman's letter from New Bedford in October 1814 [34].

Even before the British capture of Washington, the economic impact of British commercial blockades, inflation, unemployment and bankruptcies had meant that the American government was increasingly unable to borrow further sufficient funds to continue the war. As a result, Madison and his Cabinet, without the agreement of the other Republican members in Congress, agreed on 27 June 1814, to the abandonment of demands by the American Peace Commissioners in Ghent for an end to British impressment as a war aim, if a peace treaty could otherwise be obtained on a *status quo ante bellum* basis. Peace was signed at Ghent on 24 December 1814, while, without news of it, Cochrane and Lieutenant-General Edward Packenham were engaged on a disastrously unsuccessful British attempt to capture New Orleans, Cochrane's second involvement in an unsuccessful attempt to capture a land target. The treaty was passed unanimously in the Senate, and ratified by Madison on 17 February 1815.[1]

With no mention of either impressment, or the British 'right' to stop and search neutral vessels in wartime, and confiscate contraband, the Treaty of Ghent left Britain free to employ its Royal Navy to conduct blockades of a Continental enemy in both 1914 and 1939, with the interception of its merchant vessels, and the destruction of its navy.

Cochrane now receives most of the credit for the crucial fiscal, financial and ultimately political consequences of the Royal Navy's commercial and naval blockades of the United States, while Warren, having laid the foundations of their success in extremely difficult circumstances, has tended, until perhaps recently, to have been overlooked.

Editorial Note

In the documents and extracts which follow, the spelling and punctuation of the original have been retained. The names of all vessels have been italicised. Between 1812 and 1815, the £/$ exchange rate remained stable, officially at $4.44 to the £, although sometimes simplified to $4/£.[2]

[1] Arthur, *How Britain* Won, p. 207.
[2] B. Mayo, ed., *Instructions to British Ministers to the United States 1791–1812*, cited in Annual Report to American History Association (Washington, 1936), vol. 3, p. 200.

1. *A List of all Ships and Vessels, and Cargoes and parts of Cargoes, prosecuted as Prize in the name of his Majesty, in the Vice Admiralty Court at Bermuda since the month of January 1802; as appears from the Returns made from the said Court to the High Court of Admiralty of England.*[1]

Returns of Prizes adjudged between the 25th of June 1805 and 26th December following

Polly (an American ship)	His Majesty's ship *Cambrian*; John Poo Beresford, esq. Commander.
Mathilda (a French privateer)	Ditto.
Atrevida (a Spanish privateer)	Ditto.
Golden Grove (a British ship)	Captured by the *Atrevida* and recaptured by His Majesty's ship *Cambrian.*
Ceres	Ditto
Columbian Packet (an American ship)	Schooner *Whiting*; Lieutenant John Orkney
Neuestra Signora del Carmen (a Spanish vessel)	His Majesty's ship *Unicorn*; Lucius Ferdinand Hardyman, esq. commander.
James and William (an American ship)	His Majesty's ship *Cambrian*; John Poo Beresford, esq. Commander

[1] 'Lists, presented to the House of Commons of all Ships and Vessels, or Cargoes or parts of Cargoes prosecuted as Prize in the name of His Majesty, in the Vice Admiralty Courts of Jamaica, Newfoundland, Bermuda, Nova Scotia, Bombay, Bahama Islands, Barbadoes, Malta, Antigua, and Gibraltar, As appears from the Returns made from the said Courts to the High Court of Admiralty of England. Ordered to be printed 2nd May 1808', p. 25. [author's collection].

2. *Foreign Secretary Castlereagh to Augustus Foster,*
British Minister in Washington

[TNA: FO 115/23] Foreign Office
10 April 1812

. . . It is more probable that the near aspect the question has now assumed may awaken them to the [word deleted] folly of attempting either to force or intimidate Gt Br. & that alarmed at the danger seen to themselves of the former attempt & the hopelessness of the latter, they may see an opportunity of receding without disgrace.

. . . Very considerable numbers of American Ships have been able, either by avoiding the notice of our Cruisers, or by the mask of a fake destination to enter the Ports of blockaded countries & to sail from them – thus relieving the necessities of the enemy & delivering him in no small degree from the pressure of our retaliatory measures. They have also co-operated with France by prohibiting in concurrence with her, the importation of British produce and manufactures into the Ports of America. They continue to exclude British Commerce & British Ships of War from her Ports, while they are open to those of the enemy, it is then clear that we are at issue with America upon principles which upon the part of this Govt. you are not at liberty to compromise.

[*Signed*] Castlereagh

3. *Foreign Secretary Castlereagh to the Lords Commissioners*
of the Admiralty

[TNA: ADM 1/4221] Foreign Office
9 May 1812

My Lords,
In consequence of the discussion now pending between this country and the United States of North America, the amicable termination of which, not withstanding the pacific disposition of His Royal Highness the Prince Regent, is at this moment uncertain, & In consideration of the length of time that must necessarily elapse between any hostile measures on the part of the United States and any orders which the commanders of His My's Ships & Vessels upon their coasts could receive from your Lordships thereupon, I am commanded by HRH the PR to signify to you . . . that you do furnish to all commanders of HM Ships and Vessels upon that Station, Instructions & Authority to repel any hostile aggression which may be made by the Ships or Vessels of America on any part of His My's Naval

Forces, and that you require them at the same time to take especial care that they commit no Act of Aggression against the Ships & Vessels of the United States, and that they avoid as far as is consistent with the honor [*sic*] of the British Flag all occasions of dispute or misunderstanding

It is HRH's pleasure that your Lordships should further instruct these officers that in the Event of their receiving Information from Mr Foster His My's Minister to the United States of a declaration of War, by that country against H My. or from Lt General Sir George Prevost Gov of Canada or from the Lieutenant Gov of Nova Scotia or of New Brunswick that the forces of the US have invaded or attacked the said province; or if they shall learn by any Proclamation, or any other Solemn Public Instrument that the Government of the said US have declared War against H My or if it shall be certified to them that the said Government have issued letters of Marque & Reprisal against the Ships & Vessels of H My or his subjects or have attacked, entered or invaded with an armed force any part of H My's Dominions; They are authorised & commanded in any of these Specific cases to commence direct and actual hostilities with the said US & to attack & take – sink, burn or destroy, all Ships & Vessels belonging to the Same or to any of the Citizens or Inhabitants thereof, and to pursue all such measures as maybe most effective for annoying the Enemy, protecting the Trade of H My's Subjects & maintaining the honor of the British Flag & the Glory of H My's Arms.

I am further to signify to your Lordships HRH's pleasure that you do strictly command & enjoin the Commanders of H My's Ships & Vessels on the aforesaid Station to exercise all possible forbearance towards the Citizens of the US & to contribute as far as may depend upon them to the maintenance of that good Understanding which [it is] HRH's most earnest wish to maintain between the two Countries.

I have etc
[Signed] Castlereagh

4. *William Hamilton to John Wilson Croker,*
First Secretary of the Admiralty

[TNA: ADM 1/4221] Foreign Office
8 June 1812

Secret
Abstract 163

Sir,

I am directed by Lord Castlereagh [to inform you that] . . . by last dispatches received from Mr Foster HM Envoy at Washington under dates

from 23rd April to 5th May last, it appears that before the Embargo
Bill was actually passed, the Merchants shipped off nearly every barrel
of flour that was to be had in the different Seaport Towns throughout
the Union: 140 sail of vessels left New York in less than one week, &
20,000 Barrels of flour were shipped in the same period from Richmond in Virginia principally for Lisbon & Cadiz. Some excitement
has been created by an account rec'd at Washington of HMS's *Bel-
videre* [*Belvidera*] & *Guirrier* [*Guerriere*] having anchored in the
mouth of the Delaware, & having brought to several ships just after
the Embargo Act passed, & Com. Rodgers had been sent with the
Frigates *President* & *Essex* to enquire into the circumstances and act
accordingly.

Serious apprehensions are stated by Mr Foster to be entertained of an
encounter taking place between His Majesty's Cruisers off the American
Coast & those of the United States owing to the indeterminate expression of the Instructions given by the United States Government to their
Cruisers 'to protect the neutral Rights' of their Country.

As the Irritation which such an event would create would operate
most powerfully in the public feeling towards this Country, and with the
Measures consequent thereon, Mr Foster has written to Admiral Sawyer
requesting that he would use every precaution to prevent such an Occur-
rence so much to be deprecated.

His Majesty's Brig *Colibri* & the United States Brig *Vixen* lately
passed each other off St Augustine, without hailing, their men at their
Quarters & Tompions out of their Guns:– Fortunately no accidental Discharge of any of the Guns of either happened, to produce any unpleasant
affair.

Among the possible causes of a War, that arising out of the practice
of Impressment is dwelt on with particular vehemence by the papers
and parties of America, Lieut. Green having written to Mr Foster
of another of His Majesty's Seamen having been seduced from the
Gleaner by the People of Annapolis, Mr Foster made a Representation
of the circumstances to the United States Government & took occasion
to dwell on the attention shewn by this Country in the discharge of any
Seaman ascertained to be a citizen of the United States, & he requested
to be furnished with a List of all such that could be claimed on that
ground.

300,000 Dollars have been appropriated for repairing the Frigates
Chesapeake, Constitution & *Adams* and an annual sum of 200,000 Dollars are to be laid out in Timber for the Navy particularly in rebuilding
the Frigates *Philadelphia, General Green, New York* & *Boston*.

[*Signed*] Wm Hamilton

5. *Hamilton to Croker with copy of Despatch No. 30 from
Augustus Foster, the British Minister in Washington*[1]

[TNA: ADM 1/4221]   Foreign Office
8 June 1812

Despatch No 30 Secret

Washington
24 April 1812

Mr [Paul] Hamilton, Secretary of the Navy, spoke with some warmth
about the insult as he called it committed within the waters of the
United States, and frankly told me that orders had been sent by him
to Comm. Rodgers to sail with the Frigates *President* & *Essex* under
his command to question the British Commander, and oblige him to
remove. He added that he had no doubt a collision would take place
if HM's Ships were still in their waters. I have already expressed my
conviction that in order to give a tone to the publick [*sic*] feelings in
the United States, the American Government would be very satisfied
should some event take place, either on the frontiers of Canada, or off
this Coast, calculated to create considerable Irritation among the Americans & I mentioned in a former dispatch, that I had written to put Sir
George Prevost on his guard in this respect . . . Vice Admiral Sawyer
has also given me every reason to believe that he will not be wanting in
precautions on his part.[2]

Very inflamatory [*sic*] paragraphs and letters on the subject of
Impressment have lately been circulated in the American papers, and,
as the cause of war become more closely canvassed, that arising out of
practice of Impresment seems to be dwelt upon with considerable vehemence. The Members [of Congress] who are friendly to peace, assure me
that it is a much more difficult task to them to explain this point to their
Constituents than the Orders in Council.

---

[1]Paul Hamilton was American Secretary of the Navy, 1809 to Dec 1812; Cdre John Rodgers commanded the USS *President*; Sir George Prevost was Govr-Gen of British North
America, and Govr of Lower Canada, 1811–16. VA Herbert Sawyer commanded the Royal
Navy's North America station at Halifax, Nova Scotia, until replaced as Warren's second
in command in February 1813, leaving Halifax in March 1813.
[2]See Doc. No. 14.

6.   *Hamilton to Croker with copy of Despatch No. 34 from Augustus Foster, the British Minister in Washington*

[TNA: ADM 1/4221]   Foreign Office
                                                              8 June 1812

Despatch No. 34

                                                              Washington
                                                              5 May 1812

Your Ldship will no doubt perceive how much the commercial part of the community are in general averse to the idea of a War with us; and I am strongly of the opinion that if War does take place, and that we confine our operations to blockading the different Harbours, particularly those of the South, and especially the mouths of the Mississippi, we shall soon unite enough of voices to those in the North, as to form a majority for peace. An actual Attack upon the great Cities of the North, I cannot but think would be detrimental to our interests soon though we should succeed in it. It is believed that on the 4th of July finally will be decided the question of peace or war.

[*Signed*] Wm. Hamilton

7.   *Extract from President James Madison's Address to Congress, 1 June 1812*[1]

Extract

To the Senate and House of Representatives of the United States.

. . . Without going back beyond the renewal in 1803, of the war in which Great Britain is engaged, and omitting unrepaired wrongs of inferior magnitude, the conduct of her government presents a series of acts, hostile to the United States as an Independent and neutral nation.

. . . British Cruisers have been in the continued practice of violating the American flag on the great high way of nations, and of seizing and carrying off persons sailing under it; not in the exercise of Belligerent rights, founded on the Law of Nations against an Enemy, but of a municipal prerogative over British subjects. British jurisdiction is thus

---

[1]James, *A Full and Correct Account*, vol. 1, pp. 2–15; also in Dudley, *The Naval War of 1812*, vol. 1, pp. 73–81.

extended to neutral vessels in a situation where no laws can operate but the law of nations, and the laws of the Country to which the vessels belong; and a self redress is assumed, which, if British subjects were wrongfully detained, and alone concerned, is that substitution of force for a resort to the responsible sovereign, which falls within the definition of War.

. . . The practice, hence, is so far from affecting British subjects alone that under the pretext of searching for these thousands of American citizens, under the safeguard of public law, and of their national flag, have been torn from their Country, and from every thing dear to them; they have been dragged on board Ships of War of a foreign nation; and exposed, under the severities of their discipline, to be exiled to the most distant and deadly climes, to risk their lives in the battles of their oppressors, and to be the melancholy instruments of taking away those of their own brethren.

. . . Against this crying enormity, which Great Britain would be so prompt to avenge if committed against herself, the United States have in vain exhausted remonstrances and expostulations. And that no proof might be wanting of their conciliatory dispositions, and no pretext left for a continuance of the practice, the British government was formally assured of the readiness of the United States to enter into arrangements such as could not be rejected, if the recovery of British subjects were the real and sole object. The communication passed without effect.

British cruisers have been in the practice also of violating the rights and peace of our Coasts. They hover over and harass our entering and departing Commerce. To the most insulting pretentions they have added the most lawless proceedings in our very harbors; and have wantonly spilt American blood within the sanctuary of our territorial jurisdiction . . .

Under pretended blockades, without the presence of an adequate force, and sometimes without the practicability of applying one, our commerce has been plundered in every Sea; the great staples of our country have been cut off from their legitimate markets; and a destructive blow aimed at our agricultural and maritime interests. In aggravation of these predatory measures, they have been considered as in force from the dates of their notification; a retrospective effect being thus added, as has been done in other important cases, to the unlawfulness of the course pursued. And to render the outrage the more signal, these mock blockades have been reiterated and enforced in the face of official communications from the British Government, declaring, as the true definition of a legal blockade, 'that particular ports must be actually invested, and previous warning given to vessels bound to them, not to enter'.

Not content with these occasional expedients for laying waste our neutral trade, the Cabinet of Great Britain resorted, at length, to the sweeping system of Blockades under the name of Orders in Council; which has been moulded and managed, as might best suit its political views, its commercial jealousies, or the avidity of British cruisers . . .

It has become, indeed, sufficiently certain, that the commerce of the United States, is to be sacrificed, not as interfering with the Belligerent rights of Great Britain; not as supplying the wants of her Enemies, which she herself supplies; but as interfering with the monopoly which she covets for her own commerce and navigation . . .

James Madison

8.   *Foreign Secretary Castlereagh to Augustus Foster, British*
      Minister in Washington, copied to Admiral Warren[1]

[NMM: WAR 27][2]   Foreign Office
                                                  17 June 1812

No 20
<u>Most Secret</u>
Sir,

As it is desireable that you should be appraised of the intention of Government respecting the Orders in Council as early as possible I enclose a Memorandum of the Declaration of his Maj's Ministers in general terms in both Houses of Parliament.

The Steps, taken by the French Government by the publication, so repeatedly called for in vain, of a decree for the Repeal of the Berlin & Milan Decrees as far as they relate to American Vessels, appears to have afforded an opportunity of putting to trial the real disposition of that Govt to proceed towards a restoration of that usual intercourse of Nations during War, and at the same time of putting equally to the trial

---

[1]Warren had earlier distinguished himself in the blockade of France and in repelling a French attack on Ireland. He had served in St Petersburg as an 'envoy extraordinary' between 1801 and 1804. Robert Stewart, Lord Castlereagh, served as Foreign Secretary from June 1812 until Aug 1822.

[2]NMM: WAR 27, 'Papers Relating to Convoys, Transport & Trade, Commerce', pp. 66–7.

the disposition of the American Government to terminate its differences with Great Britain, & to concur with us in some amiable arrangements by which the Invasions of France upon Neutral Rights, may if she persists in them, be satisfactorily resisted.

In a few days you will receive some formal Documents upon the Subject, with Instructions as to your future Conduct towards the American Govt. In the meantime, I only intend this communication to enable you to open in Conversations the general nature of the measures about to be taken: but you will not present any Note to the American Govt, nor even read or allow to be read, the enclosed Memorandum, nor permit any minute to be taken of your conversation upon this Subject as the arrangement of its details cannot be considered as yet open to discussion.

[*Signed*] Castlereagh

9. *Extract from* The Repertory, *Boston*

[NMM: LBK/2][1]   18 September 1812

The War – We have at length received intelligence from England, of a later date than the official notice of the war. Great Britain does not appear to be prostrated by this unexpected blow, contrary to the expectations of Mr Madison and Mons [Louis] Serrurier [*sic*] [the French Minister in Washington]. Having concluded a peace with Russia & Sweden, and gained a great battle in Spain, we doubt whether she is disposed to humble herself before the ally of France: So far from this, large reinforcements are to be sent to Canada and Halifax and ships of the line are to be stationed upon our coast, and off our harbours. The war will soon begin to press upon us, in a manner we have not yet felt. We believe it will be popular in England: and as a natural consequence, it will be carried on with vigour. The shallow opinions entertained by Jefferson and Madison, that the power of England was already too much shaken to stand the shock of an American War, are just as well founded as their confidence in the power of embargoes and gunboats.

[1]NMM: LBK/2, Editorial in *The Repertory*, Boston, of 18 Sept 1812, forwarded by Warren with other cuttings to Robert Saunders Dundas, 2nd Viscount Melville, First Lord of the Admiralty, on 11 Nov 1812. Melville was to remain First Lord of the Admiralty until 1827, and between 1828 and 1830.

10.   *Alexander Howe of Nova Scotia, to his second son,*
Lieutenant Howe of HMS Theseus.[1]

[BL: Add MSS 38572, f. 310]   Halifax
                                                          20 July 1812

My Dear Sandy
   The Americans have at last declared War on the 18th June, their Congress for many days [held] Conclaves and issued the dark decrees unexpectedly, immediately their Squadron put to Sea and coming up with
the *Belvidera* attacked her (the *President, United States, Constitution* &
Hornet in Company) the *Belvidera* <u>first</u> showed her colors & Rogers [*sic*]
hoisted his & fired a Broadside, Capt Byron put before the wind & made
a gallant defense with his stern guns & in spite of their Broadsides &
Single Shots gott clear of the whole while doing them much damage.
And arrived Safely here not knowing of war & surprised us – It is said
that Rogers has gone to the Eastward of the Banks of Newfoundland
with a view to intercept our Jamaica Convoy Consisting of the *Thalia*
frigate, a vessel of 20 guns and a sloop of 18, with 111 sail under their
care, some of the merchant ships it is said have arrived.
   Our squadron here consisting of the *Africa, Shannon, Guerier* [*sic*]
Bilvedera [*sic*] *Spartan* & *Eolus*, are out and dayly sending prizes. The
Maidstone frigate arrived here on the 17th inst from Plymouth, with
news that the *Acasta, Nymphe* & *Loire* are immediately to follow her.

   Alex. Burgoyne Howe – aboard His Maj's
   Ship *Theseus* at Deal on the Downs England.

11.   *Lord Melville, First Lord of the Admiralty to Admiral*
Sir John B. Warren

[NMM: WAR/82]   Admiralty
                                                          30 July 1812

Dear Sir,
   As it will be necessary under present circumstances to provide for the
contingency of the Americans persevering [in] the War, notwithstanding

---

[1]Alexander Burgoyne Howe, 1st Lt of HMS *Theseus* (74) at the Downs, commissioned
as Lt on 28 May 1803, and present in HMS *Leviathan* (74) at Trafalgar, and later to serve
in HMS *Newcastle* (50) in North America. The American squadron actually included the
frigate *Congress* (36), <u>not</u> *Constitution* (44) and also the brig *Argus* (18). The copied letter
was later sent to Prime Minister Lord Liverpool, on 21 Aug 1812.

the revocation of the Order in Council, I have to request that you will come to Town forthwith in order to proceed without delay to the destination which I mentioned to you. Your Ship, the *San Domingo*, will be ready in a few days, as far as her equipment in Stores & provisions is concerned.

I have the honor to be Dear Sir, Your most obedient & faithful servant

[*Signed*] Melville

12. *Warren to Melville*

[NMM: LBK/2]   Upper Groso^r Street, London
                                                8 August 1812

My Lord

I beg leave to state leave to your Lordship's that having considered the Instructions that Lord Castlereagh did me the Honour of explaining to me the other day, I am anxious to have further Information, as well as the Determination & Authority of His Majesty's Government upon the following points.

First. In the Event of any alteration in the Sentiments of the Eastern States respecting Great Britain or a Separation from the General Union of the United States, Expressed by an Act or Resolution of the Legislature of any particular State to conclude Peace with Great Britain, Whether in such a case I may be authorised to suspend Hostilities with such State.

Secondly. In the event of a Union & Confederacy of the Eastern States North of the Hudson River & Seperation [*sic*] from the General Union – Whether in that case I may be authorised to Suspend Hostilities with Such States.

Thirdly. If either of the above mentioned points should take place; and that those States; who may have passed resolutions to enter into Terms of Amity & Peace with Great Britain, and should open their ports to the British Flag and require protection and Convoy for their Vessels: Whether I shall be Authorised in such a case to afford them Succour or Aid: or What Measures would my own Government Desire to have Established on such occasion; to avoid Collusion with any other States; that may remain in Hostility with Great Britain.

Fourth. If any Measures are proposed by the Several States who may Determine to enter into Terms of Amity or a closer connection, that may require immediate Decision and Co'operation against those of the American States remaining in Hostility with Great Britain, Whether I may in such a Case be authorised to Concur provisionally with Reference Home in a Requisition on the part of the State or States above alluded to.

I have mentioned the particular points in which it would afford me satisfaction to be explicitly Instructed by His Majesty's Government & as being necessary for any unforeseen Event. The only subject that remains for me to add: is that a fixed period may be stated in my Instructions for the Answer: to the proposals sent by the Flag of Truce to Mr Monroe, to prevent any unnecessary delay on the part of the American Government

I have the Honor to be
With the Highest Consideration & respect My Lord
Your Lordships faithful & obed[t] Hum[b] servant
[*Signed*] John Borlase Warren

13. *Warren to Melville*

[NMM: LBK/2]
Upper Groso[r] Street, London
9 August 1812

Private.
My Lord

I should have left Town early this morning but having been delayed until noon by a visit from Mr [William] Hamilton [of the Foreign Office] respecting the Queries: noted in my Letter to your Lordship yesterday. I shall be at Portsmouth tomorrow Evening & Embark on Wednesday & sail as soon afterwards as possible. I trust the *Junon* will be allowed to sail with me as well as the *Poictiers* being on my spot together with the *Magnet*: As the effect of our appearance on the American coast will otherwise be Destroyed.

I have the honor to be with great regard
Your Lordships sincere & obdt Humb Servant
[*Initialled*] JBW

14. *Lord Bathurst Secretary of State for War to the Lords Commissioners of the Admiralty*

[TNA: CO 43/49]
Downing Street
21 November 1812

My Lords

It is the Prince Regent's Pleasure that you do instruct the Naval Officer commanding His Majesty's Ships on the American Station, that, in the Event of the American Government having refused to conclude a cessation of Hostilities by Sea and Land, under the authority vested in him for that purpose, he do forthwith institute a strict and rigorous Blockade of the Ports and Harbors of the Bay of the Chesapeake, and of the River Delaware, in the United States of America and do maintain and enforce the same according to the Usages of War in similar Cases and in the Event of the Blockade of the said Ports and Harbors being de facto Instituted, that, he do lose no time in reporting the same, that the usual Notification may be made to Neutral Powers.

I have &^{c}

Bathurst

15. *Melville to Warren*

[NMM: WAR/82]   Admiralty

3 December 1812

Private.

Dear Sir,

I have had the honor to receive your letter of the 7th October from Halifax, & as some parts of them relate to matters of comparative inferior importance, I shall reply to these separately & shall confine myself in this letter to the public business of your command –

I regret to find that your Squadrons have hitherto been so unfortunate as not to fall in with the Enemy's frigates, though the latter appear to have been a good deal at Sea, & we have information lately of several of them being off the Western Islands. I am aware that it is impossible so to blockade all the American Ports as to prevent the occasional escape of the Enemy's Ships, & the same observation applies to the Ports of France; but it must be to our endeavour by blockading some & stationing cruisers along other parts of the coast, to make it such a hazardous enterprize as may in time produce the same affect [*sic*] upon the Americans as upon the French, viz, that their Line of Battle Ships & Frigates rarely attempt it, & that their expectations by Sea are chiefly confined to their small privateers in the Channel.

You will receive an Order for instituting a vigorous blockade of the Chesapeake & Delaware, and I must confess that I have been surprised that some measure of that Description had not been already resorted to in regard to the Enemys Ships, though of course it required an Order from hence to extend it to Neutrals. I presume there can be no difficulty in anchoring at all times of the year within the Chesapeake, & that the Delaware may also be rendered very unsafe for the Enemys Cruisers to enter. It will probably require Line of Battle Ships as well as Frigates to perform that Service; but you have already a very large proportion of the latter, considering the amount of Ships of that class which are opposed to you & six sail of the former either are or will forthwith be under your command, viz *San Domingo, Marlborough, Victorious & Ramillies.* Rear Admiral Cockburn will succeed Admiral Sawyer, & I trust you will find some more active employment for the former than merely attending to the Port Duties of Bermuda or Halifax. He is understood to be a very intelligent & enterprizing Officer, & I shall be sorry if you cannot find occupation for him, such as I have described.

I am writing to you under the supposition that the American Government shall have refused all your pacific overtures, & I think it right to apprize you distinctly that we cannot consent to the War being conducted on any other principles than those laid down on 9th May, viz the annoying the Enemy to the utmost of your power & means, & in every possible mode of legitimate warfare. You will have, & indeed have now under your command, some of the most enterprizing Captains in the Navy, & I am persuaded therefore that you will have no difficulty in undertaking any service for the success of which a reasonable prospect may be entertained. You mention the inadequacy of your force; it has however been increased, & at any rate it would have been more satisfactory if you had stated the amount which in your judgement the various duties will require. In the number of pendants under your Order, we reckon about one seventh of all sea-going vessels in the British Navy, & though there can be no necessity for your having more cruisers than will be sufficient for keeping off the Privateers (provided the Ports are properly blockaded,) it is indispensably necessary that our Trade be protected & our Naval superiority be maintained; and though it might perhaps be impracticable without weakening too much our force on other stations, to comply with the full extent of your demands, it would have been convenient to have received from you a statement in detail, & adverting to the various parts of your command, of the force which you would deem adequate.

You will have ascertained long before this letter reaches you whether the scheme of sparing the Northern States is likely to be attended with any beneficial affects [*sic*]. It must not be permitted under any circumstances (except a separation from their Southern neighbours) to extend to the protection of their trade or Ships of War; it may be more desireable to begin with destroying Shipping & levying a contributions in the Southern ports, if your force will enable you; but it will be a mischeivous [*sic*] & unsafe policy to spare any portion of the United States, if no separation is to be expected.

I have the honor to be, Dear Sir
your most obedient & faithful Servant
[*Signed*] Melville

16. *Samuel Rodman of New Bedford, Massachusetts, to his*
son-in-law William Logan Fisher of Philadelphia

[PPL: NWC, Letter 70][1]   New Bedford
30 January 1813

Dear W[m.]

. . . I heartily wish there was grounds of hope for peace but I see none –
The folly of the ruling party who seem to be in pursuit of a mere chi-
mera, mingled with their vanity pride and hatred of the Northern section
of the Union, render it morally impossible for anything tending towards
peace to emanate from them – I conceive them utterly devoid of the
characteristics to constitute real Statesmen not a trace of magnanimity
is to be discerned, and as no more overtures can be calculated upon by
the English Cabinet . . . so as to obtain loans they will in fear persist in
their mad career till they drive to desperation half the Nation . . . they
will be disappointed in men and money I am strongly inclined to believe,
and here, if I have any, rests my hope for peace. Not from their virtue, of
which I believe them to be destitute or love of Country, this is all swal-
lowed up in self, and when they prate about public good they mean their
private ends . . .

thy affectionate father
Sam[l.] Rodman

17. *Warren to Croker*

[TNA: ADM 1/502]   Bermuda
22 February 1813

Sir,

. . . There is not any Rope left in the Stores of the Royal Yard nor
any to be had in the Islands; the ships are in great want, & the Stores at
Halifax being likewise drained, I apprehend the highest inconvenience in
refitting my Squadron.

---

[1]Providence Public Library (PPL): Nicholson Whaling Collection (NWC), Letter 70.
By courtesy of the Nicholson Whaling Collection, Special Collections, Providence Public
Library, Providence, RI.

18.   *Warren to Melville*

[NMM: LBK/2, pp. 4–5]   *San Domingo*, Bermuda
                                                        25 February 1813

Private & Confidential

My Lord,
   . . . With respect to the West Indies, it is a subject which has cost me
more trouble and pain than it is easy to Describe: I mean however more
particularly by Jamaica: Where I am sorry to say that Ad. Stirling is
acting in a very unhandsome way: as he seems to aid the sort of political
intrigue or outcry attempted to be raised first against the Administration &
next to lay all the odium of every protest that the voice of Faction can
butter upon my shoulders & I trust after receiving their Lordships orders
Admiral Stirling should never [have] withdrawn a single Ship or be
absent from that District with my assuming the Command which was
unsolicited by me:[1] & I have sent the *Wanderer* to his aid the other Day.
He has ordered home Sir Lucas Yeo & his Officers for Mail & sent all
the men but 20 in the [*illegible word*], without no [*sic*] communication
with me upon the subject. When he must know that this Squadron would
have derived great benefit in having completed from this source: and no
Seamen are now sent to me by the Cartels: and the American government
seem very anxious to prevent any such assistance reaching me: I have
sent some Voluminous Despatches Taken in an unarmed Government
Schooner: from the French Ambassador Serrurrier: & hope they can
be decyphered at the Foreign Office, as it is probable they may contain
Information of Consequence: there are also others from another person
or the Office of Mr Munroe for Joel Barlow [US Minister in Paris] containing Statements of the Public Finances & among other Reports; a part
of the Committee to Examine the Foreign relations have Stated my correspondence with their Mischevous agent Mr Michell.
   I am persuaded in recurring to the business relative to Ad Stirling that
the Board will perceive the necessity of making that Officer answer for
the employment of the Ships left under his immediate Direction; as my
instructions were with the exception of the Division of New Orleans, to

---

[1]VA Stirling's Court Martial in May 1814 was to result in a 'not-proven' verdict, but he
was never to serve again.

continue to act according to his former orders: but I should not wish to have anything to do with it as a few privateers is the only warfare waged in that Quarter: & which with 13 or 14 sail of Pendants I should think he might prevent; if he employed the Ships upon the Public Service instead of convoying Money & I hope your Lordship will arrange this Disagreeable business & relieve me from such Insidious combinations that would require every Moment of my Time to resist.

> I have the honour to be my Lord
> Your humble & obd^t servant
> [*Signed*] J.B. Warren.

19.   *Rear Admiral George Cockburn to Warren*[1]

> *Marlborough,* Hampton Roads
> 23 March 1813

Sir

1st Herewith I have the honor to enclose the duplicate of my Letter and its enclosures . . .

2nd These movements of the Enemy having put it quite out of my power to attempt anything further in Elizabeth River with adequate prospects of success until we should have sufficient military Force to land at the same time on both its Banks, I determined on making a movement up James's River to distract the Enemy and to capture such of his vessels as might have taken shelter there . . . I have the satisfaction to remark, from the Prisoners taken on this occasion and from some Americans who have since been on board here with Flags of Truce, that it appears the Capture of these Ships so high up one of their Rivers, the probability of their other rivers being subject to similar visitations, the state of alarm in which our arrival has put the whole country, their late ineffectual application to Government for their means of defence, added to the rigorous blockade of the Bay, and the Delaware, and the check lately given to the Licence trade by the recent orders on that head, have caused the continuation of Hostilities with us to be now as unpopular in this as it has been in other parts of the United States and the Virginians who a few Months back so loudly called for war are beginning to be as clamorous and axious [*sic*] for Peace.

[1]Dudley, *The Naval War of 1812*, vol. 2, pp. 326–8.

3rd It may also be useful for me Sir here to state to you that in a conversation I had an opportunity of entering into the other day, with an intelligent Merchant of Richmond he fairly explained to me that the Commencement of this War could not but have been popular in this part of the world from the increased Advantages which they appeared at the moment to derive from it for he assured me he never had seen since his entering into Business such Commercial activity in America, offering such Prospects of General Profit to all concerned in it as for the four or five Months immediately following the Declaration of Hostilities he said the demands for Supplies from Europe and the West Indies had been naturally very much increased by it and the Superabundance of British Licences occasioning Plenty of them to be always in the market at as reasonable Rate, the Ship owners were able without risk to get freight the moment their ships were ready to receive it, the Merchants had more orders for Shipments to Europe &c than they could well execute, and the Farmers and Cultivation of the land consequently got higher prices for the produce of their Labor, than had been known for many years; but the late measures of our Government having (he said) not only put a stop to these advantageous prospects but having also thrown back into the Country an immense quantity of last years produce and caused an entire and complete stagnation of all Commerce to succeed so immediately to the late Scenes of activity and profit, had had a proportionate effect on the minds of the People, and there was now only to be heard from one end of the country to the other Lamentations of Individuals who were now beginning to suffering (sic) from the effects of the war. He also added with much apparent pleasure that Mr Maddison had lost all the latter measures he had proposed to congress (previous to its breaking up) for prosecuting the war with rancour, and he assured me from the present state of the Country the President would neither be enabled nor permitted to continue it . . .

I have the honor to be Sir &ᶜ· &ᶜ·

[*Signed*] G. Cockburn   Rʳ Ad

20. *Samuel Rodman to William Logan Fisher*

[PPL: NWC, Letter 71]   New Bedford
                                                        23 March 1813

Dear Wᵐ·

Government have a good criterion to judge of the popularity of the war & the confidence placed in it by the trials they have made for subscriptions to the new loan – I have no hope of peace but what arises from this source, money, [which] I believe they can't obtain without a sacrifice that the sovereign people will not consent to – men of reputation this way will neither risque their money [n]or tarnish their character by applying it to so base a use –

We have had within a week several British vessels about Block Island & the mouths of Vinegar and Long Island Sounds. Several vessels have been captured & driven on shore, three of the latter class within a few days. One at Cuttahunk another at Watch hill & one on Narragansett beach – all that I have heard of were provision vessels – that it now seems probable, our water intercourse will be nearly annihlilated, and as we have no Store of Bread Stuff. I fear we are approaching hard times.

With love to thee Mary & the Children I am
thy affectionate father
Saml. Rodman

21.   *Melville to Warren*[1]

Admiralty
26 March 1813

Private

Dear Sir,

   . . . You will receive by the present opportunity an order for blockading all the principal Ports of the United States to the southward of Rhode Island & including the Mississippi, and we calculate that your force is amply sufficient to enable you to execute this service effectually.

We do not intend this as a mere paper blockade, but as a complete stop to all trade & intercourse by Sea with those Ports, as far as wind & weather & the continual presence of a sufficient armed Force will permit & ensure. If you find that this cannot be done without abandoning for a time the interruption you appear to be giving to the internal navigation of the Chesapeake, the latter object must be given up, & you must be content with blockading its entrance & sending in occasionally your cruisers for the purpose of harassing & annoyance . . .

I have the honor to be, Dear Sir,
your very faithful & obedient servant
Melville

---

[1]Dudley, *The Naval War of 1812*, vol. 2, p. 78.

22.   *Admiralty to Warren*

[NLS: Cochrane Papers, MS 2340, ff. 49–50][1]

> By Commissioners for executing
> The Office of Lord High Admiral
> of the United Kingdom of Great
> Britain and Ireland &c

Whereas the Earl Bathurst, one of His Majesty's Principal Secretaries of State, hath by his letter of 25th Instant signified to us the Pleasure of His Royal Highness the Prince Regent, that you should be instructed forthwith to institute a strict and rigorous Blockade of the Ports and Harbours of New York, Charleston, Port Royal, Savannah and of the River Mississippi in the United States of America, and to maintain and enforce the same according to the usages of War in similar cases; And likewise that the Ministers of neutral powers should be duly notified that all the Measures authorised by the Law of Nations should be adopted and exercised with respect to all vessels which may attempt to violate the said blockade . . .

Given under Our Hands the 26th March 1813
Melville
W Domett
J S Yorke

To
The Rt Hb[l.]
Sir John Borlase Warren Bt K B
Admiral of the Blue
&[c] &[c] &[c]
Bermuda
By Command of their Lordships
[*Signed*] John Barrow

23.   *Warren to Melville*

[NMM: LBK/2]   *San Domingo*, Lynhaven Bay [*sic*]
29 March 1813

My Dear Lord,
    . . . The whole country has been alarmed, not having any idea of our coming here to remain but a great Effect has been produced by the

---

[1]By courtesy of the Trustees of the National Library of Scotland.

Measure as the Flour &Articles from these States cannot be Sold, & much Distress must arise among them. Madison is alarmed from not obtaining Cash & being so ill supported by the French & by the apprehension of the Discussions which must ensue in the Congress from the Necessity of Imposing Taxes to Pay the Interest of the Debt already Created by the War: The American Government are however so false & Crafty that little reliance can be placed on their Professions or friendly advances: & it is probable that the Mediation of Russia has been requested with a view of inducing us to Relax in our Exertions, as well as with the hope of reviving the Ancient Question of the Armed Neutrality in her Favour . . . It would be Dangerous to relax until all the Points in Dispute are conceded . . . It is possible that the everlasting Demand for Cash & Consequently Taxes may occasion Convulsions and Disorder among the Several States, Which may urge the President to more explicit and acceptable Terms, of which, should such an Event arise, Your Lordship will receive the Earliest information.

I have the honor to be Dear Sir,
Your faithful & obd[t] serv[nt.]
J.B. Warren

24. *Jonathan Fisk of New York to House of Representatives*[1]

16 June 1813

Defence of Maritime Frontier

Mr Fisk of New York, remarked, that an allusion had already been made in a petition presented today to the state of defence in one of our cities. He now rose for the purpose of calling the attention of the House to the subject generally. On recurring to this subject; it could not be denied that much had been done for the defence of our seaports, and that many of them were in a respectable, if not a perfect state of defence. But more might, doubtless, be done. If one place appeared to him to be more exposed and less effectively defended than another, it did not become him here to state it. It would be sufficient, for his present purpose, to state that three-fourths of our seacoast had been declared in a state of

[1]AC: 13–1, 165–6, *A Century of Lawmaking for a New Nation: US Congressional Documents and Debates, 1774–1875*, Washington, Library of Congress, available online at http://memory.loc.gov/ammem/amlaw/lwac.html (accessed on 08/06/2012).

blockade; that our waters were infested, and [our] coast lined with the armed boats and barges of the enemy, which were engaged in marauding and destroying the property of our citizens, with an impunity which was deeply to be regretted. He wished an investigation, for the purpose of inquiring whether any means could be devised to defend our coast from a warfare so distressing and vexatious. He needed not, he presumed, say anything more to induce the House to adopt the following resolutions:

Mr. F. then moved three resolutions as follows:

Resolved, That the Committee on Naval Affairs be instructed to inquire into the expediency of procuring and equipping such number of barges and row-galleys as may be required to aid in the defence and protection of our seacoast, and that they have leave to report by bill or otherwise.

Resolved, That the same committee be instructed to inquire into the expediency of equipping, for the public service, the gunboats belonging to the United States, not now in actual service.

Resolved, That the Committee on Military Affairs be instructed to inquire if any, and what, further provisions are required by law, for the better defence of the towns and cities on the seacoast, and that they have leave to report by bill or otherwise.

Mr. NELSON said he thought it proper to state, lest an imputation of indifference on this head should rest on the Naval Committee, that that committee had paid attention to these subjects, and had them now under consideration.

Mr. FISK disclaimed any intention to throw any censure on the Naval Committee; but the gentleman would properly appreciate the feelings of the people on the maritime frontier on this subject, which fully justified that particular attention of the House to their wishes, which Mr. F. had proposed.

The resolutions were adopted without opposition.

25. *From* The Norfolk Gazette

[NMM: LBK/2]   19 May 1813

The Publick Ledger

On Monday afternoon, the greater part of the enemy's force left the bay; there remains [*sic*] only nine, a ship of the line, four frigates, two brigs, and two schooners. It is supposed the ships that have sailed will proceed off the ports recently declared to be in blockade.

26.   *Warren's draft Proclamation*

[NMM: HUL/18]   1 September 1813

[Extract]

On His Majesty's Service to John Dougan Esq.ʳᵉ

Agent to the Commisioners for American Property Condemned as Droits to the Crown.

Admiral Sir J.B.Warren

Whereas his RH the Price Regent hath caused his pleasure to be signified to the Rt Hon the Lds Comm. of the Admiralty to direct that I should institute a strict & rigorous blockade of the ports and harbours. . .

. . . I do further declare from the 1st of September1813, all the outlets from the Albermarle & Pamlico Sounds, connected by inland navigation with the Port of Norfolk, the ports of Beaufort & Ocracocke [*sic*], North Carolina, Cape Fear river & Georgetown, South Carolina, and Sunbury and Darrien in Georgia, in a state of strict & rigorous blockade.

Given under my hand on board HMS *San Domingo* Chesapeake 1st Sept. 1813

[*Signed*] John Borlase Warren

To the Respective Flag Officers & By Command of the Admiral
[*Signed*] Thomas Fox Pro Secʸ.

27.   *Warren to Croker*[1]

Halifax
20 November 1813

No 274

Sir

Having consulted with His Excellency The Lieutenant Governor of this Province and considered the best means of enforcing the Blockade of the different Ports of the United States, I found it necessary to give full effect to the Orders of the Lords Commissioners of the Admiralty and to further their Lordships intentions therein, to direct an additional Blockade to be proclaimed which comprehends the line of Coast from the entrance by the Sound into New York to the Southern Ports and the River Mississippi – I enclose a Copy of the Same and hope it will meet

---

[1]Dudley, *The Naval War of 1812*, vol. 2, pp. 262–3, Warren to Croker, enclosing copy of Proclamation of 16 Nov 1813, citing TNA: ADM 1/504, pp. 551–3.

with their Lordships approbation – I have the honour to be Sir Your most obedient humble Servant.

John Borlase Warren

[*Enclosure*]

A PROCLAMATION

. . . I have also Ordered all that part of *Long Island Sound*, so called, being the Sea Coast lying within Montuk Point, or the Eastern Point of Long Island, and the Point of Land opposite thereto, commonly called Black Point, situate on the Sea Coast of the Mainland or Continent, together with all the Ports, Harbours, Creeks and Entrances of the East and North Rivers of *New-York*, as well as all the other Ports, Creeks and Bays along the Sea Coast of *Long Island*, and the State of *New-York*, and all the Ports Harbours Rivers and Creeks, lying and being on the Sea Coasts of the States of *East and West Jersey, Pennsylvania*, the lower Countries on the *Delaware, Maryland, Virginia, North and South Carolina, Georgia* and all the Entrances from the Sea, into the said River of the *Mississippi* to be strictly and vigorously Blockaded:- . . .

GIVEN under my Hand, at HALIFAX, the 16th Day of NOVEMBER, 1813.

John Borlase Warren,
Admiral of the Blue, and Commander in
Chief, &c, &c, &c.

To The Respective Flag Officers, Captains, Commanders, and Commanding Officers of His Majesty's Ships and Vessels, employed and to be employed on the American and West Indian Stations, and all whom it may concern.
By command of the Admiral
George Redmond Hulbert, *Secretary.*

28. *Samuel Rodman to William Logan Fisher*

[PPL: NWC, Letter 76]   New Bedford
16 November 1813

Dear Will^(m.)

. . . The present speculation rage will very probably be injurious to many concerned before it stops. I have hardly ever known it fail of proving so . . . Although I have no expectation of a speedy termination of war, yet accident may give it a peaceable turn, contrary to what I believe the wish and intention of the misrulers at Washington, whose aim I firmly believe is to prostrate the liberty of this Country and if they find, as they have hithertofore done, money'd men in the ranks of the Federalists, so lost to virtue & patriotism as to fill up the loans, I greatly fear they will effect it. – How I am astonished when I reflect on the conduct of this class of men, but for whom the wasteful war must have languished, and the tyrants of the South abandoned their wicked designs for the present – I also consider them in a pecuniary point of view to have been blinded by their cupidity, and it is very probable that the men that could not be satisfied with their funds lying dormant may yet live to see with the sacrifice of principles that would have upheld the union, they have also, for the sordid view of interest, made a sacrifice of the principal. It cannot be presumed that when a general peace takes place in Europe, which I do not think it chimerical to suppose may be produced by the eventual restraint of Bonaparte, that this country can share in commerce & revenue for a long time to come, half equal to what we may have experienced, and the people of the North who are becoming daily more disgusted with the war will not bear a heavy load of taxes.

Saml. Rodman

29. *Melville to Warren*

[NMM: LBK/2]

Admiralty
24 November 1813

Private
Dear Sir,

. . . You will receive by the present opportunity the Official intimation of the measure we have been compelled to adopt of again placing the Leeward Island and Jamaica stations on their former footing of chief commands, the former under Rear Admiral Durham who succeeds Sir F Laforey & the latter under Rear Admiral Brown. This arrangement became unavoidable (though much against my inclination) by the repeated and well founded complaints from Jamaica of the almost total want of protection on that station. This evil was also liable to be increased by the order which Admiral Brown had received from you to send away to join your flag any Vessel whose commanders might happen to die, in order that the vacancy might be filled up after such situation instead of an acting Captain being put in immediately. Under all these circumstances it became necessary to allocate a certain number of Ships to each Admiral [and] to make him responsible for their being properly disposed of, according to the wants of his station.

As the sole reason for the appointment of an Officer senior to Vice Admirals Stirling & Sawyer was the Union of the three commands, I do not think it fair either to you or to the latter officers to expect or direct that with your work in the Service you should continue merely as the successor of Admiral Sawyer on the Halifax Station. No person has yet been selected for that command, which if the latter had remained there, would actually have reverted to him; but it will probably be either Sir Alex^r Cochrane or Sir Richard Keats.

[Signed] Melville.

30. *Warren to Melville*

[NMM: LBK/2]

Bermuda
3 February 1814

Private
My Lord
I am honoured by your Lordship's Letter of the 24th Novr inform-ing me, that the Board had Determined to Divide the Command of the United Station; & that Rear Admiral Durham would succeed Sir Francis Laforey: and Sir Alexander Cochrane to this place, for the reasons thei-rin [*sic*] stated.

I am extremely surprised in being recalled at this moment after having undertaken the Command in the Situation in which I was placed at the Time, after having zealously & faithfully served my Sovereign & Coun-try, under so many Disadvantages.

I shall therefore forebear saying any further upon the Subject untill [*sic*] my arrival in Great Britain.

[Signed] Warren

31. *By the President of the United States of America,*
A proclamation[1]

Whereas it is manifest that the blockade, which has been proclaimed by the enemy, of the whole Atlantic coast of the United States, nearly 2,000 miles in extent, and abounding in ports, harbors and navigable inlets, can not be carried into effect by any adequate force actually stationed for the purpose; and it is rendered a matter of certainty and notoriety by the mul-tiplied and daily arrivals and departures of the public and private armed vessels of the United States, and other vessels that no such adequate force has been so stationed; And whereas a blockade thus destitute of

---

[1]AC: Appendix, Proclamations, 29 June 1814, No: 13, p. 76, available online at http://memory.loc.gov/ammem/amlaw/lwac.html (accessed on 08/06/2012).

the character of a regular and legal blockade, as defined and recognised by the established law of nations, whatever other purposes it may be made to answer, forms no lawful prohibition or obstacle to such neutral and friendly vessels as may choose to visit and trade with the United States; and whereas it accords with the interest and amicable views of the United States to favor and promote, as far as may be, the free and mutually beneficial commercial intercourse of all friendly nations disposed to engage therein, and with that view to afford to their vessels destined to the United States, a more positive and satisfactory security against all interruptions, molestations, or vexations whatever from the cruisers of the United States:

Now be it known that I, James Madison, President of the United States of America, do by his proclamation, strictly order and instruct all the public armed vessels of the United States, and all private armed vessels commissioned as privateers, or with letters of marque and reprisal, not to interrupt, detain, or otherwise molest or vex, any vessels whatever belonging to neutral powers, or the subjects or citizens thereof, which vessels shall be actually bound and proceeding to any port or place within the jurisdiction of the United States; but, on the contrary, to render all such vessels all the aid and kind offices which they may need or require.

[SEAL]

Given under my hand and seal of the United States at the city of Washington, the 29th day of June, A.D. 1814, and of the Independence of the United States the thirty eighth

James Madison
By the President:
Jas. Monroe, Secretary of State

32. *Warren to Croker*

[TNA: ADM 1/505, pp. 87–90]   Bermuda
                                                  30 December 1813

Sir
    . . . [I beg] to acquaint my Lord Commissioners of the Admiralty that having sent the *Barrossa* to Jamaica to carry home specie, and every other Ship that could be spared without raising the Blockaded ports of America, I lament to find that both the Leeward Islands and Jamaica are very deficient of a Force adequate to their protection, or to perform the various extensive Convoy Service required to be done in those places . . .
                                                  [*Signed*] J.B. Warren

33. *Warren to Melville*

[NMM: LBK/2][1]   Bermuda
                                                    30 December 1813

Private
My Lord,

I am sorry to say that the American Small Vessels notwithstanding the Vigilance of the Blockading Squadrons; from the severity of the weather & in the Dark Showery nights; Do get out; & it is almost impracticable to prevent it: the Assembly at Jamaica are caballing & Demonstrating about Ships; I have sent all in my power: I really am left so base to keep in check the American Cruisers and new Ships which must be soon expected out, & that I am in no Enviable State but trust you will soon reinforce the squadron with some of the large new Frigates: the *Endymion* is an Excellent Ship & also *Goliath* & *Majestic*:[2] The Extent of this Coast however is [so] immense: that to shut on all points would require Twice my Numbers.

I am sorry to say that Cruising upon the Edge off Nantucket Shoal & off Rhode Island: the cold has occasioned me a Rheumatick Illness from Which I am but just recovering.

                                    I have the honor to be with great regard
                                                    My Dear Lord,
                            your earnest friend & faithful & Humble ser[t]
                                        [*Signed*] John Borlase Warren

PS Several privateers are now
Spotted out at Carthagena
Under the American Flag.

34. *Samuel Rodman to William Logan Fisher*

[PPL: NWC, Letter 79]   New Bedford
                                                      6 October 1814

Dear W[m]
    . . . [My] Mind [is] filled with anxious cares for the protection of my family & property which the ferocious aspect of British warfare

---

[1]A draft copy of this letter exists, with slightly different wording.
[2]HMS *Endymion* (40) was one of the Royal Navy's best sailers, *Goliath* and *Majestic* (58) were both razees, cut down 74's.

lately assumed has so strengthened and increased beyond former ideas of anticipated danger at this place, that I have given less attention to pen & paper than I was once in the habit of, days often pass without my visiting the Compting [Counting] house, whence the prospect of our haul'd up and abandon'd Ships affords a dreary prospect to all that once looked to them for support, and this class, with owners, artificers &c comprises nearly all of the inhabitants of New Bedford – I have sent into the Country some of my most valuable Merchandize such as Oil, Spermacetti Candles, Duck &c, with some of the ship's appurtances [*sic* – appurtenances] – from my house I have not removed an article and should Adml Cochranes order of burning all the property accessible to his squadron be carried into effect here, I think I should suffer more than any other person in it from the kind of property that cannot be removed – There are now one 74, three frigates and two Brigs at Tarpaulin Cove, supposed to be part of the Chesapeake fleet, I hope on their way to Halifax without looking into any harbor, but as this is a larger force than has hitherto been in the vineyard sound it renews apprehensions that it is very unpleasant to foster and from which relief can only be had by their departure.

I am thy affectionate father
Sam. Rodman

CAPTAIN JOHN PASCOE GRENFELL OF THE BRAZILIAN NAVY IN THE RIVER PLATE, MARCH TO AUGUST 1826

Edited by Brian Vale

At the end of 1825, the newly independent Empire of Brazil went to war with the newly independent Republic of Argentina – then called the United Provinces of the River Plate – over control of the north bank of the Plate Estuary and consequently of the river itself. It was a replay of the long-standing dispute between the Portuguese and Spanish colonial Empires over what was confusingly called the 'Banda Oriental' (properly the 'Banda Oriental del Uruguay'). Originally a Spanish province, the area had been occupied by Brazil in the confusion which followed the Napoleonic Wars. In 1825, a rebellion against Brazilian rule brought the United Provinces into the conflict and drove the two countries to war. It lasted for two years and resulted in a stalemate – the United Provinces dominating on land, the Brazilians at sea. Eventually, the state of Uruguay was created as a compromise and a buffer between the two.

The two nations that confronted each other in the River Plate were strikingly different. The United Provinces was a republic, with a small, largely immigrant population scattered over a vast land mass politically dominated by the city and province of Buenos Aires. It had a large international trade, carried out principally in British, American and French vessels, but few maritime pretensions. Its naval forces were modest and, at the beginning of the war, consisted of no more than six small warships and a dozen gunboats for port defence. Brazil, by contrast, was a monarchy, ruled by the former Crown Prince of Portugal who, as the Emperor Pedro I, had led the country to independence in 1822–23. It was a vast country with a huge coastline, an extensive seaborne commerce and a large and experienced navy comprising some 96 ships of all sizes carrying 690 guns. The strategy of the two nations in the maritime war reflected their circumstances: Brazil's aim was to strangle the trade of Buenos Aires by blockade; while that of the United Provinces was to keep the waters of the Plate open while unleashing a swarm of privateers on Brazil's sea borne commerce.[1]

Manpower and Foreign Recruitment

A remarkable feature of the war is that the navies of both sides in the conflict relied heavily on foreign sailors – notably British and Americans – to command and man their ships. This tradition had been established during the struggles for independence from Spain and Portugal. For both Brazil and the United Provinces, command of the seas or – in the case of the latter – the waters of the Plate had been vital to success, and the creation of navies had been a priority. Suitable ships and equipment were readily available, but there was a critical shortage of local manpower. In spite of their extensive coastlines, Brazil and the United Provinces were essentially continental countries of cattle ranches, plantations and mines: there was no maritime tradition and few people had any knowledge of the sea. The problem had been solved by using foreign sources of supply, whether newly arrived migrants – as in the case of the United Provinces – or secret recruitment in England supplemented by the engagement of British and American sailors in local ports – as in the case of Brazil. The naval forces which resulted had made major contributions to securing independence. In the River Plate, Argentine sailors under the command of Irish-born Commodore William Brown had overcome the Spanish; while the Brazilian Navy, under the leadership of Lord Cochrane, had swept the Portuguese from the seas and expelled its garrisons.

When war came in 1826, the manpower problem reappeared. The situation was less acute in Buenos Aires than in Rio de Janeiro. The United Provinces needed only 54 officers and some 1,300 seamen and marines to man its small squadron – numbers that were easily found by recalling veterans of independence and drawing on the seagoing experience of the wave of migrants who had come to the Plate in the post-Napoleonic war period attracted by cheap land and good wages. As a result, the Argentine Navy was well manned, with half of its sailors and two-thirds of its officers of Anglo-Saxon origin. Most were British and Irish, but the republican hue of the regime appealed to North Americans. There were also representatives of more individualistic nationalities,

---

[1]For a complete history of the war in English, see Brian Vale, *'A War Betwixt Englishmen': Brazil against Argentina on the River Plate 1825–30* (London, 2000).

such as Frenchmen, Italians and Spaniards: though these, by and large, preferred the more free and easy life of the privateer to naval service.

Brazil needed 200 sea officers and 10,500 sailors and marines to adequately man its extensive navy. This was a tougher nut to crack. Some 100 officers of the old Portuguese Navy had thrown in their lot with Brazil but most were senior and few had wartime experience. Fortunately, 57 officers of British and 16 of American, French and Scandinavian origin remained in service after the successes of the independence period, and were available for front line commands. However the Imperial Navy remained short of junior officers and men in spite of local impressments, overseas recruitment, and the tempting of foreign sailors to desert in Brazilian ports. As before, potential prize money proved an irresistible temptation. The result, as HM Consul Woodbine Parish reflected, as he surveyed the blockading squadron in 1826, was that 'the Brazilian Navy appears so formidable to the Buenos Aireans because it is largely commanded and manned by Englishmen'.[1] By 1827, one-third of officers at sea in the Brazilian Navy and over one-sixth of the seamen were British. Indeed, that same year, Ambassador Robert Gordon complained bitterly that the conflict between Brazil and Argentina which was ruining British trade was essentially 'a war betwixt Englishmen', pointing out that 1,200 British subjects were serving in the Brazilian Navy and that the opposing commanders – Commodore James Norton[2] and Commodore William Brown[3] – were both Englishmen.[4] As was common at the time, Parish

---

[1]Parish to Canning, 20 July 1825, TNA: FO 6/9.

[2]James Norton (1789–1832). Born in Newark-on-Trent, Norton had seen service in the Royal Navy and the East India Company. In India, he married Eliza Bland, widow of a Waterloo veteran, Colonel Esme Erskine, son of Lord Erskine. Appointed a Brazilian Captain-of-Frigate in 1823, he was instrumental in the recruitment of British sailors in London. Arriving in Brazil too late to be active in the War of Independence, Norton distinguished himself during the Pernambuco rebellion of 1824. Promoted full Capt, he commanded the inshore squadron blockading Buenos Aires 1826–27, directing the battles of Lara Quilmes and Monte Santiago. Lost an arm during the capture of the privateer *General Branzden* in 1827. Commanded the *Isabela* frigate on an expedition conveying Queen Maria II to claim the Portuguese throne, and was promoted Cmdr, 1829.

[3]William Brown (1760–1857). Venerated as the Father of the Argentine Navy, Brown was born in Co. Mayo, Ireland. Emigrated to the United Provinces in 1811 and volunteered to command its small patriot navy in the successful war of independence in 1814. In disgrace after a privateering voyage in the Pacific and West Indies, he was recalled to command as a Cmdr during the war against Brazil. Promoted RA, 1827. Active during the war with Uruguay and the siege of Montevideo under the Dictator Rosas from 1841 until 1845 when the Argentine squadron was seized by the French and British. In retirement thereafter.

[4]Gordon to Dudley, no. 26, 1 Oct 1827, TNA: FO 13/39.

and Gordon – a Scot himself – used the term 'Englishmen' broadly so as to include all subjects of King George, whether English, Scottish or Irish.

John Pascoe Grenfell

One of the most outstanding of Brazil's British officers was John Pascoe Grenfell. Grenfell was born in Battersea in 1800, a member of a family whose members served with distinction in the armed forces, the Church and in the civil administration of the Crown. Unable to follow his brother, Sydney – who ended his career as a Rear Admiral – into the Royal Navy, John Pascoe briefly joined the East India Company before making his way to the Pacific to join Cochrane in 1820. He was appointed as a lieutenant in the Chilean Navy and served in some of the major engagements of the War of Independence. He was with the squadron which convoyed San Martin's invading army up the coast in August to Peru, and in November took part in one of Cochrane's greatest achievements, the cutting out of the Spanish frigate *Esmeralda* from the heavily fortified port of Callao. Hitching his wagon to Cochrane's star, in April 1821, he obtained a transfer to the flagship *O'Higgins* and was present in 1821–22 during the unsuccessful pursuit of the Spanish frigates *Venganza* and *Prueba* as far north as Mexico. With that war concluded, Cochrane accepted an offer from the Brazilians to command their navy in the liberation struggle against Portugal. In January 1823, he sailed for Rio de Janeiro accompanied by five followers. One of them was John Pascoe Grenfell.

Appointed as a Brazilian Lieutenant, Grenfell served on Cochrane's flagship, *Pedro I* during the blockade and evacuation of the Portuguese stronghold of Salvador de Bahia; then during the expedition against Maranhão, the centre of enemy influence on the northern coast. After Cochrane had tricked the Portuguese into evacuation by pretending that a huge Brazilian fleet and army were over the horizon, Grenfell was promoted commander (Capitão-Tenente) and sent to Belem do Pará at the mouth of the Amazon to secure the evacuation of the Portuguese forces there by using the same deception. In this he was successful, but at the cost of becoming embroiled in local politics.

In November 1823, Cochrane was back in Rio basking in a hero's welcome and his new title of Marquis of Maranhão. Grenfell returned some months later. They served together again in 1824–25 in the suppression of a rebellion in the north eastern province of Pernambuco. By this time Cochrane's triumphs had, as usual, been overshadowed by disputes over pay and prize money and by accusations of poor treatment. In mid-1825, he returned to England. Grenfell, like most of his British comrades remained in Brazil. High in the favour of the Emperor Pedro, and cleared of any political impropriety in Pará, Grenfell was appointed to command the three-masted schooner *Grecian*, soon renamed *Principe Imperial*.

With the outbreak of war with the United Provinces, Grenfell's first task was to escort a convoy to the River Plate. In Montevideo, Grenfell was promoted Captain of Frigate (Capitão da Fragata) and was moved to the brig of war *Caboclo*.[1] To avoid language problems and ensure efficiency, it was common for the Brazilian Navy to post its British officers and men to the same ships. *Caboclo* was no exception. When Grenfell took command, 74 out of a ship's company of 90 were British [32, 88]. His journal shows the British style of ship management which Grenfell and his colleagues brought to the Brazilian Navy – mustering and reading the Article of War (though no religious services) on Sundays; regular exercises with the guns; washing clothes and hammocks; condemning and disposing of rotten beef etc. They also show that organising a convoy made up of a motley collection of merchant captains was as difficult in the South Atlantic as in the English Channel or the Western Approaches [3–7, 9, 11].

Cat and Mouse in the River Plate

The major influence dictating the tactics of the war was the geography of the River Plate. Cutting into the side of South America like a great gash, the Plate was 200 miles wide at its mouth and 250 miles long before it joined the great southward-flowing river systems which provide the back door to the interior of the continent. However, although extensive, the Plate for most of its length was a shallow stretch of water, interspersed by mudbanks that could only be passed by using three narrow channels, the deepest of which was only 20 feet. Buenos Aires lay some 200 miles from the mouth, surrounded by shallows and with an anchorage that could only be approached via an easily defended channel three-quarters of a mile wide and 12 feet deep. All this posed obvious challenges for the Brazilian Navy whose smallest frigates needed 17 feet in which to float. It was impossible for it to deploy its full strength in the river so as to crush Brown's squadron. The inshore squadron thus consisted of its smaller vessels, few of which could get nearer than 3 miles from the city.

---

[1]Purchased in 1823, *Caboclo* was a 16-gun brig of 250 tons.

Armament too was a factor. Although large, the Brazilian Navy comprised a heterogeneous collection of ships, some very modern, some very old. Aiming to maintain a powerful 'blue water' navy, the Brazilians had chosen to arm their smaller and older vessels with heavy calibre but short-range carronades. This was unsuitable to action in the Plate, where navigational difficulties made range important, and where the arsenal in Buenos Aires had only been able to supply long guns of traditional design. This stroke of good fortune meant that Brown's ships were able to outrange their opponents.

Brazil's first naval commander in the war was the unpopular Portuguese-born Vice Admiral Rodrigo Lobo.[1] Although vastly experienced, Lobo was excessively cautious and reluctant to make any move unless backed by overwhelming force. This was a marked contrast to the aggressive attitude of Commodore William Brown, who held to the British view (shared by the Royal Navy veterans in the Imperial Navy) that the object of naval warfare was to secure the destruction of enemy warships wherever they could be found, whatever the risk.

Lobo's tactics were true to form. His reaction to the navigational problems and the challenge posed by Brown – who had already forced him into an indecisive action at Corales north of the Argentine capital, on 9 February – was to deploy his forces between Montevideo and the Punto del Indio on the southern shore, over a hundred miles east of Buenos Aires. This meant that blockade runners could take advantage of fog or contrary winds to get through. It also left Brown free to create havoc through the rest of the River Plate. On 24 February, he attacked the Brazilian outpost of Colonia and, on 11 April, raided the Brazilian base of Montevette. In this action, Brown with a corvette, two brigs and a schooner were seen off by a force headed by the Brazilian frigate *Niteroi*, commanded by James Norton. Grenfell, whose ship was being repaired, joined the *Niteroi* with two of his officers and volunteers from his crew [26].

Lobo's defeatism and timidity inevitably led to his recall and replacement by Admiral Rodrigo Pinto Guedes [30], a man of vast experience

---

[1] Rodrigo Lobo (1763–1843). Lobo entered the Portuguese Navy in 1790 and rose rapidly. He was promoted Cmdr in 1808, having accompanied the Royal Family on its flight to Brazil. In 1817, he commanded the sea forces during the Portuguese seizure of the Band Oriental; and gained unpopularity for his suppression of a revolt in Pernambuco. As RA, he commanded the small force in the River Plate on the brink of independence in 1822, joined the Brazilian cause and was promoted VA. Recalled from the Plate in April 1826, he faced a court of inquiry, was acquitted but never served again.

who was then senior naval member of the Supreme Military Council.[1] Pinto Guedes's first act was to replace five of the most timid or inexperienced captains with officers in whom he had confidence, most of them British. His next was to tighten the blockade and adopt a more aggressive policy. Accordingly, he divided his forces into three divisions and a reserve. The First Division, formed of the six heaviest ships under Pinto Guedes's direct command, provided an external line of blockade which covered the mouth of the river in the east. The Third Division, of eleven schooners, was responsible for controlling the waters of the Uruguay to the west. The Second Division, consisting of four corvettes, four brigs or brigantines and two schooners under the command of Captain James Norton in the frigate *Niteroi*, was deployed in the centre, charged with closely blockading Buenos Aires and containing Brown's squadron of warships. Grenfell and *Caboclo* were ordered to join this force [31].

The impact of Norton's inshore squadron was immediate. As Grenfell's journal shows, the Brazilians began to strangle the trade of Buenos Aires, intercepting almost everything that could float. In 1825, 387 merchant ships had entered Buenos Aires; in the last six months of 1826, only two got through. Dealing with the Argentine commander, William Brown, was more difficult. His tactics were to sail from his anchorage and advance with his small squadron towards the Brazilians who would then retreat into deeper water to gain sea room in the hope of drawing him into a fight. Brown would then withdraw in the vain hope that the Brazilians would follow so that their larger warships would ground on the mud while the smaller ones would be tempted to come within gunshot and be overwhelmed. To the population of Buenos Aires, it looked as if the enemy were fleeing the Argentine advance and were too timid to follow their retreat – an impression that was propagated in the local newspapers. He tried this trick on three occasions – 23 and 25 May and 11 June [39, 41, 56] – each of which was hailed as a victory. Brown's reluctance to enter into action and the false impression created in the newspapers was bitterly resented by Brazilian commanders [89, 90].

---

[1]Rodrigo Pinto Guedes (1762–1845). Pinto Guedes entered the Portuguese Navy in 1781, and rose rapidly. In 1798, he was a Cmdr serving with the Portuguese squadron which formed part of Lord Nelson's force in the Mediterranean. In 1805, he became RA and member of the Admiralty Board; and in 1807, VA and Chief of Staff of the Navy. 1807–08, he fled with the Portuguese Royal Family and government to Brazil. In 1822, now Adm, he embraced the cause of Brazilian independence. In the Plate, Pinto Guedes was a skilful and aggressive commander, effectively destroying the trade of Buenos Aires and the capability of its navy. Unfortunately, his actions provoked international protest. After the war, he faced a court of inquiry into the conduct of the campaign but was acquitted.

On 29 July, Brown used the tactic again at what became called the Battle of Lara-Quilmes. But this time he tried a variant, leaving Buenos Aires at nightfall in the hope of surprising and boarding *Niteroi* in the dark. The gamble did not work. The two schooners Norton had placed in the channel gave the alarm, the Brazilians withdrew as usual but turned and managed to catch Brown's ships before they reached the safety of the shallows. There was an intense exchange of fire in which the Argentines were heavily damaged and took many casualties [89, 90]. Brown abandoned his sinking flagship, *25 de Mayo*, and continued his withdrawal in the brig *Republica Argentina*. Grenfell's *Caboclo*, being fast and having a shallow draught, pursued the brig and engaged her. Legend has it that Grenfell called over to Brown with his speaking trumpet, inviting the Argentine commander to surrender and take tea in his cabin. The answer was a patriotic assertion that his colours were nailed to the mast followed by a broadside which shattered the upper part of Grenfell's right arm. He was taken to the military hospital in Montevideo and there, on 19 August, the arm was amputated [91, 92]. The last entry in Grenfell's journal is that for 28 July.

Epilogue

Grenfell made a good recovery from his injury and spent one year's leave in England. He returned to Brazil in 1828 to command the corvette *Maria Isabel*. The war was nearly over by this time, but Grenfell managed to capture the privateer *Peruana* off Rio in July. In Montevideo, on 13 February 1829, he married Maria Dolores Masini, whose sister – Maria Engracia – married another British comrade in arms, William Parker, who had served as Norton's First Lieutenant on *Niteroi*.[1] Grenfell's career went from strength to strength. In 1829, he was promoted full captain (Capitao-de-Mar-e-Guerra) and the following year commanded the new frigate *Isabela* on an expedition against the Azores in support of

---

[1]William Parker (1801–1883). Born Dumfries. Mate of his uncle's brig, the *Lindsays*, hired to convey contracted sailors to Brazil in 1823. Joined the Brazilian Navy. Served with Cochrane in the War of Independence and the insurrection in Pernambuco, 1823–24. Lt, Oct 1825. Served throughout the Buenos Aires war. Cdr, 1827. Married Maria Engracia Massini (sister of Maria Dolores, wife of John Pascoe Grenfell). Second in command to Grenfell in *Isabela* to the Azores in support of the claims of Queen Maria II of Portugal, 1829–30. Second-in-command to Grenfell in the war against the rebels in Rio Grande do Sul, 1836–39, as Capt of Frigate. Full Capt, 1842. Commanded in the River Plate, 1848–51. Second-in-command to Grenfell in war with the Argentine Dictator, Rosas, 1851. Cmdr, 1851. Port Commander Rio de Janeiro, 1855. VA, 1856. Successively commanded naval districts of Bahia, Rio and Montevideo, 1857–65. Adm (rtd), 1867. Died in Montevideo.

the claims of Pedro's daughter, Queen Maria II of Portugal. In 1836, he was promoted commodore (Chefe-de-Divisao) and spent three years in charge of the naval forces fighting the 'Farrapos' rebellion in Rio Grand do Sul. In 1841, he was made Rear Admiral (Chefe-de-Esquadra) and commander-in-chief of Brazil's Southern Naval District.

Between 1846 and 1850, Grenfell served as Consul-General in Liverpool. In addition to diplomatic and commercial dutes, one of his major tasks was to supervise the construction of a state-of-the-art steam paddle frigate *D Affonso*.[1] Built as a smaller version of the Royal Navy's HMS *Fury*, she was 186 feet in length, of 886 tons burden and had a shallow draft which made her ideal for Brazil's riverine conditions.[2] But even this relatively peaceful task was not without incident. On 24 August 1848, *Affonso* was undergoing her final trials on the Mersey under her first captain, Joaquim Marques Lisboa (later to achieve fame as the Marquis of Tamandaré, hero of the Paraguayan War). There was a galaxy of distinguished passengers on board – Grenfell himself, members of the Brazilian Royal family and of the French Royal family, to which they were related, together with representatives of the diplomatic corps and local dignitaries. The junketing was suddenly interrupted by the sight of smoke on the horizon. It proved to be the immigrant ship *Ocean Monarch* which had caught fire one day out from Liverpool. *Affonso* steamed to the rescue and plucked 160 survivors from the flames and the water to universal admiration.[3] As a warship, *Affonso* was such a success that, in 1850, Grenfell signed a contract for a second steamer to be called *Amazonas*.[4]

In 1851, he was recalled to Brazil to command the naval forces in Brazil's war against the Argentine dictator Rosas. Flying his flag in the *Affonso*, at the head of a mixed squadron of steam and sailing ships (the latter commanded by his brother-in-law, William Parker) Grenfell forced a passage through the heavily fortified narrows of Tonelero with a Brazilian army on board. As a consequence, Rosas was outflanked and defeated at the Battle of Monte Caseros. The Brazilian Government recommended that Grenfell be ennobled as a Viscount, but the Emperor refused because he had always insisted on retaining his British

---

[1]Grenfell's letter books are in the University of Liverpool Library Special Collections and Archives (ULLSCA), piece 472.

[2]Iron-framed but sheathed in timber, *Affonso* was built by Thomas Royden and Co. of Liverpool with 300 hp engines supplied by John Rigby of Hawarden.

[3]ULLSCA, piece 473–4; *Illustrated London News*, 2 Sept 1848.

[4]Built by Thomas Wilson of Birkenhead with engines by Benjamin Hicks and Co. of Bolton.

nationality.[1] Indeed, he had special permission from Queen Victoria[2] permitting him to serve Brazil.

Promoted Vice Admiral in 1852, Grenfell returned to Liverpool as Consul-General and, in 1861, attended the funeral of his old chief, Lord Cochrane, as a representative of the Imperial Government. Grenfell died in Paris in 1869, a full admiral.

Acknowledgements

The documents printed below are all in the possession of current members of the Grenfell family who have generously given permission to reproduce them. I would particularly like to thank Lt-Colonel Patrick Lort-Phillips, Dame Frances Campbell-Preston DCVO and Mr Frank Grenfell of Eton College; and also Mrs Bridget Krasinska – a direct descendent of Grenfell's brother-in-law, Admiral William Parker – who provided the transcript of the journal.

[1]Moreira de Castro to Grenfell, 18 Feb 1852, ULLSCA, piece 502–3.
[2]ULLSCA, piece 160–5.

J.P. GRENFELL'S JOURNAL AS CAPTAIN OF
THE *PRINCIPE IMPERIAL* AND *CABOCLO*
MARCH TO JULY 1826[1]

Convoy to Montevideo

1.   *Friday March the 10th*

His Imperial Majesty's schooner, *Principe Imperial*, at single anchor in the outer roads of Rio de Janeiro.

am Light airs from the NW & fine weather, at daylight hoisted the convoy signal to weigh, at 8 weighed and made sail, at 9 falling calm & the tide sweeping the vessel within the Fort Lagé, anchored, ran a warp out to the eastward, weighed the anchor & drifted out clear. At 10 moderate sea breeze, hauled up & worked out of the harbour in company with the schooner of war *Providencia*, schooners *St Domingo Eneas*, & *Urania*, & brigs *Nova Mendingue* & *St. José de Rio*, smacks *Lilia* & *Euphrasia*, & ship *Gertrudes Elizabeth*, bound to Rio Grande and Monte Video.

pm Calm. Quartered the people & passed out the small arms. At sunset a light air from the southward, hauled to the SW.

2.   *Saturday March 11th*

Light airs from the SE; hauled to the SW and burnt a blue light. At daylight convoy in shore and much scattered, hoisted the signal to close & shortened sail. At noon Sugar-loaf NNE 10 leagues. At 4 wore to join the sternmost vessels – at sunset convoy united, hauled to the SW under moderate sail.

3.   *Sunday 12th*

am Moderate breeze at ENE & fine weather, at daylight convoy all in sight but much scattered. Made sail ahead and hoisted signal to close. At 11 mustered the people and read the Articles of War. At noon no land in sight. Latitude 23° 51' S, longitude 43° 45' W.

pm Increasing breeze. At 5 *Mendingue* & *St José* very far astern, all the others well up. Rounded to & hoisted the signal to close, the *Gertrudes* not answering or shortening sail, fired the blank guns, & then

[1]Handwritten manuscript in the possession of the Grenfell family.

two shot at her when she rounded to. At 7 the convoy being all united close & steered away SSW.

4. *Monday 13th*

am Moderate breeze from the NE & cloudy weather, topsails lowered on the caps. Scrubbed hammocks & bags & washed clothes: towards noon, breeze dying away. At noon latitude 25°35'S, longitude 45°1'W.

pm At 1.30 a fresh breeze from the SW, hauled to the SE & made signal for the convoy to close . . . At sunset convoy all united. At 10 burnt a blue light, which was answered by the convoy.

5. *Tuesday 14th*

am Fresh breezes from the southward & cloudy weather. At 1 & 4 burnt blue lights, answered partially by the convoy. At sunrise convoy much scattered, the *Gertrudes* 5 miles on the quarter, schooner under double-reefed foretopsail, main trysail & forestaysail. At 9 wore & let up the weather forerigging, at 9.30 wore again. At noon latitude 25°28'S, longitude 44°1'W.

pm At 4 all the convoy in company, made the signal to tack. Tacked to the SW, all the convoy doing the same except the *Nova Mendingue*. At 5 bore up to join the ship *Gertrudes* & brig *St José de Rio*, hailed ditto & ordered them to carry more sail. At sunset *Mendingue* not in sight. During the night under easy sail, burning blue lights every two hours.

6. *Wednesday 15th March*

am Moderate breezes at SSE & fine weather. At daylight the *St Domingos Eneas* & *Mendingue* missing. Made the signal to close and bore up to join the leewardmost vessels. At 7 the *Urania* hailed us, & asked leave to part company, having the smallpox on board & neither medicines or doctor. Sent the surgeon to visit her & supplied her with necessaries & ordered her to keep company. At 11 hailed a strange smack from Rio Grande. No news. At noon the *Mendingue* in sight on the weather quarter. Latitude 25°33'S, longitude 44°22'W.

pm An increasing breeze veering round to the eastward with a rising sea. At 4 exercised with ball at a mark. At sunset all the convoy in sight except the *St Domingos Eneas*. Made the signal to close & at night burnt a blue light every two hours.

7.   *Thursday 16th March*

am Fresh breeze from the eastward in cloudy weather & passing squalls of rain. At daylight 6 sail of the convoy only in sight. At noon clearing up with fine weather. Latitude 27°21'S, longitude 45°58'W.

pm Fine weather, tacked to join the brig *Mendingue*. At 4 made her signal to close & to carry all sail. Wore & made sail and spoke the brig *St José*. Ordered her to carry all sail & steer the same course as ourselves. Made the general signal to close, & shortened sail. At night occasional squalls; burnt blue lights every two hours.

8.   *Friday 17th March*

Fresh breezes from the eastward & fine weather. At daylight all the vessels in sight, but the *Gertrudes*, the *Mendingue* & *St José* very distant. Hauled up. At 8 o'clock bore away SSW again & set the maintopsail. Washed clothes. At noon convoy in company. Latitude 29°29'S, longitude 47°34'W. By our course made good for the last 48 hours I have been every reason to think our compasses are incorrect, & in great error to the eastward.

pm Steady breeze from the NE & fine weather. Exercised with the schooner *Providencia* with blank cartridges. At sunset made the signal to close, the convoy all in company.

9.   *Saturday 18th March 1826*

Fine fresh breeze from the NE & clear weather. At daylight only 4 sail in sight, the *Gertrudes* & smack *Euphrasia* missing. At 6 saw the smack ahead. Made all sail in chase; at 6.30 saw the *Gertrudes* on the larboard bow. Made the signal to close & fired two blank guns. Schooner under all sail going 9½ knots. At 8 shortened sail & fired two shot at the *Gertrudes*, who had paid no attention to the signal. She then shortened sail & kept away to close us. Made the signal to pass us within hail & bore away to join the other vessels just in sight astern. At 10 hove to, spoke the *Gertrudes* & ordered the Master on board. Sent the surgeon to visit her sick. The *Mendingue* passed with a signal of distress flying, having broken her coppers, which we could not repair. At 11 bore away & made sail to the SW. At noon latitude obs. 31°11'S, longitude 49°22'W. Rio Grande bearing S 66°W distant 152 miles.

pm An increasing breeze. At 2 hove to and lowered the second gig to send on board the schooner *Providencia*, ditto swamped & in hoisting her up she broke her back – At sunset all the convoy in company excepting the *St Domingos Eneas* who parted company on the night of the 14th and the schooner *Urania* who we have not seen since the evening of the 17th, both having separated intentionally. At night blowing hard from the NE & a large following sea. Furled the foretopsail, the schooner running under her bare poles 7 & 8 knots. Burnt blue lights every two hours: at midnight sounded, ground at 32 fathoms, fine sand: fired a gun.

10.　*Sunday 19th March*

Blowing fresh from the NE & hazy weather at daylight. Made sail and hauled up NW for the land. During the night the *Euphrasia* parted company: the rest of the convoy all present. At 10.30 saw the land, the tower of Alalya on the bar of the Rio Grande bearing NWbyW 3 leagues. At 11 wore, hoisted our colours, fired a gun, and hove to. Several strange sail in sight & others at anchor off the bar. At 11.30 the *Euphrasia* joining company. At noon latitude observed 32°14'S, longitude per chronometer 51°46'W Rio Grande NWbyN 4 leagues. Wore and stood towards the bar.

　　At 1 pm found the schooner *Urania* at anchor with two other vessels . . . At 4 shortened sail. At sunset all the convoy in company. During the night burnt blue lights every two hours.

11.　*Monday 20th March*

Light breezes varying from SSW to SSE and fine clear weather. At daylight found that the brig *St José de Rio* had parted company. Made signal for the convoy to continue the same course, & tacked to the westward. At 7 saw a strange sail north, bore up in chase, and at 9 hailed the brig *St José de Rio*. Reprimanded the captain for his negligence & obliged him to make all sail to rejoin the convoy. At noon latitude 33°23'S, longitude 52°15'W. At 1 tacked to the SE. At 4 made sail in chase of a stranger bearing SW. At 7 brought her to, & spoke her. She proved to be a Brazilian smack from St Catharina bound to Rio Grande out 13 days. At 10 rejoined the convoy, fired a gun & burnt a blue light.

12.　*Tuesday 21st March*

Light winds from the southward and cloudy weather. Convoy all in company, passed a Brazilian sumaca. Latitude at noon 33°22'S, longitude 51°16'W.

　　Pm Exercise with ball at a cask. At night wind veering round to the NW.

13.   *Wednesday 22nd March*

am Strong breezes from the northward & clear weather. Clapped a Spanish cap on the foremast head. At noon latitude 34°2"S, longitude 51°40'W.

pm Strong breeze veering to the SW. At 1 tacked to the westward in chase of a strange brig: at 3 ditto a vessel of war, cleared for action and at 3.30 bore up alongside a French brig of war of 22 guns, steering to the NE[1]. Wore & made sail to rejoin the convoy convoy.

14.   *Thursday 23rd of March*

Moderate breezes from the westward and clear weather, under easy sail, & bearing up occasionally for the convoy. At noon lat. 35°24'S, longitude 52°22'W.

pm Exercised with blank cartridge at the schooner *Providencia*.

15.   *Friday 24th March*

Moderate breezes from the SE and clear weather. At noon Cape St. Maria S 64° W. A strong current setting to the northward.

pm Chased and brought to the English brig *Cornelius* from Liverpool to Buenos Ayres; warned her of the blockade by HIM Fleet. At night convoy much scattered.

16.   *Saturday 25th March*

Light airs from the southward & fine weather with a strong current setting NNE. Convoy in company. Boarded the American ship *Anne Maria* from Philadelphia to Buenos Ayres, warned her of the blockade. At noon Cape St Maria SW 30 miles.

17.   *Sunday 26th March*

Light airs from the eastward & fine weather. Current setting to the southward. At 8 am off the Castillos only 3 of the convoy in sight. Mustered in divisions. At noon lat.34°22'S, long. 53°36'W. Cape St Maria S 42° W, dist. 24 miles.

---

[1]The *Faune*, based at Montevideo to watch over French interests.

pm Tacked to the southward and spoke [with] the ship *Gertrudes Elizabeth*, desired her to carry all possible sail.

18.   *Monday 27 th March*

am Moderate breeze from the northward and cloudy weather. At 9 off Point Pedras, observed the convoy astern very negligent, tacked to join them. At noon lat. 34°58'S, Cape St Maria NWbyN 3 leagues.

pm Chased and spoke with the English brig *Europe* from Monte Video bound to Bahia. Exercised at quarters; during the night soundings in 20, 19 & 18 fathoms; muddy bottom.

19.   *Tuesday 28th March*

Moderate breezes from the SE and clear weather. At 6 saw the Isle of Lobos SWbyW 4 leagues. The convoy all astern. At noon off Point of Maldonado. At 6 off Point Negra. During the night, standing for Flores in 9, 8, 7 & 5 fathoms. At midnight sounding in 5 fathoms, sand, hauled up NW, contrary to the advice of the pilot, burnt blue lights for the convoy to follow our motions. Deepened our water immediately & got again on muddy bottom.

20.   *Wednesday 29th March*

Moderate breeze from the NE & clear weather. At 1 saw Monte Video bearing NWbyW. At 4 came to off Punta Brava in 6 fathoms. At 7 weighed and made sail, worked into Monte Video harbour & at 1 pm anchored in 3 fathoms water. Furled sails, & delivered the dispatches. During the afternoon all the convoy arrived. Found in the port His Britannic Majesty's ship *Doris*,[1] a French brig of war and three Brazilian schooners of war. Received orders from Pedro Antonio Nunes, the commodore of the port.

21.   *March 30th & 31st March*

At anchor in Monte Video.

---

[1]Under the command of Sir John Sinclair, the frigate *Doris* was in Montevideo watching over British interests and reporting on naval events during the whole of 1826. The French brig *Faune* and the USS *Cyane* were similarly engaged.

22.   *April 1st 1826*

Strong breeze from the SW and heavy rain. Arrived HIM. brig *Rio da Prata*[1] with her deck blown up & 30 men killed & wounded from an explosion of gunpowder in their artillery store room.

23.   *Sunday April 2nd*

Wind SE & clear weather. Arrived HIM frigate *Nitheroy*[2] from Rio de Janeiro.

24.   *Monday April 3rd*

Received orders to proceed to Admiral Lobo off Point Indio with dispatches. At 8.30 weighed with a moderate breeze at east. At 9 hove to and communicated with the *Nitheroy*. At 11 bore up and made all sail to the SW in company with the schooner *Providencia* & 5 sail of provision boats for the squadron. At 1 pm Monte Video ESE 4 leagues; saw the squadron at anchor bearing SSW. At 3 hove to & spoke HIM corvette *Maria da Gloria*. At 5.40 passed the *Liberal*, bearing the flag of Vice Admiral Rodrigo Lobo, saluted him with 15 guns, & anchored under his quarter. Twenty-four sail of pendants in company viz. frigate *Imperatrice*, corvettes *Liberal, Maria da Gloria, Macaió, Itaparica* & *Jurujuba*, brigs *Caboclo, Independencia ou Morte*, & *Real João*, two schooners and nine gunboats.

In Command of *Caboclo* at Montevideo, 5 April–15 May

25.   *Wednesday April 5th*

Light airs from the NNW. At 1 pm Captain Grenfell gave up command of the schooner *Principe Imperial* to Captain Clewly,[3] & proceeded to

---

[1]*Rio da Prata*: of 12 guns and 75 men, commanded by Lt Alexander Anderson. Anderson served through the war of independence as a Volunteer and was promoted Sub-Lt in Oct 1823. As a Lt and then a Cdr in the River Plate, he commanded the *Rio da Plata* 1824–25, then the brig *Maranhão* 1827–28. Killed ashore in Jan 1828 rounding up deserters.

[2]Previously the Portuguese *Successo*, seized at the time of Independence, *Niteroi* (which Grenfell spelt 'Niteroy' or 'Nitheroy') was originally classified as a 38-gun, 12-pounder frigate of 900 tons.

[3]Stephen Clewley (b. 1797) was a midshipman in the Royal Navy 1809–15. Served with Cochrane in Chile, and travelled with him to Brazil. Lt on *Pedro I* during the Blockade of

take command of the brig *Caboclo* by order of His Excellency the Vice Admiral, Commander of the squadron.

Memorandum. I found the *Caboclo* with her starboard gunwale all stove in, from the main chains to the second port before the gangway, thereby disabling three guns on her starboard side: her mainmast very badly chafed, her hold extremely dirty, and so full of rats, that the filled cartridges in the magazine were nearly all damaged by them. Her rigging is in a most wretched condition, worming all gone, and serving chafed off – sails full of rat holes & the brig's good sailing quite lost. I considered myself justified, therefore, in stipulating with the Admiral before I took command of her, for leave to take her to Monte Video to refit.

26. *Monday April 11 1826*

Note. *Caboclo* at Monte Video refitting; wind from the eastward, and fine weather. At 10 observed a strange ship standing towards the harbour under French colours; at 12 observed a bark & a brig in the offing. At 1 the ship[1] hoisted Buenos Ayrean colours and the broad pendant of Commodore Brown & began firing on a Brazilian smack coming in from the eastward. The *Nitheroy* set her topsails & made signal for the enemy. Put the 1st & 2nd lieutenants and 40 men into boats and took them with their arms on board the *Nitheroy*. Captain Norton shortly afterwards arrived aboard, slipped the cable & made all sail on the larboard tack after the enemy. At 2.20 the enemy tacked inshore and at 2.30 passed us to windward; tried the range of our guns but observed the shot fall short. At 2.35 enemy's brig[2] crossed our bows, & fired her broadside. The ship then tacked again, & bore down on our larboard quarter, the brig following in her wake. At 2.40 commenced action at half gunshot. The enemy's fire was smart and well directed; and soon did us considerable damage, whilst the greater part of our shot appeared to fall short & to take little or no effect on the enemy. At 5 the enemy had shot ahead so as to bring himself on our larboard bow,

---

Bahia, the capture of Maranhão and the Pernambuco rebellion, 1823–24. Cdr, Aug 1824. Served in various ships throughout the war in the River Plate. Capt of Frigate, 1828. Still in service, 1835.

[1] The corvette *25 de Mayo* (28), commanded by Capt Tomas Espora.

[2] The *Republica Argentina* (16), commanded by an American, Capt William Clark.

whilst the brig kept on our larboard quarter. The ship now bore away to cross our bows, we kept away to avoid being raked, and by this manoeuvre closed him to about 3 cables' lengths, keeping up the whole time a continued fire. Observed our shot now take effect on the enemy's hull, sails & rigging, which he supported for about half an hour, and then hauled close to the wind and made all possible sail away, followed by the brig. We hauled up & made sail after him, & kept firing our bow chase guns. But the enemy drew fast away: and it being nearly dark, none of our squadron in sight, the port of Monte Video unprotected, and a fresh vessel of the enemy working up to windward, our own vessel much crippled & people much exhausted from 3 hours constant firing, gave up pursuit of the enemy & stood back towards Monte Video. Found our loss to consist of 6 men killed, one lieutenant and 12 men wounded, about 20 shot through the hull, the sails cut all to pieces, boats in the same condition, and three guns on the main deck dismounted. During the night bent a new jib, a main topsail, kept standing off and on until daylight, and then anchored near her old berth, got hold of the end of the slipped chain, & hove up the anchor – the enemy not in sight, nor any of our own squadron. Returned with all my officers and people to the Hulk.

Force of the *Nitheroy*
16. 32 lb carronades   } Main deck
8. 18 lbr   }
14. 24 lbr carronades   } 2nd deck & forecastle   Total 40 guns
2. long 12 lbrs   }
Crew actually on board   290
Volunteers from the *Caboclo* & *29th of August*   56
                                           Total 346 men, 40 guns

Force of the enemy's ship
14 long 12lb on the lower & upper decks   }
14. 12lb. carronades on the upper deck   }   Total 28

                    Crew actually on board not less than 200

Ditto of the enemy's brig
18. 12lb carronades & long 9 lbs.
                    Crew not less than 100

Total force of the enemy – 46 guns   300 men

27.   *Tuesday May 9th 1826*

His Imperial Majesty's Brig *Caboclo* at Monte Video. Moderate breeze from the north and fine weather. Arrived in the offing HIM frigate *Paraguassú*.[1] At 4 pm received from the Hulk the original crew of the *Caboclo*, and all the officers.

28.   *Wednesday May 10th*

Fine weather. Wind at WNW. Received from the Mole all our guns. Employed painting ship, the carpenters & blacksmiths still at work on the starboard side.

29.   *Thursday May 11th*

Fine weather. Wind SE. Employed receiving stores and provisions from the Hulk and bending sails.

pm Fitted topgallant sails – artificers from the Arsenal still aboard.

30.   *Friday May 12th*

Fine weather. Wind north. At daylight crossed topgallant yards. Received our powder from the *Armonia* & schooner *Principe Imperial*.

pm Watched & quartered the people and served out the small arms. Arrived in the offing HIM ship *Piranga*[2] bearing the flag of Admiral Rodrigo Pinto Guedes, [new] Commander of the squadron of the River Plate.

31.   *Saturday May 13th 1826*

Fine weather, the wind at north. Unmoored, sent the old chains onshore, and bent our new ones to the anchors. At noon the artificers from the

---

[1]Originally the Portuguese *Real Carolina*, *Paraguassu* was a 1,200-ton, 18-pounder frigate built in Damão of teak in 1818. She was commanded by a Capt Mateus Welsh, formerly of the Portuguese Navy.

[2]Originally the Portuguese *Uniao*, *Piranga* was a 1,200-ton, 24-pounder frigate built in Bahia in 1817. She was commanded by Capt James Shepherd, who had come with Cochrane from Chile. As a Lt in the Brazilian Navy, he served through the War of Independence and the Pernambuco rebellion, 1823–24, ending with the rank of Cdr. Accompanied Cochrane to England in 1825 in the *Piranga* and commanded the frigate on its return to Brazil. He was killed leading an attack on Patagonia on 7 March 1827.

Arsenal finished the repairs of the brig. At 2 pm weighed and made sail out of the Bay. Passed the boat of His Excellency General Lecor, Viscount da Laguna;[1] saluted him with three cheers which his suit returned. At 4.30 came to on the quarter of the Admiral; veered to a short range & furled sails. Visited the Admiral and received orders to be under the command of Captain James Norton, commander of the *Nitheroy*, and of the force destined to blockade Buenos Ayres.

32. *Sunday May 14th*

Strong breezes from the NW. At 8.30 the Admiral weighed and shifted his berth further inshore. Employed cleaning arms. At 3 weighed & worked to windward. Passed through the squadron, stood into Monte Video & went on board the transport *Jurujuba* to take leave of Vice Admiral Lobo. At 5 mustered at quarters, all the arms clean and in good order. Bore up to join the Admiral and at 6.30 came to on his quarter, veered to 20 fathoms & furled sails. During this day's trial of sailing observed the brig to behave very well, sailing as fast & not so crank as formerly.

Present at muster –

Officers (commissioned)		4
Warrants		6
Petty		13
Seamen (Able)		40
(Ord)		12
Landsmen		1
Boys		9
Marines	(Sergeant)	1
	(soldiers)	4
Total		90

NB   All volunteers, and 74 of the total, English; the other 16 Portuguese & Brazilian.

---

[1]Carlos Frederico Lecor (1764–1836). Born in Lisbon, Lecor, joined the artillery in 1793 as an NCO. Promoted captain of caçadores in 1803. Lt-Col, 1805. Joined the British-raised Loyal Lusitanian Legion on the occupation of Portugal. Commanded various regiments in the Peninsular War. Brig Gen, 1811. Commanded a Brigade in the Anglo-Portuguese 7th Division, and later the Division itself, at the battles of Bussaco, Vitoria, Sorauren and Nivelle under Wellington. Maj-Gen, 1813. Lt-Gen, 1815. Commanded Brazilian forces that occupied and pacified the Banda Oriental, 1817–25. Made Viscount of Laguna. Governor of the province in the war with the United Provinces.

With the Inshore Squadron Blockading Buenos Aires

33.   *Monday May 15th 1826*

Moderate breeze from the north & fine weather. Employed washing the paintwork outside and inside, and cleaning the upper and lower decks. At 5 pm weighed per signal from the *Nitheroy* & made sail up the River in company with the frigate and the corvettes *Maria da Gloria,*[1] *Macaió,*[2] *Itaparica*[3] & *Liberal,*[4] the brigs *Piraja,*[5] *29th of August,*[6] *Independencia ou Morte,*[7] [*no number given*] sail of schooners, & a convoy of provision boats for the relief of the Colonia do Sacramento blockaded by land and sea by the rebels & the forces of Buenos Ayres. At 11 a full calm. Anchored per signal.

34.   *Tuesday May 16th*

Blowing a fresh pampero.[8] Squadron all at anchor. Monte Video bearing NEbyN 6 leagues. At 3 pm down topgallant yards and veered to 70 fathoms of chain. A heavy sea: observed many of the provision boats weigh and bear up for Monte Video. Two of our brigs in chase of a stranger in the SW. At 11.30 pm a heavy sea washed away our stern boat and before she could be secured, her painter broke & she went adrift.

35.   *Wednesday May 17th*

am Moderate breeze from the SW. Up topgallant yards. At 11 turned the hands up to muster, read the Articles of War, and punished William

---

[1]Flush-decked and of 26 guns and 450 tons, *Maria da Gloria* was built in the US for Chile as the *Horatio.* When Chile was unable to pay, she was purchased by the Portuguese in 1819 and seized by Brazil in 1822. She was commanded by a French officer, Theodoro de Beaurepaire.

[2]*Macaió*: an 18-gun flush-decked vessel built in Alagoas in 1822–23, commanded by Cdr José Ignacio Maia.

[3]*Itaparica*: of 22 guns and 360 tons, commanded by William Eyre.

[4]*Liberal*: built 1791, formerly the Portuguese *Gaivota,* seized at the time of independence. Of 22 guns, commanded by Bartholomew Hayden.

[5]Of 18 guns and 250 tons, *Piraja* was a former independence war prize, now commanded by Lt David Carter. Carter served as a Sub-Lt through the War of Independence and the Pernambuco rebellion 1823–24. Commanded *Pirajá* and *Itaparica* in the River Plate. Reprimanded for being drunk in action, but still in service 1835.

[6]*29th of August*: of 18 guns, formerly the prize *Cerqueira,* commanded by Lt Raphael de Carvalho.

[7]*Independencia ou Morte*: of 14 guns, commanded by Lt João Francisco Regis.

[8]A pampero is a sudden wind and storm peculiar to the River Plate.

Skinner, ord. seaman, with five dozen lashes for repeated drunkenness, insolence, & sedition.

pm Breeze increasing with a heavy sea, veered to 60 fathoms of chain, and at sunset down topgallant yards.

36. *Thursday May 18th*

am Moderate breeze from the SW. Up topgallant yards & shortened in cable. At 10 asked permission to shift our berth, weighed & ran down to the corvette *Liberal*. Received from her one day's water. Weighed in company with her & worked to windward to rejoin the senior officer. At 2 in stays, stove & swamped our cutter towing astern: cut her adrift. At 2.30 came to on the starboard quarter of the *Nitheroy*. Veered to 30 fathoms & furled sails. At sunset exercised at quarters & down top-gallant yards.

*   *   *

37. *Saturday 20th May 1826*

am Moderate breeze from the SSE & fine weather. At 6.30 up topgal-lant yards and weighed per signal in company with the squadron and stood up the River. Made & shortened sail occasionally. Observed the brig to be too much by the head, but she is still the fastest vessel except the *Macaió*. At 10 bore away WSW. At noon steering west in 4 fathoms water.

pm Breeze from the NNE. At 5 passed the wreck on the tail of the Chico Bank. At 8 anchored per signal in company with the squadron.

*   *   *

38. *Monday 22nd*

am Calm and thick fog. At noon clearing up with a breeze from the SE. Weighed per signal, & made sail up the River in company with the squadron.

pm Fine weather: found that our sailing is much improved, sparing every vessel except the *Macaio*, with topgallant sails, and several oth-ers royals, courses & topgallant sails. At 5 saw the church of Colonia bearing NW. Scaled the guns, but did not load them, it being impossi-ble to keep them dry. At 5.40 came to with the squadron off Colonia in

4 fathoms water, furled sails, & veered to 25 fathoms of chain. During the night washed the people's clothes.

39.   *Tuesday May 23rd*

am Strong breeze from the SE with cloudy weather. At 11 weighed per signal from the *Nitheroy* and made sail to the southward, the squadron in company.

pm Ditto weather, off the Ensenada, at 2 the *Nitheroy* made signal to follow her motions, and bore away to the westward. Bore up in company with her and at 2.40 saw several strange sail ahead, the *Nitheroy* at the same time making signal for the enemy. Set the fore topmast studding sail. At 3.30 observed the Buenos Ayrean squadron getting under weigh & consisting of a ship bearing the broad pendant of Commodore Brown, a bark, five brigs, one schooner and eleven gunboats. At 4 observed the *Nitheroy* ahead shorten sail, took in the topmast studding sail & topgallant sails, and cleared for action. At 4.10 passed the *Nitheroy*, who had hauled up to the NW on account of the shoalness of the water. The Cathedral of Buenos Ayres then bearing SWbyW distant three leagues. At 4.30 commenced firing on the enemy's flag ship, in company with the brig *Independencia ou Morte* at about half a mile's distance. At 4.45 observed the corvette *Itaparica* gallantly bearing down to our assistance, hoisted three ensigns and hauled up to close the enemy. At 4.55 bore up across the bows of Commodore Brown & fired two broadsides into him at two cables' lengths distance. When he likewise bore up to join his vessels to leeward, bringing us on his broadside and keeping up a smart fire which killed our pilot, Luis Pinto, cut our main boom in two, knocked away our fore royal mast & hulled us in three places. Finding ourselves now close on the bar, and exposed to the fire of all the enemy's squadron, with only the brig & corvette above mentioned to support us & these too hauling off, hauled our own wind on the starboard tack & set the courses. Observed the *Nitheroy* with the signal flying to follow her motions standing to the NE. During the night working to the NE under easy sail the squadron in company.

40.   *Wednesday 24th of May*

am Fresh breeze from the eastward and cold cloudy weather. Employed fishing the main boom & shifting the fore topgallant mast. Went on board the *Nitheroy* per signal: the enemy's squadron just in sight to leeward on the edge of the Banks of Buenos Ayres.

pm Ditto weather. Enemy not in sight. Standing across the River between Colonia & the Ensenada. At midnight came to & furled sail.

41. *Thursday 25th of May*

am Strong breezes from the SE and cloudy weather. At 9.30 weighed per signal & made sail to the westward in company with the squadron.

pm Moderate. At 2 saw the enemy ahead, of the same force as on the 23rd. At 3 the *Nitheroy* made the signal to tack; tacked to the eastward to draw the enemy out into deep water. At 4 the enemy coming up astern under a press of sail, the *Nitheroy* made the signal to tack again and then to make all sail, and to form the line. Wore; set the courses and topgallant sails, and hauled up to close the *Nitheroy*. Observed the enemy heave about, shorten sail & form in a very open line with their heads towards the shoals. Our own squadron at the same time paying no attention to the signals of the *Nitheroy*, to make sail & form the line, but following at a great distance under easy sail, & entirely without order. At 4.30 the enemy commenced firing on the *Nitheroy*, this brig, the corvette *Itaparica*, our brig *Independencia ou Morte*, which were the only vessels in their stations and within gunshot; the *Nitheroy* and *Itaparica* returned the enemy's fire with their long guns, we did the same with our bow gun, the only one that would reach them, and kept the rest of the people laying snug at their quarters. At 4.45 the *Nitheroy* kept away for the Buenos Ayres Commodore, [we] kept away with her, and at the same time observed Commodore Brown put his helm up & kept away to avoid us, leaving five of the vessels exposed to be cut off if the rest of our squadron had been near enough to follow him up and support us. We had now approached to about half a mile of the enemy's line when the shoalness of the water obliged the *Nitheroy* to haul her wind and heave about, Buenos Ayres bearing west by south, 4 leagues & in 3¼ fathoms water. Finding myself now exposed to the whole of the enemy's fire with only the *Itaparica* & *Independencia ou Morte* to support me, the rest of our squadron wearing and all far out of gunshot, hove about, hauled up the courses & stood after the *Nitheroy*, followed by the corvette & brig. At 5.10 passed the corvette *Liberal* which had just come up, and who fired a shot at the enemy that only just cleared our quarter deck. She then immediately wore & made all sail ahead. The *Pirajá* and *Maria da Gloria* acted in precisely the same manner, firing at the enemy when their shot did not reach half way, but dropped all about us as we retired. During the evening the enemy continued to follow us until we deepened our water to 4 fathoms. At 11 anchored between Colonia and Ensenada & furled sails. The damage sustained in the action of today consists of another shot through the main boom, one through the bulwark forward which carried away a lower shroud, one through the boat on the booms, and two or three through the sails – but fortunately no person hurt, owing to their being kept <u>lying at quarters</u>.

42. *Friday May 26th*

Moderate breeze from the SW and cloudy. At 8 o'clock got under weigh and closed the squadron, lying at anchor with Colonia bearing NWbyW. Employed repairing the damage of yesterday. At 7 pm got under weigh.

43. *Saturday 27th*

At 1.30 anchored between Colonia & Ensenada. At 9 weighed with the squadron and stood to the SE. Observed the *Nitheroy* bring to and communicate with the English packet.[1] At 11 made sail to the eastward in chase of a strange sail.

pm Moderate breeze from the SW standing down the middle passage, the chase on the other tack and on the opposite side of the Chico bank. At 12.30 tacked to the NW, the wreck on the Chico bank bearing east 2 miles, soundings in 3 fathoms, sand. At 3 made signal to the *Nitheroy* <u>for a pilot</u>. Observed the schooner *Januaria* bring to the stranger. At 8 the lights of Buenos Ayres bearing WSW. Stood towards Colonia and at 11 anchored with the squadron.

44. *Sunday 28th*

Light airs from the southward. A strange sail in the westward. At 11 mustered the crew.

pm Weighed per signal and made sail in chase of a brig under English colours. At 3 fired 3 shots at ditto, when she brought to and proved to be the *Maria* of Guernsey, bound in ballast from Buenos Ayres to Monte Video. Allowed her to proceed. Hauled our wind to the SE & at 9 anchored in 2½ fathoms water.

45. *Monday 29th*

Light variable airs from the SE. At 8 weighed and made to join the squadron. Employed stationing the people to <u>working ship</u> and <u>making sail</u>.

---

[1] The *Princess Elizabeth*, 60 days direct from Falmouth.

pm Ditto weather, making but little progress. At 8 Colonia NWbyW 3 leagues. At 9 anchored and furled sails.

46.   *Tuesday May 30th 1826*

Moderate breezes from the westward and fine weather. At daylight Ensenada bearing SbyE distant 10 miles. Observed a sail at anchor in the harbour. At 9 weighed to close the squadron. At 10 observed them all under weigh.

pm Standing over to the southern shore at 1. Saw the enemy's squadron at anchor off Buenos Ayres. The *Nitheroy* made the signal to form the line of Battle. Made sail and got close under her stern. During the whole evening observed the *Nitheroy* endeavouring to get the squadron into their stations but without effect, no line could be formed. At 4 o'clock Captain Norton hailed us and told us we were in our station. At 7 anchored off Ensenada.

*   *   *

47.   *Friday June 2nd*

Light airs from the NW. At daylight observed a strange sail to windward, the schooner *Januaria* in chase. At 10 observed ditto bring the stranger to.

pm I proceeded in the schooner *Conceição*, by order of Captain Norton, to examine the port of Ensenada. At 4 it fell calm and I went in the whale boat of the frigate to ascertain whether gunboats could enter the harbour without being much exposed to the fort – This I found impracticable, the only passage being within pistol shot of the fort on the western shore. Whilst making my observations, the fort fired two shot at me, which fell short, but soon afterwards I observed two boats pull out of a creek to the eastward, who endeavoured to cut off our retreat. We pulled out instantly but the whale boat at the same instant grounding, obliged us to shape our course in an oblique direction towards them. As soon as they were within good musket shot I fired at the headmost boat, which was quickly returned and with three cheers from both boats in English. I now altered my course so as to bring their boats on the quarter and a mutual exchange of fire was kept up for about 20 minutes, when having one of her crew wounded, she gave up the chase and at 7 o'clock we got safe on board the schooner.

48.   *Saturday June 3rd*

Light airs from the NE. Employed cleaning inside and outside thoroughly. I returned on board.

49.   *Sunday 4th*

am Calm & clear – At 11 mustered in divisions.

pm Light airs from the southward. Weighed per signal and made all sail in chase to the eastward. At 2 hove to. Stranger no. 3 gunboat from Monte Video having on board Capp. da Fragata Jacinto Roque da Senna, commander of the flotilla of the Uruguay. At 4 made sail and at 6 anchored and furled sails in company with the squadron.

50.   *Monday June 5th*

Strong breezes from the SW with sh[owers] of rain at times. Unstowed the booms, reduced the gaff and cut up the main boom which we find perfectly useless from the shots received in the 23rd & 25th ult.

51.   *Tuesday 6th*

Strong gale at west – finding the brig drive let go the best bower & veered 15 fathoms on both cables. At noon down topgallant yards per signal. At 5 Colonia bore NWbyN, Point Lara SW. A strange sail in sight WSW. Received notice from the *Nitheroy* to weigh & chase. Took up best bower & hove into 30 fathoms on the small one, when from the violence of the gale, the sea & currents, judging it impossible to work to windward, veered away again & lay quiet for the night. Observed the brig *Independencia ou Morte* weigh.

52.   *Wednesday 7th*

Strong gale at WNW. At 1 the brig driving let go the best bower. At daylight found that all the squadron had driven materially, the *Independencia ou Morte* had driven to leeward, the stranger nearer than last night.

pm More moderate. At 1 the enemy squadron in sight to windward. The *Nitheroy* made signal to make sail; crossed topgallant yards, weighed and hauled on the starboard tack. Asked leave to chase per signal which was answered in the affirmative. Made all sail after a brig right ahead. At 5 the *Nitheroy* tacked to the eastward and made signal to close, the enemy's squadron then bearing down to succour their brig who had lost her foretopgallant mast. Buenos Ayres bearing WbyS 5 or 6 leagues. At 5.15 the *Nitheroy* repeated the signal to close: tacked, shortened sail, & at 5.50 anchored near the *Nitheroy*. During the night keeping a good look out.

53.   *Thursday June 8th*

Strong breezes from the NW. Colonia bearing NbyW. Ensenada SSE. Two sail in sight to the SE.

pm Weather more moderate. The strange sails prove to be our two schooners from Colonia which bring information that the Buenos Ayrean squadron had shown itself to the westward of that port. At 2 weighed per signal and worked up towards Colonia. At 6 anchored.

54.   *Friday June 9th*

Strong breezes from the NW. At 7.30 weighed with the squadron & worked towards Colonia, the enemy in sight in the westward. At 10 observed our flotilla coming out of Colonia consisting of 16 sail.

pm Light airs. Flotilla in company. At 7 anchored and received a pilot from the flotilla.

55.   *Saturday 10th*

Light airs from the N. At 4.30 am in consequence of private instructions from Captain Norton, made the signal for the *Macaio*, schooners *Itaparica* & *Januaria*, and brig *Independencia ou Morte* to weigh. Weighed and made sail to westward. At 7.30 signal from the *Nitheroy* to pass within hail, tacked & bore away for her. At 8 *Nitheroy* hailed us & countermanded the orders: the enemy WbyS. 5 leagues. At 3 pm anchored. At 5 being out of our station, tripped our anchor & got into line.

The Battles of Los Pozes and Lara Quilmes

56.   *Sunday 11th*

At 5 weighed, per signal, and made sail to the NW. Wind moderate from the northward and fine weather. At 8 Buenos Ayres WbyS 5 leagues. At 10 observed the Buenos Ayrean squadron consisting of a ship, a bark, four brigs and six gunboats at anchor in line at the extremity of the Banco la Cidade, their line stretching across the Rosalita Channel to the Banco las Conchas. Our squadron under easy sail, forming the line.

pm Ditto weather. Several of our flotilla very far astern. At 2 sent the people to their quarters, the enemy being distant about a league. At 2.30 *Nitheroy* made signal to form in line abreast – obeyed it – at 3 the whole of the enemy's line opened their fire, but every shot fell short. At 3.10 in ¼ less three fathoms, observed the *Nitheroy* ground, & shortly afterwards the *Maria da Gloria*. Kept standing on for the headmost of the enemy's line, but shot passing over us, till we shoaled to 13 feet water, which being too little for any vessel but ourselves, and being only within long gun-shot of the enemy, hauled our wind & hove in stays. Some of the vessels followed us, others wore, and all began firing. Captain Norton having shifted to the *Itaparica*, now shifted to this brig, and shortly afterwards left us, and proceeded on board the gunboat *Doña Paula*. At this time the *Nitheroy* & *Maria da Gloria* had both floated and lay at anchor. This brig and the other vessels made short tacks between them and the enemy & for exercise I fired a few rounds. At 3.40 per order of Captain Norton made sail to windward in chase of a brig & 6 sail of gunboats coming across the River to join the enemy. At 4.10 passed the brig *29th of August* aground. At 4.20 shoaled our water to 14 feet on the bank of Camarones & by the pilot's advice wore. Observing our gunboats all retiring and five of the enemy's advanced to attack the *Nitheroy*, bore away for them, brought our broadside to bear at about half a mile's distance, and drove them away, evidently with some loss. Shoaled our water again to 13 feet, hauled our wind. Made a tack to windward, gave them a few more shots, and then observing the *Nitheroy* under weigh & standing to the eastward with the signal flying to follow her motions, wore and made sail after her accompanied by the rest of the squadron & flotilla. At 7 anchored. Buenos Ayres WbyS 4 leagues.

57.   *Monday 12th of June 1826*

Moderate breeze from the NNW and cloudy weather. At 10 the *Independencia ou Morte* in chase of a stranger ESE. At 11 observed her bring her to. Buenos Ayres WbyS 4 leagues. The enemy as yesterday.

pm At 2 weighed per signal and stood to the NE. At 6 received orders to proceed to Colonia for a new main boom. Made all sail. At 9 anchored.

58.   *Tuesday 13th*

Fresh breeze from the NW. At daylight weighed and made sail for Colonia, bearing north 3 leagues. At 8 anchored in the harbour in 5 fathoms, furled sails & moored with half a cable each way in NW & SE. Went onshore to visit the Governor. All the flotilla arrived and anchored in the port.

pm Blowing fresh, down topgallant yards & bent the short cable. Received a new main boom. <u>Discharged the pilot.</u>

59. *Wednesday 14th*

Moderate breezes from the northward. At 8 unmoored, weighed & made sail out of the port. At 10 saw our squadron bearing SW, at anchor.

pm At 1 anchored astern of the *Nitheroy*; found a strange brig, a prize, in company.[1]

[15–19 June, anchored with the squadron or sailing within sight of the enemy receiving supplies, firewood etc.]

60. *Tuesday 20th of June 1826*

Light airs from the ENE. At 5 am observed the *Nitheroy* bring to & board the English packet bound to Buenos Ayres.[2] Ensenada S½W 4 leagues.

61. *Wednesday 21st*

Light airs from the eastward, with thick fog at times. At 11 the *Januaria* & *Conceição* weighed in chase of a strange sail.

pm At 3 arrived in the squadron & anchored the schooner *Itaparica* from Monte Video.

62. *Thursday 22nd*

Strong breeze from the northward. At daylight two strange sail in sight in the east & west quarters. Weighed with the squadron and made sail in chase to the westward, the sail on the east being HIM schooner *Principe Imperial*. Under all possible sail going 9 knots & coming up with the chase, the *Nitheroy* and *Macaio* ahead of us firing at her. At 8 chase hoisted American colours, & appeared to be a vessel of 200 tons burden, rigged as a brig & painted with 8 ports a side:[3] the enemy's squadron west 4 leagues, the breeze began now to fall light, and the chase to draw

---

[1]The British *Stag*.

[2]The *Dove*, 61 days from Falmouth via Montevideo.

[3]The privateer *Oriental Argentina*, commanded by Frenchman Pierre Dautant, unsuccessfully attempting to evade the Brazilian blockade and get to sea.

away from us. At 10 the *Nitheroy* & *Macaio* gave up the chase & tacked. We continued standing on in hopes that the chase might ground, being then in 3 fathoms. The *Nitheroy* repeated our signal to tack; asked permission to continue the chase, answered by the *Nitheroy* in the negative. Stood on 5 minutes longer until the stranger got alongside Admiral Brown's ship, then shortened sail. Wore & fired two guns at him, and stood after our squadron on the other tack.

pm Anchored off Point Lara. In the evening received fresh beef for two days.

* * *

63.   *Saturday 24th*

Moderate breezes from the westward. Joined company the schooner *Itaparica* with dispatches from the Commander of the flotilla in the Uruguay.

pm Passed down the English packet:[1] ditto carried 2½ fathoms water, out from the enemy's line, but draws only 12 feet 6" aft. By the Buenos Ayrean gazettes intercepted by the flotilla, I find that on the night of the 2nd of June, I shot two men in the boats that attempted to cut off our retreat to the schooner *Conceiçäo*. The Buenos Ayreans claim the honour of great victories on the 25th of May, & 11th of June.

64.   *Sunday June 25th*

Light airs from the eastward and thick fog. Mustered the crew. At 11 weighed with the squadron and made sail to the eastward. At 2 pm anchored: at 3 weighed again; at 6 anchored and furled sails.

65.   *Monday 26th*

Moderate breeze from the northward: at daylight a strange sail under Point Lara. Weighed & made all sail in chase. At 8.30 brought the stranger to: ditto a provision boat from Monte Video bound for the squadron. Hauled our wind to rejoin the squadron. At 11 anchored per signal in line north of the *Nitheroy*.

---

[1]The *Princess Elizabeth* returning to Falmouth via Montevideo.

pm Received sundry stores from the provision craft. Observed the *Nitheroy*'s and *Liberal*'s boats in chase of a bilander to the northward. Ditto from Monte Video bound to Colonia.

* * *

66. *Thursday 29th. St. Peter's day*

Light breeze from the NNE. Squadron anchored in line south. Colonia bearing NbyW distant 3 leagues.

pm Calm. Dressed in flags in honour of the <u>Emperor's Saint</u>: & served out double allowance <u>of grog</u>.

67. *Friday June 30th 1826*

Strong breeze from the NNE. Squadron at anchor in line south of Colonia. Observed the schooners *Conceição* & *Maria Theresa* bring a Monte Video provision boat into the squadron.

pm Received two days fresh beef & firewood.

* * *

68. *Saturday 8th July*

Moderate breeze from the north & fine clear weather. At 8 loosed sails to dry. At 9 observed the brigs *Piraja* & *29th of August* weigh, pass within hail of the *Nitheroy* & make sail to the westward. At 10 Captain Norton came on board, weighed & made sail inshore towards Point Lara. At 11 in 2¼ fathoms wore to the SE & anchored at the entrance of the channel of the Ensenada. Captains Norton, Hayden[1] & myself proceeded to the

---

[1]Bartholomew Hayden (1792–1857). Born in Tipperary, Hayden served as a Royal Navy midshipman during the Napoleonic Wars. From 1817 to 1821 he was a masters mate then Second Master of *Andromache* and *Conway* on the S America station. In 1821, resigned and bought the trader *Colonel Allen*. Brought Cochrane from Chile to Brazil in 1823, where his ship was converted to a brig-of-war and he was appointed a commander in the Brazilian Navy. Served through the War of Independence and the Pernambuco rebellion, 1823–24. Commanded *Pirajá* in the River Plate 1825–26, capturing the privateer *Liberdade del Sur.* Capt of Frigate, 1826. Commanded *Liberal* as Capt of Frigate during the blockade of Buenos Aires. Commanded the Brazilian (anti-slavery) Division of the East 1828–29. Active against rebels in Pará 1835–36. Full Capt, 1836; and Cdre, May 1847. Member of Naval Armaments Commission, 1851. Died in 1857.

wreck with two masts, inshore, & cut away her mainmast for plank. At 1 pm returned on board with the same, took the boats in tow, weighed & made sail by the wind on the larboard tack. At 4 tacked to the NW, & at 7 anchored; the *Nitheroy* bearing north ¼ mile.

69.   *Sunday 9th July*

am Moderate breeze from the WNW. At 9 heard a very heavy cannonading to the westward. Weighed with the squadron per signal, & made sail to windward. At 11 mustered the crew & read the articles of war.

pm Falling calm. At sunset a light breeze. The *Paulistana* gunboat parted company for Colonia. At 6 anchored in line south of the *Nitheroy*. Today at 9 am, at noon, & at 4 pm we have heard very heavy firing, or general saluting, at Bueos Ayres.

70.   *Monday July 10th*

am Calm. Colonia NbyE 3 leagues. Went ashore with Captains Norton & Hayden; visited the Governor, Marshall Manuel George Rodriguez,[1] & at 8 pm returned on board. At night light airs from the NE & rain. At 10 pm down topgallant yards.

71.   *Tuesday 11th*

Strong gale from the ESE with constant rain, & a heavy sea. At 9 am down topgallant masts, in flying jib boom, rove the top pendants & jeers. Observed most of the squadron to have driven considerably. At 1 pm three schooners being close in our hawse, asked leave per signal to shift our berth: answered affirmative. Weighed & ran a league to the SW & anchored again. Veered to 40 fathoms of chain. Lost the *Nitheroy*'s dingy, which was hoisted up astern, by a heavy sea staving her & washing her out of the ropes. At midnight falling calm with a threatening appearance in the SW.

---

[1]General Manuel Jorge Rodrigues. Portuguese-born veteran of the Napoleonic Wars where he commanded a battalion of cacadores at Bussaco and the sieges of Ciudad Rodrigo and Badajoz under Wellington. Adhered to Brazil in 1822. As Governor of Colonia, he had defied a joint attack by Brown and land forces of the Uruguayan patriot Lavelleja in February.

72.   Wednesday 12th

Am Light airs from the NW & thick fog. At 8 up topgallant masts & yards & unrove jeers, & top ropes; got wet clothes up to dry, & fumigated the lower deck. At 11 set the topsails & topgallant sails.

pm Moderate breeze from the SW, the fog clearing away, but weather becoming rainy, found that the *Nitheroy* had shifted her berth to the south & observed the signal up to unite. Weighed & ran towards her and anchored again, she bearing south ½ a mile distant. At night blowing fresh from the SSW. Veered to 40 fathoms of chain & down topgallant yards.

73.   Thursday July 13

Blowing fresh from the south with thick rainy weather: cleaned and fumigated the lower deck, & kept the people under shelter. At 4 pm the *Nitheroy* made our signal to weigh: weighed in company with her and the *Macaio* & stood to the SW. Observed the *Itaparica* also under sail. At 5.30 seeing nothing of the squadron, & the weather continuing very thick, anchored & furled sails.

74.   Friday July 14th

Light airs from the SW with thick weather and rain at times. At 8 weighed with the squadron and made all sail to the SW. Towards midday clearing up. Saw the city of Buenos Ayres and counted 9 sail of vessels in the Pozo [anchorage], Admiral Brown appearing to be in the same situation as before. Observed the squadron in chase to the eastward, tacked after them & set the studding sails. At 4 pm anchored close to the *Nitheroy* who had brought to an American schooner[1] bound to Buenos Aires. Joined company from Monte Video HIM brig *Real João*.

75.   Saturday 15th

Light airs from the SE & thick wet weather. Squadron all at anchor.

pm Detained schooner parted company for Monte Video, taking with her the sick of the squadron, amongst them the 2nd Lieutenant John Williams[2] who has been 7 weeks on the sick list.

---

[1]The *Leonidas* from Canton.

[2]John (William) Williams. Served as a Volunteer with Cochrane at the Blockade of Bahia and capture of Maranhão in 1823. Sub-Lt on various ships, 1824–25. Lt on *Principe*

76.   *Sunday July 16th*

Moderate breeze from the northward with thick cloudy weather. Mustered the people.

77.   *Monday 17th*

am Moderate breeze from the eastward and fine clear weather. At 9.30 weighed & made sail to the southward with the squadron. At 10.30 the *Nitheroy* wore to the southward, Captain Norton came on board & we stood on towards Ensenada. At 11 hove to: went with Captain Norton on board the schooner *Doña Paula* & got her within a quarter of a mile of the land. From the schooner's masthead we could distinctly see everything in the harbour. We then went in the whale boat to sound a creek to the eastward of Point St. Iago, found plenty of water inside, but a shoal flat at the mouth only capable of floating a light boat over. We pushed on through the creek until we got a view of the vessels, which were manned with soldiers under arms to receive us. After a most complete reconnoitre, we returned to the schooner, and stood out to the squadron. In the evening made sail in chase of two vessels in the NE, which proved to be provision boats from Monte Video for Colonia & the squadron. At 7.30 anchored.

78.   *Tuesday 18th*

am Fresh breeze from the eastward with thick fog, clearing away at intervals. At 8 saw a strange sail bearing east; the *Nitheroy* made the signal to chase. Weighed, made all sail, & cleared for action. At 9, stranger bearing down upon us, fired a gun at her, when she hoisted French colours & hove to. [She] proved to be the *Courier* from Havre de Grace bound to Buenos Ayres, knowing of the blockade. Captain Norton took possession of her & at 10 anchored with the squadron in line north & south, the prize in company.
pm Ditto weather. Received fresh beef & fire wood.

Imperial then *Caboclo*, Dec 1825–July 1826. Cdr, 1827. Commanded the *Constança* schooner, 1828; assisted in the capture of the state commerce raider *General Branzden*. Died and buried in Wales, 1832.

79.   *Wednesday July 19th*

Light airs from the SE and clear weather. By order of Captain Norton proceeded with 25 men on board the gunboat *Paulistana* & took her in to reconnoitre Ensenada. Found everything as before except that the two hulks had dericks erected, but could distinguish nothing more. At night returned on board. Received 30 days beef & fire wood.

80.   *Thursday 20th*

Light breeze from the northeastward and fine weather: a strange sail to the westward. At 9 general signal for boats manned & armed to tow the gunboat *Doña Paula* and reinforce the crew of the *Paulistana*. Both boats shortly gave chase and at noon came up with and boarded the American brig *John Noble* from Buenos Ayres in ballast. Captain Norton detained her.

81.   *Friday 21st*

Strong breezes from the ESE & cloudy weather. At 2 am the detained brig parted company for Monte Video. At 9 weighed per signal in company with the squadron: received orders to chase to windward and recall the American. Made all sail by the wind, tacking occasionally. At noon saw three strangers to windward; the same proved to be the French ship, *Thale*, & schooner *Itaparica* that sailed from the squadron on the 18th inst. At 2 pm after two shot, brought the chase to & bore up with her for the squadron, making all sail. At 5 passed close to the *Nitheroy* at anchor, shortened sail & came to on her quarter.

*   *   *

82.   *Sunday July 23rd 1826*

Moderate breeze from the southward & fine dry weather. Dried clothes, bedding, sails &c. At 10 weighed, shifted our berth nearer to the *Nitheroy* & at 11 anchored.

pm Received from a provision boat sundry stores from Monte Video. Came down the river and anchored in the squadron a French brig in ballast from Buenos Ayres.[1] This vessel and the American report that the

---

[1]The *Junon*.

American brig that escaped us on the 22nd of June was the *Homer* from Rio de Janeiro bound to Valparaiso, & put in under pretence of distress. The enemy's squadron they say are anchored in the <u>Canneleta Portuguesa</u> and not in <u>Three fathom Hale</u>. If this is the case <u>(which I doubt)</u> they may be easily destroyed. Captain Norton sent an officer to take the French brig to Monte Video.

83. *Monday 24th*

Moderate breeze from the ESE & fine weather.

pm Hove overboard 11 casks of the salt beef last received, it being perfectly unfit for use. Made a report of the same to the commander of the division.

84. *Tuesday 25th*

Light winds from the NE and fine weather. Squadron at anchor with Point Lara bearing S distant 3 leagues. Attended a survey on some salt beef on board the *Nitheroy*, the whole of which was pronounced bad by every person but Captain Norton who insisted on its goodness, and ordered it to be served out to the people.

85. *Wednesday 26th*

Light breezes from the SW & fine dry weather. At 9 weighed & made sail by the wind on the starboard tack. At 1 pm moderate breeze; tacked to the NW. At 2 anchored in line, & furled sails. Buenos Ayres in sight from the masthead, bearing WbyS.

86. *Thursday 27th*

Moderate breezes from the northward and fine weather. Joined company from Colonia, Captain da Fragata Jacinto Roque da Senna, with five gunboats. At night blowing fresh, veered to 40 fathoms.

87. *Friday 28th July*

Fresh breeze at NNE. At 7 weighed per signal from the *Nitheroy*, & made sail in chase of a ship to the eastward, in company with the corvette *Macaió*. At 8 tacked under the lee of the stranger and proved to be the *Maria da Gloria* from Monte Video. At 9 anchored in our station south of the *Nitheroy*.

88. *List of personnel who were aboard the brig* Caboclo *since its armament, and during the command of Captain of Frigate John Pascoe Grenfell, to show entitlement to a share of the prizes taken by the River Plate Squadron*[1]

Capt of Frigate John Pascoe Grenfell
Lieut John Williams
Sub Lieut Robert Mackintosh
Pilot William MacErwing
Surgeon Thomas Wilson
Purser Antonio Maria Marques
Clerk Estivão Antonio Chaves
Master John Henry
Carpenter Peter Wooley
Mid Benjamin Brown
Mid James Edward
Purser's Steward Januario de Agudo
Cook Harrigan Morron
Petty Officers
Fuller Caltrop
Peter Parker
Samuel Austin
William Collister
Arthur Anspar
Benjamin Miller
Samuel Norton
James Perkins
William Page
Able Seamen
William Almond
Nathaniel Mathias
John Jones
William Skinner
Richard Hollands
Manuel Domingos
Charles Hansard
Charles Morrison
Roberto Pernes
Joseph Robson

Robert Williams
Thomas Jacobs
Lawrence Atkins
James Davies
William Williams (2)
John Moira
John Macbane
Carlos S Pereira
Manoel Costas
Ordinary Seamen
William White
George H Wilder
Thomas Gibson
Thomas Williams
John William Perkins
Peter Adams
Hilario Oliveira
John Davies
Harry Goodwin
John Scarman
Peter Miller
James Cockran
Henry Lancaster
Boys
John Patterson
Herman Croman
Vicente Pereira
John Henry
Frederico Fernandes
Manoel dos Pasos
Andre Pilz
John Ferreira
James Cristie
Marine Artillery

---

[1]Handwritten manuscript in the possession of the Grenfell family.

Benjamin Thomas
Charles Bremen
John Ingram
William Wilson
John Knight
John Springman
Joze Antonio
Luis Beltrão
Frederico Lasdoff
John Anderson

George Griffiths

Sergt
Fransisco Pereira Maia
Privates
Luis Pires
Joze Simplicio
Bazilio Magno Basid
Manoel Anto do Bonfim
Albino Joze

On board the brig Caboclo anchored at
Montevideo, 4 August 1826
(Sgn) Estivão Antonio Chave

Preliminary Report on Battle of Lara Quilmes, 29–30 July 1826

89. *Pinto Guedes to the Marquis of
Paranaguá, Minister of Marine*

[XM 293, Arquivo Nacional (AN), Rio de Janeiro][1]   3 August 1826

Most Illustrious and Excellent Sir

Although I have not received dispatches from Captain Norton, commanding the Division before Buenos Aires, or the commanders of the ships deployed there with which I could give Yr Excellency an exact account of the combat which took place between our Division and the Squadron of that Republic on the night of 29 June and the following morning, I can say with certainty that it was fought between forces which were equal, or with little difference between them. I had arranged it this way so as to prevent any excuse of being outnumbered seeing that the enemy had previously been unwilling to unmoor and leave the port while our Division remained anchored in front of the bar.

Brown therefore saw himself obliged to accept the gauntlet and left during the night, exchanging shots as he did so, and the following morning he fought an action whilst fleeing under full sail without maintaining either his position or his honour, always keeping close to the mudbanks over which he could flee if he got into trouble: emulating the behavior of a regular naval officer is not important to him, and he always takes the path of the guerrilla or the footpad.

[1]Printed in the *Diario Fluminense*, no. 53, 2 September 1826.

The result of this petty ambush was that he was only able to reply to our broadsides with intermittent fire. Consequently, his corvette was left like a sieve, without yards on his mainmast and with no maintopmast, no mizzentopmast, no foresail and no foretopmast – but with what was left, it was driven by a strong wind towards the bar with such rapidity and in such confusion that it ran aground at the entrance. All our ships were punished by the strength of the wind which increased to such a violent *pampeiro* that our Division was unable to carry sail, anchored before the bar, and remained there except the *Caboclo* which, taking advantage of the wind, headed for Montevideo carrying her commander.

We suffered considerable loss. As the *Caboclo* draws less water, she was able to get near the bar and to harass the fleeing corvette and, passing an enemy brig-of-war which, with his other ships was following the precipitate flight of their admiral, fired and received cannon shots which left 1 dead and 5 wounded. Alas, this number included the valiant and daring Grenfell, who still lives but whose prognosis is poor, and whose disappearance would leave a gap that would be difficult to fill. Lieutenant Taylor[1] was also shot through the stomach from the right side wounding the intestines, and his injury is thought to be mortal. Lieutenant Rafael de Carvalho of the brig *29 de Agosto* was wounded by a shot in the left arm. There are further casualties and dead among the seamen but I do not have exact information.

In others of my letters, I have told Yr Excellency the facts, which are that the enemy can navigate in shallower water than our ships, which enables him to flee by putting himself between the mudbanks, and allows him to leave when the wind is favourable; but he seldom leaves the shelter of the banks, relies on their artillery which is longer range than ours. We, who have to remain under sail and to enforce a blockade stretching from Colonia to Ensenada, run great risks if we try to do the same.

Rodrigo Pinto Guedes
On board the frigate *Piranga*

---

[1] Of the *Niteroi*. A former Royal Navy midshipman, Taylor served during the Pernambuco rebellion of 1824. Promoted Sub-Lt in 1825 and posted to River Plate. Made a complete recovery and was promoted Lt in 1829. Still in service, 1832.

Supplementary Report on Battle of Lara Quilmes, 29–30 July 1826

90. *Pinto Guedes to the Marquis of Paranaguá,*
Minister of Marine

[XM 293, AN, Rio de Janerio]   11 August 1826

Most Illustrious and Excellent Sir

I can add little to what I wrote in my letter no 50 [of 3 August] about the events of 30 July in which our division and the naval forces of Buenos Aires met in battle. For further information however, Yr Excellency must permit me to relate a little story repeated with few changes from the *Correio de Buenos Aires* of 14 July.

On 13 July, a Buenos Aires lady called D. Maria de Mendeville, Secretary of the local Charitable Association, in the midst of a great gathering at the House of Assembly, presented Brown with a flag of the Republic in embroidered silk, accompanied with an appropriate speech. Brown thanked her for it and replied with another (I believe of equal eloquence) in which he pledged his word that within two months the trade of Buenos Aires would be free and that the Imperial flag would no longer be seen in the River Plate.

Great cheers and applause accompanied this declaration – and another that the flag would never be allowed to fall into the hands of the enemy. The journalist reported this arrogant boast and then used it as an opportunity to refer to the deeds of the Roman Heroes, claiming that they were pale in comparison [with those of Brown]; he then reported that the scene ended with tears in the eyes of all participants, praise for both speakers and the bestowal on Brown of the accolade 'Hero of the 11th June!' (In fact, this was a day of shame for him as reported in my letters of 21 and 23 June 1826).

[Pinto Guedes goes on to explain that he had reduced the size of the blockading squadron to one of equality with the enemy so as to give Brown no opportunity to refuse action.]

I will now narrate the events of that day using the latest information.

Brown thought that by leaving at night when it was dark, he would be able to board the *Niteroi* and, to that end, it is said that he had assembled 500 men on his corvette. However, Norton had posted the schooners *Dona Paula* and *Conceição* in the channel to warn of any movement – which they did . . . Brown was thus unable to carry out his plan, and after some firing, he withdrew. At dawn his position was revealed and he was obliged to resort to flight. As usual he had the advantage of being near the banks over which he could flee if in danger. But on this occasion, Brown had become separated from the brigs which were unable to support him with broadsides.

The corvette *25 de Mayo* was attacked by *Niteroi* – and Norton reports that he was given all possible assistance by Captain of Frigate Grenfell in the *Caboclo*, and Captain of Frigate Jacinto Roque da Senna [Pereira] who, on this day, was embarked in the schooner *Leal Paulistana* – until she could follow no further as she touched bottom and momentarily went aground. *Maria da Gloria*, commanded by Captain of Frigate Theodoro de Beaurepaire, seconded the *Niteroi* and continued her vigorous fire until halted by for the same reason; *Itaparica*, commanded by Captain of Frigate William Eyre[1] . . . lost her foretopmast in which state she was attacked by the brigs and defended herself with extraordinary bravery. *Liberal* under Captain of Frigate Bartholomew Hayden, being now the nearest vessel, was ordered to attack and destroy the damaged vessel [*25 de Mayo*]; but the order could not be obeyed as she could not get near enough to do so. *Maria de Gloria* then went in pursuit of the enemy brigs to windward coming within cannon shot and losing her foretopmast.

To demonstrate the state of the *25 de Mayo*, which fled . . . and went aground with masts and rigging badly damaged and only her foremast standing, I can only repeat Brown's official report to the Minister if War and Marine as follows:

'Most Excellent Sir,
   Provoked into sailing we had fought but have not surrendered to the enemy: permit me to inform Yr Excellency that our national ships are still free; though it behoves me to report that there are many dead and wounded including my brave [flag] captain Espora.

---

[1]William Eyre (1798–1850) served in the Royal Navy during the Napoleonic Wars and was an Admiralty Midshipman on *Conway* in South America, 1819–22. He resigned to join the Brazilian Navy and served through the War of Independence and the Pernambuco rebellion, 1823–24, ending with the rank of Cdr. In command of *Itaparica* in the Plate, 1826. Captured in an unsuccessful attack on Patagonia in 1827. As a Capt of Frigate he commanded major warships, 1829–33. Served against the rebels in Para and Rio Grande do Sul, 1835–7. Cdre, 1847.

The *25 de Mayo* is completely destroyed and a list of the dead and wounded will be sent as soon as possible.

I am, Yr Excellency's most odedient and humble servant

William Brown.'

Rodrigo Pinto Guedes
On board the frigate *Piranga*

Medical Reports on Captain J.P. Grenfell

91. *Pinto Guedes to the Marquis of Paranaguá, Minister of Marine*

[XM 293, AN, Rio de Janerio][1]   4 August 1826

Most Illustrious and Excellent Sir

I have just received a letter from the most able Dr José Pedro D'Oliveira (whom I ordered to attend with all the medical and surgical skills available on sea and land) about the state in which he found Grenfell and, the better to convey the situation, it behoves me to quote his own words:

'The casualty Grenfell runs no risk to his life even if it proves necessary to perform an amputation. The wound runs from the middle of the right arm to the armpit. From outside to inside and from below to above, affecting most of the bicep muscles and fracturing the humerus, but the bracial artery and the median nerve – which respectively nourish and stimulate the limb – are undamaged. The period of recuperation could be long, but the patient is vigorous and spirited, so that a good result can be hoped for.'

I bring this good news to Yr Excellency with great pleasure as I know you esteem him highly, and with good reason.

Rodrigo Pinto Guedes
On board the frigate *Piranga*

[1]Printed in the *Diario Fluminense*, no. 53, 2 September 1826.

92. *Dr José Pedro D'Oliveira to Pinto Guedes*

[XM 293, AN, Rio de Janerio]   20 August 1826

Most Illustrious and Excellent Sir

I have the honour to bring to Yr Excellency's attention that, examining the wounds of Grenfell yesterday, I found the humerus fractured up to its head in the shoulder socket and that the damage was much greater than I had thought when the limb was swollen as a result of inflammation. Because of this, and because the patient is being weakened by complicated suppuration of the wound and partial spasms of the affected muscles, I decided to carry out an immediate amputation. I have to report that this took place at 11 o'clock in the morning of yesterday being the only way of saving the life of this distinguished officer, who up to the point of the operation had showed spirit, courage and valour.

I remain etc

Dr José Pedro D'Oliveira
                    Surgeon General, Montevideo

VII

LORD NORTHBROOK'S 1885 RESPONSE TO WILLIAM T. STEAD'S CRITICISMS OF NAVAL PREPAREDNESS IN THE *PALL MALL GAZETTE*

Edited by John Beeler

Thomas George Baring, 1st Earl of Northbrook[1] has generally been regarded as one of the least effectual First Lords of the Admiralty of the Victorian era. Appointed to the post in 1880 by William Gladstone,[2] he was, according to John Henry Briggs,[3] of the same economical and ideological stripes as Gladstone himself:

> Lord Northbrook was a politician, and, what is more, a very strong party man. From the date of his entering into public life he imbibed the extreme views advocated by his [Liberal] party in regard to economy and retrenchment; he was at all times disinclined to incur any expense which he thought might be inconvenient or embarrassing to the Ministry, and was consequently far more solicitous to keep down the estimates [i.e., expenditures] than add to the strength of the navy.[4]

Briggs's credentials to pass judgment on the First Lord appear impeccable. Both he and his father were career Admiralty civil servants, their combined tenures spanning much of the nineteenth century. Briggs

---

[1]Thomas George Baring, 1st Earl of Northbrook, F.R.S., G.C.S.I. (1826–1904). MP for Penryn and Falmouth, 1857–65. Private Sec to First Lord of the Admiralty Francis Baring, 1st Baron Northbrook, 1849–51; Civil Lord of the Admiralty, 1857–58; Undersec of State for India, 1859–61, 1861–64; Undersec of State for War, 1861, 1868–72; Undersec of State for the Home Dept, 1864–66; First (Political) Sec to the Admiralty, 1866; Viceroy of India, 1872–76, First Lord of the Admiralty, 1880–85.

[2]William Ewart Gladstone, F.R.S., F.S.S. (1809–98). MP for Newark, 1832–45; for Oxford University, 1847–65; for South Lancashire, 1865–68; for Greenwich, 1868–80; for Midlothian, 1880–95. Undersec of State for War and the Colonies, 1835; Vice-President of the Board of Trade, 1841–43; President of the Board of Trade, 1843–45; Sec of State for War and the Colonies, 1845–46; Chancellor of the Exchequer, 1852–55, 1859–66, 1873–74, 1880–82; Lord High Commissioner of the Ionian Islands, 1859; Lord Privy Seal, 1886, 1892–94; Prime Minister, 1868–74, 1880–85, 1886, 1892–94.

[3]John Henry Briggs, Kt (1808–1897). Admiralty clerk, 1826; Chief Clerk, 1865.

[4]John Henry Briggs, *Naval Administrations 1827 to 1892: The Experience of 65 Years*, ed. Elizabeth Briggs (London, 1897).

himself served almost forty-five years at Whitehall, of which more than thirty-five were spent assisting the Board itself.[1] Thus, his boast that he 'had the honour of serving with fifteen First Lords and upwards of fifty Admirals' lends apparent credence to his subsequent claim that he 'was cognisant of all that was taking place throughout the department'.[2]

Having retired in 1870, Briggs was, unless clairvoyant, no longer 'cognisant of all that was taking place throughout the department' by the time that Northbrook assumed office, and historians have long been aware that his account of the Admiralty's doings, even when he was present, is often profoundly unreliable: marred by blatant partisanship, factual errors, and near-libels of many distinguished and capable Navy officials.[3] And yet his allegations continue to inform modern judgments of many of those administrators, none more so than Northbrook.

Oscar Parkes, long-time editor of *Jane's Fighting Ships*, appropriated not only Briggs's verdict but enough of his words to warrant accusations of plagiarism: 'Northbrook was a politician and a very strong party one at that. Having from early days imbibed the extreme views of economy and retrenchment associated with Liberalism, he was always more solicitous to keep down the Estimates than to incur any expenses which he thought might be embarrassing to the Ministry.'[4] More recently, N.A.M. Rodger has stated that Northbrook was 'uninterested' in the Navy and 'so long as the Estimates were kept down' was 'content to leave the running of the Navy to those, like [First Naval Lord Astley Cooper] Key[5] who enjoyed it'.[6]

But Briggs's strictures upon Northbrook would probably not have gained such traction amongst historians had a major 'naval scare' not erupted during the closing months of the second Gladstone ministry. This episode was provoked by a series of articles titled 'The Truth about

---

[1]First as Deputy Reader – i.e., the clerk who read incoming correspondence to the assembled Board during formal meetings and minuted their replies – then as Reader, and finally as Chief Clerk of the Admiralty.

[2]Briggs, *Naval Administrations*, p. xx.

[3]For instance, he wrote of Sir George Cockburn, First Naval Lord 1828–30 and 1841–46, '[a]lmost every opinion he expressed, every measure he devised, and every step he took, were retrograde in their tendencies'(75). Of this indictment Dr Roger Morriss's entry for Cockburn in the *Oxford Dictionary of National Biography* tersely states 'far from being the reactionary as which he was later depicted by Sir John Briggs, he ensured that the latest steam and screw technology adopted by the Royal Navy was appropriate to its requirements'. See http://www.oxforddnb.com/view/article/5770?docPos=2.

[4]Oscar Parkes, *British Battleships, 1860–1950* (London, 1957), p. 307.

[5]Astley Cooper Key, C.B., K.C.B., G.C.B. (1821–88). Entered, 1833; Lt, 1842; Cdr, 1845; Capt, 1850; RA, 1866; VA, 1873; Adm, 1878. Dir of Naval Ordnance, 1866–69; First Naval Lord, 1879–1885.

[6]Nicholas A.M. Rodger, 'The Dark Ages of the Admiralty, 1869–1885 Part III: Peace, Retrenchment and Reform, 1880–85', *Mariner's Mirror* 62/2 (1976): p. 121.

the Navy and its Coaling Stations by One who Knows the Facts' published in the *Pall Mall Gazette* beginning on 15 September 1884.[1] The anonymous author was the *Gazette*'s editor, muck-raking journalist William T. Stead,[2] who drew on information furnished by disgruntled navy officers, chief among them then-Captain John Arbuthnot Fisher.[3]

The picture painted by Stead was grim: Britain, whose national and imperial survival depended upon 'command of the sea' had, as 'One who Knows the Facts' claimed, a bare margin of superiority in armoured vessels over the French Navy alone, and would have been inferior to a combination of France and another naval power. Meanwhile, '[t]he naval expenditure of other Powers has increased 40 per cent . . . our trade [has increased] 40 per cent., our wealth 40 per cent., our shipping 30 per cent., and our possessions have been enormously increased. Yet in [the] face of all these increased responsibilities and increased danger our naval expenditure has been slightly diminished.'[4] In sum, '[o]ur naval supremacy . . . has ceased to exist . . . We have not even a navy of . . . "irresistible superiority" to that of France . . .'[5]

Stead's series provoked other writers to enter the fray, and the final months of 1884 and opening months of 1885 witnessed a small avalanche of articles critical of Northbrook's administration.[6] The public and political furore reached so great a level that the government was pushed to bring forward a Supplementary Vote of £5,525,000, of which £3,100,000 was devoted increasing the material strength of the navy.

---

[1] 'What is the Truth About the Navy?' (15 Sept 1884); 'The Truth About the Navy By One Who Knows the Facts' (18 Sept); 'The Truth About Our Coaling Stations By One who Knows the Facts' (16–17 Oct); 'What Ought to be Done for the Navy By One who Knows the Facts' (13 Nov). These were later compiled and published as a pamphlet (London: Pall Mall Gazette Office, 1884).

[2] William T. Stead (1849–1912). Journalist, newspaper editor and spiritualist. Editor of the Darlington *Northern Echo*, 1871–80; of the *Pall Mall Gazette*, 1883–90; of the *Review of Reviews*, 1890–1912; of the *Daily Paper*, 1904. The impetus for Stead's series was furnished by journalist and politician Hugh Oakeley Arnold-Forster (1855–1909).

[3] John Arbuthnot, 1st Baron Fisher of Kilverstone, K.C.B., G.C.B., O.M., G.C.V.O. (1841–1920). Entered, 1854; Lt, 1861; Cdr, 1869; Capt, 1876; RA, 1890; VA, 1896; Adm, 1901, AoF, 1905. Dir of Naval Ordnance, 1886–91; Third Naval Lord and Controller, 1892–97; Second Naval Lord, 1902–03; First Naval Lord, 1904–10, 1914–15.

[4] *The Truth About the Navy* (pamphlet), p. 16.

[5] Ibid., p. 56.

[6] See Anon., 'The Navy and the Empire', *Quarterly Review* 159, no. 317 (Jan 1885), pp. 201–19; H.O. Arnold-Forster, 'The People of England vs. Their Naval Officials', *The Nineteenth Century* 16, no. 93 (Nov 1884), pp. 702–14; *Ibid.*, 'England or the Admiralty', *The Nineteenth Century* 18, no. 101 (July 1885), pp. 160–76; Edward J. Reed, 'The British Navy', *Contemporary Review* 46 (Nov 1884), 61733; Robert Spencer Robinson, 'The Navy and the Admiralty', *The Nineteenth Century* 17, no. 95 (Jan 1885), pp. 185–99; W.H. Smith, 'The Navy and Its Duties', *National Review* 4, no. 21 (Nov 1884), pp. 289–99.

This outcome, and subsequent assessments of Northbrook's tenure at the Admiralty, suggests that Stead's charges were fundamentally accurate.[1] Northbrook's entry in the *Oxford Dictionary of National Biography*, for instance, states:

> he and his Admiralty board were famously indicted by W. T. Stead in the *Pall Mall Gazette* (September 1884) for their comparative neglect of the fleet. Writing half a century afterwards, the leading modern historian of the Victorian navy [Arthur J. Marder] found Northbrook and his board guilty as charged of the gradual decline of the Royal Navy as a fighting force. France and Germany between them had more first-class ironclads than Britain; Russia and Italy were expanding their navies. Amid gathering international tensions, the public took fright. The reaction to Stead's articles compelled Northbrook to announce a dramatic increase in spending on construction and ordnance.[2]

Moreover, it has been pointed out that Northbrook was brought into the Cabinet more for his knowledge of India (he served as Viceroy 1872–76) rather than his familiarity with naval administration (he had served as Private Secretary to his father, Sir Francis Baring, when the latter was First Lord, 1849–51, and had subsequently occupied the posts of Civil Lord and Parliamentary Secretary of the Admiralty), Rodger remarking that he 'was an expert on India, the colonies, and finance, and his advice in these matters was more sought after by his Cabinet colleagues than his work in a department which neither he nor they valued highly'.[3] Indeed, when the Stead articles appeared Northbrook was on a troubleshooting mission in recently occupied Eygpt, and Arthur Marder claims that he 'apparently . . . did not read details of the *Pall Mall* scare until on his way back to England'.[4]

---

[1]The 'Truth About the Navy' campaign is the subject of a Ph.D. dissertation by Harvey Blumenthal, 'W.T. Stead's Role in Shaping Official Policy: The Navy Campaign of 1884' (George Washington University, 1984), but the author never questions the accuracy of Stead's allegations.

[2]David Steele, 'Baring, Thomas George, First Earl of Northbrook', *Oxford Dictionary of National Biography*, http://www.oxforddnb.com/view/article/30586?docPos=19. See also Arthur J. Marder, *The Anatomy of British Sea Power: A History of British Naval Policy in the Pre-Dreadnought Era, 1880–1905* (New York, 1940), p. 122. Marder states: 'In 1884 England still possessed the largest navy in the world, but the situation was clearly full of danger. The French fleet was growing rapidly, and if, as had happened before, the English had to face alone a European coalition at sea, the situation would be desperate. The Italians and Russians were creating big fleets, and the new German Empire was already showing naval ambitions. A combination of Germany and France alone would outnumber the English in first-class ships.'

[3]Rodger, 'Dark Ages, Part III, p. 121.

[4]Marder, *The Anatomy of British Sea Power*, p. 122.

As a further indicator of Northbrook's apparent indifference, contemporaries seized on a remark he made in the House of Lords prior to his departure for Egypt to the effect that, were the Navy Estimates to be raised by three or four million pounds, '[t]he great difficulty the Admiralty would have to contend with . . . would be to decide how they should spend the money', suggesting to critics that he thought such expenditure unnecessary.[1] In fact, Northbrook was referring to the confounded state of naval architecture and of an utter lack of consensus within the Admiralty about the continued utility of heavily armoured and armed battleships. This fact did not stop Briggs, among others, from wholly misrepresenting his meaning.[2]

Stead's charges, however, were wildly exaggerated. True, foreign naval spending was on the increase. For example, the Italian Navy's budget had grown from £1.8 million in 1868 to £2.3 million in 1884, but the British Navy received almost £11.5 million in the latter year. In fact, the Royal Navy's 1884 budget was more than £2.5 million above those of Italy, Austria, Germany, and the United States combined. The French Navy, the second largest in the world, received £7.8 million, scarcely two-thirds of the Royal Navy's figure. The combined naval expenditures of France and Russia (£4.89 million in 1884), the third-largest navy, came to about 10 per cent more than Britain's, but it can be claimed with little exaggeration that in terms of spending the latter was close to the 'two-power standard' generally deemed requisite for the maintenance of national and imperial security.[3]

The materiel situation was similarly unthreatening. While it is impossible to find a consensus among contemporary commentators as to the numerical strength of the British or other battlefleets, owing to the rapid pace of technological change and the extreme heterogeneity of those fleets, in general terms it can be stated that Britain had a lead over France in first-class armoured vessels (battleships) of twenty-six to sixteen, in second-class armoured vessels (armoured cruisers) of sixteen to twelve, and in third-class armoured vessels (small ironclads designed for coastal defence and assault) of fourteen to eleven. No two navies, with the exception of a French-German combination (scarcely a possibility), could have posed a challenge to Britain's lead in first-class armoured vessels.[4]

---

[1]Northbrook's speech, 10 July 1884, quoted in Bernard Mallet, *Thomas George Earl of Northbrook, G.C.S.I. A Memoir* (London, 1908), p. 200.

[2]Briggs, *Naval Administrations*, p. xviii.

[3]All of the figures in this paragraph are drawn from John Beeler, *British Naval Policy in the Gladstone-Disraeli Era, 1866–1880* (Stanford, CA, 1997), pp. 192–3.

[4]Ibid., p. 198. For a detailed assessment of Britain's naval position vis-à-vis possible rivals during the period, see pp. 191–209.

Stead's charges would have had more accurate had they been aired a few years earlier. While there were, as of 1884, areas in which Britain's resources required augmentation, especially swift cruisers for the protection of commerce and torpedo vessels for the defence of commercial ports, the situation regarding the battlefleet was much improved over that of 1881 or 1882, thanks entirely to Northbrook's Board.

During the late 1870s and early 1880s the French undertook an ambitious programme of naval construction to replace the substantial but thoroughly obsolete ironclad fleet of Napoleon III, built in the late 1850s and early 1860s. Between 1875 and 1880, they laid down thirteen battleships and four coast defence/assault vessels, more than doubling the total number – seven – begun by Britain during those years. In 1877, Controller of the Navy William Houston Stewart[1] hyperbolically claimed that the French 'are rapidly going ahead of us, and unless it is decided to lay down *12* Armoured Battle Ships to be completed by the end of 1881, that year will find the Navy of France decidedly superior to that of Great Britain in ships and guns'.[2]

So, far from being ignorant of or indifferent to the state of the navy, Northbrook's Board was fully alive to the narrowing lead in battleships almost from the moment it assumed office in May 1880, and took substantive and effectual steps to counter the French building programme. In June 1880, the British naval attaché in Paris informed the Board that the French had 'definitely decided to build four more [battleships] of 10,300 tons load displacement' in addition to those already under construction.[3]

This report prompted Parliamentary Secretary George John Shaw Lefevre,[4] to make a comparative assessment of the two battle fleets. He concluded that, unless the British increased the number of battleships building:

> there cannot be a doubt that the strength of the French Fleet would by [1885] equal if not exceed our own, unless considerable additions be made to the latter in the interval [hence] . . . It appears that it will

[1]William Houston Stewart, G.C.B. (1822–1901). Entered, 1835; Lt, 1842; Cdr, 1848; Capt, 1854; RA, 1870; VA, 1876; Adm, 1881. Controller of the Navy, 1872–81.

[2]Comments of Houston Stewart on Captain Nicolson's Report #18, 'The Comparative Strength of the English and French Fleets', 15 Nov 1877, TNA: ADM 1/6424.

[3]Rice to Foreign Office, 18 June 1880, in bound papers relative to decision to build 'Admiral' class, Surveyor's Branch, 1 Aug 1881, TNA: ADM 1/6608.

[4]George John Shaw Lefevre, 1st Baron Eversley, F.S.S. (1831–1928). MP for Reading, 1863–85; for Bradford Central, 1886–95. Civil Lord of the Admiralty, 1866; Sec to the Board of Trade, 1868–71; Undersec of State for the Home Dept, 1871; Sec to the Admiralty, 1871–74, 1880; First Commissioner of Works, 1881–85, 1892–94; Postmaster General, 1884–85; President of the Local Government Board, 1894–95.

not be safe to maintain for the next 5 years the rate of construction of iron clads of the last 6 years, namely 8000 tons a year . . . and that in order to maintain a reasonable superiority over the French fleet we must considerably increase the construction of iron clads during the next few years, and so long as the French maintain their present rate of progress.[1]

Debate about the types of ships most needed and their designs consumed much of 1880 and early 1881, but by March of the latter year the Board authorised two armoured cruisers – *Warspite* and *Imperieuse* – to counter enemy commerce raiders, and on 1 August 1881 Northbrook himself issued a directive calling for 'Two *Collingwoods* [type battleships] to be laid down'. Furthermore, ongoing concern over the French construction programme led the Board to authorise an additional three *Collingwood*-class vessels in 1882.[2]

The French construction programme also slowed precipitously after 1882. As Theodore Ropp states in his study of French naval policy in the late nineteenth century, '[t]he expansion of the French Navy in the early 1880s, along with many other capital improvements, was financed by loans. When these dried up, the navy was forced to take a major cut in its budget, which fell from 217.2 million francs in 1883 to 171.6 million in 1885. As a result, the whole armoured shipbuilding program nearly ground to a halt.'[3] Insofar as French battleship building posed any threat to British naval supremacy, that threat peaked in 1881. By 1884, the relative balance between the two fleets was much altered in Britain's favour. The 'Truth About the Navy' panic broke out after the situation had taken a dramatic turn for the better.

In sum, as John Knox Laughton, the most knowledgeable contemporary authority on the Royal Navy, and one of the few commentators unequivocally to condemn Stead's efforts to sow the seeds of panic, put it in the wake of the scare:

The alarm has really sprung from ignorance and misrepresentation: ignorance of the facts of the navy as it has been, misrepresentation of

---

[1]Shaw Lefevre memorandum 'Programme of Works for Building of Armoured Vessels, 1881–2. Comparison Between English and French Armoured Fleets', 29 Oct 1880, in bound papers relative to decision to build 'Admiral' class, Surveyor's Branch, 1 Aug 1881, TNA: ADM 1/6608.

[2]Northbrook memorandum, 1 Aug 1881, in bound papers relative to decision to build 'Admiral' class, Surveyor's Branch, TNA: ADM 1/6608.

[3]Theodore Ropp, *The Development of a Modern Navy*, ed. Stephen Roberts (Annapolis, MD, 1987), p. 140.

the state of the navy as it is. That much of this misrepresentation has been made in perfect good faith, there is no reason to doubt; that some at least of it has been made to serve some hidden party or personal end, there is also no reason to doubt. But panic is the child of darkness and ignorance; with light and knowledge comes a return of steadfast courage and sober judgment.[1]

So far from being in thrall to the Gladstonian imperatives of economy and retrenchment, Northbrook's Board between 1881–82 and 1884–85 spent on average £1,121,215 per year on armoured shipbuilding, whereas the preceding Conservative Board averaged £984,828, including a substantial extraordinary augmentation in 1878 when sums from a Vote of Credit were used to purchase four ironclads building in private shipyards.[2] And so far from allowing naval supremacy to dwindle, Northbrook and his colleagues did precisely the opposite.

Stead stoked up a public furore, based not on reliable information, but on special pleading from a source whose professional dissatisfaction with political treatment of the navy should have been taken as a given and discounted. This was not accurate reporting: it was scandalmongering alarmism. This situation should come as no surprise; Stead was in the business of selling newspapers, and he followed the 'Truth about the Navy' campaign with other sensationalistic exploits, including the notorious 'Maiden Tribute of Modern Babylon',[3] which detailed his purchase of an adolescent girl on the 'white slavery' market. That his, and by extension Briggs's, allegations about the state of the navy were largely without foundation can be perceived in the placid response of two informed Admiralty insiders, Parliamentary Secretary Henry Campbell Bannerman[4] and First Naval Lord Cooper Key. The former wrote to the Chancellor of the Exchequer in early October 1884:

[1]John Knox Laughton, 'Past and Present State of the Navy', *Edinburgh Review* 161, no. 330 (April 1885), p. 513. The whole of Laughton's piece is well worth reading as a contemporary corrective to charges which for the most part were and continue to be accepted uncritically

[2]See 'Expenditure on Shipbuilding, 1875–76 to 1885–86', appended to Appendix IV, below. Without the 1878 Vote of Credit the figure for the 1874–80 Conservative government would have been £745,817 per annum, scarcely two-thirds of the Liberals' annual expenditure 1881–85.

[3]A series which Ronald Pearsall describes as 'the death knell of responsible journalism'. The same charge could be applied to 'The Truth About the Navy'. See Pearsall, *The Worm in the Bud: The World of Victorian Sexuality* (New York, 1969), p. 373.

[4]Henry Campbell Bannerman, G.C.B. (1836–1908). MP for Stirling Burghs, 1868–1908. Financial Sec to the War Office, 1871–74, 1880–82; Sec to the Admiralty, 1882–84; Chief Sec for Ireland, 1884–85; Sec of State for War, 1886, 1892–95; Prime Minister, 1905–08.

It is the iron-clad Fleet that is generally most discussed in the House of Commons, but I do not think it is on this that my [naval] colleagues would spend . . . money if they had it . . . [I]t may be that a period has come, or is coming, when owing to the definite program the French have been recently working up to, our margin of superiority may be for the moment less than it should be. When their programme is accomplished, we should, of course, by going on steadily year by year, recover our ground.[1]

And Cooper Key, the highest-ranking naval officer at the Admiralty, wrote to a colleague in December 1884:

We now have twenty-seven ironclads in commission. The French have eleven. We could commission thirteen more within a month. I cannot find that the French have more than two ready and one of these has her boilers condemned . . . Many of our ships are of obsolete types – so are many of theirs. Moreover, being of wood theirs cannot last long. I should have no fear whatever of war with France and Russia now, so far as our Navy is concerned . . .[2]

Yet, notwithstanding their utter lack of alarm, and notwithstanding Laughton's eloquent and persuasive denunciation of the 'ignorance and misrepresentation', Briggs and Stead put forward a portrait of Northbrook and his Board which has for the most part persisted to this day.

For this reason alone, the memorandum that follows is of immense significance for coming to a more accurate and balanced understanding of Northbrook's stewardship of the navy. It was composed on his departure from the Admiralty in July 1885, for the information of his Conservative successor, Lord George Hamilton.[3] In terms of the navy's materiel situation it echoes and amplifies the calm and deliberate

---

[1] Campbell Bannerman to Hugh Childers, 2 Oct 1884, printed in J.A. Spender, *The Life of the Right Hon. Sir Henry Campbell-Bannerman* (Boston, 1923), vol. 1, p. 54.

[2] Cooper Key to Geoffrey Phipps Hornby, 2 Dec 1884, printed in Parkes, *British Battleships*, p. 328.

[3] George Francis Hamilton, G.C.S.I. (1845–1927). MP for Middlesex, 1868–85; for Ealing, 1885–1906. Undersec of State for India, 1874–78; Vice-president for the Committee on Education, 1878–80; First Lord of the Admiralty, 1885–86, 1886–92; Sec of State for India, 1895–1903. Perhaps because of its recipient, or because of his desire to avoid the appearance of partisanship, Northbrook eschewed placing blame for the situation he found upon taking up the First Lordship on his Conservative predecessors, George Ward Hunt and W.H. Smith, although the latter had manifestly failed to act on the warnings from his professional advisors about the narrowing ratio of British to French battleships. See Beeler, *British Naval Policy in the Gladstone-Disraeli Era*, pp. 243–4; *Ibid., Birth of the Battleship: British Capital Ship Design, 1870–1881* (London, 2001), pp. 157–8, 168–70.

assessments of Laughton, Campbell-Bannerman and Cooper Key. Likewise, it makes clear that Northbrook's administration addressed the subject of imperial defence, and demonstrates that the reforming impulses associated with Gladstonian Liberalism were evident in many other spheres: the Board's policies on personnel matters such as corporal punishment and otherwise improving the service conditions of enlisted men were unmistakably progressive, as was their reintroduction of competitive entrance examinations for officer aspirants.

Finally, while Northbrook was at times absent from Britain as a colonial troubleshooter, it would be difficult to find a more conscientious and qualified group of Parliamentary Secretaries than the four who served under him: Shaw Lefevre, George Otto Trevelyan,[1] Campbell Bannerman and Thomas Brassey.[2] The first two had served at the Admiralty during the first Gladstone Ministry and thus were intimately familiar with its workings, Campbell Bannerman was a future Prime Minister, and Brassey's name remains a byword for all things naval. The Admiralty was in capable hands whether or not Northbrook himself was present.

---

[1]George Otto Trevelyan, Bt (1838–1928). MP for Tynemouth and North Shields, 1865–68; for Hanwick Burghs, 1868–86; for Glasgow Bridgeton, 1887–97. Civil Lord of the Admiralty, 1868–70; Sec to the Admiralty, 1880–82; Chief Sec for Ireland, 1882–84; Chancellor of the Duchy of Lancaster, 1884–85; Sec for Scotland, 1886, 1892–95.

[2]Thomas, 1st Earl Brassey, F.S.S., K.C.B., G.C.B. (1836–1918). MP for Devonport, 1865; for Hastings, 1868–86. Civil Lord of the Admiralty, 1880–84; Sec to the Admiralty, 1884–85; Govr of Victoria (Australia), 1895–1900. Published *The British Navy: Its Strengths, Resources and Administration* in 1882 and founded the *Naval Annual* in 1886.

MINUTE by THE EARL OF NORTHBOOK
on the
ADMINISTRATION OF THE NAVY
FROM 1880 TO 1885
WITH
APPENDICES[1]

I informed my colleagues of the Board of Admiralty[2] that I would write a paper dealing with some of the more important matters which have come before us during the last five years; and I shall proceed to do so, taking, as the most convenient arrangement, first the *Personnel*, next the *Materiel*, and lastly the *Administration* of the Navy.

I. PERSONNEL

First, then, as regards the *Personnel* of the Navy. No important changes have been made in the regulations respecting the promotion and retire-ment of Officers. The scheme which Mr. Childers[3] framed in 1870, with the modifications since introduced,[4] has, on the whole, worked well. Promotion from the rank of Captain to Admiral has been fairly regular; the numbers on the Captains' and Commanders' lists are by no means excessive as compared with the demands, and afford to Officers a very considerable amount of employment in both those ranks. To increase either the list of Captains or that of Commanders by any considerable extent would not be to the advantage of the Service, because the result must be to keep Officers longer on half-pay.

A small alteration was introduced in the year 1881[5] by which an addition of five was made to the number of annual promotions from the rank of Lieutenant to that of Commander. This was done to give some additional promotions to the Lieutenants. There can be no doubt that the great difficulty with respect to the promotion of Officers is to give

---

[1]Only Appendix IV, on shipbuilding, is included in this edition.

[2]Footnote in original text: 'See Board Minute of July 3, 1885.'

[3]Hugh Culling Eardley Childers (1827–95). MP for Pontefract, 1860–85; for Edin-burgh South, 1886–92. Civil Lord of the Admiralty, 1864–66; First Lord of the Admiralty, 1868–71; Chancellor of the Duchy of Lancaster, 1872–73; Sec of State for War, 1880–82; Chancellor of the Exchequer, 1882–85; Sec of State for Home Affairs, 1886.

[4]Footnote in original text: 'The last Order in Council is that of August 1875, which makes certain arrangements which are to be re-considered after ten years from that date.' For an account of Childers's retirement scheme, see John Beeler, '"Fit for Service Abroad": Promo-tion, Retirement, and Royal Navy Officers, 1830–1890', *Mariner's Mirror* 81, no. 3 (1995), pp. 300–312.

[5]Footnote in original text: 'Order in Council of January 5, 1881.'

sufficient advancement to Lieutenants of long and good service. It is, however, one of those cases which it is impossible to remedy without destroying the efficiency of the superior ranks by placing more Officers on the higher lists than it is possible to employ. In the year 1884 an addition was made to the pay of the senior Lieutenants as some recognition of the value of their services.

As regards promotions I wish to observe that it is very necessary, in the interests of the Service, that care should be taken to promote a certain number of young Officers both to the rank of Captain and that of Commander. The natural inclination of a First Lord of the Admiralty must be to give the weight which is due to long service, but it would be detrimental to the interests of Navy if a certain number of young Officers should not be advanced, and the upper ranks of the Service should be composed of men of uniform and somewhat advanced age. I have, therefore, taken every fair opportunity of advancing young Officers that presented itself to me, and there have been in the last five years promoted to the rank of Captain 11 Commanders of the age of 36 and under, and to the rank of Commander 21 Lieutenants of the age of 32 and under.

Another remark I wish to make regarding promotions is this. Although, shortly before the Board was formed in 1880, the old regulations under which certain periodical promotions for gunnery duties were awarded had been cancelled and no regulation providing for such promotions remained in force, I have taken care every year to recognize, pretty nearly in the same proportion as when that regulation existed, the services of the Gunnery Staff of the *Excellent* and *Cambridge*. I attach very great importance to this; for unless the services of the Officers engaged upon these instructional and scientific duties are recognized, it cannot be expected that the best of the young Officers will willingly undertake them. I have also taken into consideration from time to time the services of Officers employed in the Torpedo School as well as the recommendations of the Hydrographer with respect to Officers employed on Surveys; and speaking generally as regards promotions, it has been my endeavour not only to give due weight to the claims of individual Officers, but also to take into consideration the desirability of distributing promotions among the different squadrons, in order that Officers employed in all parts of the world might feel that their claims were not overlooked, as well as among the different branches of the Service.

I do not believe that since the regulations of 1870 [were introduced] there has ever been occasion to consider the question of how the services of Officers rendered in action, or during military operations, should be dealt with. No provision has been made for what used under the old system to be termed 'Board Promotions,' as distinguished from promotions made in ordinary vacancies. After the action at Alexandria, in 1882,[1] this question had to be considered, and we represented to the Treasury that the regulations for promotions in ordinary times could not be adhered to under such circumstances. We therefore proposed, and with some modification our suggestion was accepted by the Treasury and carried into effect, that in such cases the promotions made for gallant and meritorious conduct should be in addition to those made in ordinary vacancies, but that the additional promotions should be absorbed gradually during a term of years. The same arrangements were made in November, 1882,[2] on the conclusion of the operations in Egypt, and again in 1884, after the operations at Suakin.[3] I presume that a similar course will be followed in respect to the operations on the Nile and at Suakin which have recently been concluded, but the full reports respecting which had not been received when we left office.

As regards entries into the Navy, we re-introduced, I believe to the advantage of the Service, the principle of limited competition in the examination of candidates for Naval Cadetships,[4] and we have been obliged recently (in consequence of actuarial calculations showing that the number of entries of Naval Cadets was not sufficient to secure the required number of Lieutenants and Sub-Lieutenants) to increase somewhat the annual entries.

Considerable difference of opinion has been expressed among Officers as to the age on entry into the Navy, the course of education on board the '*Britannia*,' and the subsequent training of young Officers before attaining the rank of Sub-Lieutenant.[5] During the last five years, having taken every opportunity in my power of asking Officers of all ranks in the Service who have returned from active service afloat their opinion of the merits and qualifications of the junior Officers, I received

---

[1]The Navy's Mediterranean Squadron bombarded the fortifications in Alexandria harbour on 11 July 1882. For an account of the action, see William Laird Clowes et al., *The Royal Navy: A History from the Earliest Times to the Death of Queen Victoria* (London, 1903), vol. 7, pp. 321–36.

[2]Footnote in original text: 'Order in Council, November, 30, 1882.'

[3]Footnote in original text: 'Order in Council, August 11, 1884. There have been specially promoted in all, under these arrangements, 11 Commanders to the rank of Captain and 24 Lieutenants to the rank of Commander. Of these 9 Captains and 20 Lieutenants have been absorbed up to the 30th of June last.' 'Suakin' refers to 1884 operations in the Sudan, in particular the Second Battle of El Teb (29 Feb 1884), in which a naval brigade and Royal Marines participated. For an account, see Clowes, *The Royal Navy*, vol. 7, pp. 350–55.

[4]Footnote in original text: 'A few exceptions from competition are allowed in the case of sons of Officers who have lost their lives in the Service or who have had long and distinguished service.'

[5]This difference of opinion was longstanding. See John Beeler, ed., *The Milne Papers*, vol. 1 (NRS vol. 147, 2004), pp. 606, 637–8, 641, 655–64.

but one answer; that as regards practical knowledge of their profession and performance of their duties there was nothing to be desired. I have not felt therefore at all keen in promoting alterations of a system the results of which have no doubt been highly satisfactory. But recently a Committee has been appointed under the presidency of Admiral Luard,[1] the President of the Royal Naval College at Greenwich, to consider the whole subject, and I do not doubt that some useful suggestions will be obtained from their report.

The recommendations of the report of the Committee appointed by our predecessors, presided over by Sir A. Hoskins,[2] as regards Medical Officers, have been carried out with great advantage to the Service: by the regulations issued in June, 1881, their full pay, half-pay, and retired pay have been increased. By these changes the position of the Medical Officers of the Navy has been so much improved that the difficulties formerly experienced in obtaining candidates possessing high professional qualifications are no longer experienced.

By an Order in Council of November, 1882, improvements were made in the pay allowances, and prospects of advancement of Engineer Officers.

Shortly after the formation of the Board our attention was directed to the condition of the promotion of Officers of the Royal Marines. The Subalterns had then to wait before attaining the rank of Captain sometimes as long as 16 years. This was remedied by adopting for their promotion the rule which obtained with respect to promotion in the scientific corps of the Army, and they are now promoted after 11 years' service, if they have not received their promotion earlier through vacancies.[3] The regulations under which Officers of the Royal Marines are employed on the Staff of the Army have been re-considered.

A well-deserved compliment has been paid to the Royal Marines in the appointment by the Queen of His Royal Highness the Duke of Edinburgh[4] to be Honorary Colonel of the Corps.

The numbers of Warrant Officers have been re-adjusted between the different ranks, and the total number increased in order to meet the

---

[1]William Garnham Luard, C.B., K.C.B. (1820–1910). Entered, 1833; Lt, 1841; Cdr, 1850; Capt, 1857; RA, 1875; VA, 1879; Adm, 1885. President of the Royal Naval College, 1882–85.

[2]Anthony Hiley Hoskins, K.C.B., G.C.B. (1828–1901). Entered, 1842; Lt, 1849; Cdr, 1858; Capt, 1863; RA, 1875; VA, 1885; Adm, 1891. Junior Naval Lord, 1880–82; Second Naval Lord, 1885–88; First Naval Lord, 1891–93.

[3]Footnote in original text: 'See Appendix I. for a full explanation of the reasons for the changes then made in the regulations affecting the Corps; the term of service was first fixed at 12 years, and reduced to 11 years.'

[4]Prince Alfred Ernest Albert, Duke of Edinburgh, Duke of Saxe-Coburg and Gotha, K.G., K.T., K.P., G.C.B., G.C.S.I., G.C.M.G., G.C.I.E., G.C.V.O. (1844–1900). Entered, 1856; Lt, 1863; Capt, 1866; RA, 1878; VA, 1882; Adm, 1887; AoF, 1893.

increased demands upon the instructional staff of the Gunnery and Torpedo ships. A considerable boon has been conferred upon Warrant Officers by the repeal of the regulations known as the 'other ships clause'[1]
and the number of Greenwich Hospital Pensions allotted to Warrant
Officers has been greatly increased. No provision was made for the children of Chief Gunners, Carpenters, and Boatswains, or of Warrant Officers who were drowned, killed, or who died from injuries received in
the Service. This has now been remedied. Compassionate allowances,
varying in amount from £5 to £10 a year, have been allowed under [the]
Order in Council of the 24th June, 1885.

In respect to the Petty Officers and Seamen considerable changes have
been made. The increased pay and allowances which of recent years
have been given to the Non-Commissioned Officers of the Army made it
necessary in our opinion to take the same question into consideration as
regards similar ranks in the Navy, and after a very careful examination
of the subject considerable additions were made in the pay and allowances of the Chief Petty Officers and Petty Officers of the Fleet, thereby
anticipating the complaints which could not fail to have arisen upon this
subject. Similar improvements were made in the pay and allowances of
the Non-Commissioned Officers of the Royal Marines.

The scale of pay of Engine Room Artificers has been re-classified and
improved, and the rating of Chief Stoker has been established.

The sick berth staff has been recently re-organized,[2] and Nursing Sis-
ters introduced into the Naval Hospitals.[3]

With a view to improving the dietary [sic] in Her Majesty's ships,
and offering increased encouragement to sobriety, Seamen have been
encouraged to take other articles in lieu of rum by increasing the quantities of tea, chocolate, and sugar allowed as substitutes for it.

Savings Banks have been established at the principal Naval Ports.

A very great benefit has been conferred on the Seamen and Marines
by new regulations which have been made as respects the manner in
which the widows of men who lose their lives in the Service were treated.
The loss of the *Atalanta*[4] brought this question prominently forward.

---

[1]The 'other ships clause' referred to Admiralty regulations by which warrant officers
serving in harbour vessels were paid less than those in seagoing ships. The clause was abolished in 1882 and warrant officers henceforth paid on the same scale whether in harbour or
at sea. See *Hansard's Parliamentary Debates* 3rd ser., vol. 267, cols. 1094–5.

[2]Footnote in original text: 'Circular 5, of February 4, 1885.'

[3]For the introduction of female nurses, see David McLean, *Surgeons of the Fleet: The
Royal Navy and its Medics from Trafalgar to Jutland* (London, 2010), pp. 212–14, 221–2.

[4]HMS *Atalanta*, a training ship, was lost at sea in Feb 1880, bound from Bermuda to
Falmouth.

The former regulations only admitted of gratuities being given in such cases, and the amount of provision which these widows received depended upon the result of subscriptions which, however liberal, varied in accordance with the circumstances of the case and the public notice which such calamities excited. This did not appear to be right, and it is now provided that in all such cases pensions will be given out of Greenwich Hospital funds to the widows of men who lose their lives in the Service, and allowances are given to their children.

A Committee, presided over by Vice-Admiral H.R.H. The Duke of Edinburgh, who has taken great interest in the subject, is considering whether a system of ensuring the lives of Seamen against ordinary risks, for the benefit of their widows, can be established with some assistance from the Funds [*sic*] of Greenwich Hospital.

We have found it necessary to increase the number of boys annually entered into the Navy. We found that the reduction which was made in the year 1879 in the number of boys had the effect of producing a gradual falling off in the number of bluejackets. In fact, the arrangements then made did not give a sufficient number of annual entries to provide for the maintenance of 19,000 Seamen, which has been agreed not to be excessive in times of peace. The present arrangements as to the number of entries are based upon actuarial calculations of the necessary provision for the maintenance of that number of Seamen.

The increasing charge for pensions was prominently brought to our notice by the report of the Pension Committee, which was appointed in 1881 to consider the large and growing charges for non-effective services. The exhaustive report of the Committee has been from time to time under our consideration, and several important changes have been made in accordance with their recommendations, the most important being that under an Act of Parliament, passed in 1884, the period of service for the first continuous service engagement has been extended from 10 to 12 years, so that the long service pension will not be acquired by men who enter the Service after the passing of the Act until after 22, instead of as present after 20 years.

Many improvements have been made by Sir Cooper Key with regard to the *personnel* of the Service, and some of them, which bear principally upon encouraging the education of Officers in professional subjects and the instruction of men in the various and complicated duties which the progress of science has applied to Naval Warfare, are described in a Memorandum which has been prepared for me by the branch.[1]

---

[1]Footnote in original text: 'See Appendix II.'

Instructions have been issued under which Officers in command of the different foreign squadrons have assembled as far as possible all the ships under their command every year for the purpose of exercising manoeuvres and reporting on the quality of ships concerned [*sic*].

Naval Officers are constantly put into trying situations abroad, and have to exercise their judgment in respect to undertaking operations on the requisitions of Consular and Diplomatic Officers. On the West Coast of Africa especially such questions have been frequently raised and present considerable difficulty. I was able to make an arrangement with the Foreign Office by which a distinct procedure was laid down to be followed by both Consular and Naval Officers before resorting to hostilities against the Petty Chiefs on the coast. A question somewhat of the same kind occurred with respect to hostilities on the East India Station which was arranged with the India Office.

In accordance with the policy of Her Majesty's Government as regards the infliction of corporal punishment in both Services, all existing regulations authorising Captains of Ships to award corporal punishment were cancelled soon after the Board was appointed, and Courts-Martial were recommended not to award sentences of flogging. In case such punishment is awarded, it is not to be carried out without the previous approval of the Board. While the discipline of the Service had in many respects been most satisfactory, there can, I fear, be no doubt that the abolition of corporal punishment has caused some increase in the offence of striking superior officers. The prevalence of such offences made it necessary for Courts-Martial to deal very severely with them, and sentences of five years' penal servitude have been awarded for this reason in certain cases which have been prominently brought to public notice in Parliament and elsewhere.[1] The Board was obliged, in the interests of the Service, to resist the pressure put upon them to treat such cases lightly but we hoped that as the offence became less frequent it would ordinarily be sufficiently met by imprisonment.

The procedure of Courts-Martial has been revised, and an Admiralty Memorandum has been issued for the guidance of Officers in framing charges. Directions have also been given with a view to securing an uniform system in recording proceedings.

In the year 1884 an Act was passed to amend the Naval Discipline Act, by the extension of the power of awarding summary punishment, by facilitating the assembly of Courts-Martial abroad, and some other minor amendments of the previous Acts. In 1883, in consequence of

[1]See *Hansard's Parliamentary Debates*, 3rd ser., vol. 281 (1883), cols. 927–32.

some Parliamentary discussion with respect to the proceedings of a Court-Martial,[1] it was prominently brought to our notice that the decisions of the Board in the revision of Courts-Martial were not fortified, as is the case with the Army, by the opinion of a professional legal advisor; and although in the case in question, which was referred to the law officers of the Crown, the decision of the Board of Admiralty was supported by the highest legal authority, we thought it was desirable in future to secure legal advice. We therefore arranged to refer all Naval Courts-Martial to the Judge-Advocate of the Fleet, the constitutional advisor to the Board of Admiralty in such matters, and all general Courts-Martial of the Royal Marines to the Judge Advocate-General.

An Order in Council was obtained on the 30th of December, 1884, under which increased and better defined powers were given to the Board for the purpose of placing Officers who may have committed repeated acts of misconduct upon the retired list, with a reduced rate of half pay.

Revised regulations were issued this year for the Naval Prisons at home and abroad.

We trusted, by an arrangement with the Home Office, by which part of the Bodmin Prison is to be transferred to the Admiralty, to secure sufficient accommodation to obviate the necessity of sending to Civil Prisons any men who are to revert to the Service on the expiration of their sentences.

No change of importance has been made in respect to the Naval Reserves, with the exception of equalising the numbers of the first and second class at 10,000 each.[2] There has been some difference of opinion with respect to the relative value of these two classes of Reserves. The Duke of Edinburgh, when he was Admiral-Superintendent of Naval Reserves, attached greater value to the second class than his successor, Sir Anthony Hoskins.

Speaking generally, the position of the Navy in respect to Reserves of Seamen is satisfactory, as will be seen from the Report which was made by the Duke of Edinburgh at the expiration of his term of service, which was laid before Parliament in 1882, from which the following is an extract:– '20,000 R.N. Reserve with Fleet-men of the Coast Guard[3] and Seamen Pensioner Reserve numbering 5,500, will, as regards blue

---

[1]For this case, see *Hansard's Parliamentary Debates*, 3rd ser., vol. 283 (1883), cols. 1373–443.

[2]First-class reserve men were recruited from merchant seamen engaged in oceanic trades, those in the second class from coastal shipping and fishermen. On the creation of the Naval Reserve, see R. Taylor, 'Manning the Royal Navy: The Reform of the Recruiting System, 1852–1862', *Mariner's Mirror* 44 (1958), pp. 302–13, and 45 (1959), pp. 46–58.

[3]The Coast Guard had been brought under Admiralty control in 1856 as a means of supplementing the enlisted manpower available to the Navy in the event of a crisis. See Beeler, *The Milne Papers*, vol. 1, pp. 605, 642–50, 651–3.

jackets, be ample to meet any emergency, and with this number of trained men the Fleet of the Royal Navy could be expanded to any extent required on the sudden outbreak of a war.'[1]

The force required to man all the available ships of the Navy formed the subject of special examination in 1883, when the details were carefully worked out.[2]

By an Act of Parliament, passed in the present year, the payment of the Naval Pensioners has been transferred from the War Office to the Admiralty, so that we shall be able in future to have a more complete record of the residences of the Pensioners, so as to be able to lay our hands upon them in time of war.

We have found some difficulty in dealing with the Royal Naval Artillery Volunteers. The three existing corps have shown great public spirit, and their efficiency has been well reported on, but until some steps were taken to organize the defences of the commercial harbours it was difficult to assign any precise duty for them. Recently, in consequence of the greater public attention that has been directed to this subject, the opportunity has arisen for action in the matter, and Vice-Admiral Hamilton[3] was appointed to visit the ports to ascertain what number of suitable boats are available for use in the Naval part of the defence, and what forces of Volunteers would be required to man them. It is probable that some capitation grant[4] will be necessary, and it was my intention, upon the receipt of Admiral Hamilton's report, to have considered the regulations under which it should have been given. Care will have to be taken to prevent the Naval Volunteers interfering either with the Naval Reserves, or with the Artillery Volunteers under the War Office; for the maintenance of the latter force is essential to man the batteries, which must form the most important part of the defences of the commercial harbours.

A most important question connected with the Reserves is that of the supply of Officers of junior ranks from the Mercantile Marine to supplement the Navy in time of war. It is impossible to employ in time of peace a sufficient number of Lieutenants and Sub-Lieutenants to perform the

---

[1]'Report on the naval reserves and coast-guard, by Rear-Admiral His Royal Highness the Duke of Edinburgh, K.G., K.T., K.P., &c., &c., &c., on resigning the command, 21st November 1882', *Parliamentary Papers*, 1882, vol. 40, pp. 491–500.

[2]Footnote in original text: 'See the Report of the Committee on Naval Matters, 1883.' This committee report was not published in the *Parliamentary Papers*.

[3]Richard Vesey Hamilton, C.B., K.C.B., G.C.B. (1829–1912). Entered, 1843; Lt, 1851; Cdr, 1857; Capt, 1862; RA, 1877; VA, 1884; Adm, 1887; Dir of Naval Ordnance, 1878–80; Second Naval Lord, 1888–89; First Naval Lord, 1889–91.

[4]A grant funded by a per-head levy such as a poll tax. Whether the grant was to be applied to paying the volunteers themselves or for the hire of their boats is unclear from the text.

work which would be required of those ranks of Officers in war time, and therefore it is most important to establish a connection between the Navy and the Mercantile Marine with a view to securing the services of Officers in those ranks. We did something to draw together the two Services by passing a regulation in 1882 under which every year young gentlemen educated on board the *Conway* and *Worcester* training ships for Officers of the Mercantile Marine are admitted to the Royal Navy as Midshipmen, the education on board these ships being taken in lieu of that which is given on board the *Britannia*.[1]

During the recent experimental cruise of the fleet under Sir Geoffrey Hornby,[2] a certain number of Officers from the Royal Naval Reserve were attached to different ships, and the experiment has been so successful that I trust some arrangements may be made by which it may be continued annually. Sir Cooper Key has recently written a Memorandum, in which he has made some valuable suggestions for the purpose of arranging for the supply of junior Officers of the Navy from the Mercantile Marine in time of war.

The subject of the assistance which can be given to the Royal Navy in time of war from the different Colonial Naval Forces is connected with the Reserves. It is well known that several of our Colonies, especially the Australasian Colonies, have of late years taken a great interest and made considerable sacrifices in defending their harbours from the possible attacks of an enemy. They have not only organized land forces and established batteries on shore, but they have also purchased Torpedo vessels and other craft to aid in the defence, and the Admiralty have cordially co-operated with them in the selection of the proper description of vessel and also by permitting Naval Officers to assist in the organization of the local forces. Sir Cooper Key has paid particular attention to this subject, and in the autumn of last year he wrote a Memorandum, a copy of which is in the Appendix.[3] This Memorandum received the

---

[1]Footnote in original text: 'The young officers who have entered under this regulation have been well reported on, and the last cadet from the *Worcester* took a creditable place at the Examination.'

[2]Geoffrey Thomas Phipps Hornby, K.C.B., G.C.B. (1825–95). Entered, 1837; Lt, 1844; Cdr, 1850; Capt, 1852; RA, 1869; VA, 1875; Adm, 1879; AoF, 1888. Second Naval Lord, 1874–77. In 1885 a Special Service Squadron under Hornby's command was fitted out in preparation for possible hostilities with Russia. After the crisis was resolved it was dispatched on an experimental cruise to test the qualities of its constituent ships.

[3]Footnote in original text: 'Appendix III.' The appendix is not included in this collection, nor was it published in the *Parliamentary Papers*, but a synopsis of its clauses can be found in 'Proceedings of the Colonial Conference, 1887. Vol. II. (appendix). Papers laid before the conference', *Parliamentary Papers*, 1887, vol. 56, p. 817.

concurrence of the Secretary of State for the Colonies and the Chancellor of the Exchequer, and it formed the basis of the instructions which were given to Admiral Tryon,[1] when he proceeded to take command of the Australian station, last winter. He was instructed to discuss the matter demi-officially [*sic*] with the Governments of the different Colonies, with the knowledge that H.M.'s Government were prepared to agree to any proposals that might be acceptable to the Colonies on the lines laid down in Sir Cooper Key's memorandum. This year the patriotic spirit shown by the Colonies in coming to the aid of the Mother Country in the Soudan Expedition, led the Government to think that the time had arrived for official communication to be opened upon the subject, and the Secretary of State for the Colonies has addressed a Circular Letter to the Governors embodying the proposals which were made by Sir Cooper Key.[2]

It will be observed that these proposals referred in the main to the organization of local defensive forces, and that their object was to secure the thorough efficiency of these forces. The further question of the provision under any arrangements with the Imperial Government of a seagoing Navy by the Colonies presents much greater difficulty. The principle which successive Boards of Admiralty have maintained is that no restriction can be placed in time of war upon the use which the Admiralty or the Officers commanding the British Naval Forces abroad may make of the ships and vessels which may be under their command; while, on the other hand, it is unlikely that any seagoing Navy will be provided by a Colony without the stipulation that the services of the ships are to be limited to the neighbourhood of the Colony by which the force is maintained.

[1]George Tryon, K.C.B. (1832–93). Entered, 1848; Lt, 1854; Cdr, 1860; Capt, 1866; RA, 1884; VA, 1889. Private Sec to First Lord of the Admiralty George J. Goschen, 1871–74; Second (Permanent) Sec to the Admiralty, 1882–84; C-in-C Australia Station, 1884–87. Died when his flagship was rammed and sunk by a squadron-mate in 1893 while executing a manoeuvre ordered by him.

[2]For the course and outcome of these negotiations, see 'Proceedings of the Colonial Conference, 1887. Vol. II. (appendix). Papers laid before the conference', *Parliamentary Papers*, 1887, vol. 56, pp. 817–68, and 'A bill for defraying the expenses of carrying into effect an agreement for naval defence with the Australasian colonies, and providing for the defence of certain ports and coaling stations, and for making further provision for imperial defence', *Parliamentary Papers*, 1888, vol. 3, pp. 365–76. For initiatives on imperial defence co-operation in the late Victorian and Edwardian eras, see D.C. Gordon, *The Dominion Partnership in Imperial Defence, 1870–1914* (Baltimore, MD, 1965).

II. MATERIEL.

The shipbuilding policy of the Board of Admiralty has been freely crit-icised in the Press and elsewhere, and it is therefore desirable to place it on record as clearly as possible. For this purpose I must revert to the condition of the shipbuilding as we found it; in so doing I have no desire to criticise the policy of our predecessors,[1] but it is necessary to state the facts in to explain the course we have taken. When the Board was consti-tuted, in May, 1880, we found that reports[2] had been made in September, 1879, to our predecessors, by Mr. Barnaby, the Director of Naval Con-struction, and Sir Houston Stewart, Comptroller of the Navy, shewing the condition of the Navy as respects armour-plated ships as compared with France. Those reports showed that while England possessed a supe-riority over France in respect to such ships for the time, yet that the French Admiralty had during the last preceding years laid down more ships of that class than we had, and there were 18 French ships build-ing as compared with 9 English; so that, unless measures were taken to redress this inequality, the time must arrive when we should be run very close. The condition of things will be seen clearly from the following list, which shows that since the year 1876 there had been laid down by France more than twice as many such ships as by England. This inequal-ity was somewhat redressed by the purchase, in the year 1878, of four ships, the *Neptune*, *Superb*, *Belleisle*, and *Orion*; but this addition was made outside the ordinary Naval Estimates, and the provision for ship-building for the year 1880–81 was exceptionally low.

[1]Footnote in original text: 'Speaking on the subject in the House of Lords on the 12th of April, 1883, I used the following words: "I am bound to say that I think it is desirable to increase very materially the amount of construction; but I must explain to your Lordships that, in saying that, I by no means wish to lay any blame upon the Board of Admiralty which we have followed, because, some years ago, it was discovered that greater power was produced in a gun by means of the use of slower [burning] powder, which very much revolutionized the construction of ships, by making it necessary to place much thicker armour upon the ships. Then, again, there have been important improvements in engines and other matters with which I need not trouble your Lordships; all of which changes may have delayed construction, and I have no doubt they had a material effect upon the policy of the Board of Admiralty which we succeeded."' Northbrook was being charitable. During his tenure as First Lord, W.H. Smith took almost no steps to counter the ambitious French battleship building programme then underway. See Beeler, *Birth of the Battleship*, pp. 157–8, 168–9.

[2]Footnote in original text: 'Printed paper: "Discussion resulting in the order to build the *Collingwood*." Sir Houston Stewart, after comparing the armour-plated ships afloat and building of England and France, summed up in the following words:– "The armoured Navy of France is equal to that of England, and the policy appears to be to increase it."' For a gloss on British assessments of French shipbuilding, see Beeler, *Birth of the Battleship*, pp. 157–58, 168–70.

ARMOUR-PLATED SHIPS LAID DOWN 1876–80.

	England.		*France.*
		1876	
	Ajax.		*Turenne.*
	Agamemnon.		*Devastation*
			Bayard.
			Foudroyant.
		1877	
			Amiral Duperré.
			Tonnant.
			Furieux.
		1878	
	{ *Neptune.*		*Terrible.*
Bought from	{ *Superb.*		*Duguesclin.*
Vote of Credit	{ *Belleisle.*		*Requin.*
	{ *Orion.*		*Indomptable.*
			Caiman.
		1879	
	Conqueror.		*Formidable.*
	Edinburgh.		*Vauban.*
	Colossus.		*Amiral Baudin.*
		1880	
	Collingwood.		
Total	{ 6 laid down.		15 laid down.
	{ 4 bought.		

We assumed office after the Navy Estimates had been introduced, and we did not think it desirable to make great change in the ship-building, programme, but, as explained in Mr. Lefevre's speech on the 7th June, 1880,[1] we made certain modifications and a slight addition for the purpose of proceeding more rapidly with the armour-plated ships on the stocks.

[1] *Hansard's Parliamentary Debates*, 3rd ser., vol. 252, cols. 1385–9.

In the course of the year we examined carefully into the figures before us, and we saw that it would be necessary to make a considerable addition to the rate of shipbuilding upon armour- plated ships, and that has been the policy we have since steadily pursued. In 1881 we laid down the *Warspite* and *Imperieuse*. In 1882 we laid down the *Howe*, *Rodney*, and *Camperdown*, and ordered the *Benbow* by contract. In 1883 we laid down the *Anson* and *Hero*; and in 1885 we ordered by contract the *Sanspareil* and *Renown*.[1] In five years we have therefore commenced ten armour-plated ships. This would have been insufficient if the French had continued the rate of building which they had been following during the five previous years, but a change took place in the financial arrangements of the French Admiralty. They had supplemented their shipbuilding votes by borrowed money, but that system ceased in 1881, and their rate of expenditure, and what is still more important, their rate of progress, which we carefully watched, fell off considerably. In the five years during which we laid down ten armour-plated ships the French have only laid down five, as will be seen from the following list, so that during the period under review we have laid down two armour-plated ships for every one laid down by the French; and the condition as respects forwardness of the ships we have laid down during that period is more advanced than that of the French. Of our ships the *Imperieuse* and *Warspite* are nearly complete, and the *Howe*, *Rodney*, and *Benbow*, have been launched; whereas none of the French ships have yet been launched.

ARMOUR-PLATED SHIPS LAID DOWN 1880–85.

	England.	*France.*
	1881	
Nearly completed	*Imperieuse.*	*Hoche.*
ditto	*Warspite.*	
	1882	
Launched	*Howe.*	*Neptune.*
ditto	*Rodney.*	*Marceau.*
ditto	*Benbow* (contract).	
	Camperdown.	

[1]Subsequently renamed HMS *Victoria*.

1883

Anson.   *Magenta.*

Hero.

1884

Charles Martel (no work
is being done on this ship.

1885

Renown.   }

Sanspareil. } (contract).

Another important question relating to shipbuilding is the efficiency, especially as regards speed, of our cruisers; and here we found that the French cruisers were of greater speed than our own.[1] This appeared to us to be a serious deficiency, and our attention has been directed to remedy it, as was stated by Mr. Lefevre in his speech of June 7th, 1880. The Board of Admiralty which we succeeded had arranged to order in the year 1880 three fast cruisers, the *Leander*, *Phaeton*, and *Arethusa*; we followed these by the *Amphion* of the same class, and then by the new class of 'protected' ships, *Thames*, *Forth*, *Mersey*, and *Severn*. We also built two fast cruisers of about 1,400 tons – the *Scout* and the *Fearless* – and we have gradually increased the speed of the smaller vessels.

Our policy as regards shipbuilding, and the necessity we felt for an increase both in armour-plated ships and in fast cruisers, was explained by me in some evidence I gave before the Royal Commission on the Defence of our Colonies and Commerce in the year 1881.[2] Our action up to last year is explained in detail in a Memorandum and Tables, prepared under the directions of Sir Thomas Brassey, which are printed in the Appendix.[3] It will be seen from the figures which are there given that the expenditure upon shipbuilding has been largely increased by us; and the increase must, in order to carry out our programme, have occasioned

---

[1] Footnote in original text: 'Sir Houston Stewart, in his report of September, 1879, wrote:– "I conclude by expressing my opinion that the unarmoured Navy of France is better provided with efficient cruising ships, both as to number and quality, than we are."'

[2] The Carnarvon Commission. The Commission's three reports were at this point classified 'strictly confidential'. An expurgated version, lacking among other things the minutes of evidence, was published in 1887, for which see *Parliamentary Papers*, 1887, vol. 56, pp. 899–942. For a description of the Commission, its work and its reports, see Donald M. Schurman, *Imperial Defence 1868–1887*, ed. John Beeler (London, 2000), pp. 83–125.

[3] Footnote in original text: 'Appendix IV.'

a further large increase in the Estimates for 1885–86, apart from circumstances to which I shall now advert.

In the autumn of 1884 public attention was very much directed to the condition of our Navy, especially in comparison with that of France, and the facts, of which the Board was well aware before, were prominently brought to public notice. The Government took advantage of this state of feeling in order to push on still further the construction of the class of ship which we most required, viz., fast cruisers for the protection of our commerce. The sum of £3,100,000 was allotted to be spent by contract in the next four or five years upon shipbuilding, in addition to the programme which we should have been able to carry out if we had gone on building at the ordinary rate. This sum was intended to provide for the addition to our programme of one armour-plated ship, five belted cruisers, ten fast cruisers of the class of the *Scout*, and thirty first-class torpedo boats; but it was explained that the division of the building between the Dockyards and the trade would depend upon circumstances. We have actually ordered, by contract, two armour-plated ships, five belted cruisers, six *Scouts*, and fourteen torpedo boats, which will expend the sum of £3,250,000.[1] A considerable number of fast boats, which will be fitted as torpedo boats, have been ordered out of the Vote of Credit of this year.

When the Board of Admiralty left office we had not decided upon the type of two armour-plated ships which were to be laid down at the end of the financial year in the dockyards, or of the rams of the type of the *Polyphemus*, which we intended to build.[2] There was no immediate necessity for arriving at our conclusions on their designs, for it was desirable to push on as fast as possible all the ships on the stocks, especially with a view to the state of political affairs at the commencement of the year.[3] I intended to discuss these questions after the conclusion of Sir Geoffrey Hornby's cruise, for I expected to obtain valuable help from his reports, particularly as to the design of the rams.[4]

No question has probably caused more anxiety to successive Boards of Admiralty or thrown upon them greater responsibility than the choice

---

[1]Footnote in original text: 'See Appendix V for the details.'

[2]The two battleships were HMS *Nile* and *Trafalgar*, heavily-armoured coast-assault vessels. The rams were never built.

[3]A reference to the Penjdeh border crisis, precipitated by Russian advances in Afghanistan that appeared to threaten the northwest frontier of British India.

[4]Footnote in original text: 'Our attention was recently particularly directed to the best class of vessel to accompany fleets to protect them against attack by torpedo boats, and on the 7th of May we ordered a design to be prepared of such a vessel, with a draft of water not exceeding 8 feet, so that she should not be subject herself to attack by the Whitehead torpedo. The design had not been submitted when we left office.' The vessel, the torpedo gunboat HMS *Rattlesnake*, was begun in Nov 1885.

of the designs of first-class armour-plated ships.[1] In the ships of the Admiral class we have laid down, we have followed the main features of the *Collingwood*, which was ordered by our predecessors early in 1880, adding slightly to the thickness of the armour and increasing the weight of the armament, and the number of the light guns. Sir Edward Reed has lately criticised the design of these ships somewhat roughly; he has also advocated a design of his own, a correspondence respecting which will be found in the office. The technical questions in dispute are, very fairly stated in two lectures delivered at the Royal Naval College, by Mr. Smith,[2] of the Construction Department, which have been lately published. We saw no reason to be dissatisfied with the disposition of the armour adopted in the Admiral class.[3]

The *Imperieuse* and *Warspite* were designed specially for service on foreign stations as the most powerful cruisers afloat.

The two new ships just ordered by contract have been so recently described in Parliament that I need not say more than that their design has been generally approved.[4]

We have paid particular attention in all these ships to the element of speed, and we expect them to have a knot greater speed than the French armour-plated ships.

We ordered for three of them the heaviest Naval gun hitherto designed, viz., the 110-ton gun, manufactured by the Elswick Ordnance Company. This appeared to us to be desirable, for guns of that weight are carried in some of the Italian ships,[5] and France is arming some ships with guns of 75 tons. The success of the hydraulic mountings, which is greatly due to Mr. George Rendel,[6] has removed the difficulty of handling these

---

[1]Northbrook was referring to this perplexity when he made the 10 July statement in the House of Lords that if the Board had an additional three or four million pounds at its disposal, 'the great difficulty . . . would be to decide how . . . [to] spend the money'. In other words, his remark had nothing to do with the strength of the navy and everything to do with the utter lack of consensus as to the future of naval architecture.

[2]William E. Smith, Draughtsman in the Dept of the Controller of the Navy.

[3]Footnote in original text: 'Board Minutes, February 28, 1885.'

[4]See *Hansard's Parliamentary Debates*, 3rd ser., vol. 294 (1884–85), cols. 455–6.

[5]Footnote in original text: 'The power of this gun was somewhat quaintly described in the *Moniteur de Rome* of the 4th of October, 1884, after the trial at Spezia as follows:– "La puissance développée par une telle charge et évaluèe à 14 millions de kilogrammes, c'est à dire à une force capable de soulever en uno senonde à 1 mêtre de hauteur 200 mille soldats complètement armes." A more forcible way of expressing the shock of the shot on the target would, Mr. Rendel, noted, be to compare it with that of an express train. It would take four "Flying Scotchmen" charging the target together to deliver a blow of the same energy as that of the shot fired at Spezia from the 100-ton gun.'

[6]George Wightwick Rendel (1833–1902). Civil Engineer; Civil Lord of the Admiralty, 1882–85.

heavy weights, and there are circumstances under which the power of the heaviest guns must be of great use.

We have resisted considerable pressure in the direction of an increase in size of our armour-plated ships. Eminent Naval architects are naturally anxious to emulate the *Italia*, of nearly 14,000 tons, built some years since by the Italian Government. But the French, since the *Formidable* and *Amiral Baudin*, of 11,200 tons, were laid down, in 1879, have not embarked in more ships of so great displacement. We have, therefore, been satisfied with a displacement of about 10,000 tons for our first-class ships.

In a general statement of the proceedings of the Board of Admiralty, during the past five years, it is impossible altogether to omit any notice of the provision of guns for the fleet, although that service is provided for out of the Army Estimates, and the Secretary of State for War is, therefore, immediately responsible, and not the Board of Admiralty; but, of course, as a Member of the Cabinet, the First Lord of the Admiralty is responsible for the whole. I append a statement prepared for me by the Director of Naval Ordnance on the subject, which has been a source of great anxiety to us. The very effective system of muzzle-loading guns, which has been carried out for many years at the Royal Arsenal at Woolwich, the safety and efficiency of which was proved at the attack, by Sir Beauchamp Seymour's[1] squadron, on the forts of Alexandria, in 1882, where there was hardly one gun disabled and no accident happened, naturally induced the authorities at Woolwich to be reluctant to change their system for the breech-loading system, which had been adopted on the Continent by other European nations. And it is possible that their views would have been found correct, and that we should have maintained the muzzle-loading system until the present time, if it had not been for the introduction of the slow burning powder, for the full utilization of which it was necessary to lengthen the guns, which obliged the breech-loading system to be adopted for Naval guns. In the year 1880 hardly anything had been done in deciding upon the patterns of the breech-loading guns for the Fleet, but since that time I believe that every endeavour has been made consistent with the security of the guns to develop the breech-loading system with the greatest rapidity possible. In this we have utilized the resources of the Elswick factory of Sir William

---

[1]Frederick Paget Beauchamp Seymour, C.B., K.C.B., G.C.B., 1st Baron Alcester (1821–95). Entered, 1834; Lt, 1842; Cdr, 1847; Capt, 1854; RA, 1870; VA, 1876; Adm, 1882. Private Sec to First Lord of the Admiralty Hugh Childers, 1868–70; Junior Naval Lord, 1872–74; Second Naval Lord, 1883–85. Seymour commanded the Mediterranean Squadron at the bombardment of Alexandria, 11 July 1882.

Armstrong and Co., as well as those of the Arsenal at Woolwich. The 110-ton guns which are to be placed on board the *Renown*, and *Sanspareil*, will be made at Elswick; the Company had experience in the manufacture of those guns from having supplied guns similar type to the Italian Navy. The difficulty as to the patterns of the breech-loading guns has to a certain extent delayed the completion of the ships on the stocks, but not very seriously;[1] and I trust that the difficulties in respect to the patterns of these guns have now been nearly, if not quite, solved, so far as our present knowledge goes; but in a science which has so rapidly developed of late years, we must expect to see changes perhaps as great in the future as those with which we have had to contend during the last five or six years.

It has been frequently suggested that the provision for guns should be made in the Navy Estimates instead of in the Army Estimates, thereby transferring the responsibility for the manufacture of guns from the Secretary of State for War to the Board of Admiralty. There is much to be said in favour of this change, because it would undoubtedly place clearly responsibility where it should be placed. I have not, however, felt able to make any recommendation of the kind to the Government. The subject is a very large one, the responsibility is very serious, the organization which would have to be made in order to enable the Board of Admiralty to carry out the duty properly would require a considerable extension of the Department, and I am not certain whether it might not be wiser to revert to some system like that which prevailed when there was a Board of Ordnance, by establishing a Department which should be assisted by the most capable civil manufacturing experience, distinct from either the War Office or Admiralty, to which Department the manufacture of guns and the supply of Ordnance stores should be entrusted both for the Army and for the Navy.

We made an arrangement, in the year 1884 that the supply of gun mountings, which used to be divided between the Army, if they were manufactured at Woolwich, and the Navy if they were received from contract, should be altogether transferred to the Naval Votes, leaving the responsibility entirely with the Board of Admiralty. I am satisfied that this change was a desirable one, and since it has been made the provision of gun mountings has been more simple and the responsibility more direct. There was some difficulty at first in arranging that the Admiralty might make use of the Royal Arsenal at Woolwich as their manufacturers

---

[1]Again, Northbrook was being charitable. The Admiralty experienced huge delays and obstruction from the War Office in the provision of heavy breech-loading guns. See Beeler, *Birth of the Battleship*, pp. 79–81.

for such gun mountings as we desired to order there; but this has now fortunately been removed, for it is very necessary, in order to check the prices and work of manufacturers, that we should be able to resort to the Royal Arsenal where the work is unexceptionable. We have recently taken steps by which we hope that other contractors, besides the Elswick Company, may be induced to take up the manufacture of gun mountings. We are very grateful for the assistance which Mr. Vavasseur[1] and the Elswick Company have given to us in this matter, but both on the grounds of economy, and also in order that there may be a greater reserve of manufacturing power for a time of war, we attach great importance to extending the business to other firms.

The same remarks apply to the manufacture of torpedoes, and we have recently made arrangements with a capable firm for the purpose of manufacturing torpedoes, so that we may not be entirely dependent on Woolwich Arsenal and on foreign manufacturers for their supply.

While on the subject of shipbuilding, I will say a few words on the subject of the Mercantile Auxiliaries.[2] The history of the movement made for the purpose of utilising, in the event of war, the fastest of the Mercantile steamers will be found in a paper which I directed to be drawn up in August, 1881. The movement was commenced when Mr. Ward Hunt was First Lord of the Admiralty, and continued by my predecessor, Mr. Smith, who in 1878 made arrangements for the arming of 30 ships of this class, if war had then broken out, for the purpose, as he justly expressed it, 'of securing a certain number of fast cruisers which would be capable of meeting and disposing of a similar class of vessels equipped by the enemy in order to prey on our commerce.'

Sir Nathaniel Barnaby[3] deserves great credit for the manner in which, with the assistance of Mr. Dunn,[4] he has induced our great shipbuilders so to construct their magnificent vessels as that they may be used with the greatest advantage in time of war. The present Board gave further development to the system by sending guns to certain stations abroad, so that they should be ready when required, and arrangements were made last spring, which fall more properly into the history

---

[1] Josiah Vavasseur, C.B. (1834–1908). Civil engineer and ordnance specialist, especially with regard to gun mountings.

[2] On efforts to utilise merchant auxiliaries, see John Beeler, 'Plowshares Into Swords: The Royal Navy and Merchant Marine Auxiliaries in the Late Nineteenth Century' in Greg Kennedy (ed.), *The Merchant Marine in International Affairs, 1850–1950* (London, 2000), pp. 5–30.

[3] Nathaniel Barnaby, C.B., K.C.B. (1829–1915). Dir of Naval Construction (Chief Constructor), 1872–85.

[4] James Dunn, Assistant Constructor and Chief Draughtsman.

of the Naval preparations, for utilising a considerable number of our fastest cruisers. I will only make here two further observations on the subject.

(1). It has been suggested that some system of subsidy should be introduced whereby the Admiralty might have a lien on such steamers as would be most useful in the event of war. After considering the subject very carefully and communicating at Liverpool with many of the persons most concerned, I decided against the introduction of any such system, and the experience of this year has shown that there was no difficulty in obtaining all the ships that we required, and that there was no serious danger of their falling into the hands of a foreign power.

(2). The view of the Board of Admiralty has been that too great reliance should not be placed on these steamers: undoubtedly they would be capable of dealing effectively with any ships of the same class that might be fitted out for the purpose of preying on our commerce, but it is not to be expected that with so many of their vital parts exposed they would be capable of holding their own against fast cruisers built as ships of war, and it is to the increase of the latter class of vessel that we must mainly look for the efficient protection of our commerce in time of war.

Several important improvements have been introduced during the last five years in the Administration of the *materiel* of the Navy.

Much has been done by Mr. McHardy,[1] the Director of Stores, in respect to the arrangement, classification, check upon issue, and audit of stores, as will be seen from a Memorandum which he has prepared at my request, and which is appended.[2]

No change has been made in the principles upon which the business of Contract Department has been conducted. The Director of Contracts has constantly visited the manufacturing districts with advantage to the economical purchase of stores, and in 1883 enlarged powers were given him for the transaction of current business.

The Constructive Staff of the Admiralty and at the Dockyards has undergone revision, and a Royal Corps of Naval Constructors has been established. The scheme originated in certain proposals from Sir Houston Stewart, which were viewed with favour by the late Board. Further inquiry was, however, needed; and a Departmental Committee was

[1]Coglan McLean McHardy (1838–1909). Dir of Stores, 1869–89.
[2]Footnote in original text: 'Appendix VII.'

appointed under the Presidency of Sir Thomas Brassey. In conformity with their suggestions, a corps has been created with the title of the Royal Corps of Naval Constructors, comprising the shipbuilding Officers of every grade above the rank of foreman. In the junior ranks substantial additions of pay have been given, and the salaries have been equalised as between London and the Dockyards. These changes will facilitate inter-change of duties, and lead to a more general combination of practical and theoretical knowledge. The regulations affecting that valuable class of public servants, the foremen of the yards, were left unchanged by the Committee, but all foremen under fifty years of age who can be recom-mended, and can pass an elementary examination in ship design, will become assistant-constructors, and their promotion in the corps will be by selection according to merit, and not as now by a competitive literary examination. The Comptroller's Department invited the special attention of the Committee to the case of the leading men of the Dockyards. Their position has been raised, and their emoluments improved.

Last year we appointed a Committee, over which Lord Ravensworth[1] presided, to inquire into the system under which ships are ordered to be built and repaired in the Dockyards and by contract. We adopted some useful suggestions from their report in our recent invitations of tenders for ships from the trade; and we have issued revised regulations with the view of preventing unnecessary work being done upon ships when they are paid off, and prepared for re-commission in the Dockyards.

So much attention has lately been attracted to the manner in which, during many years, the progress of ship-building has been calculated in the Navy Estimates and Returns presented to Parliament, that I will make a few remarks on the subject. We found a method of calculation in force by which an exceptional use is made of the term 'ton' as the measure of work done. The 'ton' in these calculations does not represent a part of the total displacement of a ship, but of the weight of the hull of a ship unfitted and unarmed. Moreover, the estimates of progress are not based upon the whole cost of a ship, but only upon the expenditure upon the labour employed in her construction. Such calculations are imper-fect, and requiring, as they do, revision from year to year if more labour should be required to complete a ship than was expected at first, must

---

[1]Henry Liddell, 2nd Earl of Ravensworth (1821–1903). Conservative politician. MP for Northumberland South, 1852–78. For the committee's report, see 'Report of the committee appointed to inquire into the conditions under which contracts are invited for the building or repairing of ships, including their engines, for Her Majesty's navy, and into the mode in which repairs and refits of ships are effected in Her Majesty's dockyards. With minutes of evidence and appendix', *Parliamentary Papers*, 1884–85, vol. 14, pp. 125–365.

necessarily be incomplete until a ship is finished. We were fully alive to the imperfection of the system, which has been fully explained by Mr. Campbell Bannerman on several occasions in the House of' Commons.[1] He also gave the reasons which induced us to retain, for what it was worth, this imperfect system rather than undertake the task of revising calculations to which Members of the House of Commons were accustomed, and which affected the shipbuilding transactions, not only of the Board of Admiralty of the day, but of former Boards.

But, having observed this year that, notwithstanding the explanations which had been given, these tonnage returns seriously misled persons who could hardly be expected to master the details of a technical and complicated system, we undertook to revise it; and the best method of doing this was under consideration when we left office. For my own part I do not see my way to the useful adoption, as the basis of Returns to be laid before Parliament, of any system by which the progress of shipbuilding is calculated by tonnage or percentages of a ship (which latter is the French practice). I am disposed to prefer giving in the Annual Estimates the first estimate of the cost of a ship, the sums already spent or required to be spent upon her year by year, and whenever the first estimate is exceeded, the amount of the increased estimate; somewhat in the same way as the estimates for public works are given.

For practical purposes there are three stages in the construction of our own ships, and those of foreign nations, upon which attention should be mainly fixed:– First, when a ship is laid down; next, when she is launched; and last, when she is ready for sea.

It must not be supposed, because the calculations to which I have referred are open to criticism, that the same observations apply to the accounts of expenditure upon shipbuilding. The calculations to which I have referred are not 'accounts' in the proper sense of the word. The accounts are based upon the actual expenditure upon labour and materials; they have been carefully revised from time to time by the able and experienced Accountant Officers of the Admiralty; they are subject to audit, and to the observations of a Standing Committee of the House of Commons, whose reports can readily be consulted upon the subject.

It has been our desire to limit the expenditure upon the Works Vote as far as possible, because we desired to apply all the money that we

---

[1]Footnote in original text: 'See Mr. Campbell Bannerman's speeches of May 7, 1883, and March 20 and May 8 1884.' For these, see *Hansard's Parliamentary Debates*, 3rd ser., vol. 279 (1883), cols. 137–9; vol. 286 (1884), cols. 371–3; vol. 287 (1884), cols. 1781–3.

had at our disposal for the purpose of increasing the expenditure upon Shipbuilding; and as the Extension Works at Chatham and Portsmouth approached their completion, we were enabled to effect a considerable reduction of expenditure under the Works Vote. It was reduced, indeed, from £467,000 in 1879–80 to £386,000 in 1884–5. We have, however, undertaken and carried on several new works of importance, principally the Barracks for Seamen at Keyham and a new Dock at Malta for armour-plated ships of the largest class. At Hong-Kong we have successfully concluded negotiations for providing a Dock capable of receiving the ships of that class. We have been endeavouring to make a similar arrangement at Halifax, and we have impressed upon the Government of India the importance of constructing a Dock of the same class at Bombay. Sir John Coode[1] is about to visit that port for the purpose of reporting upon the best site for a Dock, upon which there are some differences of opinion.

III. ADMINISTRATION.

The Board of Admiralty, as formed on the 13th of May, 1880, consisted of the following members:– Admiral Sir Cooper Key, Vice-Admiral Lord John Hay,[2] Rear-Admiral A. H. Hoskins, and Mr. T. Brassey, MP.

When Rear-Admiral Hoskins was appointed second in command in the Mediterranean in July, 1882, he was succeeded by Rear-Admiral Sir Frederick Richards[3] who had just returned from the command of the Cape and West Coast of Africa Station. On the expiration of Admiral Lord Alcester's command in the Mediterranean, in March, 1883, Vice-Admiral Lord John Hay was appointed to succeed him, and Lord Alcester took Lord John Hay's seat on the Board. Lastly, Sir Frederick Richards having been appointed Commander-In-Chief of the East India Station in May last, was succeeded on the Board by Vice-Admiral Sir Wm. Hewett,[4] whom he relieved in that command.

---

[1]John Coode, K.C.M.G. (1816–92). Civil Engineer. Authority on harbour construction, chiefly responsible for the harbours at Portland, England, and Colombo, Sri Lanka.

[2]John Hay, C.B. (1827–1916). Entered, 1839; Lt, 1846; Cdr, 1851; Capt, 1854; RA, 1872; VA, 1877; Adm, 1884; AoF, 1888. MP for Wick, 1857–59; for Ripon, 1866–67, 1868–71; Naval Lord of the Admiralty, 1866, 1868–71; Second Naval Lord, 1880–83; First Naval Lord, 1886.

[3]Frederick William Richards, C.B., K.C.B., G.C.B., D.C.L. (1833–1912). Entered, 1848; Lt, 1855; Cdr, 1860; Capt, 1866; RA, 1882; VA, 1888; Adm, 1893; AoF, 1898. Junior Naval Lord, 1882–85; Second Naval Lord, 1892–93; First Naval Lord, 1893–99.

[4]William Nathan Wrighte Hewett, V.C., K.C.B., K.C.S.I. (1834–88). Entered, 1847; Lt, 1852; Cdr, 1858; Capt, 1862; RA, 1878; VA, 1884. Naval Lord of the Admiralty, 1885.

Sir Thomas Brassey remained the Civil Lord until November, 1884, when he was succeeded by Mr. Caine, MP.[1]

But, besides these changes, an important alteration was made in the constitution of the Board in April, 1882. The Comptroller of the Navy was made an additional Naval Lord of the Admiralty by virtue of his office, and the new appointment was created of an additional Civil Lord who should, to quote the words of the Order in Council, 'possess special mechanical and engineering knowledge as well as administrative experience,' and should 'assist the Comptroller in the business relating to the *materiel*' of the Navy. To this office Mr. George Rendel was appointed, and he gave the Board most valuable assistance in respect to many difficult questions connected with the armament of our ships and shipbuilding generally, uniting, in a remarkable degree, the qualifications specified in the Order in Council.

In 1880 Vice-Admiral Sir Houston Stewart was Comptroller of the Navy. His term of office expired in 1881, when he was succeeded by Rear-Admiral Brandreth,[2] who had recently been Admiral-Superintendent of Chatham Dockyard.

The position of Financial Secretary was first filled by Mr. Shaw Lefevre; on his advancement to the office of First Commissioner of Works, in November, 1880, Mr. Trevelyan succeeded him. Mr. Trevelyan was appointed Chief Secretary to the Lord Lieutenant [of Ireland] in 1882, and was succeeded by Mr. Campbell Bannerman, who was also Chief Secretary for Ireland in November last, and was succeeded by Sir Thomas Brassey. The office of Naval Secretary to the Board was abolished on expiration of the term of service of Vice-Admiral Hall[3] in 1882, and the old appointment of Permanent Secretary was revived, to which office Mr. (now Sir Robert) Hamilton,[4] who had

---

[1] William Sproston Caine (1842–1903). MP for Scarborough, 1880–85; for Barrow-in-Furness, 1886–90; for Bradford East, 1892–95; for Camborne, 1900–1903. Civil Lord of the Admiralty, 1884–85.

[2] Thomas Brandreth, K.C.B. (1825–94). Entered, c. 1838; Lt, 1845; Cdr, 1858; Capt, 1863; RA, 1878; VA, 1884; Adm, 1889. Third Lord and Controller of the Navy, 1882–86.

[3] Robert Hall, C.B. (1817–82). Entered, 1833; Lt, 1843; Cdr, 1852; Capt, 1855; RA (Ret.), 1873; VA (Ret.), 1878. Private Sec to First Lord of the Admiralty the Duke of Somerset, 1863–66; Naval Lord of the Admiralty, 1871–72; Naval Sec of the Admiralty, 1872–82; Permanent (Second) Sec of the Admiralty, 1882–83.

[4] Robert George Crookshank Hamilton, C.B., K.C.B., L.L.D. (1836–95). Civil Servant and Colonial Administrator. War Office clerk, 1855–57; Office of Works clerk, 1857–61; Education Dept Accountant, 1861–69; Accountant to the Board of Trade, 1869–74; Assistant Sec, Civil Service Inquiry Commission, 1872–74; Sec, Civil Service Inquiry Commission, 1874–78; Accountant-General of the Navy, 1878–82; Member of the Carnarvon Commission on Imperial Defence, 1879–82; Permanent (Second) Sec of the Admiralty, 1882; Permanent Undersec for Ireland, 1882–86; Govr of Tasmania, 1887–92.

filled for some time the appointment of Accountant-General of the Navy, was appointed.

The murder of Lord Frederick Cavendish[1] and Mr. Burke,[2] at Dublin, on the 6th May, 1882, involved considerable sacrifices in the administration of the Navy. It was necessary to find men who under those trying circumstances should take the places of the Chief Secretary and Under Secretary to the Lord Lieutenant. Mr. Trevelyan succeeded Lord Frederick Cavendish, and Mr. Hamilton Mr. Burke. The circumstances respecting the latter appointment are somewhat remarkable. Mr. Hamilton had just received the appointment of Secretary to the Admiralty, to which he had looked forward, when at ten o'clock on the morning of the 8th of May, I mentioned to him the possibility that he might be asked to go to Ireland. Although the work was not to his taste, and he would obtain no advantage in respect to salary, he at once said that he was ready. The appointment was settled in the course of the afternoon, and he started by the mail train that evening for Dublin, as fine an instance (as I noted at the time) of public spirit as I know. Vice-Admiral Hall was good enough to resume his old post temporarily, pending Mr. Hamilton's absence; but he died very soon after, and was succeeded by Captain Tryon. Mr. Hamilton finally elected in May, 1883, to remain in the important post he was filling at Dublin. On Captain Tryon's promotion to the rank of Rear-Admiral, in April, 1884, he was succeeded by Mr. Evan MacGregor,[3] who had for some time well filled the office of Head of the Military Department in the Admiralty.

The office of Private Secretary to the First Lord is one of considerable importance, and I am under great obligations to the Officers who have filled it. Captain Codrington[4] was kind enough to remain

---

[1]Frederick Charles Cavendish (1836–82). Liberal politician. MP for the West Riding of Yorkshire, 1865–82. Private Sec to Lord Granville, 1859–64; to William Gladstone, 1872–73; Lord of the Treasury, 1873–74; Financial Sec to the Treasury, 1880–82; Chief Sec for Ireland, 1882. Assassinated on 6 May 1882 in Phoenix Park, Dublin, a few hours after his arrival in the city.

[2]Thomas Henry Burke (1829–82). Permanent Undersec for Ireland, 1869–82. Assassinated in Phoenix Park, Dublin, with Lord Frederick Cavendish.

[3]Evan MacGregor, C.B., G.C.B. (1842–1926). Appointed Admiralty clerk, 1860; Private Sec to a succession of Naval Lords, including First Naval Lords Sydney Dacres (1869–72), Alexander Milne (1872–76), Hastings Yelverton (1876–77), and George Wellesley (1877–79); Permanent (Second) Sec to the Admiralty, 1884–1907.

[4]William Codrington, C.B. (1832–88). Entered, c. 1848; Lt, 1855; Cdr, 1864; Capt, 1869; RA, 1886. Private Sec to First Lords George Ward Hunt (1876–77), William Henry Smith (1877–80), and Lord Northbrook (1880); Dir of Naval Ordnance, 1882–83; Naval Lord of the Admiralty, 1885–86.

for a short time at first. He was succeeded by Captain Erskine,[1] Captain Erskine by Captain Hopkins,[2] and Captain Hopkins by Captain Beaumont.[3]

No changes of importance have been made during the last five years in the regulations under which the business of the Admiralty has been transacted. The Department had been re-organized in 1879, and its working was successfully tried during our tenure of office upon three occasions of very considerable pressure: the operations in Egypt in the years 1882 and 1884, and the preparations which we have recently had to make to meet the contingency of a war with Russia.[4] I have already expressed, through the Secretary to the different Heads of Departments, my sense of the manner in which the duties of all Branches of the Admiralty have been conducted.

Some supplementary measures have been taken to complete the reorganization, principally affecting the Departments of the Comptroller, the Director of Naval Ordnance, the Director of Works, and the Hydrographer.

New regulations have been made whereby all messengerships in the Admiralty have been confined to pensioned Seamen and Marines.

There have been considerable changes made in the Royal Hospital, Greenwich. During the time when Sir Thomas Brassey was Civil Lord of the Admiralty the School was re-organized and the dietary [sic] considerably improved. Several alterations have been made in the distribution of the Greenwich Hospital pensions; and this year, in accordance with the report of a Committee which was appointed to consider the subject, a fresh scheme has been sanctioned for the administration of the Hospital.

An addition of very great importance has been made by us to the Administration of the Navy by the constitution, in 1883, of an Intelligence Department.

[1]James Elphinstone Erskine, K.C.B. (1838–1911). Entered, 1852; Lt, 1859; Cdr, 1862; Capt, 1868; RA, 1886, VA, 1892, Adm, 1897, AoF, 1902. Private Sec to Lord Northbrook, 1880–81.

[2]John Ommanney Hopkins, K.C.B. (1834–1916). Entered, 1848; Lt, 1854; Cdr, 1862; Capt, 1867; RA, 1888; VA, 1891; Adm, 1896. Private Sec to Lord Northbrook, 1881–82; Dir of Naval Ordnance, 1883–86; Naval Lord of the Admiralty, 1888–92.

[3]Lewis Anthony Beaumont, K.C.B., G.C.B., K.C.M.G., F.R.G.S. (1847–1922). Entered, 1860; Lt, 1867; Cdr, 1876; Capt, 1882; RA, 1897; VA, 1902; Adm, 1906. Private Sec to Lord Northbrook, 1882–85; Dir of Naval Intelligence, 1894–99.

[4]On plans for possible war with Russia, see Barbara Jelavich, 'British Means of Offense Against Russia in the Nineteenth Century', *Russian History/Histoire Russe* 1, pt. 2 (1974), pp. 119–35.

Shortly after my connection with the Admiralty, I received a letter from General Charles Gordon,[1] calling my particular attention to the want of Intelligence Department for the Navy. I found that the subject had been considered,[2] but owing to the difficulty of making any definite arrangement, no such Department existed. With the valuable assistance of Captain Tryon, a Committee was organized[3] for the collection and record [sic] of intelligence under Captain Hall,[4] presided over by the Senior Naval Lord, and it has now been in active operation during the last two years. A most interesting report from Captain Hall has been placed by me in the hands of my successor, in which the work of the Department is described, and not only has information been collected bearing upon possible Naval operations in all parts of the world, and circulated to the different Commanders-in-Chief for the purpose of supplementing deficiencies, but upon several occasions during the recent operations in Egypt, and also while we were preparing for a war with Russia, the use [sic: 'utility'] of the Department has been demonstrated. It is possible that some additions to its strength be desirable, but I trust that these additions will be made gradually, and with care will be taken to prevent the Department from absorbing any of the executive duties of other Departments, so that its work may be confined to the record of information and to the preparation of memoranda and suggestions bearing upon Naval operations. The Department must necessarily be in constant communication with the Hydrographer, Naval operations being essentially connected with the peculiar information for which the Hydrographical Department of the Admiralty is responsible.

A summary of the Navy Estimates for the last five years will be found in Appendix VIII. The main feature of our financial administration has been to check increases of expenditure upon other branches of the Service in order to devote as much as we could to the increase of shipbuilding, and it will be seen a considerable sum has been so applied in addition to the increase which we have made in the Navy Estimates.

[1]Charles George Gordon, C.B. (1833–85). 2nd Lt, 1852; 1st Lt, 1854; Capt, 1859; Major, 1862; Lt Col, 1864; Col (Egyptian Army), 1874; Major Gen, 1882. Extensive military and administrative experience in China and Africa, especially Egypt and the Sudan. Died at Khartoum, January 1885.

[2]See N.A.M. Rodger, 'The Dark Ages of the Admiralty, 1869–85 Part III: Peace, Retrenchment and Reform, 1880–85', Mariner's Mirror 62, no. 2 (1976), pp. 123–4.

[3]Footnote in original text: 'Board Order, 5th December, 1882.' On the creation of the Naval Intelligence Department, see Matthew Allen 'The Foreign Intelligence Committee and the Origins of the Naval Intelligence Department of the Admiralty', Mariner's Mirror 81, no. 1 (1995), pp. 65–78.

[4]William Henry Hall (1842–95). Entered, c. 1855; Lt, 1862; Cdr, 1875; Capt, 1882.

In the year 1882 an alteration was made in the manner in which receipts for sales of stores, &c., are brought to account. The sums received are applied in aid of the Naval charges of the year instead of being paid into the Exchequer.

The reports of the Auditor-General, and of the Standing Committee of the House of Commons, which examines the annual accounts of expenditure, have, on the whole, been satisfactory.

This is not the place for attempting to give an account of the Naval operations on the Coast of Albania in 1880,[1] of the successful attack on the Forts of Alexandria in 1882, the subsequent operations in the Suez Canal in that year, the Suakin Expedition in 1884, and that of the present year. I would only observe that throughout all these operations nothing so far as I am aware was found wanting in the arrangements made by the different Departments of the Admiralty.

I have directed a Memorandum to be prepared showing the measures that were taken in consequence of the preparations for a war with Russia. The mobilisation of the Navy is a subject which has occupied a good deal of our attention, and elaborate Tables were drawn up under Lord Alcester's directions, assisted by Admiral Tryon, in the year 1883, which were of great service when the question had to be practically dealt with.

While I do not propose here to enter into any history of Naval operations, I must refer shortly to the services rendered by the Royal Marines in aid of the Civil Power. A strong battalion of the Light Infantry was employed in the Cork district in Ireland from 1880 to 1882, and Sir Thomas Steele;[2] who was in command of the Forces in Ireland, mentioned, in an official report, 'the admirable behaviour of the battalion, subjected as it was to especially trying duties, most of the detachments being in out of the way places, often, with miserable accommodation.' He said, that notwithstanding this, 'their soldier-like bearing and excellent discipline gained for the corps universal admiration, and the moral effect of their presence in very disturbed and disaffected districts undoubtedly had a very marked effect in maintaining order and checking outrages.' A force of Royal Marines has subsequently been engaged on a delicate and difficult service in Skye,[3] which was very well performed.

---

[1] A joint demonstration by Britain, France, Austria, Russia and Italy to pressure the Ottoman Empire to cede Dulcigno to Montenegro. For a brief description of the operation, see Clowes, *The Royal Navy*, vol. 7, p. 314.

[2] Thomas Montagu Steele, C.B., G.C.B. (1820–92). Ensign, 1838; Lt, 1844; Capt, 1844; Major, 1860; Lt Colonel, 1862; Major Gen, 1865; Lt Gen, 1874; Gen, 1877. Cdr of British Forces in Ireland, 1880–85.

[3] In response to the 1882 Skye 'rent strike', in which crofters on that island sought concessions similar to those granted Irish tenant farmers by the Irish Land Act of 1881.

In December, 1882, a still more remarkable duty was performed by the Royal Marines. The Lord-Lieutenant consulted me as to the assistance which could be given in order to protect Dublin against a large number of desperate men who were banded together to plot assassination, and I arranged with him that 300 volunteers from the Royal Marines should be placed at his disposal for the purpose of helping the Dublin police. This force remained in Dublin till the end of July in the following year. The arrangements under which they were employed were made by Colonel Herbert (afterwards Sir Herbert) Stewart,[1] and his opinion, as expressed in a letter to the Under-Secretary to the Lord-Lieutenant, of the services, performed by the men, their good conduct, their determined manner of doing their duty, and their self-restraint, was highly complimentary. The Under-Secretary was also directed to write to the Secretary to the Admiralty expressing His Excellency's warm acknowledgments of the services rendered by the Royal Marines at a time of unprecedented danger and difficulty.

I trust that while the Corps of Royal Marines will doubtless in future be utilized for services which are outside Naval operations proper, no future Board of Admiralty will, forget that the Corps essentially belongs to the Naval Forces of the country, forming indeed an important portion of the reserves for the Navy; and that it is, therefore, essential that the Marines should not be engaged upon any such service from which they cannot be promptly withdrawn in the event of war.

When I observed that no change had been made in the regulations under which the business of the Navy has been transacted, I alluded to a Order in Council, passed when Mr. Childers was First Lord, under which, subject to the constitutional functions of the Board of Admiralty, the business was divided into three parts, the *Personnel*, for which the Senior Naval Lord, the *Materiel*, for which the Comptroller, and the Finance, for which the Financial secretary are respectively made responsible to the First Lord. This division of business has worked well, accompanied, as it has been, by frequent communications between the three responsible officers: such communications are very necessary, for the current business of the Comptroller greatly depends upon the composition and distribution of the Fleet which is under the charge of the Senior Naval Lord, while financial considerations affect all branches of the administration.

---

[1]Herbert Stewart, C.B., K.C.B. (1843–85). Ensign, 1863; Lt, 1865; Capt, 1868; Brevet Major, 1879; Brevet Lt Col, 1880; Brevet Col, 1882; Brevet Major Gen, 1885.

The only change in the present arrangements which has occurred to me as desirable, is that the permanent financial element in the administration should be somewhat strengthened. The Financial Secretary is a Parliamentary Officer, and is therefore liable to frequent change. In fact, owing to the great ability and Parliamentary success of our Financial Secretaries, the Board has been deprived of the services of no less than three of them since 1880 by their well deserved advancement to higher functions. It was, therefore, my intention to have placed the Accountant-General in the position of assistant to the Financial Secretary in order to supply that permanent financial assistance of which I have felt the want somewhat under the present arrangements.

In conclusion, although I hope that this record of work done will show we have effected some not unimportant improvements in the Service, and we have vigorously maintained the Naval strength of the country, I am sensible that much still remains to be done, part of which we might have taken in hand if so much of our time and attention had not been occupied by the urgent calls of providing for actual and probable military operations. To one circumstance I desire gratefully to allude, and that is the unremitting devotion and constant harmony with which Sir A. Cooper Key and the other Members of the Board have done their duty, both in the transaction of the details of the administration of the Navy which mainly devolve upon them, and in initiating and advising upon other and larger questions, during the last five years.

NORTHBROOK.
July 1885.

APPENDIX IV.
Shipbuilding 1880–84.
By SIR THOMAS BRASSEY, K.C.B., MP

The aggregate expenditure under the shipbuilding votes has risen from £3,106,000 for 1879–80, and £3,083,000 for 1880–81, to £3,615,264l in 1883–4, and £3,998,320 for 1884–5, as will be seen from the annexed table drawn up by Mr. Lambert.[1]

---

[1]George T. Lambert. Admiralty clerk and Brassey's Private Sec. For Lambert's table, see the last page of this document.

Under the present Board the expenditure for new construction has been raised to a point only surpassed in one year during the last quarter of a century. In that year, 1876–7, the expenditure on building was £2,121,960. It fell to £1,388,607 in 1879–80, since which a steady advance has been made from £1,682,500 in 1881–2 to £1,930,000 for 1883–4, and £1,984,250 in 1884–5. The expenditure on shipbuilding in 1876–7 exceeded that of 1884–5 by £137,710, but by a redistribution, as between armoured and unarmoured ships, the expenditure on armoured building for 1884–5 exceeded that of 1876–7 by no less than £344,382. Following the same policy, we have in 1884–5 as compared with 1880–81 a reduction in unarmoured building of £28,000, and an increase in armoured of £585,902.

While the construction of ironclads has been largely increased, the cost of building has advanced in still greater proportions.

Confining ourselves to the type now generally accepted for our battleships, the cost per ton weight of hull has increased from £48 for the *Devastation*, constructed in 1869–73, to £68 per ton for the *Dreadnought*, constructed between 1870–79, while for the ships in the building programme last submitted to Parliament, the cost is £80 for the *Collingwood* and £72 for the *Camperdown*. The tons weight of hull in the *Devastation*, *Howe*, and *Rodney* are identical, but the cost for materials has increased from £182,000 to £250,000, and for labour from £106,000 to £190,000. The increase is distributed over all the elements of cost.

The mean cost of the armour per ton was £50 for the *Devastation*, £95 14s. for the *Colossus*, and £95 12s. for the *Collingwood* and *Rodney*.

The propelling machinery of the *Devastation* cost £63,200, whereas that of the *Colossus* cost £93,433, that of the *Collingwood* £87,500, and that of the *Howe* £103,000.

The cost of the hydraulic gun mountings in the *Collingwood* is £38,882[,] a large sum for which there was no corresponding charge in the ships of the date of the *Devastation*.

The increase in the calibre of the heavy guns, with a consequent necessity for hydraulic loading, the addition of a large superstructure, the light broadside armament, the machine guns, the torpedo fittings and electric lights have been forced upon us by the progress of invention, and the result has been an enormous addition to the cost, and an ever-increasing difficulty of maintaining the output of tonnage at the amount laid down as necessary by the Chancellor of the Exchequer

(Mr. Childers), when First Lord of the Admiralty.[1] Twelve thousand tons of *Devastation*s would have cost £576,000; twelve thousand tons of *Collingwood*s cost £960,000.

With so great an increase in the cost of building, the additional construction could only have been rendered possible by the liberality of Parliament, but the Board have endeavoured to check the increase of expense by every means in their power. With this view, while carefully considering every suggestion for improvement, they have avoided as far as possible those repeated changes of design which can only be justified by the promise of a substantial gain in efficiency.

The programme for 1884–5 consists for the most part of types well known in the dockyards. Four types only are represented in the 11 ironclads actually in progress. For the first class we have six ships of the 'Admiral' type. For the second class we have in the *Hero* a repetition of the *Conqueror*. The *Warspite* and *Impérieuse* were specially designed for distant foreign service. The *Collingwood*[2] and *Edinburgh* were laid down under the late Board.

In the selection of types we claim that marked progress has been realized in the most important features of fighting efficiency. All the more recent first-class ships have a designed speed of at least 16 knots, as compared with the 14 knots of the *Inflexible*. The *Conqueror* type has a speed only a fraction below 16 knots.[3]

The *Colossus*, *Edinburgh*, and the 'Admiral' class are built on nearly the same lines. These ships have an extreme breath of 68 feet, as compared with 66 feet in the *Ajax*, but their length has been extended from 280 feet, as in the *Ajax*, to 325 feet. With these more favourable proportions of length to breadth an additional speed of nearly two knots has been obtained without increasing the horse-power.

In the 'Admiral' class, as compared with the *Colossus*, we find an important change in the disposition of the armour. In the central citadel turret ship it forms the wall of the citadel. In the *Collingwood* it is taken

---

[1]Childers had instituted a standard for construction while First Lord, which called for 20,000 tons a year, 12,000 of them to be armoured vessels, the remainder unarmoured. This standard became a reference point for subsequent naval administrations' shipbuilding programmes through the mid-1880s. See Beeler, *British Naval Policy in the Gladstone-Disraeli Era*, pp. 84–5.

[2]Brassey may have meant HMS *Colossus* rather than *Collingwood*.

[3]There follows a table detailing the particulars and cost of the armoured vessels laid down between 1874 and 1884. The information it contains can be found in Oscar Parkes, *British Battleships, 1860–1950* (London, 1957).

away from the central citadel, and formed into separate fixed barbette towers. The towers are placed 140 feet apart, and the guns 22 feet above the water. The enclosed turrets of the *Colossus* are 80 feet apart, and the guns are 12 feet above the water.

In the *Collingwood* the length of the belt is 140 feet; in the *Colossus* 123 feet. In the *Collingwood* the belt protects the machinery and the communications from the magazines to the barbettes. It descends 5 feet below, and rises 2 feet 6 inches above the water.

In the *Inflexible, Ajax, Agamemnon, Colossus, Edinburgh, Collingwood*, and new armoured cruisers, the belt armour stops short of the ends, and the protection of vitals is continued by an under-water deck. In the *Collingwood* a steel-faced deck plating is for the first time introduced. In the *Collingwood*, and new cruisers, the armoured deck does not rise above the lower deck. In the other ships it is one deck higher.

The tons weight of armour, including deck armour, are:–

Ajax	2223
Colossus	2364
Conqueror	1720
Armoured cruiser	1446
Collingwood	2548

The trim, or the proper relation between the drafts of forward and aft is maintained after perforation by the water-tight deck below the water, subdivision above it, and a certain reinforcement of these divisions by solid packing.

In the *Collingwood* the heavy guns are to be mounted *en barbette*. Various modifications have been proposed for the substitution of enclosed for barbette turrets. The additional expense involved ranged from £40,000 to £100,000, and considerable delay would have resulted from any material alterations. The improvements anticipated did not appear to be sufficient to justify the loss of time and the heavy outlay.

The introduction of barbettes into our Navy, when first proposed, led to much anxious discussion. The additional weight required for the armoured citadel, which must surround the unprotected base of the turret, can be better used in increasing the speed and the coal endurance, and in mounting a greater number of powerful guns, and also auxiliary guns. Turret guns cannot be mounted as high above the water as guns *en barbette*. The latter, therefore, will be sooner free from smoke, and the gunners will have a better field of view. As a means of protection against the effects of shell fire, it is proposed in the 'Admiral' class to fix a revolving shield, machine-gun proof, at the level of the top of the barbette wall. This shield will revolve with the turntable, and the guns will elevate and depress through openings in the shield, which will be of steel.

The minor armament forms an important and novel feature in the 'Admiral' class. Between the barbettes and above the true upper deck is a large unarmoured battery, protected by one-inch steel plating from the fire of machine guns, and containing six 6-inch breech-loading guns, fought at ports 14 feet above the water. The battery is protected from a raking fire by winged bulkheads, plated with six inches of steel-faced armour. In this respect the *Collingwood*'s battery resembles the batteries of the *Nelson* and the *Shannon*. The crew will be berthed in the upper battery, and will have accommodation infinitely superior to that of any turret ship. On the deck above the upper battery, there is ample space for boat stowage, and all the ordinary working of the ship. The ventilation of the machinery, and the stoke-holes in action, is provided for in the *Collingwood* by down-cast shafts through armoured tubes, at the inner ends of the barbette. In most armoured ships the provision for the ventilation of machinery in action is deficient, and must inevitably result in a serious loss of speed.

Having described the *Collingwood*, it will be sufficient to observe that in the succeeding ships all the general features of the type have been retained. It has been attempted to make some improvement by giving to the *Benbow*, *Camperdown*, and *Anson*, five feet more length, with a displacement of 10,000 tons, as compared with 9,600 in the *Howe* and *Rodney*, and 9,150 in the *Collingwood*. The armour on the barbettes will he increased from 11½ inches to 14 inches. The *Collingwood* will be armed with 43-ton guns, and the other ships of the class (with the exception of the *Benbow*) will have 64-ton guns. In the *Benbow* two of the 110-ton guns of the Elswick pattern will be substituted for the 64-ton guns.

These changes are summarised in the following table:

DIFFERENCES IN THE 'ADMIRAL' CLASS.

Collingwood:–

> 18 inches compound armour at W[ater] L[ine]
> 11½ inches and 10 inches armour on two sloping barbettes.
> Armament four 43-ton in towers and six 6-inch guns.
> Speed, 16 knots.

Rodney and *Howe*:–

> 18 inches armour at W.L.
> 11½ inches, and 10 inches armour on two sloping barbettes.

Armament four 64-ton guns in towers and six 6-inch guns.
Speed, 16 knots.

Camperdown and *Anson*:–

18 inches armour at W.L.
14 inches and 12 inches armour on two sloping barbettes.
Armament four 64-ton guns and six 6-inch guns.
Speed 16 knots.

Benbow:–

Armament two 110-ton guns and ten 6-inch guns.
In other respects same as *Camperdown*.

Only one new type of ironclad, being that represented by the *Impérieuse* and *Warspite*, has been originated under the present administration.[1] It was described to Parliament by Mr. Trevelyan, in moving the Estimates in 1881,[2] as follows:–

'In our opinion it is necessary to produce a vessel which shall not only have the heels of others [*sic*], but which shall be able to meet, on at least equal terms, almost anything she is likely to catch. Great pains have been spent, over the form and attributes of a vessel which, in the words of the designer, is intended –

"Especially for independent service on foreign stations, where fast unarmoured ships may have to be opposed, and where the second-class ironclads of an enemy may have to be met and engaged."

'On such service it is considered desirable to secure the following conditions:– A speed of 16 knots; a comparatively large number of guns, some of them capable of penetrating the thickest armour of second-class ironclads at long ranges, armour of proof to protect the vitals of the ship; her coal supply must also be large, and the vessel must have auxiliary sail power to economise fuel, and a coppered bottom to make her independent of docks. Such a vessel, fit to keep the sea and to sweep the sea, the Admiralty believe they have got. Her length is to be 315 feet, her extreme breadth 61 feet, and her tonnage about 7,300. Her horsepower is to be 8,000; her bunkers will hold 900 tons (now increased to 1,200 tons), and her speed on the measured mile will be 16 knots. (1.) She has the great advantage of a twin-screw. (2.) She will have a

---

[1]On the deliberations leading to the design of *Warspite* and *Impérieuse*, see Beeler, *Birth of the Battleship*, pp. 194–202.
[2]*Hansard's Parliamentary Debates*, 3rd ser., vol. 259 (1881), cols. 1390–1.

conning tower of steel-faced armour. (3.) She will carry an armament of four 18-ton 9.2 inch breech-loading guns mounted in barbettes, with protection against bullets, which at 1,000 yards will pierce 16½ inches of iron armour, and more than 13 inches of steel-faced armour. (4.) She will carry likewise six 6-inch breech-loading guns, equal in range to those which have carried at a distance of five miles into the Peruvian harbours;[1] she will be equipped with boat guns, torpedoes, field guns, machine guns, and will probably be fitted a couple of torpedo boats in addition,[2] and she will have room for over 400 men to work her and fight her. (5.) She will combine the speed of the *Leander*, with guns of greater power than the *Thunderer* or *Devastation*, and the Admiralty, with some confidence, submit her to the criticism of a nation which thinks little of a vessel which cannot travel far and fast, and fight sharply and long. She will rank high among cruisers, and high among second-class ironclads, and, in the hope that she will meet the ends for which she is designed, it is proposed to lay down one such vessel this year at Portsmouth, and another at Chatham. Her hull and engines will cost £400,000, as against £550,000 of the *Collingwood*, and £150,000 of the *Leander*.'

The design thus described by Mr. Trevelyan was subjected to a severe criticism in the House of Commons. It was not claimed for the new vessels that their armour is sufficient completely to protect their buoyancy and stability, or, that they have the armament of battle-ships. Every design for a ship of war must be more or less a compromise. In insisting upon a speed unapproached in any armoured ships except those building in Italy in a vessel of little more than half the dimensions of the Italian ships, we were compelled to give up some features which we might have desired to retain.

As compared with the *Collingwood*, the disposition of the belt and deck armour is very similar, but the thickness is reduced from 18 inches to 10 inches. The belt in each case extends along more than two-fifths of the length. It will protect the machinery and magazines, and will incidentally assist in protecting the stability and buoyancy. The armour of the barbettes protects the mechanism of the guns, and the guns' crews are also screened from horizontal fire. The ends of the ship before and abaft the citadel are protected with an under-water deck. A large part of the unarmoured space above the armoured deck can be used as a supplementary coal-bunker. If the water should penetrate while the auxiliary

---

[1]During the War of the Pacific (1879–83), in which Chile fought and defeated Peru and Bolivia and the Chilean Navy blockaded several Peruvian ports.

[2]Footnote in original: 'It has been decided to omit the torpedo boats.'

bunkers are full, the quantity which can be admitted will be inconsiderable. If the coal has been burned out more water will be admitted, but the vessel will have been lightened of a burden of coal. In any case the submersion of the ship will be arrested soon as the armoured part gains a displacement equal to that of the unarmoured part which has become water-logged [*sic*].

The absence of armour round the water line was criticised. It was said that the protected cruiser was specially designed to chase, and that the bow might be exposed to a destructive fire from a retreating enemy. It is difficult to hit a ship at or near the water line. It was never done even in the long engagement between the *Huascar* and the *Almirante Cochrane* at close quarters.[1] Again, protection by thick armour in the bow means additional weight, and an alteration in form which would not be favourable to speed. Protection by thin vertical armour is inferior to the under-water deck, and numerous compartments into which the unarmoured ends of the cruiser are subdivided.

The French constructors have displayed their unfailing skill and ingenuity in the endeavour to protect their ships by a continuous belt of armour. But in attempting to protect the water-line, they have been compelled to accept armour tapering away from amidships, until at the extremities, it becomes too thin to afford an effective protection.

The plating of the *Richelieu*, which is 500 tons larger than our protected cruisers, is 8½ inches amidships, tapering away to 7 inches at the stem, and 6¼ inches over the battery.

The comparatively light armament suggested another objection. The percentage of weight in armament is 5 per cent. for the new cruiser, and 6.77 per cent. for the *Nelson*. The justification for the reduction is to be found in the additional speed[2]; and it is important to observe that, when we extend the comparison to the unarmoured vessels of Foreign Powers, we stand on a footing of equality. The percentage of displacement in armament is 4 per cent. in the French *Duguay Trouin*, a 16-knot ship, but without armour; and it is the same in the Russian *Yaroslav*, of decidedly inferior speed. In the new cruiser, the inferiority in the aggregate weight of armament, as compared with the *Nelson*, is largely compensated by the superior penetrative power. It is estimated that the new breech-loading 18-ton gun will pierce 18¾ inches of iron, and be equal to the

---

[1] In the Battle of Angamos, 8 Oct 1879.

[2] And in the substitution of compound armour (a steel face over iron) for wrought iron, which enabled a thinner swath of the former to have the same resistive power as a greater thickness of the latter.

Service 38-ton gun. The muzzle-loading 18-ton guns of the *Nelson* have a penetrative power of 14¾ inches.

As the heavy guns will be breech-loading, and of great length, the French system of mounting in armoured barbette towers with an all round fire has been adopted. The French Constructors attach great importance to the elevation of their barbette guns to as great a height as possible. The *Nelson* carries her 18-ton guns at a height of 13½ feet. The armoured cruisers' 18-ton guns are 21 feet 5 inches above water. Even at this considerable elevation the guns are slightly lower than those of the latest French ships of the *Vauban* class, with inferior displacement.

When the design for this vessel was originally described in Parliament, an objection was raised that the coal endurance was inadequate.[1] With 900 tons of fuel on board, the *Warspite* will have 1 foot 9 inches, and with 1,100 tons 1 foot 4 inches of armoured freeboard. If none of the 900 tons of coal were consumed, and the ends were water-logged, the armour would be level with the water, but the vessel would still have a 15-knot speed, a good range of stability, and the batteries would be high out of [the] water. The quantity of coal proposed for the speed trials was 400 tons, but every effort will be made to secure 16 knots with a much larger supply. The conditions in relation to coal endurance are almost identical in the *Collingwood*, the *Colossus*, and the new cruiser. All these vessels carry 1,200 tons of coal, and can easily steam across the Atlantic.

It has been contended that the armoured cruiser should have had greater length. The constructors tell us they could not have made her

---

[1]It is not clear why Brassey switched from discussing coal endurance to floatation between the topic and second sentences in this paragraph, although he returned to the former topic in the latter part of the paragraph. This portion of the appendix would appear to make more sense if re-arranged thusly:

> The French Constructors attach great importance to the elevation of their barbette guns to as great a height as possible. The *Nelson* carries her 18-ton guns at a height of 13½ feet. The armoured cruisers' 18-ton guns are 21 feet 5 inches above water. Even at this considerable elevation the guns are slightly lower than those of the latest French ships of the *Vauban* class, with inferior displacement.
>
> With 900 tons of fuel on board, the *Warspite* will have 1 foot 9 inches, and with 1,100 tons 1 foot 4 inches of armoured freeboard. If none of the 900 tons of coal were consumed, and the ends were water-logged, the armour would be level with the water, but the vessel would still have a 15-knot speed, a good range of stability, and the batteries would be high out of [the] water.
>
> When the design for this vessel was originally described in Parliament, an objection was raised that the coal endurance was inadequate. The quantity of coal proposed for the speed trials was 400 tons, but every effort will be made to secure 16 knots with a much larger supply. The conditions in relation to coal endurance are almost identical in the *Collingwood*, the *Colossus*, and the new cruiser. All these vessels carry 1,200 tons of coal, and can easily steam across the Atlantic.

longer without making her more costly for performing the same work. As the length is increased, so is the weight of hull, in proportion to its cubical contents, a serious objection, where heavy armour protection is attempted. At high speeds there is economy in steam power from fineness of form. As the speeds are reduced, the advantages of great length in relation to horse-power disappear. It was necessary to keep down the length with a view to engagements with the short and handy second-class ironclads of Foreign Powers.

It may be argued, however, that with the actual proportions of length to breadth, we might have given more protection to the proposed cruiser, by lowering the unarmoured side, and applying the weight thus saved in the superstructure in extending the belt of armour. If such an alteration were made, it would involve a reduction in the height of the gun[s] above the waterline, and would have been especially objectionable in the case of guns mounted en barbette.

Turning to the ironclads of earlier design, the speed of 15½ knots attained in the trials of the *Conqueror* was a most satisfactory performance. The *Conqueror* is a valuable addition to the Navy, being well-armed and armoured, an effective and handy ram, and a thorough sea-going ship. By their number and superior manoeuvring qualities, such vessels must be formidable in battle, and they will always be required for the general duties of the Fleet. Recognising the value of these features, a repetition of the *Conqueror*, the *Hero*, was laid down in 1883.

Having referred to the new ships we may point with satisfaction to the improvements lately made in the *Hecate*.

On the outbreak of the Franco-German War it was thought necessary to strengthen the Navy in vessels of moderate draught. A Vote of Credit was obtained for this purpose, and the *Gorgon, Hecate, Cyclops*, and *Hydra* were constructed. They were double-turreted monitors on the American model, but with more elevated turrets protected by a breastwork. Questions having been raised as to the stability of these and other vessels, a Committee of Inquiry was appointed by the Admiralty. Their report was favourable to the *Gorgon* class, considered as harbour defence or strictly coast-service vessels. It was suggested that the addition of a superstructure would add materially to their stability, and, in short, raise them from simple coast-service vessels into sea-going ironclads, able to make passages in all weathers; and, from their moderate draught, peculiarly adapted for operations on the line of our communications with the East. The cost of the superstructure recommended is £12,000, and it is not going too far to affirm that this expenditure yields a larger return in fighting strength for the Navy than it is possible to obtain from any other appropriation of the same amount of money. This alteration has been carried out in the case of the *Hecate* with satisfactory results. It is intended to take one vessel of the *Hecate* type in hand every year.

Turning to the unarmoured construction, we have maintained our ship building at an amount fully equal to the average produced under the former administration. Special efforts are being made to build fast and well-protected vessels. The programme for 1880–1 included only three vessels which had a speed exceeding 13 knots. The present unarmoured programme includes four 17-knot, seven 16-knot, and two 14-knot vessels . . .[1]

Comparisons of the unarmoured vessels in the British Navy with those of Foreign Powers have recently been made in an unfavourable sense. In justice to the able constructors, who are responsible for the efficiency of the designs produced for our Service, it should be pointed out that such comparisons can only be made fairly when vessels of corresponding dates are selected. Under equal conditions as to date, power to carry sail, and armament, the English designs compare favourably with the French. The progress realised in the later types of our ships is of a marked character. The speeds have been increased in the larger types from 13 to 17 knots, in the corvettes and sloops from 10 to 13 knots.

Having given in a tabular form the general results of our successive proposals, it remains to give further details of the more important types, adopted by the present Board.

The type represented by the *Mersey* may be described as a protected twin-screw steel corvette, having no vertical armour except on the conning towers, which will be protected with 10-inch plates, but having an under-water armoured deck extending right through the ship, and varying in thickness from 2 to 3 inches. By this deck and by internal subdivision buoyancy and stability would be effectually protected. The *Mersey* is of the same general type as the *Leander*, and has the same principal dimensions and the same form underwater except as modified to give a ram bow, and to keep the machinery below the protected deck. Unlike the *Leander*, the *Mersey* will have no rig, but only two pole masts for signalling.

The speed expected under forced draught is about 17 knots, practically the same as the *Leander*'s and exceeding the *Conqueror*'s by 1½ knots, an advantage of the utmost importance in enabling the heavier ships, to which the *Mersey* may be attached, to bring on an action.

The *Mersey* class are capable of carrying heavy armour-piercing guns, and it has been decided to give them two long 7" guns of a new type,

[1]There follows two tables: one classifying unarmoured cruisers laid down between 1874 and 1884 by speed, the other those laid down between 1880 and 1884 by type. These are not included in this edition.

mounted on the poop and forecastle, and commanding a large range of fire. They have besides ten 6" guns, which are also capable of piercing armour of moderate thickness.

The *Severn* and the *Mersey* were originally projected for the use of the torpedo as the principal arm. The uncertainty attending the discharge from the broadside has led to an alteration in the armament, and these vessels have now become powerfully armed fast gun-vessels with the torpedo. If a question may be raised as to the capability of the new class of protected ships for battle, as supports to the armoured ships, it is certain that they would be effective for the protection of commerce. If we have in the Mercantile Marine great resources for self-defence, the Navy must be prepared to lead and to co-operate in the task. It was for this service that the ships of the *Leander* class were lately built. In the *Mersey* we have the cruising qualities of the *Leander*s, combined with more complete protection and superior fighting efficiency.

The coal-carrying capacity of the *Mersey* class is 750 tons, and their endurance at a speed of 17 and 10 knots is as follows:–

Speed.	I.H.P.[1]	Consumption of Coal in 24 hours.	Endurance in Knots.
Knots.		Tons.	
17	5,500	148	2,000
10	1,050	22½	8,000

For the police of the seas the Admiralty has accepted the *Heroine* type, of which no less than seven are now building, having a displacement of 1,420 tons. We prefer these vessels to the larger types lately in vogue. As cruisers under canvas the smaller vessels have a great advantage. The speed under steam is 13 knots in the *Cordelia*, and 13.11 in the *Heroine*, and the cost is £72,347 in the *Heroine* against £117,873 in the *Cordelia*.

In addition to the protected cruisers we have introduced into our programme a seagoing torpedo vessel, the *Scout*, of a much more powerful type than any we have yet built. The *Scout* was described as follows by Mr. Campbell Bannerman, in moving the Estimates on the 20th March, 1884:[2]

'She will be a vessel of 1,430 tons, 220 feet in length, and 34 feet in beam, with a coal capacity of 300 tons, which in case of necessity may be filled up to 450 tons, which would enable her to steam at 10 knots

---

[1]Indicated Horsepower.
[2]*Hansard's Parliamentary Debates*, 3rd ser., vol. 286 (1884), cols. 375–6.

speed, 4,600 miles, and 7,000 miles respectively; her estimated speed with forced draught will be 16 knots; and she will carry a light armament of guns and machine guns, but will be chiefly formidable owing to her power in torpedo discharge. She is designed for the employment of the Whitehead torpedo, and, in fact, she represents the cheapest vessel that can be produced for this service with the speed I have named; and with sea-going qualities. The question of constructing such a vessel has been hindered in solution by difficulties regarding the under-water discharge of torpedoes at full speed: and for the settlement of this important question the *Polyphemus*, has afforded us the means for the most valuable experiments and investigation, great progress having been made in overcoming the difficulties of the problem. The *Scout* is entirely open and unprotected (by armour) and protection would, of course, greatly increase the weight and cost of the vessel.'

Captain Harris,[1] in a recent paper read at the United Service Institution, says:–

'In the latter moments of the sea-fights of the future a prominent part will be taken by swift rams and torpedo vessels. Amidst the roaring of escaping steam, the din and confusion of a heavy fire, and its consequent clouds of smoke, will exist the opportunity for small swift vessels. It is in these moments that numbers will tell more than individual strength.'

If the *Scout* proves successful, similar vessels will be attached to our squadrons in considerable numbers.

The marked increase in the building as shown in the statistics given in the earlier pages of this report has not been obtained by neglecting repairs. The number of men employed on repairs has been increased from 4,566 in 1879–80 to 5,803 in the Estimates for 1884–5. In July, 1884, we have in the home ports ready for sea immediately, or within a few weeks, 18 ironclads, including such ships as the *Dreadnought*, *Devastation*, *Ajax*, *Agamemnon*, and *Conqueror*. At the foreign yards we have in reserve the *Thunderer*, *Scorpion*, *Wivern*, and *Orion*.

The unarmoured vessels now ready include the *Mercury* and *Bacchante*, 13 corvettes, several of these ships being the finest of their class afloat, nine gun vessels for general service, and 29 for coast defence.

With the exception of the *Warrior*, *Black Prince*, *Resistance*, and *Waterwitch*, and eight wood-built unarmoured vessels, as to the re-armament of which some doubt exists, every defective vessel not actually in commission is included in the repairing programme.

<hr>

[1]Robert Hastings Penruddock Harris, K.C.B., K.C.M.G. (1843–1926). Entered, 1856; Lt, 1863; Cdr, 1870; Capt, 1879; RA, 1891; VA, 1901; Adm, 1904.

Expenditure on Shipbuilding, 1875–76 to 1885–86

Year	Ascertained Expenditure on Shipbuilding and New Machinery		Number of Men Employed on Shipbuilding in Dockyards at Home		Ascertained Expenditure on Repairs at Home and Abroad	Men employed on Repairs in Dockyards at Home and Abroad	Men employed in Dockyards at Home	Expenditure on Naval Ordnance (Army and Navy Estimates)	Total Expenditure under Votes 6 and 10	Total Expenditure on Shipbuilding and Ordnance
	Armoured	Unarmoured	Armoured	Unarmoured						
	£	£			£			£	£	£
1875–76	1,058,463	554,755	3,592	1,997	953,677	5,265	15,780	246,198	3,540,092	3,772,601
1876–77	940,318	1,181,642	3,142	3,007	807,656	4,776	15,807	416,865	3,929,846	4,301,711
1877–78	1,948,472*	973,970*	2,308	3,345	1,069,425	5,413	16,074	369,348	5,123,591	5,458,839
1878–79	631,195	876,854	3,228	2,764	1,064,151	5,471	17,177	507,000	3,810,737	4,269,737
1879–80	631,724	756,883	3,545	2,688	822,220	4,566	16,381	397,000 *211,745***	3,106,563	3,460,563
1880–81	698,798	727,551	4,632	2,206	841,710	4,708	16,894	377,968 *248,975*	3,082,803	3,425,803
1881–82	949,313	733,187	5,306	2,557	691,080	4,465	17,192	458,686 *290,719*	3,318,555	3,736,669
1882–83	990,710	776,304	5,718	2,675	881,810	5,486	18,924	740,691 *534,695*	3,472,953	4,156,644
1883–84	1,260,137	669,953	5,922	2,742	929,236	5,888	19,610	792,023 *509,429*	3,615,264	4,245,382
1884–85***	1,284,700	699,550	5,193	3,200	958,680	5,803	18,849	794,497 *512,549*	3,998,320	4,607,237
1886–86***	1,590,000	1,431,440	5,012	3,227	875,862	5,308	18,702	1,399,232 *856,908*	5,047,320	6,102,652

* These amounts include the cost of armoured and unarmoured tonnage purchased out of Vote of Credit.

** The figures in *italics* do not include cost of ammunition and small arms.

*** Estimated only.

VIII

CONVEYING THE EMPEROR HAILE SELASSIE INTO EXILE

Edited by Paul G. Halpern

The invasion of Ethiopia – often referred to as Abyssinia at the time – in October 1935 by Fascist Italy under the dictatorship of Benito Mussolini was a major test of the League of Nations to which Ethiopia belonged. The failure of the League to protect one of its members was a major step in the decline of the League as a serious institution for the preservation of peace and a blow to the concept of collective security.[1] The British Government and a sizeable segment of British public opinion were strong supporters of the League and a concentration of British naval forces in the Mediterranean resulted. As Malta was considered vulnerable to air attack, the majority of British naval forces were based at Alexandria.[2] There was much talk of war should the League enact painful sanctions against Italy. Nevertheless, support of the League was not as strong as it seemed. The British Foreign Secretary Sir Samuel Hoare and his French counterpart Pierre Laval in December 1935 seemed ready to enter into an agreement with Mussolini that would have resulted in a partial dismemberment of Ethiopia, the so-called Hoare-Laval Pact. When news of this leaked out, there was great public indignation and Hoare was forced to resign, although in June 1936 he was back in the Cabinet as First Lord of the Admiralty. Nevertheless the Hoare-Laval Pact was a preview of things to come. The League enacted sanctions against Italy but failed to enact those that would be truly effective or likely to provoke war.

---

[1] Valuable studies of the subject are George W. Baer's *The Coming of the Italian Ethiopian War* (Cambridge, MA, 1967) and *Test Case. Italy, Ethiopia and the League of Nations* (Stanford, 1976).

[2] The naval aspects of the Ethiopian crisis are covered in Stephen Roskill, *Naval Policy between the Wars*. Vol. II: *The Period of Reluctant Rearmament, 1930–39* (London, 1976), chapter 4; and Arthur J. Marder, *From the Dardanelles to Oran: Studies of the Royal Navy in War and Peace, 1915–1940* (London, 1974), chapter 3. For the Italian side see: Robert Mallett, *The Italian Navy and Fascist Expansionism, 1935–1940* (London, 1998), chapter 1; and John Gooch, *Mussolini and his Generals* (Cambridge, 2007), pp. 279–96.

The French government, in theory an equally strong supporter of the League, was anxious to maintain good relations with Italy in the face of a resurgent Germany. The Fascist conquest continued unchecked and by late April 1936 the Italian army was closing in on Addis Ababa, the capital of landlocked Ethiopia. The question of the fate of Haile Selassie,[1] the Emperor of Ethiopia now became acute. At first the Emperor asked the British to ensure the safety of the Empress and his younger children and grandchildren but then extended the request for himself and a larger entourage [1, 4]. With the consent of the French government, the imperial party was to be evacuated in a British warship through Djibuti, the major port of neighbouring French Somaliland [5]. The initial intent was to use only a sloop from the East Indies station and carry the Empress as far as Aden with onward passage to Suez in a P. & O. liner. This left open the possibility that with public opinion in Italy 'in a state of excitement and exultation' the Italians might interfere with and search the British liner creating 'an awkward incident'. The Cabinet decided it would be better to use a British man-of-war for passage direct to Suez.[2] When the Imperial party expanded to include the Emperor and a larger entourage, a cruiser was substituted for the sloop and the destination changed at the Emperor's request from Suez to Haifa in the Palestine mandate where it was expected the Emperor would find asylum in Jerusalem [2, 4].

Enterprise and her sister ship *Emerald* on the East Indies station were the last of the British cruiser war programme – a third ship was cancelled after the Armistice. Laid down in 1918, their construction proceeded very slowly after the war and they did not enter service until 1926. *Enterprise* was 7,580 tons standard displacement and had a primary armament of seven 6-inch guns, distinguished from *Emerald* by having the two forward guns mounted in a twin turret. The ship had been modified from 1934–35 including the fitting of an aircraft catapult in place of a flying-off platform. Her normal complement was listed as 572.[3]

The Admiralty arranged for *Enterprise* to have distant support from *Emerald* and three 'D' class destroyers: *Diana, Decoy* and *Dainty* [6].

---

[1]Haile Selassie I (1892–1975). Born Tafari Makonnen. Regent of Abyssinia (Ethiopia), 1916–30; Emperor of Ethiopia, 1930–74; in exile during Italian occupation, 1936–41; deposed by military coup, Sept 1974; died in prison, Aug 1975.

[2]Extract from Cabinet Conclusions 30(36), 22 April 1936, TNA: FO 371/20195. The British ambassador in Rome thought feelings against Britain so high that he would have been more comfortable if a French ship was available to convey the Emperor to Suez, Sir E. Drummond to Foreign Office, 3 May 1936, ibid.

[3]Alan Raven and John Roberts, *British Cruisers of World War Two* (London, 1980), pp. 93–7, 241.

The 'D' class belonged to the 8th Destroyer Flotilla on the China Station from which six temporarily reinforced the East Indies Station during the Ethiopian crisis. There were similar security arrangements, including aerial reconnaissance, for passage through the Gulf of Suez and the Mediterranean, the latter facilitated by the fact the Mediterranean Fleet would sail from Alexandria for fleet exercises [9, 10]. The emphasis was on discretion rather than an ostentatious show of force. The Foreign Office discounted the possibility of any Italian attempt to interfere with the Emperor's voyage on the grounds that technically Ethiopia and Italy were not at war and the Italians could not, therefore, claim belligerent rights.[1]

The destroyer *Diana* (1932, 1,375 tons) was ordered to Djibuti to make preparations for the Emperor's embarkation and serve as a communications link since the British Vice Consul in Djibuti lacked a cypher. The report of proceedings by *Diana*'s commander, Lieut. Commander W.H. Selby, is reproduced [19]. The lengthy report of proceedings by Captain C.E. Morgan on *Enterprise*'s voyage from Djibuti to Haifa forms the heart of this chapter and includes his polite refusal to embark the Emperor's two pet lion cubs and his description of the living conditions. At times during the voyage, he found it hard to believe he was aboard a warship of the Royal Navy [21]. The portrait of the Emperor is, on the whole, flattering.

However charming the Emperor might have been in the *Enterprise*, he posed a delicate problem when he asked to continue on to London in the ship [7, 13, 17]. The request was hardly practicable and politely declined [16, 18]. The Admiralty and Foreign Office were also careful to prevent the Emperor making any unauthorised communications from the *Enterprise* and insisted he refrain from statements or actions which might be construed as carrying on the war while a 'guest' of the British on board *Enterprise* or while in Palestine, a situation that resembled somewhat a sort of mild internment [12]. The Emperor would also travel incognito during his voyages to avoid the delicate question of rendering salutes.

After Haile Selassie arrived in Palestine and was comfortably ensconced in the King David Hotel in Jerusalem there came the problem of his future. In conveying him in a British warship to British-controlled territory the British Government had assumed a certain responsibility for him. The Foreign Office view was that under the rules of neutrality neither the Emperor nor any of his entourage should be permitted to

---

[1] Extract from Cabinet Conclusions 33(36), 4 May 1936, TNA: FO 371/20195.

leave while hostilities in Ethiopia continued.[1] On the other hand he had been received in Haifa by a guard of honour, something beyond what a defeated general taking refuge in a neutral country might normally receive. Furthermore, there were embarrassing questions in the House of Commons as to whether or not he should be treated under the rules of neutrality or as the head of a state which was a member of the League of Nations and entitled to the protection of the League Covenant. Prime Minister Stanley Baldwin could only reply that the issues were complex and must be the subject of careful consideration.[2] When pressed with a provocative question that the real so-called 'practical grounds' for not altering *Enterprise*'s programme was to avoid popular demonstrations in favour of Abyssinia, Baldwin replied that the offer of passage in a cruiser had been 'a special act of courtesy' but had entailed a good deal of inconvenience to keep a ship of that class from her normal duties and it was impractical having detached her for a week from her duties to change the programme still further. He added that, had it been possible and had they possessed an unlimited number of cruisers, they might have done more.[3]

The Emperor repeated his requests to come to England, mostly but not exclusively on grounds of health. He also intended to continue on to Geneva to plead his case before the League Council in June. The British Government realized they could not prevent his departure indefinitely but there remained the practical problem of how the journey was to be accomplished. Passage in a liner involved the risk of Italian interference, although the Foreign Office was inclined to discount this since the Italians had not attempted to exercise belligerent rights and had, moreover, proclaimed that the fighting in Ethiopia was over. Air travel at this time via Imperial Airways normally meant a stop in Italy and overland travel avoiding northern Italy would have required numerous permissions from governments, perhaps not always forthcoming, and the journey itself would likely involve considerable publicity. The Foreign Office would have preferred to see the Emperor embark in a French ship but the Emperor refused to land in Marseilles with its large Italian population, fearing for his life. In the end, the Government reluctantly decided to allow the Emperor to proceed as far west as Gibraltar in a British cruiser, but it would be explained to the Emperor that 'service requirements' at

[1] Foreign Office to Colonial Office, 6 May 1936, ibid.

[2] Parliamentary Question by Mr Arthur Henderson and suggestions for reply, 8 and 9 May, 1936, TNA: FO 371/2196.

[3] Parliamentary Question by Miss Wilkinson, 11 May 1936, ibid.

the present time prevented the ship from going further west and he would have to make his own arrangements from Gibraltar to England.[1]

The Admiralty ordered the Mediterranean Commander-in-Chief, Admiral Sir Dudley Pound, to select a suitable cruiser [22]. Pound chose H.M.S. *Capetown* [23]. There was a good amount of opportunism in the choice and more than a little penny-pinching. *Capetown* had been on the China Station and was on her way back to England to re-commission. Pound hoped he 'did not embarrass the Admiralty by using *Capetown*' but 'it seemed such a waste of fuel to use one of the Mediterranean ships'.[2] *Capetown* was the last of the numerous 'C'-class cruisers, laid down in February 1918, but not launched until after the Armistice in 1919 and not completed until 1922. At 4,200 tons standard displacement, armed with six 6-inch guns and an average complement of 334, the ship was smaller and less impressive than the *Enterprise*, hence Pound's apologetic comment.[3] The Emperor and his suite of seven – a contrast to the large entourage in *Enterprise* – embarked in *Capetown* at 2000 on 23 May and the ship proceeded to sea a little over half an hour later. The *Capetown* went to Night Defence Stations the first four nights, that is until past Malta, Pantellaria and Cape Bon.[4] Shortly after the ship left Haifa the Emperor was given a message from the Foreign Office that, while they anticipated no interference after he left Gibraltar, the British Government could not give any guarantee of his personal safety. The Emperor had assumed that measures for his safety would have been taken when embarking in a merchant ship and, alarmed, asked that he might be allowed to continue on to England in the *Capetown* [24, 25, 28]. This, not surprisingly, was refused although the Emperor was informed that if he did not wish to embark in a British liner he was free to make his own arrangements for overland travel via Spain and France. Furthermore, the Governor of Gibraltar[5] was informed that as he would be incognito there would be

---

[1]Paraphrase telegrams from High Commissioner for Palestine to Secretary of State for the Colonies, 10, 15 and 21 May 1936; Note for Secretary of State's use in Cabinet on future movements of the Emperor of Ethiopia, 16 May 1936; Colonial Office to Sir A. Wauchope (Jerusalem), 19 May 1936; Extract from Cabinet Conclusions 38(36), 20 May 1936, TNA: FO 371/2196.

[2]Pound to Chatfield, 30 May, 1936, NMM, Greenwich, Chatfield MSS. CHT/4/10.

[3]Raven and Roberts, *British Cruisers*, pp. 67, 406–7.

[4]Log of H.M.S. *Capetown*, 23–29 May 1936, TNA: ADM 53/95482.

[5]General Sir Charles Harington (1872–1940). Deputy Chief of Imperial General Staff, 1918–20; C-in-C Army of the Black Sea, 1920–21; C-in-C Allied Forces of Occupation in Turkey, 1921–23; C-in-C Northern Command, 1923–27; C-in-C Western Command, India, 1927–31; C-in-C Aldershot Command, 1931–33; Govr and C-in-C Gibraltar, 1933–38.

no salutes or guard of honour for the Emperor, nor would there be any official entertainment. He was not to be lodged in Government House or in any sense be considered a guest of the British Government and, while the Governor was free to provide unofficial hospitality, it would be out of the Governor's own allowance. As a Foreign Office official put it, the Emperor 'would be on his own' after leaving the ship.[1] There was one concession – the Admiralty was asked and agreed to the Emperor and his suite remaining aboard *Capetown*, safely berthed in the dockyard, until his liner, the Orient Line's *Orford* (1928, 19,941 tons), was due to sail [29]. The Admiralty exercised strict control over the Emperor's communications while in the *Capetown*. Any messages he desired to send were to be transmitted in naval cypher directly to the Admiralty [26, 27]. When an American magazine tried to query the Emperor on the forthcoming meeting of the League Council, the message was only to be handed to the Emperor as he left the ship at Gibraltar [30, 31].

The Emperor was not entirely snubbed. Shortly after *Capetown* secured alongside the wharf in the Gibraltar dockyard on the morning of 29 May Admiral Sir Roger Backhouse, Commander-in-Chief of the Home Fleet under whose orders *Capetown* now came, paid a courtesy call on the Emperor. He was followed by the Abyssinian ambassador from Paris. Haile Selassie disregarded the advice to remain in the ship until his liner sailed two days later and decided to lodge at the undoubtedly more comfortable Rock Hotel. This was probably a great relief to those officers in the ship who had to vacate their cabins to accommodate the Imperial party. At 1255 the Emperor and his suite left the ship and *Capetown* returned to her normal routine.[2] The Royal Navy's role in the unfortunate ruler's journey into exile was over. The impression given by *Enterprise*'s report of proceedings is that her captain and his officers were far more sympathetic to the Emperor than the professionals in the Foreign Office as reflected in their docket minutes. The diplomats gave the impression that the Emperor was becoming a nuisance and Ethiopia a lost cause. They were primarily concerned with legalisms and diplomatic considerations. Great Britain had taken the lead in support of the League and had carried out a major and expensive concentration of naval

---

[1]Governor of Gibraltar to Sec of State for the Colonies, 25 May 1936; and Sec of State for the Colonies to Govr of Gibraltar, 25 May 1936, TNA: ADM 116/3045; Foreign Office Minute of Conversation with Mr. Dawe of the Colonial Office [*illegible signature*], 25 May 1936, TNA: FO 371/20196.

[2]Log of H.M.S. *Capetown*, 29 May 1936, TNA: ADM 53/95482.

strength, but that had not saved Ethiopia and it was time to move on and readjust to the new situation.

The Emperor lunched informally with the Governor at Government House on the day of his arrival.[1] Backhouse received orders from the Admiralty to hold *Capetown* for a sufficient interval after *Orford* had sailed on the evening of the 31st so as to avoid the impression that he could have come home in the cruiser, or that the latter was in attendance upon him [32]. *Capetown* therefore did not sail for Devonport until the morning of 2 June.

Haile Selassie was one of a number of former sovereigns the Royal Navy had carried into exile in the period between the two World Wars. He had followed the Dowager Empress of Russia, the Emperor and Empress of Austria-Hungary and the last Sultan of Ottoman Turkey. Unlike his predecessors, however, he would have the distinction of being restored by British and British Empire arms in 1941.

Note

All Documents printed are from Adm 116/3045 in The National Archives, Kew. All but 19, 20 and 21 are Telegrams. All Adm [Admiralty] and FO [Foreign Office] documents are likewise in The National Archives, Kew.

---

[1]Governor of Gibraltar to Sec of State for the Colonies, 28 and 29 May, 1936, copies in TNA: ADM 116/3045.

1. *Admiralty to C-in-C East Indies*[1]

21 April 1936

SECRET

IMMEDIATE

Request you will hold a sloop in readiness to transport the Empress of Ethiopia, her two daughters, two sons aged 12 and 4, and eight small grandchildren from Jibouti to Aden. In addition there will be an entourage of six persons at most, none of whom will be males of military age.

1336/21

2. *Admiralty to C-in-C East Indies*

22 April 1936

SECRET

IMPORTANT

My 1356 of 21st April and your 1758/21. It has been decided that should this service be required a cruiser is to be used and that the party is to be taken to Suez where connection with Palestine can be made by railway.

1314/22

3. *Admiralty to C-in-C East Indies*
[Repeated C-in-C Mediterranean,[2] H.M.S. Enterprise]

2 May 1936

SECRET

IMMEDIATE

My 1433/2 to C.-in-C. East Indies.

Destroyer at Perim is to proceed to Djibouti so as to arrive by 0900 local time tomorrow Sunday. She is to deliver following confidential message from Foreign Office to British Vice Consul Djibouti. Begins.

---

[1]VA Frank Forrester Rose (1878–1955). Commanded destroyer *Laurel* in Helgoland action, 28 Aug 1914; commanded 3rd Destroyer Flotilla, Atlantic Fleet, 1921; Dir of Operations Division, Admiralty, 1925–27; commanded RN Barracks, Portsmouth, 1928–29; RA commanding Destroyer Flotillas, Mediterranean Fleet, 1931–33; C-in-C East Indies, 1934–36; invalided, 1937.

[2]Adm [later AoF Sir] Alfred Dudley Pickman Rogers Pound (1877–1943). Commanded battleship *Colossus* at Jutland, 1916; Dir of Plans Division, Admiralty, 1922–25; Chief of Staff in Mediterranean Fleet, 1925–27; Assistant Chief of Naval Staff, 1927–29; RADM commanding Battle Cruiser Squadron, 1929–31; Admiralty representative on League of Nations Advisory Commission, 1932; Second Sea Lord, 1932–35; temporary Chief of Staff, Mediterranean Fleet, 1935–36; C-in-C Mediterranean Fleet, 1936–39; First Sea Lord and Chief of Naval Staff, 1939–43.

Inform Emperor of Abyssinia on arrival at Djibouti that the matter raised by him with Sir S. Barton[1] is engaging the earnest consideration of His Majesty's Government whose final decision will be communicated to him with no avoidable delay. Ends.

Destroyer is to remain at Djibouti until further instructions to act as wireless link with British Vice Consul.

French Authorities are being informed.

Report name of destroyer and repeat back times.

1815/2

4. *Admiralty to H.M.S.* Diana

[Repeated C-in-C East Indies, C-in-C Mediterranean,
H.M.S. Enterprise]

3 May 1936

SECRET

IMMEDIATE

You should either in conjunction with British Vice Consul at Djibuti, or by yourself, make following communication in writing to the Negus.[2] H.M. Government are prepared to give effect to request which Your Majesty made to Sir S. Barton and to convey Your Majesty, the Empress, your son and your immediate entourage to Palestine and to afford the necessary asylum in Jerusalem.

For this purpose H.M.S. *Enterprise* will call at Djibuti within the next few hours. Your Majesty will appreciate the fact that H.M. Government make these offers on the express understanding that neither Your Majesty, who will be travelling incognito, nor any of your entourage, will while in Palestine participate in any way actively or passively in the furtherance of hostilities. You should add that it is necessary for navigational reasons for *Enterprise* to sail as near noon (Monday May 4th) local time as possible, you should ask His Majesty and party to embark with immediate despatch.

2138/3

---

[1] Sir Sidney Barton (1876–1946). Interpreter and assistant political officer in China Field Force during Boxer Rebellion, 1900; Chinese sec, Peking, 1911–22; Consul-General, Shanghai, 1922–29; Minister in Addis Ababa, Ethiopia, May 1929–May 1936; retired, 1937.

[2] Amharic title, meaning 'king', used here for the sovereign of Abyssinia.

5. *Admiralty to C-in-C East Indies*
[*Repeated C-in-C Mediterranean, H.M.S.* Enterprise,
S.N.O. Port Said, S.N.O. Haifa]

3 May 1936

SECRET

IMMEDIATE

His Majesty's Government have decided with concurrence of French Government to convey Emperor of Abyssinia and party comprising members of Imperial Family and Staff from Djibuti to Haifa. *Enterprise* is to proceed immediately to Djibuti for this purpose. Emperor has already been informed through *Diana*.

It is expected that party will number about twelve. If any number greatly in excess be proposed Captain of *Enterprise* should fix his own limit. Emperor and party should not be allowed to dispatch messages from *Enterprise*. *Enterprise* should keep Haifa informed of her movements and hour of arrival in time to permit High Commissioner, Palestine[1] to arrange for reception of party. After leaving Djibuti *Enterprise* is to proceed at requisite speed so as to arrive at entrance to Suez Canal at daylight Thursday May 7th necessary arrangements being made for her to pass straight through the Canal.

2146/3

6. *Admiralty to C-in-C East Indies and C-in-C Mediterranean*
[*Repeated H.M.S.* Enterprise]

3 May 1936

SECRET

IMMEDIATE

Government desire that support should be available for *Enterprise* as a precaution, but that such support should not be unduly in evidence. C.-in-C. East Indies is therefore to proceed in *Emerald* accompanied by *Decoy*, *Dainty* and *Diana* so as to escort *Enterprise* through the Red Sea keeping at maximum supporting distance to the eastward. *Diana* should be instructed to leave Djibuti subsequent to departure of *Enterprise* as

---

[1]Major General Sir Arthur Grenfell Wauchope (1874–1947). British representative on Military Inter-Allied Commission of Control in Germany after World War I; High Commissioner of Palestine, 1931–38.

requisite to rendezvous with you. On arrival of *Enterprise* at entrance to Gulf of Suez you should return to Aden with escorting ships. C.-in-C. Mediterranean is to arrange for *Enterprise* to be similarly escorted from Port Said to Haifa.

2330/3

7.   *H.M.S.* Enterprise *to Admiralty*
[Repeated C-in-C East Indies, H.B.M. Minister, Addis Ababa]

4 May 1936

SECRET

IMPORTANT

H.M. The Emperor requested that following messages which have been translated from the French be passed to British Government. Begins.

We send our deepest thanks to H.M.B. Government for having so quickly acceded to our request and for granting us H.M.S. *Enterprise* for our voyage. We should be particularly grateful to H.B.M. Government if it could permit us to continue our voyage direct to London. During our stay in London we will abstain from any act in furtherance of the war in Ethiopia. We continually hope and pray that H.B.M. Government, which has never ceased to devote its efforts towards maintenance of the principles of the League of Nations, will uphold our peaceful attempts to prevent a member of the League of Nations being destroyed solely at the will of a state unanimously condemned as an aggressor. Ends.

1701/4

8.   *Admiralty to H.M.S.* Enterprise
[Repeated C-in-C East Indies]

4 May 1936

SECRET

IMPORTANT

Should Emperor ask to send any signals whilst onboard *Enterprise* you should inform him that you are unable to comply without reference to Admiralty. Any new message is to be reported at once to Admiralty for instructions.

1850/4

9. *Pound to Admiralty*
[*Repeated C-in-C East Indies, H.M.S.* Enterprise]

4 May 1936

SECRET.

202. My 1228 18th April and my 2223 29th April to Admiralty only[1] and Admiralty's 2146 and 2330 both of 3rd May. Intend reconnaissance of Gulf of Suez by flying boats of No. 4 Wing on Wednesday 6th May and that H.M.S. *Venetia* should provide an unobtrusive escort throughout Gulf of Suez.

Reconnaissance of Alexandria, Port Said, Haifa, Cyprus areas will be carried out by No. 4 Flying Boat Wing on Thursday 7th May.

Fleet exercise originally arranged for 5th May and 6th May has been postponed until 7th May and 8th May on account of arrival of His Majesty King Farouk[2] on Wednesday 6th May.

Fleet proceeding to sea is common knowledge and I intend adhering to Fleet exercise working fleet to eastward to cover passage of H.M.S. *Enterprise* from Port Said to Haifa during night of Thursday 7th May Friday 8th May.

H.M.S. *Delhi* will be the only ship at Haifa when H.M.S. *Enterprise* arrives.

1851/4

10. *Pound to S.B.N.O. Suez Canal Area*
[*Repeated* Venetia, Enterprise, *S.N.O. Haifa,*
S.N.O. Port Said, R.A. (D)]

5 May 1936

SECRET.

IMPORTANT

Reference Admiralty telegram 2146 3rd May to S.N.O. Port Said but not to S.B.N.O. Suez Canal Area. *Enterprise* with Negus and party on board is due Suez daylight Thursday 7th May. Request you will arrange for her to pass straight through Canal.

Venetia is to leave Suez and proceed to vicinity of Shadwan arriving there 1800 6th May. She is to get into touch with *Enterprise* and escort her to Suez not closing her within 15 miles unless ordered to

---

[1]Not reproduced. They concern Mediterranean Fleet exercises.
[2]Farouk I (1920–65). King of Egypt, 1936–52. Forced to abdicate by military coup, July 1952. Farouk had just succeeded his father Fuad, who died 28 April.

do so. *Enterprise* will not be escorted through the Canal but *Wolsey* is similarly to escort her from Port Said to Haifa. Air reconnaissance of Gulf of Suez by flying boats of Number 4 Wing is being carried out on 6th May.

1008/5

11. *S.B.N.O. Suez Canal to Admiralty*
[Repeated C.-in-C. Mediterranean, C.-in-C. East Indies]

5 May 36

SECRET

IMMEDIATE

Admiralty Message 2146 3rd May. Daylight passage of Negus through Canal will cause crowds and possible disturbances. Therefore suggest *Enterprise* arrives Suez 1900 Thursday and passes quickly as possible to Port Said in darkness.

Should I offer any civilities to Negus on behalf of C.-in-C. Mediterranean?

1031/5

12. *Pound to H.M.S.* Enterprise
[Repeated C-in-C East Indies, Admiralty, N.O.i.C. Haifa,
S.B.N.O. Suez Canal, S.N.O.A. at Haifa, S.N.O.A. at Port Said,
S.N.O. at Suez, N.O.i.C. Port Said]

5 May 1936

SECRET

IMPORTANT

Whilst in H.M.S. *Enterprise* not only are the Emperor and party not to be allowed to despatch messages but steps are to be taken to ensure that they hold no communication whatsoever with anyone from shore.

1245/5

13. *H.M.S.* Enterprise *to Admiralty*
[Repeated C-in-C East Indies, British Minister Addis Ababa]

5 May 1936

SECRET

The Emperor has requested that following message may be passed to H.B.M. Minister Addis Ababa. Begins.

Confident that British Government will consider favourably our request telegraphed yesterday 4th May with a view to permitting us to proceed direct by the same ship to London instead of going to Palestine: we await a reply which we hope will be communicated to us as soon as possible. Signed Emperor. Ends.

1539/5

14. *Admiralty to Pound*
[*Repeated C-in-C East Indies, S.B.N.O. Suez Canal*]

5 May 1936

SECRET

IMPORTANT

Reference S.B.N.O. Suez Canal 1031/5.
It is not necessary to make any alteration in *Enterprise*'s programme.
1714/5

15. *Admiralty to C.-in-C. East Indies*
[*Repeated C-in-C Mediterranean, H.M.S.* Emerald,
H.M.S. Enterprise]

5 May 1936

SECRET

IMPORTANT

My 2330/3 not to *Emerald*.
It is no longer considered necessary for *Enterprise* to be escorted in force but a courtesy escort of one destroyer is to proceed in company with *Enterprise* as far as the entrance to the Gulf of Suez. Remaining ships of escort are therefore to return now to Aden.
1725/5

16. *Admiralty to C.O., H.M.S.* Enterprise
[*Repeated C-in-C East Indies*]

5 May 1936

SECRET

Your 1701 of May 4th.
Following from Foreign Office:

Please inform the Emperor that H.M. Government regret that they do not feel it practicable at any rate at the present moment to give effect to His Majesty's request that he shall continue his voyage to London.

2038/5

17.   H.M.S. Enterprise *to Admiralty for Foreign Office*
[*Repeated C-in-C East Indies*]

6 May 1936

SECRET

IMMEDIATE

The Emperor has requested following message may be given to H.M. Government. (Begins). Having considered British Government's reply to our telegram of 4th May from Djibouti with regard to our request to continue direct to London in H.M.S. *Enterprise*. Our wish to proceed to London was made known to British Minister before leaving Addis Ababa. We had intended to continue the journey after leaving our family at Jerusalem. However, pressed by reasons of health we wish to carry out a small change in this programme.

Our family and most of the suite will go to Jerusalem while we carry straight on to London from Haifa in H.M.S. *Enterprise*. Once again we earnestly entreat that the British Government will be kind enough to consent to this request in consideration, above all, of our health.

Then if the British Government thinks fit we will be glad to point out to them certain things that to us appear useful both to British and Ethiopian interests.

1215Z/6

18.   *Foreign Office via Admiralty to*
C.O., H.M.S. Enterprise

7 May 1936

SECRET

Please inform the Emperor that His Majesty's Government have received the Emperor's message conveyed to them in your telegram of May 6th.

His Majesty's Government feel obliged to make it clear that, while the position will be reviewed in the near future, it is not at present practicable for them to depart from the decision already conveyed to His Majesty in Admiralty telegram to you of May 5th or to modify plans which were originally made in accordance with what they understood to be His Majesty's wishes.

In the circumstances His Majesty would be well advised to accompany the Imperial Family to Jerusalem and remain there for the present and until the position can be further considered.[1]

2020/7

19. *Lieutenant Commander W.H. Selby[2] to*
C-in-C East Indies Station

No. 444/J

H.M.S. *Diana*, at Aden
8 May 1936

I have the honour to submit the following report of proceedings of H.M. Ship *Diana*, under my command, on 3rd and 4th May, 1936.

2. In accordance with orders received by Admiralty signal 1815/2 *Diana* proceeded from Perim to Djibouti, arriving at 0900 on Sunday, 3rd May. As no one from the town had come on board by 0930 I landed and met Mr. Lowe, the British Vice Consul, who was on the point of coming to see me, accompanied by the French Chef de Cabinet. Mr. Lowe told me that news of the Emperor's train was very unreliable and that he had already been waiting most of the previous night at the station. The latest news was that there were two trains, one arriving at 1130 and the other at 1330.

3. We returned on board *Diana* while I prepared for a visit to the Governor,[3] which was paid at 1030. His Excellency knew no more exact

---

[1]The Emperor had also sent a personal message to King Edward VIII requesting that he come to England. The message apparently was in similar terms and the Foreign Office provided the King a draft of their reply. King Edward then sent a reply, 'as kindly worded as possible' expressing his regret that he did not feel justified in asking his Ministers to reconsider their decision. Foreign Office Memorandum, 7 May 1936, TNA: FO 371/20196. A copy of the King's telegram sent through the Foreign Office to the CO, H.M.S. *Enterprise* is in TNA: ADM 116/3045

[2]Lt Cdr [later RA] William Halford Selby (1902–94). Commanded destroyers *Restless*, 1932–34, *Veteran*, 1934, *Diana*, 1934–36, *Wren*, 1939–40, *Mashona*, 1940–41, *Onslaught*, 1942–44; Chief Staff Officer to Cmdr (D), Western Approaches, 1944; Chief of Staff to Naval Officer-in-Charge, Londonderry, 1945; Capt (D), 3rd Destroyer Flotilla in *Saumarez* (mined in Corfu Channel, 1946), 1945–47; Deputy Dir of Operations Division, 1948–50; Capt-in-Charge Simonstown (South Africa) and Capt Superintendent H.M. Dockyard, Simonstown, 1950–52; Head of British Naval Mission to Greece, 1953–56.

[3]Armand Léon Annet (1888–1973). Governor of French Somaliland, 1935–37; Lt Govr of Dahomey, 1938–40; Gov-Gen of Madagascar, 1941–42. A strong supporter of Marshal Petain and the Vichy Government, Annet led a bitter six-month struggle against the British invasion of Madagascar before finally surrendering.

time of the Emperor's arrival than did Mr. Lowe. I asked for permission to use W/T, which was granted at once. At 1130 the Governor sent his Administrateur to return my call as by then it was known that the train by which the Emperor was travelling was due at 1400.

4. The Emperor, Empress, family, staff and servants, with all the baggage, were on this train which had apparently stopped for eleven hours at Diredawa while the Emperor conferred with his southern Chiefs. (This is not confirmed.) The railway and roads were heavily guarded by French native troops when the Emperor arrived and he was driven straight to the Residency. His staff were put up in the Ethiopian Consulate.

5. Mr. Lowe and I waited until 1700 when we were granted an audience; I read out the terms of H.M. Government (communicated by Admiralty's Signal 1815/2) and left a copy of the letter with the Secretary. His Majesty seemed to be very disappointed with the terms but cheered up when I said that we were in touch with London and would bring ashore any further communications. He was particularly interested in the size of *Diana* and asked whether there was an Italian warship in the harbour as well. The only Italian vessel there was the *Somalia*[1] which arrived at 1000 and left at 1730. He also expressed a wish that we should go direct to him or his Secretary with any communications as he did not appear to have much confidence in the safety afforded him by the French authorities and wished to keep them out of all negotiations.

6. I returned to the Vice Consulate with Mr. Lowe to see whether there was any news from Sir Sydney Barton; nothing had come through nor was he on the train which arrived later, about 1730. We returned on board at 1830 and Mr. Lowe remained to supper. He went ashore at 2300 and I arranged to call him if any signals came during the night.

7. His Majesty's Government's decision was stated in Admiralty's Signal 2138/3[2] which was decyphered by 0300, and I went ashore with it at once. After calling Mr. Lowe we both went to the Residency at 0400 and were able to walk right in; only one sentry was awake and he took no notice of us.

8. I roused the night watchman and, as the Secretary was not there we were received by the Emperor at 0440 and I gave him the decision of His Majesty's Government. He asked me the probable time of arrival of *Enterprise* which I gave as between 0700 and 0900, and also required to know the number she would accommodate as eighty-one people had travelled with him from Addis Ababa; I told him, that I had received no

---

[1] Probably the steamer *Somalia* (1918, 2,700 tons) of the 'Tirrenia' group which traded between Genoa and East African ports.

[2] Doc. No. 4.

instructions but thought that the maximum possible numbers that could be embarked would be about fifty.

9. Mr. Lowe and I returned on board at 0500 to collect any further information and went ashore at 0630 with the news of the time of arrival of *Enterprise*. At this time some members of the French Residency were about and we had difficulty in getting an audience until 0715. His Majesty was now anxious to know whether he could signal to London and get a reply before he sailed. I informed him that there would be every chance if the signal was ready within an hour and that he could get a reply on board if necessary. This signal was not ready for despatch until the afternoon.

10. I went over to *Enterprise* on her arrival and turned over all the information I had obtained to Captain C.E. Morgan, D.S.O.[1] whom I accompanied on his visit ashore during Monday forenoon.

11. A great deal depended upon the cyphering and decyphering of signals and in this respect I would like to draw attention to the excellent work done by Lieutenant J.A. Stewart-Moore and Sub-Lieutenant W.F.B. Webb who carried out the whole of this work.

12. The attached list of passengers on the royal train was received from the French railway officials. Communications are dealt with in an appendix.[2]

20.   *Captain J. G. Crace[3] to C-in-C East Indies*

No. 4249/191.

H.M.S. *Emerald*, at Aden
9 May 1936

I have the honour to submit the following report of Proceedings for H.M. Ship under my command for the period 4th to 7th May, 1936.

2. In accordance with your message timed 0340/4, *Emerald* raised steam with all despatch, and sailed at 1000 from Aden at 22 knots, with

---

[1]Capt [later Adm Sir] Charles Eric Morgan (1889–1951). Fleet Navigating Officer in battleship *Nelson*, Home Fleet, 1932; commanded cruiser *Enterprise*, 1936–38; Dir of Navigation, Admiralty, 1938–40; commanded battleship *Valiant*, 1940–42; RA commanding Iceland, 1942–43; Flag Officer Taranto and Adriatic, 1944–45; Deputy Chief of Naval Personnel and Admiral Commanding Reserves, 1945–47; retired 1948; Staff Capt (Merchant Navy) in Blue Funnel liner *Clytoneus*, 1948.

[2]The list and appendix are not reproduced.

[3]Capt [later Adm Sir] John Gregory Crace (1887–1968). Commanded Anti Submarine School (H.M.S. *Osprey*), Portland, 1924–25; commanded destroyer *Valhalla*, 1929–30; Capt Anti Submarine and Commanding Officer, Anti Submarine School, Portland, 1930–32; Dir of Tactical Division, Admiralty, 1932–34; commanded cruiser *Emerald*, 1934–37; Naval Assistant to Second Sea Lord, 1937–39; RA commanding Australian Squadron, 1939–42; Adm Superintendent H.M. Dockyard, Chatham, 1942–46.

H.M. Ships *Decoy* and *Dainty* in company, to rendezvous with H.M.S. *Diana* off the Gulf of Tajura.

3. Reaching the rendezvous at 1400, speed was reduced to 10 knots, and the ship steamed up and down between the rendezvous and Masha Island.

4. At 1930 H.M. Ships *Enterprise* and *Diana* were sighted coming from the direction of Djibuti. *Diana* joined destroyers in company, who were then stationed one mile ahead of *Emerald*. *Emerald* took station approximately 10 miles astern of *Enterprise*, who was proceeding at 22 knots. *Emerald* and destroyers assumed third degree of readiness, having been darkened since sunset.

Enterprise was ordered to alter course 180° and join *Emerald* at full speed should necessity for support arise.

5. Perim was passed at 2330, and at daylight on 5th May the ship was off Jebel Zubair Island; destroyers were then stationed astern, and speed reduced to 17 knots, until *Emerald* was in station 20 miles on the starboard quarter of *Enterprise*. Throughout the day course and speed were adjusted to maintain this station.

6. At 1600 speed was increased to 25 knots to close *Enterprise* for the night.

7. At 2016, Admiralty message timed 1725/5[1] was received and at 2120 *Dainty* was ordered to join *Enterprise*, while remaining ships altered course 180°, and reduced to 15 knots to return to Aden. At the same time, ships ceased to be at 3rd degree of readiness.

8. Whilst off Perim, at 0545 on 7th May, aircraft was catapulted to search for S.S. *Glengarry*, who had naval mails for Aden, but was not calling at that port. *Decoy* was detached to board S.S. *Glengarry* at 0630; she rejoined some 2 hours later.

9. *Emerald*, with H.M. Ships *Decoy* and *Diana* in company, arrived at Aden at 1200 on 7th May; *Emerald* anchored in Z.1 berth, and destroyers proceeded alongside R.F.A. *Montenol* to fuel.

21. *Captain C.E. Morgan to C-in-C East Indies*

H.M.S. *Enterprise*, at sea

No. 166   16 May 1936

I have the honour to forward the following letter of proceedings of His Majesty's Ship under my command in continuation of my letter No.191A

---

[1]Doc. No. 15.

dated 2nd May, 1936 reporting the work done at Perim between 29th April and 3rd May.

2. On 28th April I was sent to Perim, to complete the new canteen and bathing pool and to be ready at four hours notice for full speed for any emergency. There I had in company with me the destroyer *Diana*, also at short notice for full speed.

The Commander-in-Chief had informed me that it was possible that the Emperor of Abyssinia might be leaving his country, in which event I should probably be required to embark him at Djibuti and convey him to an unknown destination. My original instructions were that the party would probably consist of the Empress, Crown Princess, four children, six grandchildren and an entourage of eight or ten servants male and female. The original port of disembarkation was mentioned as Suez.

3. Nothing happened for 3 or 4 days but it was obvious from the Press News that the Emperor was about to leave his country, and provided that the Government agreed to convey him in a British warship, I knew that it was only a matter of hours before I should be required.

Early on Sunday morning, 3rd May, *Diana* was ordered to proceed with all despatch to Djibuti to deliver a message to the Emperor when he arrived, to the effect that the British Government had agreed to convey him, his family and his staff in a British warship, and that H.M.S. *Enterprise* had been detailed for this duty. On Monday, 4th May, at 0245 I was ordered to proceed to Djibuti, so as to arrive at 0800, embark the Royal Family and staff and convey them to Haifa in Palestine.

4. I anchored at Djibuti at 0800, saluted the country and immediately landed with the Captain of the *Diana,* to call on the Governor and to have an audience with the Emperor. The Emperor, Royal Family, Staff and servants, baggage and bullion had arrived at 1600 the day before and were living with the Governor at the Palace. The total numbers were said to be 150, not including the Emperor's dog and two lion cubs. In the Admiralty message I was informed that the party would probably consist of 12!, but that if this number was greatly exceeded I was to fix my own limit as to the numbers embarked.

5. After about half an hour's conversation with the French Governor of Djibuti, I was told that the Emperor was ready to receive me. There were present at the audience the Emperor, the interpreter, Emperor's legal adviser, the British Vice Consul at Djibuti, the Captain of the *Diana*, Lieutenant Tillard,[1] the officer whom I had told off to act as the

---

[1]Lt [later Lt Cdr] Rupert Claude Tillard (1910–41). Also Flying Officer, RAF, Jan 1932; commanded 808 Squadron, FAA, July 1940–May 1941; Tillard reached ace status

Emperor's personal A.D.C. during the time he was on board, and myself. I also told off Midshipman C.A. James[1] to act as a 2nd A.D.C. to the Emperor because I knew that with the Emperor living aft and myself on the bridge, I could not deal direct with all the thousand and one things which would have to be arranged and settled. It was a very interesting experience for these two officers as they were in constant personal attendance on His Majesty and his staff, and I can only say that they carried out their duties from start to finish with the utmost efficiency and extreme tact. I could not have done without them because with the ship steaming at high speed, I only left the bridge when I had to go aft to see the Emperor, and except for matters which had to be communicated by me personally to the Emperor or when he wished to see me, I left the arrangements and programme entirely in their hands. As far as I know, I don't think they made a mistake, which is very creditable, because besides being in personal attendance on the Emperor they had to make all the arrangements for the accommodation, messing and private affairs of 46 Abyssinians, some of whom had never seen the sea before.

6. My first impression on being presented to His Majesty on Monday morning was, how very tired he looked. I felt somehow that he was almost at his last gasp and from his first few remarks I knew he was a very frightened man. He had a hunted look in his eye and he seemed only too glad to sit down as soon as the presentations were over.

I was glad to notice that his hands were all right, because we had heard a rumour that he had been gassed and that his hands were all bandaged from mustard gas burns. Such beautiful hands too, I have never seen such delicate hands on any man, and I should think his fingers must have been nearly twice as long as mine. As a matter of fact all the Royal Family had beautiful hands and I believe they take a great pride in them.

7. His first questions were about his own personal safety on board and I assured him at once, that as soon as he stepped over my gangway he would be as safe as the Bank of England. That was the first time

and was credited with 6.5 enemy aircraft but was shot down and killed with his observer (Lt Mark Somerville, nephew of Adm Sir James Somerville, Flag Officer, Force H), 8 May 1941.

[1]Midshipman [later Capt] Christopher Alexander James (1916–69). Son of Adm Sir William ('Bubbles') James (1881–1973). Served in Coastal Forces and commanded M.T.B. *29*, Felixstowe, 1940–41; credited with sinking enemy merchant ship near Flushing, Dec 1940; commanded M.T.B. *30* and Signal Officer in 4th Motor Torpedo Boat Flotilla, Felixstowe, 1941; Signal Officer in destroyer *Milne*, 1943; Signal Officer, RN Air Station H.M.S. *Condor*, Arbroath, 1943–44; Signal Officer on Staff of C-in-C British Pacific Fleet, 1944–45; on directing staff, RN Staff College, Greenwich, 1951–52; commanded destroyer *Concord*, 1953–54; Dir of the Signal Division, Admiralty, 1957.

I saw him smile and I shall never forget it. There is something about his smile that you cannot resist, and you are always hoping that you will say something of which he approves or do some little thing that will please him, so that you can see him smile again.

8. He then asked if he would be escorted up the Red Sea and I told him that the escort was already waiting outside. I told him that it would consist of a cruiser and three destroyers and although they would keep out of sight, they would be in close support. He then asked if he would be escorted up the Gulf of Suez and I told him a destroyer for that had been arranged. He then asked if arrangements had been made to escort him from Port Said to Haifa, and I told him a destroyer had already been detailed for that duty. When he heard all that, he appeared very much happier.

9. The Emperor himself speaks his own language of course, he speaks French well and understands English. I found it was much the best and quickest to speak to him in English through his interpreter, who was also his own private doctor and speaks English perfectly. As a matter of fact the Emperor generally got the sense of what I was saying before he got it from Doctor Malakou, and his head was already in the air listening to the advice or opinion of his legal adviser, a man called Gorges, who never left His Majesty's side. As soon as he got the sense of a conversation he used to look up to the ceiling and Gorges would lean over and whisper in his left ear and as soon as he had made up his mind or decided, down would come his head and if it was approval he would smile and bow. If it was otherwise he would give me the answer through the interpreter.

The next question to be settled was numbers. The problem I was immediately faced with was a request from the Emperor that I would take 150 persons male and female, two lions, one dog, about 15 tons of baggage and about 150 cases of Maria Theresa dollars, between 250,000 and 300,000 of them and valued at about £17,000.

The original signal you will remember had suggested that the party would consist of about 12, but I was prepared for something like this, because these eastern potentates never move about without a huge retinue and I had discussed it with the Commander before we landed. We had decided that in view of the fact that we might strike bad weather, in which event they would all have to be stowed down below, we could not possibly manage more than 50 bodies.

10. I therefore told the Emperor that I could not take the lions, but that I would accept the dog, the baggage and the bullion, but that the party to embark must be cut down to 50. When this information was communicated I thought the throne room in the Palace was going up in a cloud of smoke. They all held up their hands in horror and said it could

not be done. I pointed out that H.M.S. *Enterprise* was not a passenger ship, and that every person who came on board would displace an officer or man from his normal accommodation and that as half the party would be females it would be extremely difficult to arrange for even 50. I pointed out too that my Government had informed me that the party would probably consist of 12 and that 50 was the very maximum I could possibly take.

The Emperor looked so very weary and fragile that I felt a perfect brute for screwing him down.[1] If I could have got the lot into my cabins he should have brought them all but that was, of course, quite impossible and I had to stick to my number.

11. The next question to be discussed was the time he was to embark. I told him my orders were to leave at noon, that the escort was waiting outside, the Suez Canal would be clear of shipping for our passage, from 0700 on Thursday 7th May and that the escort had been ordered to be at Port Said accordingly. The Emperor said he was very sorry, but that he just could not do it. By then it was about 1030 and it was obviously quite impossible for him to settle up all his private and the affairs of his country and embark in one and half hours. Also, now that he knew I could only take 50, he would have to go into conference with his ministers to see who was to go and who was to be left behind. When that had been decided all the baggage would have to be sorted out and that belonging to those who were going, had to be loaded into a lighter and taken off to the ship.

12. I pointed out that if we went at noon we could do the trip at 20 knots, but that every hour we delayed we should have to go faster and it would therefore be more uncomfortable for him living aft, as I had to be at the entrance to the Suez Canal at 0700 on Thursday. He saw that point and after a short conference with his ministers he said the earliest possible moment he could embark, was at 5.30 p.m. and I think it was rather marvellous that he walked over our starboard gangway at 5.29 p.m. Actually the baggage and the bullion were the biggest problem, it took rather longer than we expected to load it into the lighter and hoist it all on board. So that finally we did not go ahead until 7.20 p.m. which meant a speed of 22 knots to adhere to our programme.

13. The Commanding Officer of H.M.S. *Diana* reported to me that he was then 110 tons of fuel short. I therefore ordered him alongside

---

[1]This was one of the phrases the Admiralty was careful to omit in the extensive excerpts from the report forwarded to the Foreign Office.

and completed him to full stowage, so that he would be ready for any emergency.

14. On leaving Djibuti I made a signal reporting our departure and giving a nominal list of all the passengers.

15. I won't go into any detail about the Emperor's arrival on board. I received him with a Royal Guard, the band playing the Ethiopian national anthem. He walked down and inspected the front rank of the Guard. I then conducted him to the after end of the Quarter Deck which I had prepared as a sort of sitting room with easy chairs, carpets and small tables, with the awning curtains round to enclose it all in, if necessary.

I took him to the most comfortable chair, held the cushion up for him and as he sat down he went fast asleep, and the awning curtain across the after end of the Quarter Deck fell on Act I.

16. In Act II, I include our trip from Djibuti to Haifa in Palestine. According to the Empire broadcast from the B.B.C., the journey was made without incident. This is certainly not a true statement as far as events on board were concerned, because every hour of the day and night was fully occupied from the moment we left Djibuti until 1130 a.m. on Friday, when His Majesty's train left for Jerusalem.

17. It was my intention that the Emperor should be worried as little as possible during the time he was on board and that he should do what he liked when he liked. I warned the Officers and ship's company that on no account was any attempt to be made to photograph the Emperor, and that nobody was to visit the after part of the ship except on duty. The arrangements for accomodating the party were made out by the Commander and First Lieutenant Commander assisted by the two A.D.C.s, Lieutenant Tillard and Midshipman James, but it was not until we got the party on board, and we had found out how they wished to bed down, that the organisation could be completed. The arrangements for victualling the party were very thoroughly & efficiently carried out by the Accounting Branch, under the direction of the Paymaster Commander.

18. Very roughly, my idea was that my cabins were at the disposal of the Emperor and that, as far as possible, the after part of the ship should be isolated and screened from view. The Commander and Commander (E) turned out of their cabins and the First Lieutenant Commander and three other officers turned out of theirs, so as to leave the centre cabin flat available for Ministers and high officials and their families. The Gunroom was used as a general sleeping space for all those officers who had turned out of their cabins.

19. The Gunroom and Warrant Officers turned out of their messes and lived in the Wardroom, and No. 6 Gun Deck was reserved for the servants

and retinue. Luckily, they had no objection to males and females sleeping together in the same space, which helped a lot, but even so it was a tight fit. Luckily too, the weather remained fine, so that all those not supplied with cabins were able to sleep on camp beds on deck. Service stretchers were used to make up the requisite number of beds.

It was my intention, if the weather turned bad, to clear the Marine Barracks so as to accommodate the party sleeping on deck. However, it would have been a very tight squeeze and I am very glad we did not have to put this plan into effect.

20. As far as messing was concerned, the following were included at my table:–

The Emperor and Empress, the Crown Prince and Crown Princess, the Duke of Harrar (2nd son of the Emperor), Isash Work (niece of the Emperor), Princess Sehaie (daughter of the Emperor), Haile Sellassie (uncle of the Emperor), Ras Cassar (A.D.C.), Madam Cassar and Ras Guetatceou (2nd A.D.C.), eleven in all.

The remaining 36 were victualled by the Wardroom and were divided into two groups. One, the Ministers, their wives and some of the children who messed in the Warrant Officers Mess and the other, remainder of the children, nurses and servants, who had their meals at the forward end of the Quarter Deck on the Port Side.

21. The Empress slept in my sleeping cabin, and the Emperor, the 2nd and 3rd sons and one of the princesses slept on the couch and camp beds in my day cabin. The remainder of the Royal Family and most of the principal ministers and members of the suite were provided with cabin accommodation. As far as I can gather, most of the Royal Family used my bathroom, and luckily there is another bathroom and lavatory in the lobby outside the Commander's cabin which was used by those accommodated in the Commander's and Commander (E)'s cabins. The Warrant Officers' lavatories and bathroom were turned over for the use of the remainder of the party.

22. It can well be imagined what the after part of the ship was like at about 0600. I went there only once at this time and found a seething mass of humanity consisting of Officers dressed, undressed or dressing, nurses, children dressed and naked, Abyssinian Generals in full uniform, sentries, Marine servants and Goanese stewards taking round iced lemon squashes. I only wish I could have had a photograph of it; it had to be seen to be believed, that you were really on board a British Man of War.

23. There were, of course, very many amusing incidents. One of the Warrant Officers told me that one morning he went Aft at about 0500, to try to get a bath, and a sentry told him that there was a lady in the Warrant Officers' bathroom who had been there for the last half hour. As there

was no water on in the bathroom and hadn't been since the night before, he didn't know, he said, why she was taking so long over her bath!!

24. I should here like to put in a word of praise for the Emperor's little dog. My Coxswain told me that the Emperor always used to put him out every night before he went to bed, and that he never moved until the Emperor came for him in the morning. I used to go the rounds of the after part of the ship each night about 2300 and I always found him lying in the Quartermaster's lobby. I used to pat him and tell him he was a very good little dog and he just used to look up and wag his tail, but he never moved. Incidentally, he was never observed to commit either the major or minor offence the whole time he was on board; perhaps he was like the proverbial canary.

25. Before leaving his country, the Emperor, so they said, spent the last three days in the front line, trying to get shot. Eventually they dragged him out, unwounded, but his little dog was wounded by his side, and I should say that from the look of his left eye, he had lost the sight of it.

26. As far as the entertainment of the party was concerned, my hope that they would never have a dull moment on board was fully realised. On Tuesday, 5th May, I presented all the Officers to the Emperor, and on Wednesday 6th May, he inspected the Ship and Ship's Company. During his inspection of the ship he was accompanied by the Empress and all the Royal Family. The Empress managed to get as far as the Pom Pom Deck but she 'conked out' at the foot of the ladder leading to the Flag Deck. While she was waiting for the rest of the party to inspect the bridges her best spring hat blew off and looked like it was going over the side. However an enterprising Somali Boy leapt on to the waist awning and the hat and the situation were saved.

27. The Emperor had two Officers to lunch and two Officers to dine with him every day. The band generally played for him twice a day; and the pictures when he asked for them. On the Thursday night, the night before we arrived at Haifa, he was to have had the band after dinner, but I had a message in the Dog Watches from him to ask if I would mind very much if he cancelled the band programme, because after dinner he really must do some work.

28. During the trip from Djibuti to Haifa we were observed with the keenest interest by everyone. All ships going the same way and sighting us coming up astern hauled over, so that we should pass close to them and ships going in the opposite direction made a bold alteration of course as soon as they sighted us, so that they should pass close.

29. Suez, Ismailia, Port Said and the banks of the canal were crowded with people the whole way along and wherever the road runs close to the Canal, we were escorted by a force of police on motorcycles.

I think the Emperor was a little bit afraid at being potted at in the Canal. At Suez he was not on deck, but at Ismailia and Port Said he came and sat close alongside me on the Compass Platform. Very nice for me if this was his idea, but as the eyes and glasses of everyone on shore were focussed on the Empress and the remainder of the Abyssinians sitting in chairs on the Quarter Deck, it was perhaps rather clever of him.

30. The silver bullion was to have been landed at Port Said. It took me two days to make the necessary arrangements for guards, representatives of the Bank of Egypt to come on board to take it over, a lighter to land it and stopping and securing while it was being landed. As it was the Emperor's wish that we should stop and land it there, I also made arrangements to replenish our stock of provisions, as we had not any for ten days and were nearly down and out and also to take in fresh water, because these Abyssinians are great washers and we were using more water each day than we could distill on board. However, one hour before arriving at Port Said the Emperor got cold feet at the idea of losing sight of the money and decided that he would take it on to Haifa with him. This meant cancelling all the arrangements for stopping and securing for landing the money and for taking in provisions and filling up with fresh water and I went straight through Port Said, only slowing down to pick up our mails and a folio of Mediterranean Charts which were required for Haifa.

31. The destroyer *Wolsey* took up escorting duties after we had cleared the breakwater and we proceeded at 12 knots so as to arrive at Haifa, in accordance with the wishes of the High Commissioner, at 0830 on Friday, 8th May. The night passed without incident, we arrived as requested exactly at 0830 and so ended Act II.

32. Act III, which is only a short one, deals with our arrival and the departure of the Emperor for Jerusalem.

33. H.M.S. *Enterprise* was berthed alongside the Railway Pier at Haifa by 0900 and the Officer of the Guard came on board for the programme of the morning's events. The Royal Train was drawn up opposite the ship and immediately on arrival we commenced hoisting out the baggage and bullion.

34. Incidentally, during the voyage the baggage was stowed on the port side of the upper deck. They were continually going to it to get things out and there was a lot of re-packing done during the time they were on board. There was about ten tons of it altogether and as it consisted mostly of old boxes and dilapidated suitcases, with here and there a brand new one, it was lucky the weather remained fine.

35. At 1000 I presented to His Majesty the High Officials of the Port after which he retired to his cabin to compose himself for the final ordeal of leaving the ship and entraining for Jerusalem.

36. It was then that the most extraordinary event of the whole voyage occurred. If there is still anyone who is doubtful that the truth is stranger than fiction, this must surely convince him for good and all.

During the voyage the Emperor had received many messages and telegrams of sympathy, congratulations and condolence from all parts, and I am sure he was greatly affected and touched by them, especially one saying 'You put your faith in the Great White Nations and they have let you down. Sincerest sympathies and heartiest congratulations on your splendid efforts', handed in at Alexandria and signed 'A crowd of Britishers'.

However, on Friday morning just after he had returned to his cabin, the Captain of the *Wolsey*, the destroyer which had escorted us from Port Said, came on board and behind him was an Able Seaman with an Engine Room glove on carrying a large hawk and attached to the hawk's leg by a piece of string was a message for the Emperor written on a piece of stiff paper, like chart paper. I took it straight in to the Emperor and he actually himself removed the message from the hawk's leg. I asked him what I should do with the hawk; would he like to keep it or should I release it and as he seemed undecided, I suggested that my official photographer should take some pictures of the Captain of the *Wolsey* holding the hawk and I should send a dozen copies to him in Jerusalem. After that we released the hawk, but even then it was too done to fly far.

I have many times seen birds, including hawks on board a ship, but I have never seen one so exhausted that you could go to it and pick it up, and when this one fell on the deck of the *Wolsey* it was so done that the Able Seaman went straight to it and after picking it up he put it in the meat safe, while he reported the incident to his Captain. Also, there must have been twenty ships in the harbour and surely it was rather extraordinary that the bird should have alighted on board the escorting destroyer just as she was entering harbour astern of *Enterprise*.

Further, where had the bird come from? It has been suggested that it had flown from Abyssinia but I cannot believe this as it is 1,500 miles from Haifa. However, I understand that the homing pigeons can and do fly up to this distance in America.

The message was a 'Welcome' message with three words written in French, with the signature at the bottom but I don't think that there is any doubt that it was meant for the Emperor.

37. The Royal Family, Ministers and all the Servants and Valets left the ship at 1100, walked over and took their seats in the train. At 1115, the Emperor, the Crown Prince, and the Emperor's second Son left the ship. I paraded a Royal Guard and the band played the Ethiopian National Anthem. The Party walked to the saluting base, took the salute from the British Regiment stationed at Haifa and the Emperor then inspected the Guard. After that he walked over towards the train and all the local civilian officials, including the Mayor of Haifa, were presented to him by the District Commissioner.

38. An incident then took place which is typical of His Majesty's thoughtfulness and courtesy. After the final presentations were over he walked towards the train and stopping at the entrance to his Saloon he turned round and said 'I wish to speak to the Captain of H.M.S. *Enterprise.*' I went up to him, he said what he had to say, and I replied. He then said 'I wish to speak to Lieutenant Tillard and Mr. James', his two A.D.C.s. He spoke to them and again thanked them and they replied. He then turned round, walked into his carriage, the steps were removed and the train steamed out of the Station.

39. I have seldom been so impressed with any man, black or white, and his consideration, courtesy and above all his dignity, has left a very deep impression on every officer and man in the ship. The night before he left the ship he sent for me and gave me a replica, about the size of a five shilling piece, in pure gold, of his coronation medal. In handing it to me he said 'It is not the value of the thing that matters; it is the sentiment that counts'. His two A.D.C.s were also presented with similar but smaller replicas.

40. Before he left the ship, I presented His Majesty with a roller blotter which had been made on board during the four days he was with us, as a memento of his voyage. It was made of teak and the screw on top to keep it together was a model of a Capstan. It was really beautifully finished and in presenting it to His Majesty I explained how every department in the ship had helped towards the making of it. One department had carved the teak, another had turned the barrels of the Capstan, another had made the screw through the middle, another the silver pawls and another the silver whelps. It therefore contained a portion of every bit of the *Enterprise* and in accepting it His Majesty appeared very delighted and touched.

41. I have referred elsewhere to His Majesty's extreme dignity but this applied to all the Royal Family. The Princess Sehaie for instance, quite a good looker,[1] educated in England and speaking perfect English could, had she wished, have mixed freely with the Officers and had a wonderful time but as far as I know, she never once forgot herself, and her behaviour was, at all times, correct and dignified.

42. None of the party were any trouble or bother and the children were quiet and well looked after. Although the accommodation was crowded and far from ideal there were no complaints from any of them, and as far as I know no requests for something different. They were a happy and contented lot and seemed only too glad to make the best of the position in which they found themselves. They all thoroughly enjoyed the trip and their thanks

---

[1]The Admiralty also cut this phrase in the excerpt for the Foreign Office.

at the end of it were moderate but genuine. They talked little but never got excited but they seemed to be able to convey appreciation without the use of words. Savages perhaps, but very attractive and well behaved ones.

43. After the Emperor and party had left at 1130 on Friday, 8th May, I took in 1,000 tons of oil fuel, completed with fresh water and provisions and gave four hours leave to the Ship's Company.

44. I left Haifa at 1830 on Friday, 8th May, proceeded through the Canal the next day and arrived at Suez at 2000, after anchoring for an hour in the Great Lake. Ship was berthed alongside at Port Ibrahim, and 48 hours leave, which was much appreciated, was given to each watch.

45. I called on His Excellency Mohamed Nadim Bey, Governor of Suez on Monday, 11th May, and he returned my call on Wednesday 13th May.

46. *Enterprise* left Suez at 1700 on Wednesday, 13th May for Aden.

22. *Admiralty to Pound*
[*Repeated S.N.O. Haifa, R.A. Gibraltar*]

22 May 1936

SECRET

IMPORTANT

Emperor of Abyssinia has accepted invitation of H.M. Government to travel from Haifa to Gibraltar in one of H.M Cruisers, travelling incognito with suite limited to six persons.

Request you will make necessary arrangements with High Commissioner, Palestine and report ship selected and programme.

1730/22

23. *Pound to Commanding Officer H.M.S.* Capetown[1]
[*Repeated Admiralty, R.A.C. 3rd Cruiser Squadron, C-in-C Home Fleet, Rear Admiral, Gibraltar, S.N.O. Afloat Port Said*]

22 May 1936

SECRET

IMPORTANT

322. Proceed Haifa and embark Emperor of Abyssinia and convey him to Gibraltar. Emperor will travel incognito with suite limited to six persons.

---

[1]Capt [later RA] Douglas A. Budgen (1889–1947). Capt, H.M.S. *Defiance*, Torpedo School, Devonport, 1936–38; Dir of Tactical Division, Admiralty, 1938; Dir of Local Defence Division, Admiralty, 1939; Senior Naval Officer and later Flag Officer-in-Charge, Simonstown, South Africa, 1940–42; retired 1942.

Rear Admiral Commanding 3rd Cruiser Squadron[1] is requested to arrange with High Commissioner, Palestine for embarkation of Emperor as soon as possible after arrival of H.M.S. *Capetown* at Haifa.

H.M.S. *Capetown* to report to Rear Admiral Commanding 3rd Cruiser Squadron as soon as possible time of arrival and in due course report programme.

2223/22

24. *H.M.S.* Capetown *to Rear Admiral 3rd Cruiser Squadron*[2]
[Repeated C-in-C Mediterranean]

24 May 1936

SECRET

IMPORTANT

Your message from General Secretary Jerusalem has been explained to the Emperor of Abyssinia. It has caused considerable concern as to the prudence of embarking in a merchant ship which he only contemplated after having been informed by the High Commissioner that all measures for his safety would be taken by the British authorities. He now wishes that the High Commissioner be asked to arrange passage to be continued to United Kingdom in this ship.

1530/24

25. *Rear Admiral 3rd Cruiser Squadron to*
C-in-C Mediterranean

24 May 1936

SECRET

H.M.S. *Capetown* 1530 has been passed to High Commissioner.
Following message was given to *Capetown*. Time of origin 1907/23.
(Begins). Following received from Chief Secretary Jerusalem.
(Begins) It should be explained to Emperor that H.M. Government cannot give a guarantee of his personal safety but that it is not anticipated there will be any interference to His Majesty between Gibraltar

---

[1]RA [later Adm Sir] George Hamilton D'Oyly Lyon (1883–1947). Assistant Dir of Plans, Admiralty, 1923–25; Dir of Physical Training and Sports, Admiralty, 1927; Head of British Naval Mission to Greece, 1929–31; Cmdr (D) commanding Home Fleet Destroyers, 1932–34; RA commanding 3rd Cruiser Squadron, 1935–37; C-in-C Africa Station, 1938–40; C-in-C, The Nore, 1941–43.

[2]For reasons of clarity Docs Nos 24 and 25 have been extracted from Pound to Admiralty, 2148/24 where they were combined in a confusing fashion.

and England. It is assumed that His Majesty will decide to sail from Gibraltar in an English liner. (Ends)

1828/24

26.   *Pound to Admiralty*

24 May 1936

<u>SECRET</u>

Following message has been received from H.M.S. *Capetown.*

(Begins). IMPORTANT. I have received request from Emperor of Abyssinia to pass a long signal to Ethiopian Legation London in native language. I have respectfully conveyed to His Majesty that I am not authorised to make in plain language signal in his name and that if he will give me his wishes in English or French I will endeavour to pass them to an authority in code who will convey them to their destination. Request information whether you wish such a signal passed to Admiralty direct or to C.-in-C. Mediterranean. (Ends)

On receipt of this I sent my 1903/24.[1]

2103/24

27.   *Admiralty to H.M.S.* Capetown
[Repeated C-in-C Mediterranean]

24 May 1936

<u>SECRET</u>

Your 1705 24th May addressed C.-in-C. Mediterranean and C.-in-C. Mediterranean's 1903 24th May. Any message that the Emperor may wish to make to anybody is to be passed in Naval Cypher direct to Admiralty.

2300/24

28.   *H.M.S.* Capetown *to Admiralty*

25 May 1936

<u>SECRET</u>

IMPORTANT.

Following message addressed to Ethiopian Legation in London from His Majesty the Emperor of Ethiopia.

---

[1] 'No repetition no communication whatever from Negus should be sent without prior Admiralty approval.'

(Begins). Before departure from Jerusalem we asked His Excellency the High Commissioner of Palestine to request His Britannic Majesty's Government in our name to make journey from Gibraltar to London by another ship or aircraft. High Commissioner promised to take this step when on 23rd May the Secretary informed us that H.M.S. *Capetown* was waiting for us at Haifa and that we must leave Jerusalem the same day. Now we receive on board a communication from Secretary to the High Commissioner Palestine which says that the British Government does not guarantee safety of your Majesty and he thinks your Majesty has decided to take an English ship on arrival at Gibraltar. Not having properly understood the sense of this communication, besides considering it would be imprudent on our part to embark in British ship *Orford* which we had intended to take in order to arrive London on 4th June, we therefore ask you to see His Excellency the Minister of Foreign Affairs and request him to inform you of the signification of communication and subsequently renew our request to continue our voyage to London in the same ship. If that is impossible request His Excellency that all measures be taken in the *Orford* in order to assure our safety. We have already addressed this request to the High Commissioner Palestine. (Ends)

1005/25

29. *Admiralty to H.M.S.* Capetown
[*Repeated Rear Admiral Gibraltar, C-in-Cs Mediterranean and Home Flee*t]

26 May 1936

SECRET.

Emperor may, if he wishes, remain on board *Capetown* with his suite until he embarks in the *Orford*.

1152/26

30. *Vice Admiral Malta*[1] *to Admiralty*

27 May 1936

SECRET

Requesting instructions on message not yet transmitted to *Capetown*. The *Literary Digest*, American national magazine, would like to know

---

[1]VA [later Adm Sir] Wilfred Frankland French (1880–1958). RA in 2nd Battle Squadron, 1931–32; VA-in-Charge, Malta, 1934–37; Member of Executive Council of Malta, 1936–37; retired list, 1938; British Administrative and Maintenance Representative in Washington, D.C., 1941–44.

by radio if Emperor will appear before League Council in June and statement of attitude towards League.

1031/27

31.   *Admiralty to Vice Admiral Malta*

27 May 1936

SECRET

Message should be transmitted to *Capetown* with instructions it should be handed to the Emperor when the Emperor finally leaves the *Capetown* at Gibraltar.[1]

1751/27

32.   *Admiralty to Pound*
[*Repeated C-in-C Home Fleet, Rear Admiral*
Gibraltar, H.M.S. Capetown]

29 May 1936

SECRET

211. *Capetown* should not leave Gibraltar until reasonable period has elapsed after departure of Emperor in *Orford*. It is desirable to avoid emphasising possibility that Emperor might have come home in *Capetown*, or creating impression that *Capetown* is in attendance upon him.

1805/29

---

[1]The Admiralty consulted the Foreign Office semi-officially on the question. The Foreign Office view was that 'our special responsibility for the utterances of the Emperor ceases as soon as he leaves the *Capetown*' and suggested the message be handed to him when he goes on board the *Orford* or finally lands at Gibraltar, Minute [*signature illegible*] on Admiralty docket, 27 May 1936, TNA: ADM 116/3045.

CONTENTS OF PREVIOUS *NAVAL MISCELLANY* VOLUMES

VOLUME II, edited by Professor Sir John Laughton
(N.R.S. series volume number 40)

Voyage of the *Barbara* to Brazil, anno 1540, edited by R.G. Marsden.

The Sea Scene from the complaynt of Scotlande, edited by Alan Moore.

The taking of the *Madre de Dios*, anno 1592, edited by C. Lethbridge
  Kingsford.

A narrative of the battle of Santa Cruz, written by Sir Richard Stayner,
  Rear-admiral of the Fleet, edited by Professor C.H. Firth.

Extracts from a Commissioner's note book, annis 1691–1694, comprising:

  I.   Scheme of stations for cruisers
  II. Explanations of some Dockyard terms
  III. Reflections on our naval strength
  IV. The fight with the French, anno 1692; written by the Earl of
       Nottingham
  V.   The attempt on Brest.

The journal of M. de Lage de Cueilly, Captain in the Spanish Navy,
  translated from the French by Lieutenant T.G. Carter, RN.

Sale of Dead Man's effects on board H.M. Ship *Gloucester*, 1750.

The Mutiny at the Nore: letter from James Watson to Admiral Robert
  Digby.

From the letter-books of Sir Charles Thompson, Bart., Vice-admiral,
  selected and edited by Admiral Sir T. Sturges Jackson, K.C.V.O., with
  sections on:

  The tactics of Sir John Jervis;

  The French ambassador at Madrid to Godoy.

Orders by Sir John Jervis.

Some letters of Lord St. Vincent.

VOLUME IV, edited by Christopher Lloyd
(N.R.S. series volume number 92)

The Spanish Armada, edited by George P.B. Naish, comprising:

1. Spanish documents
2. Narrative of P. Ubaldino
3. A song attributed to Queen Elizabeth I.

The journal of John Weale, 1654–1656, edited by Reverend J.R. Powell.

Boscawen's letters to his wife, 1755–1756, edited from the Falmouth papers by Peter K. Kemp.

The reminiscences of Lieutenant Malmsköld, 1756–1763, translated and edited by Dr. R.C. Anderson.

Prince William and Lieutenant Schomberg, 1787–1788, edited from the Hood papers by B. McL. Ranft.

The log of the *Guardian*, 1789–1790, edited from the journal of Captain Riou by Ludovic Kennedy.

Corsica, 1794, edited from the Nelson–Hood letters by Admiral J.H. Godfrey.

Congreve's rockets, 1805–1806, edited by Christopher Lloyd and Hardin Craig, Jnr.

Letters of Lord St. Vincent to Thomas Grenville, 1806–1807, edited by Hardin Craig, Jnr.

VOLUME V, edited by Dr. N.A.M. Rodger
(N.R.S. series volume number 125)

Further papers from the Commission of Enquiry, 1608, edited by A.P. McGowan.

The Earl of Warwick's voyage of 1627, edited by Nelson P. Bard.

The Management of the Royal Dockyards, 1672–1678, edited by R.V. Saville.

Benbow's Last Fight, edited by John B. Hattendorf.

Naval aspects of the landings on the French coast, 1758, edited by A.W.H. Pearsall.

VOLUME VII, edited by Susan Rose
(N.R.S. series volume number 153)

The Provision of Ships for Edward I's Campaigns in Scotland, 1300–1306: Barges and Merchantmen, edited by Susan Rose.

Lord Admiral Lisle and the Invasion of Scotland, 1544, edited by C.S. Knighton and David Loades.

The Journal of the Voyage of the *Marigold* to Iceland, 1654, edited by Evan T. Jones.

Neutrality, Sovereignty and Jurisdiction: Two Cases in the Admiralty Court, 1798–1805, edited by Richard Hill.

The Supply of Timber for the Royal Navy, *c*.1803–*c*.1830, edited by P.K. Crimmin.

The Journal of Lieutenant George Bedford, 1835–36: Surveying on the West Coast of Africa edited by Matthew Sheldon.

The Journal of Lieutenant Charles Knowles in the River Niger, 1864, edited by Robert Wilson.

The Diary of Signal Bosun Henry Eason: The Naval Brigade in the Zulu War, 1879, edited by Paul Quinn.

The Autobiography of Chief Gunner Alexander Grant: HMS *Lion* at the Battle of Jutland, 1916 edited by Eric Grove.

Australian Naval Defence: Selections from the Papers and Correspondence of Captain W.H.C.S. Thring, 1913–34, edited by David Stevens.

The Relief of Admiral North from Gibraltar in 1940, edited by Robin Brodhurst and Michael Simpson.

The Development of an Independent Navy for Australia: Correspondence between the First Naval Member and the First Sea Lord, 1947–59, edited by Alastair Cooper.

INDEX

II. More Documents for the Last Campaign of the *Mary Rose*

**III. The Royal Navy and the
    Enforcement of the Stamp Act
    1764–5: the Account of Capt
    Archibald Kennedy RN**

V. Sir John Borlase Warren and the Royal Navy's blockades of the United States in the War of 1812

VI. Captain John Pascoe Grenfell of the Brazilian Navy in the River Plate

NAVY RECORDS SOCIETY – LIST OF VOLUMES
(as at 1 March 2017)

Members wishing to order any volumes should write to Robin Brod-hurst, The Mill, Stanford Dingley, Reading, RG7 6LS or email him at robinbrodhurst@gmail.com.

Those volumes marked **OP** will be printed from scanned copies or original discs. For other titles the Society still retains some original copies.

1. *State Papers relating to the Defeat of the Spanish Armada, 1588,* Vol. I. Ed. Professor J.K. Laughton. (£15.00)
2. *State Papers relating to the Defeat of the Spanish Armada, 1588,* Vol. II. Ed. Professor J.K. Laughton. (£15.00)
1 + 2 Combined Volumes. (£20.00)
3. *Letters of Lord Hood, 1781–1783.* Ed. D. Hannay. **OP**
4. *Index to James's Naval History, 1886,* by C.G. Toogood. Ed. by the Hon. T.A. Brassey. **OP**
5. *Life of Captain Stephen Martin, 1666–1740.* Ed. Sir Clements R. Markham. **OP**
6. *Journal of Rear Admiral Bartholomew James, 1752–1828.* Ed. Professor J.K. Laughton & Cdr. J.Y.F. Sullivan. **OP**
7. *Hollond's Discourses of the Navy, 1638 and 1659 and Slynges-bie's Discourse on the Navy, 1660.* Ed. J.R. Tanner. **OP**
8. *Naval Accounts and Inventories of the Reign of Henry VII, 1485–1488 and 1495–1497.* Ed. M. Oppenheim. **OP**
9. *The Journal of Sir George Rooke, 1700–1702.* Ed. O. Browning. **OP**
10. *Letters and Papers relating to the War with France, 1512–1513.* Ed. A. Spont. **OP**
11. *Papers relating to the Navy during The Spanish War, 1585–1587.* Ed. J.S. Corbett. (£15.00)

12. *Letters and Papers of Admiral of the Fleet Sir Thomas Byam Martin, 1733–1854*, Vol. II. (For Vol. I see Vol. 24) Ed. Admiral Sir R. Vesey Hamilton. **OP**

13. *Letters and Papers relating to the First Dutch War, 1652–1654*, Vol. I. Ed. S.R. Gardiner. **OP**

14. *Dispatches and Letters relating to the Blockade of Brest, 1803–1805*, Vol. I. Ed. J. Leyland. **OP**

15. *History of the Russian Fleet during the reign of Peter The Great, by a Contemporary Englishman, 1724.* Ed. Vice–Admiral Sir Cyprian A.G. Bridge. **OP**

16. *Logs of the Great Sea Fights, 1794–1805*, Vol. I. Ed. Rear Admiral Sir T. Sturges Jackson. **OP**

17. *Letters and Papers relating to the First Dutch War, 1652–1654*, Vol. II. Ed. S.R. Gardiner. **OP**

18. *Logs of the Great Sea Fights, 1794–1805, Vol. II.* Ed. Rear Admiral Sir T. Sturges Jackson. (£15.00)

19. *Letters and Papers of Admiral of the Fleet Sir Thomas Byam Martin, 1773–1854*, Vol. III. Ed. Admiral Sir R. Vesey Hamilton. OP

20. *The Naval Miscellany,* Vol. I. Ed. Professor J.K. Laughton. (£15.00)

21. *Dispatches and Letters relating to the Blockade of Brest, 1803–1805*, Vol. II. Ed. J. Leyland. **OP**

22. *The Naval Tracts of Sir William Monson,* Vol. I. Ed. M. Oppenheim. **OP**

23. *The Naval Tracts of Sir William Monson,* Vol. II. Ed. M. Oppenheim. **OP**

24. *Letters and Papers of Admiral of the Fleet Sir Thomas Byam Martin, 1773–1854*, Vol. I. Ed. Admiral Sir R. Vesey Hamilton. **OP**

25. *Nelson and the Neapolitan Jacobins.* Ed. H.G. Gutteridge. (£25.00)

26. *A Descriptive Catalogue of the Naval Mss. in the Pepysian Library,* Vol. I. Ed. J.R. Tanner. **OP**

27. *A Descriptive Catalogue of the Naval Mss. in the Pepysian Library,* Vol. II. Ed. J.R. Tanner. **OP**

28. *The Correspondence of Admiral John Markham, 1801–1807.* Ed. Sir Clements R. Markham. **OP**

29. *Fighting Instructions, 1530–1816.* Ed. J.S. Corbett. **OP**

30. *Letters and Papers relating to the First Dutch War, 1652–1654*, Vol. III. Ed. S.R. Gardiner and C.T. Atkinson. **OP**

77. *Letters and Papers of Admiral the Hon. Samuel Barrington,* Vol. I. Ed. D. Bonner-Smith. (£15.00)
78. *Private Papers of John, Earl of Sandwich,* Vol. IV. Ed. G.R.T. Barnes & Cdr. J.H. Owen. **OP**
79. *The Journals of Sir Thomas Allin, 1660–1678,* Vol. I, *1660–1666.* Ed. R.C. Anderson. (£15.00)
80. *The Journals of Sir Thomas Allin, 1660–1678,* Vol. II, *1667–1678.* Ed. R.C. Anderson. (£15.00)
81. *Letters and Papers of Admiral the Hon. Samuel Barrington,* Vol. II. Ed. D. Bonner-Smith. **OP**
82. *Captain Boteler's Recollections, 1808–1830.* Ed. D. Bonner-Smith. **OP**
83. *The Russian War, 1854: Baltic and Black Sea.* Ed. D. Bonner-Smith and Capt. A.C. Dewar R.N. **OP**
84. *The Russian War, 1855: Baltic.* Ed. D. Bonner-Smith. **OP**
85. *The Russian War, 1855: Black Sea.* Ed. Capt. A.C. Dewar. **OP**
86. *Journals and Narratives of the Third Dutch War.* Ed. R.C. Anderson. **OP**
87. *The Naval Brigades of the Indian Mutiny, 1857–1858.* Ed. Cdr. W.B. Rowbotham. **OP**
88. *Patee Byng's Journal, 1718–1720.* Ed. J.L. Cranmer-Byng. **OP**
89. *The Sergison Papers, 1688–1702.* Ed. Cdr. R.D. Merriman. (£15.00)
90. *The Keith Papers,* Vol. II. Ed. C. Lloyd. **OP**
91. *Five Naval Journals, 1789–1817.* Ed. Rear Admiral H.G. Thursfield. **OP**
92. *The Naval Miscellany,* Vol. IV. Ed. C. Lloyd. **OP**
93. *Sir William Dillon's Narrative of Professional Adventures, 1790–1839,* Vol. I, *1790–1802.* Ed. Professor M. Lewis. **OP**
94. *The Walker Expedition to Quebec, 1711.* Ed. Professor G.S. Graham. **OP**
95. *The Second China War, 1856–1860.* Ed. D. Bonner-Smith & E.W.R. Lumby. **OP**
96. *The Keith Papers,* Vol. III. Ed. C.C. Lloyd. (£15.00)
97. *Sir William Dillon's Narrative of Professional Adventures, 1790–1839,* Vol. II, *1802–1839.* Ed. Professor M. Lewis. **OP**
98. *The Private Correspondence of Admiral Lord Collingwood.* Ed. Professor E. Hughes. **OP**
99. *The Vernon Papers, 1739–1745.* Ed. B.McL. Ranft. **OP**
100. *Nelson's Letters to his Wife and Other Documents, 1785–1831.* Ed. G.P.B. Naish. (£15.00)

101. *A Memoir of James Trevenen, 1760–1790.* Ed. Professor C.C. Lloyd. **OP**

102. *The Papers of Admiral Sir John Fisher,* Vol. I. Ed. Lt. Cdr. P.K. Kemp R.N. **OP**

103. *Queen Anne's Navy.* Ed. Cdr. R.D. Merriman R.I.N. **OP**

104. *The Navy and South America, 1807–1823.* Ed. Professor G.S. Graham & Professor R.A. Humphreys. (£15.00)

105. *Documents relating to the Civil War.* Ed. Rev. J.R. Powell & E.K. Timings. **OP**

106. *The Papers of Admiral Sir John Fisher,* Vol. II. Ed. Lt. Cdr. P.K. Kemp R.N. **OP**

107. *The Health of Seamen.* Ed. Professor C.C. Lloyd. **OP**

108. *The Jellicoe Papers, Vol. I, 1893–1916.* Ed. A. Temple Patterson. (£15.00)

109. *Documents relating to Anson's Voyage Round the World, 1740–1744.* Ed. Dr G. Williams. **OP**

110. *The Saumarez Papers: The Baltic 1808–1812.* Ed. A.N. Ryan. **OP**

111. *The Jellicoe Papers,* Vol. II, *1916–1935.* Ed. A Temple Patterson. (£15.00)

112. *The Rupert and Monck Letterbook, 1666.* Ed. The Rev. J.R. Powell & E.K. Timings. **OP**

113. *Documents relating to the Royal Naval Air Service, Vol. I, 1908–1918.* Ed. Capt. S.W. Roskill. (£15.00)

114. *The Siege and Capture of Havana, 1762.* Ed. Professor D. Syrett. **OP**

115. *Policy and Operations in the Mediterranean, 1912–1914.* Ed. E.W.R. Lumby. **OP**

116. *The Jacobean Commissions of Enquiry, 1608 and 1618.* Ed. A.P. McGowan. (£15.00)

117. *The Keyes Papers, Vol. I, 1914–1918.* Ed. Professor P.G. Halpern. (£15.00)

118. *The Royal Navy and North America: The Warren Papers, 1736–1752.* Ed. Dr. J. Gwyn. **OP**

119. *The Manning of the Royal Navy: Selected Public Pamphlets, 1693–1873.* Ed. Professor J.S. Bromley. (£15.00)

120. *Naval Administration, 1715–1750.* Ed. Professor D.A. Baugh. (£15.00)

121. *The Keyes Papers, Vol. II, 1919–1938.* Ed. Professor P.G. Halpern. (£15.00)

122. *The Keyes Papers, Vol. III, 1939–1945.* Ed. Professor P.G. Halpern. (£15.00)

123. *The Navy of the Lancastrian Kings: Accounts and Inventories of William Soper, Keeper of the King's Ships, 1422–1427*. Ed. Dr S. Rose. (£15.00)

124. *The Pollen Papers: The Privately Circulated Printed Works of Arthur Hungerford Pollen, 1901–1916*. Ed. Dr J.T. Sumida. (£15.00)

125. *The Naval Miscellany*, Vol. V. Ed. Dr N.A.M. Rodger. (£15.00)

126. *The Royal Navy in the Mediterranean, 1915–1918*. Ed. Professor P.G. Halpern. (£15.00)

127. *The Expedition of Sir John Norris and Sir Francis Drake to Spain and Portugal, 1589*. Ed. Professor R.B. Wernhan. (£15.00)

128. *The Beatty Papers, Vol. I, 1902–1918*. Ed. Professor B.McL. Ranft. (£15.00)

129. *The Hawke Papers, A Selection: 1743–1771*. Ed. Dr R.F. Mackay. (£15.00)

130. *Anglo-American Naval Relations, 1917–1919*. Ed. M. Simpson. (£15.00)

131. *British Naval Documents, 1204–1960*. Ed. Professor J.B. Hattendorf, Dr R.J.B. Knight, A.W.H. Pearsall, Dr N.A.M. Rodger & Professor G. Till. (£25.00)

132. *The Beatty Papers, Vol. II, 1916–1927*. Ed. Professor B.McL. Ranft. (£25.00)

133. *Samuel Pepys and the Second Dutch War*. Ed. R. Latham. (£25.00)

134. *The Somerville Papers*. Ed. M. Simpson with assistance from J. Somerville. (£25.00)

135. *The Royal Navy in the River Plate, 1806–1807*. Ed. J.D. Grainger. (£25.00)

136. *The Collective Naval Defence of the Empire, 1900–1940*. Ed. Professor N. Tracy. (£25.00)

137. *The Defeat of the Enemy Attack on Shipping, 1939–1945*. Ed. Dr. E.J. Grove. (£25.00)

138. *Shipboard Life and Organisation, 1731–1815*. Ed. B. Lavery. (£25.00)

139. *The Battle of the Atlantic and Signals Intelligence: U-boat Situations and Trends, 1941–1945*. Ed. Professor D. Syrett. (£25.00)

140. *The Cunningham Papers, Vol. I: The Mediterranean Fleet, 1939–1942*. Ed. M. Simpson. (£25.00)

141. *The Channel Fleet and the Blockade of Brest, 1793–1801*. Ed. Dr R. Morriss. (£25.00)

162. *The Milne Papers. Papers of Admiral of the Fleet Sir Alexander Milne 1806–1896*, Vol. II, *1860–1862*. Ed. Professor J. Beeler. (£40.00)

163. *The Mediterranean Fleet, 1930–1939*. Ed. Professor P.G. Halpern. (£40.00)

OCCASIONAL PUBLICATIONS.

O.P. 1 *The Commissioned Sea Officers of the Royal Navy, 1660–1815*. Ed. Professor D. Syrett & Professor R.L. DiNardo. (£25.00)

O.P. 2 *The Anthony Roll of Henry VIII's Navy*. Ed. Dr C.S. Knighton & Professor D.M. Loades. (£25.00)

Robin Brodhurst
The Mill,
Stanford Dingley,
Reading, RG7 6LS.

robinbrodhurst@gmail.com